a ♡ healthy book

Scrapper's Soup

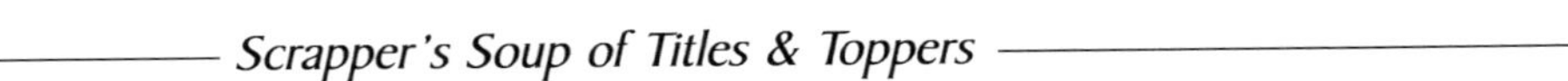

Scrapper's Soup of Titles & Toppers

a ♡ healthy book

Cheryl Bradbury

Check out my other book,

"Page Patterns"

Vol. I

A book loaded with more than 600 page patterns to help make your layouts fast, fun & easy, just the prescription for that painfully annoying disease afflicting all us scrapbookers called, "Layout Block"

It contains 215 Single and 386 Double Page Pattern ideas free of all the other distractions that may cloud Your Scrapbooking Vision!

Author Introduction

Leaving my Legacy and Heritage through Scrapbooking has been my passion for over thirteen years and I have seen the industry just explode with a multitude of products. The one thing that has always been a must on my pages is a title that almost explains the page layout. My favorite kinds of titles are the ones that are a 'play-on-words' which gives them a playful impact. Coming up with little sayings, one liners, expressions, etc. for my titles are like the cherry on a sundae to me.

I used to write down sayings and such for titles on scraps of paper and collect them for my upcoming layouts which would inevitably get lost. My first few searches for any books of titles was slim and frustrating for me. I did find a few, but I wanted more so with my family and friends encouragement, I decided to write my own book and in May 2005 Totally Toppers & Titles was born. That book includes quotes, poems, prayers and more and is terrific. Being that I love collecting titles my own personal book was getting crammed full of additions, as I had added thousands of titles since the book was released. I wanted to share this collection of over 22,000 titles so I decided to write another book of just titles...Scrapper's Soup of Titles & Toppers.

This book is the largest resource of Titles & Toppers with more than 22,000 in over 400 categories to choose from. Cross-referencing and ideas are incorporated wherever possible providing you with an optimal array of options. You will never be at a loss for a title with this book in your hands, as there are 22,000 of them. You may even find yourself creating layouts based on a great title you read, giving you a memory you may not have experienced had you not read this book. I hope you enjoy using this encyclopedia of titles as much as I do in helping your pages to tell their story in a great title.

Have a Scrappin' 4 Memories Day
Cheryl Bradbury

Table of Contents

ACTING TITLES
(SEE SHOW BUSINESS)

ADOPTION TITLES
(SEE ALSO BABY, BOY, CHILDREN & GIRL)

A Chosen Heart
Adopted In Love
Adoption Option
Born Into Our Hearts
God Brought Us Together
Happy Adoption Day
However Motherhood Comes, It's A Miracle
Laced Into Our Lives & Hearts
Made Of The Imagery Of My Heart
Our Special Flower
Special Delivery
Specially Picked By Mom & Dad
Two Mommies Love You...1 Of Heart & 1 In Memory

____
____
____
____
____

AGE TITLES
(SEE ALSO BIRTHDAY)

Age Before Beauty
The Age Of Innocence
Aged To Perfection
Aging Like Fine Wine...Complex & Full Bodied
An Oldie But A Goodie
As Old As Methuselah
Awkward Age
Born In The USA...A Long Time Ago!
Classified Antique
Coming Of Age
Dark Ages
The Dawn Of A New Age
Fine Like Wine
Forever Young
A Golden Age
Golden Oldies
Golden Years Of Glory
Holding Back The Years
I Don't Want To Grow Up...
Ice Aged
I'm Not Getting Older...I'm Getting Better
I'm Not Old...I'm A Vintage Year
In Dog Years...I'm Dead!
Like Fine Wine...
Look Who's The Dinosaur Now!
Middle Aged
My Get Up & Go Has Got Up & Went
Old As Dirt
Old As The Hills
Old Timers
Older Than Dirt
Over The Hill
Over The Hill & Still Running Wild
Recycled Teenager
Spacey Aged
Still Young At Heart
Stone Aged
The More Candles...The Bigger The Wish
Truth Be Told...You're Growing Old
Two Old Crows Live Here
When I Was Your Age...
World's Oldest Teenager

____
____
____
____
____

AIRPLANE/FLYING TITLES

- *Place title on a banner trailing behind an airplane.*
- *A small simple Airplane makes a cute "T".*
- *Hang a Pilot's Hat on a letter in the title.*
- *Make a Plane flying thru clouds with title in them.*

Action Man
Aim High
Are You Ready To Fly?
Aviation Adventures
Born To Fly
Come Fly With Me
Cool Your Jets
Dreams Of Flight
Endless Flight
Feel Like Flying
Feelings Of Flying
First Class Fun
A Flight For 'Soar' Eyes
Flights Of Fancy
Fly Beyond Imagining
Fly By Night
Fly By The Book
Fly By The Seat Of Your Pants
Fly, Fly Away
Fly Girl
Fly Like An Eagle
Fly Me To The Moon
Fly The Friendly Skies
Fly With The Wind

Fly With Wings Of Peace
Flyin' High
Flyin' Into The Blue Skies
Flyin' On Auto Pilot
Flyin' Thru The Clouds
Flyin' Thru The Starry Night
Flying Home
Flyin' Near Heaven
Flying On The Wings Of Tenderness
Flying Thru The Air
Flying With The Angels
Free Flight
Future Dum-Dum Operator
God Is My Co-Pilot
He's Got A Ticket To Fly
High Above The Clouds
I Believe I Can Fly
If Only I Could Fly...
If You're Gonna Fly...
It's A Pilot's Life For Me
Jr. Pilot In Training
Just Plane Cute
Just Plane Fun
Landings Should Equal Take-Offs
Leavin' On A Jet Plane
Let 'Em Fly
Let Him/Her Fly
Let Me Fly
Let Your Dreams Take Flight
Let Your Soul Be Your Pilot
Let's Fly Away
Love Lite In Flight
Night Flights
The Night Of Our Flight
No Peeling Out On The Runways
No Trick Stunts Over Tall Buildings
Off We Go Into The Wild Blue Yonder
Oh Beautiful, For Spacious Skies
Oh To Fly
On A Natural High
On A Wing & A Prayer
On The Fly
Passed With Flying Colors
Pilot In Training
Pilot To Paradise
Signal Ahead
Spread Your Wings & Fly
Take Flight
Take Me To The Pilot
The Wildest Wish To Fly
Those Magnificent Men In Their Flying Machines
To Live Is To Fly
Up & Flying
Up, Up & Away
Wing Nuts
Wishin' I Could Fly
You Make My Heart Fly

AIRSOFT SHOOTING TITLES

Air Ballers
Air Shooter
Air Shot
On The Hunt
Pellet Packer
Pellet Packin' Playtime
Perfect Aim
Practice Makes Perfect
Ready, Aim, Fire!
Right On Target
Quick Draw McGraw
Sharpshooter
Straight Shooter
Sure Shot
What A Softy!

ALLIGATOR TITLES

(SEE CROCODILE)

AMERICA TITLES

(SEE FLAG, JULY 4th, MILITARY & PATRIOTIC)

AMUSEMENT PARK TITLES

(SEE ALSO CAROUSEL & DISNEY)

- *Place title on top of a Roller Coaster.*
- *For Circus pages, use a Seal's Ball or Popcorn for an "O"*

3-Ring Circus
A Day At The Circus
A Land Of Imagination
A Whale Of A Time
Around & Around
Breakneck Speedster
Bump'em! Crash'em! Smash'em!
Carousel/Coaster Fanatics
Circus Act
Circus Circus
Clowning Around

Coaster Crazy
Coaster Fanatics
Coaster Zombies
Coastin' The Coasters
Corny Dogs & Turkey Legs
Cotton Candy Crazy
Country Fair
Do It Again!!!
Don't Look Down
Drive Safely...No Bumping!!!
"E" Ticket Ride *(Old Disneyland tickets)*
Everybody Loves A Circus/Clown
An Af"fair" To Remember
A Family Af"fair"
Fast, Faster, Fastest!
This Is A FUN House?
Get Set To Get Wet
Give It A Whirl
The Greatest Show On Earth
Hang On!
He's Got A Ticket To Ride...
High Anxiety!!!
Hurl-A-Whirl
I Almost Lost My Tummy
I Feel Like A Crash Test Dummy
I've/We've Gotta Ticket To Ride
Let The Good Times Roll
Let The Magic Begin
Let's Go Again & Again & Again
Life In The Fast Lane *(Roller coaster pics)*
Lions & Tigers & Bears, Oh My!
Look Ma, No Hands!
Loop-D-Loop
Loop-The-Loop
Loopty-Loop
The Man On The Flying Trapeze
A Need For Speed
Oh, What A Circus
Our Favorite Thrills
Over The Top
Pushing The Envelope
Pushing The Limits
Puttin' The Petal To The Metal
Rode The Vomit Comet
Screamin'
Send In The Clowns
Silly Clown, Tricks Are For Kids!
Splash Down
Take It To The Limit
Take Me To The Barf Wagon
Tears Of A Clown
A Thrill A Minute
The Thrill Of It All
Thrill Ride
Ticket To Ride
Top Speed
Toss & Turn
Twirler Whirler
Twist & Turn
Twist & Shout
The Ultimate Thrill Ride
Under The Big Top
Up & Down & 'Round & 'Round
View To A Thrill
What A Bunch Of Characters
What Goes Up Must Come Down
Whip It Good
White Knuckle Rider
A White Knuckler
Wild & Wacky Water Ride
A World Of Adventure

CIRCUS

Clowns
Ice Cream
Ringmaster
Cotton Candy
Unicycle
Sideshows

CLOWN

Crazy
Laugh
Outrageous
Wacky
Nutty

ANGEL TITLES

(SEE ALSO HEAVEN)

- *Put a Halo over the top of the "A".*
- *Use an Angel in place of the word.*

All I Want Is An Angel
American Angel
An Angel Came To Me
An Angel Is As An Angel Does
An Angel Of The Lord
An Angel Too Soon
An Angel With Wings Of Grace
Angel Among Us
Angel Baby
Angel Bound
Angel Dusted
Angel Eyes

Angel Face
Angel From Paradise
Angel Heart
Angel In Blue Jeans
Angel In Disguise
Angel In My Heart
Angel In The Clouds
Angel In The Sky
Angel In The Snow
Angel Love
Angel...My Little Angel
Angel Of Love
Angel Of Mercy
Angel Of Mine
Angel Of My Dreams
Angel Of My Soul
Angel Of The Morning
Angel On My Shoulder
Angel Sweet
Angel Whose Smile Is Like The Sun
Angel Without Wings
Angel's Delight
Angel's Night
Angels Watching Over Us
Angels We Have Heard On High
Another Angel Gets It's Wings
Beautiful Angel
Believe In Angels...Believe In Me
Blue Jean Angel
Breath Of An Angel
Christmas Angel
Concrete Angel
Cowboys & Angels
Crazy Angel
Dark-Eyed Angel
Devil Or Angel
Dream Angel
Earth Angel
Fly On, Sweet Angel
Forever An Angel
God's Littlest Angel
Good Friends Are Angels On Earth
Goodnight My Angel
Guarded By Angels
Hark, Our Herald Angel Sings...
Heart Of An Angel
Heavenly Angel
Heaven's Missing An Angel
Honky Tonk Angel
House Of Angels
I Believe In Angels
I Wanna Be Your Love Angel
I'm Holding An Angel
I'm No Angel!!!
In Love With An Angel
In The Arms Of An Angel
I've Been Loved By An Angel
Kiss An Angel Good Morning
Lips Of An Angel
Little Angel
Look For The Angels In Your Life...They're Everywhere...
Looks Like An Angel
Lord Send Me An Angel
Love Of An Angel
Mother...Another Word For Angel
My Angel Is Here
My Baby's Got Angel Eyes
My Darling Angel
My Guardian Angel
My Love-Sent Angel
Night Angel
On The Wings Of An Angel
A Perfect Angel
Precious Angel
Pretty Little Angel Eyes
Real Angels Don't Have Wings
She Walks Like An Angel Walks
Shhh...Angel Sleeping
Snow Angel
Sprinkled With Angel Dust
Still Earning My Wings
Sunshine Angel
Teen Angel
This Is How An Angel Sleeps...
Tiny Angel
Touched By An Angel
Undercover Angel
Unlikely Angel
Waiting For An Angel
Walkin' With An/My Angel
Wayward Angel
We Believe In Angels
When Angels Fly
When Angels Sing...
Wild Angels
Won't You Call Me Angel
You Angel You
You Make Me Feel Like An Angel Inside
You Must Be Angel
You're My Angel

____
____
____
____
____

ANIMALS TITLES

(SEE ALSO FARM, ZOO & SOME SPECIFIC ANIMALS)

5 *(any #)* Little Seals Sitting On The Rocks
All Creatures Great & Small...
...And God Created
Animal Crackers
Animal Farm/House
Animals...Animals...Animals
Best Of Breed
Billy Goat Gruff
A Breed Above The Rest
Breed All About It
Bungle In The Jungle
Bunny Love
Buzzy As A Beaver
Come On A Safari With Me
Counting Sheep
Crazy Critters
Creature Comforts
Cute Critters
Dandy Lions
A Day Among The Animals
Dolphin Majesty
Dr. Doolittle
Duck 'N Run
Elephant Raggae
Elephant Talk
Ewe Are Furr-ever Loved
The Facts Of Animal Life
Feelin Squirrelly
Funky Furr
Furr-ever Friends
Fuzzy Memories
God's Creatures
Going Wild
The Golden Goat
Grunt & Squeak & Squawk With The Animals
I Am The Walrus
I'll Work For Peanuts
I'm Not A Packrat...I'm A Collector *(Squirrel)*
In The Swing Of It
It's A Jungle Out There
King Of The Jungle
Leaping Lizards
Licks Of Love
Lions & Tigers & Bears, Oh My!
The Lions Game
Little Bunny "Foo-Foo"
The Lion Sleeps Tonight
The Lions Den
The Mane Attraction
Mice Are Nice
My 'Fur'vorite Animal Is...
Night Owl
Not A Creature Was Stirring
Octopus's Garden
Our Private Zoo
Out Of Africa
"Owl" Always Be There For You
Party Animal
Paws & Enjoy The Animals
Peanut Gallery
Penguin's Prance
Petopia
Pet Palace/Paradise
Pink Elephants
Prancing Penguins
Proud As A Peacock
Proud Penguins
Quiet As A Mouse
A Real Swinger
Sitting Duck
Squirrel Vision
A Squirrelly Tale
Strong As A Bull
Suburban Safari
Talk To The Animals
Tall Tales
A Trunk Full Of *(Food)*
Turtle Blue
Turtle Toddle
Urban Safari
Walk With The Animals
Where The Buffalo Roam!
Wild Thing
You Quack Me Up!

ANNIVERSARY TITLES

(SEE ALSO HEART, LOVE, MARRIAGE & WEDDING)

- *Use a Heart in place of the word Heart.*
- *Replace an "A", "O", or "V" with a Heart.*

Always & Forever
Always Have, Always Will!!!
Born To Be Together
Choose Thy Love...Love Thy Choice!
Endless Love
First Love, Last Love
Forever Together Forever
Happy Anniversary My Love
Happy Memories...Happy Times...Happy Anniversary
Happy Yesterdays, Happier Tomorrows

I Will Always Love You
Just The Two Of Us
Looks Like We've Made It
Love Is Everlasting
Lucky To Have Each Other
Of One Heart
One Heart, One Mind
Our Love Is Tied With Heartstrings
Our Special Day
Sharing The Love
So Happy Together
Still Together Forever
Through The Years
A Time To Remember
Together, Forever, Always
True Love Never Grows Old
Undying Love
Walk Forever By My Side
We Are Blessed
Yesterme, Yesteryou, Yesterday
You Mean The World To Me
(Years) Of Wedded Bliss

ANTIQUE TITLES

A Grandma Is An Antique Little Girl
A Grandpa Is An Antique Little Boy
It's Not Junk, It's A Collection
Junque & Antiques
Nostalgia Isn't What It Used To Be
An Oldie But A Goodie
One Person's Junk Is Another Person's Treasures
This Isn't Clutter...These Are My Antiques!
A Timeless Treasure!!!
Today's Junk...Tomorrow's Antiques

ANTS TITLES

(SEE BUGS)

APPLE TITLES

(SEE FOOD)

AQUATIC TITLES

(SEE ALSO ANIMALS, BEACH & FISH)

Any Fish In There?
Crabby Critter
Dancing With The Fishes
Dolphin Dance
The Dolphins & Me
Fish Stories Told Here
Fish Tales
Look At The Dolphins
Ocean Wonders
I Sea You
The Shamu Adventure
"Star"Fish
Three Little Fishes
Twinkle, Twinkle Ocean Star
A Whale Of A Time
The Whales & Me
Wishin' On A Sea Star

ARCHERY TITLES

- *Use an Arrow in place of an "I" or "L".*
- *Use a Target Board for an "O".*

Arrow Of Deliverance
Arrow Of Love
Broken Arrow
Bullseye
Crossbow Queen/King
Cupid's Arrow
Easy Target
Flirty Flyer
Hit The Moving Target
On Target
Petticoat Point
Poison Arrow
Right On Target
Sitting Duck
Straight As An Arrow
Target Practice

ARMED FORCES TITLES

(SEE MILITARY)

ART TITLES

(SEE ALSO CHALK & COLORING)

- *Use a Paintbrush, Crayon or Chalk for an "I".*
- *Use a Paint splat for an "O" or to dot an "I".*

A Budding Picasso
A Pigment Of Imagination
An Artist At Heart
An Artist's Apprentice
Art & Illusion
Art & Soul
Art Appreciation
Art For Art's Sake
Art Imitates Art/Life
Art Of Color
Art Of Persuasion
Artist At Work
Artist In Training
The Artistic Styling's Of *(Child's name)*
Artists Do It Creatively
Baby...That's Art!!!
Be Bold...Color Outside The Lines
Brushing Up
Budding Artist/Picasso
Caution: Artist At Work
Cement Rembrandt
Chalk Board Chalk Art
Chalk It Up To Talent
Chalk Talk
Creating A Masterpiece
A Creative Mess
Exceptional Artistry
How Beautiful Thou Art
How Fun Thou Art
How Great Thou Art
How Sweet Thou Art
I'm Not Messy, I'm Creative!
The Imagination Factory
To Imagine Is Everything
Imagine That!
Just A Pigment Of My Imagination
Just Add Water
A Little Dab Did Ya!
Little Picasso
Look What I Made!
A Lotta Dabs Did Ya!
The Magic Paintbrush
Masterpiece
The Next Picasso
Oh, For Arts Sake
Our Little Artist
Our Very Own Mini Monet
Paint Me A Picture
Pavement Picasso
Peewee Picasso
A Picasso In The Making
Pint-Sized Picasso
Pretty Picasso
A Real Piece Of Work
Rustic Rembrandt
Shhh...Artist At Work
Sidewalk Picasso
Stand Back & Give Me Room
State Of The Art
Strokes Of Genius
What A Creation!!!
A Work Of Art
A Work Of Heart
You Did It With Flying Colors

ASPIRING/ASPIRATIONS TITLES

(SEE ALSO DREAMS, HOPES & WISHES)

Against All Odds
Carpe Diem *(Seize The Day)*
Count Your Blessings
Follow The Yellow Brick Road
Follow Your Heart
High Hopes
Hope Costs Nothing
Hope Is The Parent Of Faith - *(Cyrus A. Bartol)*
Hugs & Kisses & Stars For Wishes
I Believe In Miracles!
If At First You Don't Succeed, Try, Try Again!
Keeping The Faith
Leap Of Faith
Life...Put Your Heart In It!
On The Wings Of A Snow White Dove
Our Aspirations Are Our Possibilities.
(Robert Browning)
Reach For The Stars
Reach High & Touch The Stars
Seize The Day
The Sky's The Limit
To Imagine Is Everything
We Believe In Miracles
When You Wish Upon a Star...
Where There's A Will, There's A Way
Wishin' & A Hopin'
With God, All Things Are Possible!

ATTITUDE TITLES

Altitude Is Determined By Attitude
Attitude Is Everything
Attitude Is Me
Attitudes 'R Us
Bad Attitude
Big Badditude Dude
Big Shot
Cocky
Darling Diva
Funny Is An Attitude - *(Flip Wilson)*
Groucho *(Child's name)*
Here Comes Trouble!
Hot Dogger
I Have Attitude & I Know How To Use It
I'm In Charge Here!
I'm The Boss
I've Risen, But I Won't Shine!
Mr./Miss Personality Plus
Needin' An Attitude Adjustment
Nooooooo!!!!
On The Tude Again!!!!
Quite A Character
Stubborn As A Mule
The Maker Of Much Mischief
Too Cute For My Own Good
Too Cute For Words
Tude Dude
Tuff Stuff!!!
Why?????
Wild Thang

____
____
____
____
____

AUNT TITLES

AUNT = **A**lways
Understanding
Naturally
Terrific
Aunt Pile
Auntabulous

____
____
____
____
____

AUTUMN TITLES

(SEE ALSO FALL/LEAVES & HARVEST)

- *Use a Leaf in place of an "A" or "O".*
- *Punch out title letters from leaf paper.*

Amazing Autumn Grace
Another Autumn Frolic
As Autumn Leaves...
As Autumn Leaves Turn...
Autumn Angels
Autumn At The *(Surname)* House
Autumn Colours
Autumn Days
Autumn Days Are Here Again!!
Autumn Frost
Autumn Harvest
Autumn Leaves
Autumn Leaves Are Falling Down
Autumn Of My Life
Autumn On My Mind
Autumn Potpourri
Autumn Splendor
Autumn...The Year's Last Loveliest Smile
Autumn Time
Autumn Turns Over A New Leaf
Autumn's All Around Us
Autumn's Here
Autumn's Palette
Autumn's Song
Autumn's Twilight
Autumn's Winds
Autumn's Winds Before The Rain
Awesome Autumn
Baskets Of Fun
The Beauty Of Fall
Bonfires Of Autumn!
The Break Of Autumn
Bushel Basket Harvest
Bushel Of Blessings/Fun
Buried Treasures *(Kids under leaves or hay)*
Chillin' In Autumn
Color Me Autumn
Colorful Autumn
Colorful Days Of Autumn
Color's Of The Wind
Crazy Days Of Autumn
Crisp Autumn Nights
Crisp, Cool & Autumn
Cuddled Up On An Autumn Night
Fall Into Autumn
For Goodness Sake, Grab A Rake!
Glorious Days Of Autumn
Glorious Golden Leaves
Golden Autumn Days
In Love With Autumn

It's An Autumn-Magic Day
Lazy Autumn Days
Misty Autumn Morn
Natures Bounty
Pieces Of Autumn
Piles Of Autumn Smiles!
A Rainbow Of Autumn Colors
Red, Green, Gold & Brown...Autumn Leaves Are On The Ground
A Riot Of Color
Season Of Change
Seasons Of My Life
Shades Of Autumn
So Fell Autumn's Rain
Starry Nights Of Autumn
Summer "Falls" Into Autumn
When Autumn Leave's...

AWARD TITLES

And The Oscar Goes To *(Name)*
And The Winner Is *(Name)*
Blue Ribbon Affair
Everybody Loves A Winner
Gold Medalist
I Am The Champion
My Award Winning *(Noun)*
New Blue Champion
Pinned Again
Principle's List Pupil
Red Ribbon Rider *(Horse or bike)*
Silver Medalist
The Winner's Circle
The Winners Takes It All
Trophy Time
We Are The Champions

BABY TITLES

(SEE ALSO ADOPTION, BIRTH ANNOUNCEMENTS & CHILDREN)

- *Replace letters with Baby Toys like a rattle or bottle.*
- *Place letters inside of connectable or stackable baby blocks.*

7 lb. 2 oz. Miracle
8 Lb. Baby Melts 200 Lb. Man's Heart
A Baby's Story
A Baby's Touch
A Boy Is A Joy
A Child Is Born
ABC...123...Baby You & Me
ABCDEFG...Tell Me What You Think Of Me?
The Age Of Innocence
Ain't She/He A Cutie Oh Me, Oh My!
All About Me
All American Boy/Girl
All By Myself
All Decked Out
All Of God's Grace...In One Little Face
All Wrapped Up
An Answered Prayer
...And Baby Makes Three
...And The Story Begins
...And Then There Was You
Angel Among Us
Angel Baby
Angel Eyes
Angel Face
Angel Picked
Angelicious
Awake & Alert
Babblin' Bambino
Babe In Arms
Babies Are A Beautiful Way To Start People
Babies Are Angels From Heaven
Babies Are For Hugging
Babies Are God's Greatest Gifts
Babies Are Hugs Sent From Heaven
Babies 'R Us
Babies Touch The World With Love
Baby Babble
Baby B'gosh
Baby Blues
Baby Boomer
Baby Bumpkin
Baby Crossing
Baby Days/Daze
Baby Faces
Baby I'm Yours
Baby It's Cold Outside!
Baby Me!
Baby Melts World
Baby Meets World
Baby Of Mine
Baby Of Mine...Don't Cry
Baby, Oh! Baby
Baby On The Move *(Put pics of baby in circles & create a caterpillar)*
Baby's Big Adventures
Baby's Day Out
Back In My Arms Again
Bald Is Beautiful
Bare Bottoms Welcome Here
Bare Necessities
Basket Case *(Baby in bassinet or basket)*
Be My Little Baby
Beboppin' Baby
Better Late Than Never
Bikini Baby
Blessing From Above
Born To Boogie
Born To Cause Trouble
Born To Drool
Born To Eat
Born To Play
Born To Pout
Born Yesterday
Bottoms Up
Brand New Blossom
Our Bundle From Heaven Above
Bundle Of Joy
Busy, Busy Baby
A Button Nose, Sweet Lips & Ten Tiny Toes
A Child Is Born
Circles Of Love *(Use circles as mats for the title letters & cut misc. pics into circles)*
Could It Be A Miracle?
Could It Be Magic?
Covered With God's Fingerprints
Cradle Of Love
The Cradle Will Rock
Crib Climber
Cute & Dangerous
The Cute Things I Do
Cutest Little Bug On The Rug
Cutie Patootie
Daddy's Mini Me
Diaper Duty
Doin' The Diaper Dance
Our Dream Come True...Little You
Dreams Really Do Come True
Drinkin' Buddies *(2 babies with bottles)*
Extra! Extra! Read All About Me!
Feature Presentation
Feelin' Pampered!

Finger Food
The First Time Ever I Saw Your Face...
Food Frenzy
From Small Beginning's, Come Great Things
From The Beginning
Funny Faces
Fussy Fellow
Future Ballerina *(Baby up on toes)*
Get A Grip *(Baby tightly gripping a toy or hair)*
A Gift From Above
Giggles & Curls
God Broke The Mold The Day You Were Born
God Created You With His Precious Hands
God Danced The Day You Were Born
God's Greatest Gift
God's Greatest Work Of Art
Golden Grin
Got Milk?
Great Things Come In Small Packages
Growing Like A Weed
Handle With Care
Heaven Sent
Here Come The Tears
He's Here!!!
Here Grows Another Generation
Hip, Hip Hooray, *(Name)* Was Born Today!
Homecoming
How Sweet I Am
Hug Me, I'm All Yours
Huggies Bug
I Am A Child Of God
I Coo, I Goo, I Poo, That's All I Do!
I Knew I Loved You Even Before I Met You
I Know I'm A Handful...
I Love My Milk
I Sometimes Leak!
I'll Roll/Tumble For You!
I'm A Handful
I'm A Little Stinker!!!
I'm A Little Swinger
I'm The Baby...Gotta Love Me
I'm Thumbody Special
I'm Too Sexy For My Diaper
In The Beginning...
In The Beginning, We All Started Out Small
In The Swing Of Things
Infant Driver
Into Everything
Introducing Our Newest Team Member
Introducing Our Superstar!
Introducing The World's Most Beautiful Baby
Isn't She Lovely?!
It's A Boy/Girl!
It's All In The Jeans

The Joy Of A Baby Boy
Just Plain/Plane Cute
King Of The Sandbox
Labor Day
A Labor Of Love
Let Me Entertain You
Let The Good Times Roll *(Baby rolling)*
Life Has Begun...
Little Bitty Pretty One
Little Boy Blue
Little Charmer
Little Darlin'
Little Me...Little You
Little One
Little Streaker
Our Little Stocking Stuffer *(Baby born on Christmas Day)*
Little This & Little That
Our Little Treasure
The Littlest Wiseman
Look At This Face
Look What I Can Do
Love Me Tender
Love My Luvs
The Love Of Our Lives
Lying In The Lap Of Luxury
Mama's Boy
Miles Of Smiles
Miles To Go Before I Sleep
Milk, It Does A Baby Good
The Miracle Of Life
Miracle On Our Street
Mommy Asked For An Angel...
Mommy's Little Love
Mommy's Little Monster
Mommy's Little Precious
Mommy's Little Squirt
Mommy's Mini Me
More Than Wonderful
My Name Is *(Name)*
My Turn On Earth
Natural Beauty
Nature Boy/Girl
Need Milk...Or Will Cry
Our New Arrival
A New Face At Our Place
New Kid On The Block
New Life...New Love
Nobody Could Fill Your Booties
Now Appearing...
Queen Of The Sandbox
Oh Baby...My Baby!
On The Roll Again!!!
One Moment's Proof Of Heaven's Existence

Our Bundle Of Joy
Our Dream Come True
Our Family Has Grown By Two Feet
Our Little Angel
Our Little Ray Of Sunshine
Our Little Sweetie
Our Perfect Angel
Outer Joy...Inner Peace
Peek-A-Boo...I See You
Perfect 10
The Perfect Gift
The Perfect Handful
Perfection!
Pool Of Drool
Our Precious Bundle Of Joy
Precious Treasure
Presenting...
Pretty As A Picture
Prisms Of Love
QT Pie
Ray Of Sunshine
Ready Or Not, Here I Come
Rollin', Rollin', Rollin' See That Baby Rollin'
See What I Can Do!
Seeing Is Believing
Shake That Bootie
Shake, Rattle & Roll
She's A Superstar
She's Here!
Simply Irresistible
Simply Magical
Small Blessings Make Life A Joy
Small Is Beautiful
Snack Time!
So Big!
So Dog-Gone Cute!
So Much To Coo About
So Precious To Me...Baby Of Mine
Softly & Tenderly
Someone To Love
Something To Talk About
Our Special Delivery
A Special Gift Has Come From Afar...
Spit Happens!!!
A Star Fell From Heaven
The Star In Our Sky
A Star Is Born
Sweet As Can Be...Baby Of Mine
Sweet Beginnings
Sweet Cheeks
Sweet Heart
Sweet Pea
Sweet Talk
Sweetie Pie
Taster Of All
Tell Me Again About The Day I Was Born
Temptations Of Tots
Thank Heaven For Bibs
Thank Heaven For Little Boys/Girls
The Way We Were...The Way We Are *(Pics of before and after baby)*
There's No Other Like My Baby
There's No Such Things As Too Much Hugs. *(Pooh)*
There's Nothing Like A Baby To Make You Smile
They Call Me Mellow Yellow
They Call Me Trouble
Think Pink
Those Eyes Melt My Heart
Thumbody Loves Me/You
Tickle Me *(Child's name)*
Time For A Change
A Time To Be Born...And The Story Begins...
Tiny Hands & Feet...Oh, So Sweet
Tiny Tot
They Call Me Precious
Too Cute For Words
Too Cute To Pout
Too Pooped To Scoot
Twinkle, Twinkle From Afar, *(Name)* Is Our Little Star
Up, Up & Away
Watch Me Grow
We Are Born Innocent...
We Heard The Angels Sing On *(Birthdate)*
We Made A Wish, & You Came True
A Wee Bit Of Heaven
We're Just Wild About Our New Child
We've Entered A Changing World *(Diapers)*
We've Expanded Our Home By Two Feet!
We've Only Just Begun
Welcome Little One
Welcome To The World Baby Boy/Girl
What A Busy Baby
What A Wonderful World
What Did They Do Before Me?!
What Is All The Fuss About?
When A Child Is Born, The Angels Sing
When Do We Eat?
Which Way To Hollywood?
Who Loves Ya, Baby?
A Whole New World
Will Smile For Food
The Wonder Of It All
Worth Every Contraction
Worth The Wait
Yes Sir, That's My Baby

You Are Cut From A Pattern I Love
You Are God's Masterpiece
You Are God's Work Of Art
You Are My Special Angel
You Are My Sunshine
You Are So Beautiful
You Are So Beautiful To Me
You Are So Precious To Me
You Bet I'm Cute!
You Light Up My Life
The Young & The Restless
You're One In A Million
You've Got The Cutest Little Baby Face
Yummy, Yummy, I've got *(Food)* in My Tummy!
(Sibling's name) Has A New Hand To Hold
(Sibling's name) Has Just Been Promoted To Big Brother/Sister

BAKING TITLES

(SEE COOKING & FOOD)

BALL TITLES

- *Place letters inside of Balls.*
- *Place letters as if Bouncing.*

B-Ball
Ball & Chain
The Ball's In My Court
Balls To The Wall
Fall Ball
Beach Ball Bounce
Belle Of The Ball
Bouncin' Off The Wall's
Crystal Ball
Curve Ball
Get On The Ball
Havin' A Ball
Knocked The Cover Off The Ball
Play Ball!
Red Rubber Ball
Speed Ball
That's The Way The Ball Bounces
The Whole Ball Of Wax
Wrecking Ball

BALLOON & HOT AIR TITLES

- *Make the "O" into a Balloon.*
- *Place a circle mat under each letter, as if a Balloon, with a dangling String hanging from each.*

A Sight for "Soar" Eyes
Above The Clouds
Balloonists Get High On Hot Air!
Champagne Flight
Chariot Of Fire
Dreams In The Sky
Flights Of Fancy
Floating About So Freely
Floating Among The Clouds
Floating On Air
Full Of Hot Air
Helium High
High Hopes
High In The Sky
Hot Air Festival
Hot Air Happiness
It Takes A Lot Of "Hot Air" To Get Into The Air
Love In A Hot Air Balloon
Magical Ride
Natural High
Peaceful...Calm...Serenity
Riding On A Chariot Of Fire
Up With The Birds
Up At Dawn's Early Light
Up, Up & Away In A Beautiful Balloon
What Goes Up Must Come Down
Would You Like To Ride In My Beautiful Balloon?

BARBECUE TITLES

(SEE COOKOUT & PICNIC)

BARN TITLES

(SEE COUNTRY & FARM)

BASEBALL TITLES

(SEE ALSO SPORTS)

- *Use Baseballs for an "O".*
- *Replace an "I" & "L" with a Bat.*

1...2...3 Strikes You're Out!!!
2nd Base Thief
All-Star
All-Star In Training
Angel In The Outfield
Around The Horn
Backyard Baseball
A Barn-Burner Win
Baseball & Boys Go Hand In Hand
Baseball Diamonds Are A Boys Best Friend
Baseball Is My Life!!!
Baseball...It's America's Pastime
Bat Boy
Batter Up
Better At The Ballpark
Blew Him Away
The Boys Of Summer
Can Of Corn Catch
Our "Casey" At The Bat
Catch Some Fun
Clutch Player
Couldn't Buy A Hit
Daisy Picker
Dark Horse Winner
A David vs. Goliath Game
Double Play
Earned His Bragging Rights
Field Of Dreams
Fly Ball
Foul Ball
Game Day
Goin' Yard
Going...Going...Gone!!!
Got Beat Like A Drum
Got Game!?!?
Got Good Wood!!!
Got The Bases Covered
Grand Slam
A Grand Slam Day
Great Catch
Havin' A Ball
Here We Come!
He's Got Game!!!
Hey...Batter, Batter, Batter!
Hit & Run
Hit The Fat Pitch/Lollipop
Hits Happened
Home Stretch
Homerun!
If You Can't Win, You Shouldn't Play
If You Hang It, They'll Bang It
In A League All Your Own
Inched Out The Win
It Was A Clean Sweep
It's Not Just A Bat, It's My Launching Stick
Just A Swingin'
He Knocked The Cover Off The Ball
A Knock-Out Blow
Knuckle Baller
The Last Hit
Let's Play Ball
Life Lessons Learned In Little League
Lil' Slugger
Little Big Leaguer
Little Major
Little Peanut Batter At Play
Little Slugger
Major/Minor League Fun
Major Leagues, Here I Come!
M-V-P
My Favorite Season...Baseball Season
A Nip & Tuck Game
Nobody Loves The Ump!
On A Roll
On Fire
Pepper Play
Pickle
Pitching In
Play Ball
Played Good "D"
Put Me In Coach...I'm Ready To Play!
A Rifle Arm Pitcher
The Rookie
Rookie Of The Year
Root, Root, Root For The *(Team name)*
Saw Ball, Hit Ball
Stealing Second Is My Game
Second Base Stealer
Set The Table For The Homerun
Seventh Inning Stretch
Slide, Slide, Slide Into Home
Slider...
Slidin' Down The Line
Slugger Boy
Safe At The Plate
SSSSSSSafe!!!
Step Up To The Plate
Steeeeerike!!!
Strike It Up
Suicide Squeeze
Take Me Out To The Ball Game!
That's A Bomb!
The Boys Are Back In Town
There's No Crying In Baseball

Those Little Spike Shoes
Ridin' The Pine
Three Strikes, You're Out
Throwin' The Heat
Triple Player
Touched 'Em All!
Went Yard!!!
What A Catch
Whiff!
Won In The 11th Hour
World Series Here We Come
World Series Or Bust
World Series Wonders
You're Out!!!
(Name) Went Yard

____
____
____
____
____

BASKETBALL TITLES

(SEE ALSO SPORTS)

- *Use Basketballs or Stars for an "O".*

3-Second Violation
Air Ball
Alley Oop To The Hoop!
Around The Rim
Around The World
Bank Shot Ball
Baskets Of Fun
B-Ball
Beat Him At The Jump!
Block That Shot!
Chairmen Of The Boards!
Clutch Player
Couldn't Buy A Basket
Dark Horse Winner
A David vs. Goliath Game
Dishin' & Swishin'
Doin' It Like Mike!!!
Double Dribbling
Dribble It...Pass It...Made The Shot
Dribblin' Down The Line
Fast Break
For The Love Of The Game
Full Court Press
Get In Your Zone!
Go For The Three!
Goin' Coast To Coast
Got Beat Like A Drum
Got Mugged
Guard Your Man!
Half Court Hoopsters
Hands Up! Block That Shot!
Hang Time
Harlem Globe Trotter In Training
He Shoots...He Scores!
Heee-eey, Hey, Hey...Gooo-ood Bye
His Prayer Was Answered
Hit It At The Buzzer
Hit The Net
Hole In One
Hook Shot
Hoop Dee Doo
Hoop Dreams
Hoop Heaven
Hoop It Up
Hoop King
Hoop Stars
Hoop, There It Is!
Hoopla Hoops, Anyone?
The Hoopster
Hot Shot
I Felt That Sinkin' Feelin'
I'm A Basket Case
In The Air Tonight
In The Paint
Intentional Foul
It's Not How Big You Are, It's How Big You Play
It's Not The Hype, It's The Hoop!
Jam Session
Jump Ball
Jump Shot
Keep On Sinkin'
Keep That Ball Alive!
Kiss The Rim!
A Knock-Out Blow
Laying Bricks
My 3 Is An Art Form!
M-V-P In Training
A Nip & Tuck Game
No Harm...No Foul
Nothin' But Net
Open Shot
OT Fun
OT Win!!!
Pass...Shoot...Score
Pass This Way
Played Good "D"
Pop-The-Rock
Poppin' The 3
Pound The Boards!
Put It Thru For Two!
Reject That Shot!
The Rim Reapers!
Rip Off The Tip Off!
Shootin' Hoops

Sinkin' Sensation
Sink & Win
Sink It & Win!
Sink That Shot!
Slam Dunk
Slam Dunk King
Slam The Competition!
Slammin' & Jammin'
Space Jam
Swish
Swoosh
Take It To The Hoop!
Takin' It Home
That Was A Slam Dunk!!!
Throw-The-Stone
Time Out Time
To "Air" Is Human!!!
Turning The Team Around 360 Degrees
Went Coast To Coast
We've Got The Hoopla!
Whoop It Up
Zero Gravity

BATH/BATHTIME TITLES

(SEE ALSO BUBBLES & WATER)

- *Make the "O" into a Bubble.*
- *Place letters inside of Vellum Bubbles.*

All Comes Off In The Bath Wash
All Washed Up
Au Naturale
Bare Bottoms Welcome Here
The Bare Necessities
Bath & Body Works
Bathing Beauty
Bathtime Blues
Bathtime Is Just Ducky
Bathtime Is Splash Time
Bathtub Brawl
The Bathtub Gang
Bear Hugs & Back Scrubs Welcome Here!
Beyond Bubbles
Bubble Baby
Bubble Bash
Bubble Bath Fun
Bubble Maker
Bubble Trouble
Bubble Your Troubles Away
Bubbles, Bubbles Everywhere
Bubblin' Baby Boy
Bubbly, Bubble Fun
Calgon...Take Me Away
Caution: Cleaning Crew At Work!
Clean As A Whistle
The Clean Machine!
Conserve Water...Bathe With A Friend!
Dirt Destruction
Don't Forget To Wash Behind The Ears!
Finally "Wet" Behind The Ears
A Flood Of Fun
Fresh & Clean & Smelling Sweet
From Grubbin' To Tubbin'
Good Clean Fun
I Love My Rubber Ducky
I'm All Washed Up
It's A Wash
Just Add Water
Lather Up
Let's Make Waves
Little Mermaid
Little Streaker!!!
Makin' A Big Splash
Makin' Waves
May Your Day Bubble Over With Fun
Mr. Bubbles To The Rescue
Mr. Bubbles Would Be Proud
Mr. Clean
Mr. Towel Man
One Little Squirt Won't Hurt!
Rub-A-Dub Dub
Rub-A-Dub Dub...A Dirty Boy/Girl In The Tub
Rub-A-Dub Dub...I Love The Tub
Rub-A-Dub Dub...My First Time In The Tub!
Rub-A-Dub Dub Splashing In The Tub
Rub-A-Dub Dub The Dirt Into The Tub!
Scrub-A-Dub Dub
Scrubbin' Scene...Getting Clean
Scrubbin' Session
Scrubbly Bubbly
Slippery When Wet
Soak & Scrub...Do It In The Tub
Soap Opera
Soap Shock
Soapy Siblings
Splash Dance
Splish Splash, I'm Takin' A Bath
Splishin' & A Splashin'
Squeaky Clean
Suds Buds
Suds Up
Threw In The Towel
Towel Man
Towel Swami
Tub Time

Tub Tyrant
Tubby Time
Wash Your Bubbles Away
Washin' The Bubbles Away
Water Baby
Water Bugs
Water Works Wonders
Wet Behind The Ears
Wet-N-Wild
Wishy Washy
You Scrub My Back & I'll Scrub Yours!

BEACH TITLES

(SEE ALSO AQUATIC, POOL, SUMMER, SUN, SUNBATHING, SURFING & SWIMMING)

- *Put different Shells in place of some letters.*
- *Make tops of letters look like Water & bottoms like Sand.*
- *Punch letters from Bubble, Ocean, Water or Sandpaper.*

20,000 Leagues Under The Sea
As The Sun Falls Into The Sea...
At One With The Sea
At The Deep Blue Sea
At The Sea Shore
Attack Of The Crabs
Baywatch Babe/Baby
Beach Babe/Baby
Beach Ball Babe/Baby
Beach Blanket Babe/Baby
Beach Blanket Napper
Beach Boy Blues
Beach Boys
Beach Bums
Beach Combing
Beach Party
Beachy Keen
The Beautiful Rolling Sea
Beauty & The Beach
Behold The Sea
Beyond The Sea
Bikini Brigade
Blue Bayou
Boy On The Beach
Bring On The Sunshine
Building Sand Castles By The Sea
Buried Treasure
By The Sea Shore
Can You Dig This?
Castle Crashers
Castles In The Sand
Castles Of Sand...Memories Of Gold
Catch A Wave
Catch A Wave & You're Sitting On Top Of It!
Children Of The Sea
Coastal Craze/Crazy
Commotion By The Ocean
A Crabby Adventure
Crabby Critter
The Deep Blue Sea
Discovering The Wonders Of The Waves
Dig This!
Diggin' For China
Down By The Bay
Down By The Ocean/Sea
Down By The Sand & Sea
Dreamin' Of The Sea
Escape To The Cape
Face To Face With The Fishies *(Snorkeling)*
Feelin' Crabby
Feelin' Under The Water
Footprints In The Sand
Friends By The Sea...Just You & Me
From Sea To Shining Sea
The Girls On The Beach
Got Baked At The Lake
Hand In Hand Walking In The Sand
Hangin' 10
Happiness Is...A Day At The Beach
Happy As A Clam
Harbor Lights
Having A Crabby Day
Having A Sandsational Time
Heaven Seems A Little Closer At The Beach
Hit The Beach
Home By The Sea
I Sea You
If You Build A Sand Castle, The Waves Will Come!
In The Cool Clear Water
Island Paradise
It Came From Beneath The Sea
Jewel Of The Sea
Jewels By The Sea
Just Beachin' It
Just Beachy
Let The Good Tides Roll
Let's Go Surfin' Now...
Let's Hit The Beach
Life's A Beach
Linger By The Sea
The Little Boy/Girl & The Sea
Little Sandman
Looney Dunes

Lounging By The Lake
Lovin' The Sea, Sand & Surf
The Lure Of The Sea
Makin' Waves
The Motion In The Ocean
Mr. Sandman
The Musical Sea
My Favorite Place To Be Is Shorely By The Sea
My First Bikini
Near The Sea, We Forget To Count The Days
Neptune's Dream
Now This Is A Sandbox! *(Child playing in sand)*
Ocean Adventures
Ocean Of Love
Ocean Waves Here I Come
Ocean Wonders
The Ocean's Roar
Official Beach Bum
The Old Man & The Sea
On The Boardwalk
On The Waterfront
Our Little Mermaid
Over The Waves
Peek-A-Boo, I "Sea" You!
Please Leave The Sand At The Beach
A Prince & His Sandcastle
A Princess & Her Sandcastle
Ridin' The Waves
The Sand & The Sea
Sand, Surf & Me Down By The Sea
Sand Dudes
Sand Man
Sand Surfer
Sand + Sun = Fun
The Sands Of Time
A "Sand"sational Day
"Sand"sational Memories
"Sand"tastic Fun
Sea Breezes
Sea Of Dreams
Sea Of Green
Sea Of Joy
Sea Of Love
Sea Of Tranquility
Sea Ya Later
Seascape Of Fun
Seascape Of Sun & Seagulls
Seascape Of Wonder
Seashell Search
A Seashell Search On The Seashore
Seashells By The Seashore
Seaside Fun
Seaside Sun
Seaside Treasure
Secrets In The Sea
She Found Seashells Down By The Seashore
Shell Games
Shell Seekers
Shellabrate Good Times
Shore Fun
Shore Is Fun
Shore Party
Shore Things
Sittin' On The Dock Of The Bay
So Crabby
Spirit Of The Sea
A Splashing Good Day
Splashing Thru The Waves
Splish Splash
Summer At The Seashore
Sun, Sea & Surf
Surf & Sand...Ain't Life Grand
Surfer Girl/Boy
Surfin' Safari
Surf's Up
Takin A Quick Dip
Testing The Water
Tidepool Treasures
Tides Of Change
Toes Dancin' In The Sand
Treasures From The Sea *(Seashells)*
Treasures In The Sand *(Kids buried in sand)*
Tropical Fun
Under The Boardwalk
Under The Sea
Underwater Brilliance
Underwater Fun
Underwater Harmony
Underwater Splendor
Unofficial Beach Bum
Up A Creek
Voyage To The Bottom Of The Sea *(Sub)*
Walkin' Along The Shore
Watchin' The Tides Roll Away
Water World
Wave Reviews
Wave Riders
We Shore Had Fun
Wet & Wild
A Whale Of A Time

Wide Ocean Spaces
The Wild, Wild Sea
Wipe Out!!!
Wishin' On A Sea Star
What A Sandbox!!!
Wonders Of The Sea
You & Me By The Sea

____
____
____
____
____

BEAR/TEDDY TITLES
(SEE ALSO ZOO)
- *Create a Bear to hold the title.*

Bear Bottoms
Bear Hug
The Bear Necessities
Bear With Me
Bear-ly *(Age)* Years Old
The Beary Best Of Friends
Beary Beary Sweet
Beary Cute
Beary Sleepy
Beauty Is In The Eyes Of The "Bear"holder
Beary Special
Don't Be A Bear...Smile
Friends Make Life Bearable
Fuzzy Wuzzy Was The Bear
Guardian Teddy On Duty
Grin & Bear It
Happiness Is A Beary Big Hug
I Couldn't "Bear" It If You...
I Love You Beary Much
I'll Share Everything In Life Except My Teddy!
I'm Beary Special
Let Me Be Your Teddy Bear
Li-Bear-ty
Love Bears All Things
Love Makes All Things Bear-able
Me & My Teddy
Please Bear With Me
Polar Bear Prowl
A Pooh-rrific Friend
Pooh's My Tubby Little Cubby
Running Bear
I'm Someone Beary Special!
A Teddy Bear Will Always Care
Teddy Bears Are For Cuddlin' & Lovin'
A Teddy's Heart Is As Big As His Smile
Unbearably Cute!
We All Need A Little Tender Loving Bear
You Make Life Bear-able
You're Unbearable

____
____
____
____
____

BEAUTY TITLES
(SEE ALSO CUTE & GRACE)
A Love So Beautiful
Ageless Beauty
All The Lovely Ladies
All Things Bright & Beautiful
American Beauty
American Beauty Rose
As Beautiful As The Day Is Long
Bald Is Beautiful!
Bald Is Neat
Bathing Beauty
Be Your Own Kind Of Beautiful!
Beautiful & Lovely
Beautiful Addiction
A Beautiful Awakening
Beautiful Baby
Beautiful Boy
Beautiful Dreamer
A Beautiful Feeling
Beautiful Flower
Beautiful Girl
Beautiful In My Eyes
A Beautiful Life
Beautiful...Loved...Blessed
A Beautiful Mind
A Beautiful Night
A Beautiful Noise
Beautiful Obsession
Beautiful One
Beautiful People
Beautiful Smile
Beautiful Star
Beautiful World
Beautiful You
Beauty & The Beast
Beauty & The Mess
Beauty Is Deeper Than Skin
Beauty Is In The Eye Of The Beholder

Beauty Is Only Skin Deep
Beauty Like This Doesn't Require Clothes
The Beauty Of You
The Beauty Of Your Soul
Beauty Pageant Princess
Beauty Queens
The Beauty That I Love
Beauty Within
Black Beauty
Cause You're So Beautiful...
Crazy Beautiful
Deeper Than Beauty
Drop Dead Gorgeous
Enchanting Beauty
Feel Pretty
Good Morning Beautiful
Goodness Is Better Than Beauty
Grace Finds Beauty In Everything
Great Big Beautiful Eyes
Hey Pretty Girl
Hot Stuff
How Beautiful It Is To Me
How Could Beauty Be So Kind
How Pretty You Are
Innocent Beauty
Isn't She Lovely
It's A Beautiful World
Just Another Pretty Face
Let Your Beauty Come Alive
Let Your Beauty Shine
Little Bitty Pretty One
Little Lovely
Lost In Your Beauty
Love & Beauty
Love Is A Beautiful Thing
A Lovely Girl In A Lovely World
Lovely Lady
Lovely, Lovely
Lovely One
Lovely To Look At
Modern Day Delilah
The Most Beautiful Girl
My Eyes Are Beautiful Because They're
Looking At You
Oh, How You Sparkle, Oh, How You Shine
Oh, Pretty Woman
Oh What A Beautiful Morning
Pretty As A Picture
Pretty Baby
Pretty Boy
Pretty Girl
Pretty In Pink
Pretty Little Thing
Pretty Maids All In A Row
Pretty Woman
Pretty Young Thing
Pure Beauty
She Don't Know She's Beautiful
She Is So Lovely
She's A Beauty
Simply Adorable
Sleeping Beauty
Such A Beautiful Child
Sweet Beauty Sleep
Too Beautiful For Words
True Beauty
We Have A Beautiful Thing
What Makes You Different Makes You Beautiful
When You've Got It...Flaunt It!!!
Wonderous Beauty
You Are So Beautiful To Me
You Must Have Been A Beautiful Baby
You're Lookin' Good
You're Lookin' Mighty Fine

BEE TITLES

(SEE ALSO BUGS)

- *Make a "Bee" with a dotted line as its trail flying around & through the title.*
- *Create the title with a dotted line to look like the Bee's Trail spelled it.*

Our "Bee"utiful Daughter/Girl
Our "Bee"utiful Son/Boy
Bee Boppin' Around
Bee Good
Bee Happy
A Bee In My Bonnet
Bee Joyful
Bee Mine
Bee My Honey
Bee Sweet
Bee Tender
Bee-cause I Love You
Bee-ing Cute
Bee-ing The Best
Bee-ing With You Makes Me Buzzy
"Bee"sy Spring
"Bee"utiful
Bee-utiful Kids
Bumblin Bee
Busy As A Bee
Busy Bee's
The Buzz

Buzzzzz Off!
Buzzwords
Can They Bee Any Cuter
Don't Worry...Bee Happy!
Got Buzzed
Got The Latest Buzz!?
Here's The Buzz!
Honey Business
Honey Do's
Honey I Love My Kids
Honey Of A Day
Hunny Bee Nice!
Hunny, I'm Stuck On You!
I "Bee"lieve I Can Fly
Just Bee Bopping Along
Just Buzzing Around
The Latest Buzz
Mad As A Hornet
My "Bee"utiful Kids
My Heart "Bee"longs In *(Your State)*
My Honey Bee
My Honeycomb Or Yours
Queen Bee
Some Honey Loves You
As Sweet As Can "Bee"
Sweet As Hunny
There's No Place I'd Rather Bee
Un"bee"lievably Cute
We "Bee"lieve In Love
We "Bee"lieve In You
What A Buzzy Boy!
What's The Buzz?
You Bee-long To Me
You're My Honey Bee

____
____
____
____
____

BERRY TITLES

*(SEE **FOOD**)*

BEVERAGE TITLES

(SEE ALSO FOOD)

2 4 Tea
99 Bottles Of Beer
...And The Drinks Flowed
Better Latte Than Never
Bye Bye Bottle, Hello Cup
Caffeine Crazy
Coffee Has Its Perks
Don't Cry Over Spilt Milk
Down The Hatch
Drink, Drank, Drunk!!!
Drink, Drink & Be Drunk
Drink, Drink & Be Merry
Drink Up!
Drinkin' Buddies
Eat, DRINK & Be Merry
Eat, DRINK & Be Scary
Expresso Yourself
That Frosty Mug Sensation
Got Milk?
Got Frappuccino...Will Survive!!!
Got Stress?...Drink Wine!
Have A Drink On Me
I Can't Believe I Drank The Whole Drink
If Life Gives You Lemons, Make Lemonade!
I'll Drink To That
In The Drink
Instant Human - Just Add Coffee
It's Always Happy Hour Somewhere
It's 5:00 Somewhere
Java Junkie
Milk, It Does A Body Good!
Obey Your Thirst
Plop, Plop...Fizz, Fizz
Sip Slurppin' Away
Sippin' Soda
So Thirsty, Gotta Drink
Summer Wine
Tea For Two
That's Brisk Baby
Thirst Quenching Satisfaction
The Uncola
With Enough Coffee...Anything Is Possible

____
____
____
____
____

BICYCLE/BIKING TITLES

(SEE ALSO DIRT BIKE, MOTORCYCLES & RIDING)

- *Make an "O" into a Bicycle Wheel.*
- *Replace the word Bike with a Bike.*

An Awaaaay She/He Goes!
Backyard Bike-A-Thon
Balancing Act
Bicycle Act
The Bicycle Is A Curious Vehicle
Biker Babe/Baby/Buddy/Dude
Biking Buddies
Born To Bike/Ride
Breaking Away
Easy Rider
First Set Of Wheels

Go Speed Racer
Good-bye Trike...Hello Bike!
Have Some Balance In Your Life
I Can Do It
I'm So Far Behind, I Thought I Was Ahead
Look Mom, No Training Wheels!!!
Look Out...Here I Come!
Makin' Tracks
On A Bicycle Built For *(Child's name)*
On Your Mark...Get Set...Go!
One Wheeler
Pedal Practice
Pedal Pushin'
The Peddler
Puttin' The Pedal To The Metal
Ready...Set...Go!
Ride Like The Wind
Rollin', Rollin', Rollin'...Keep Those Wheels A Rollin'
'Round & 'Round
Spinning Your Wheels
Steady As She Goes
Steady...Steady
Steering Clear
Tandum Duo
There's No Looking Back Now
Trail & Error
Trail Blazer
Training Progress
Training Wheels *(Put the saying inside a circle with a diagonal line through it)*
Two Wheel Travelin'
Uneasy Rider
Unicycler
Watch Me Go
The Wheels On My Bike Go 'Round & 'Round
Wheely Fun

BILLIARDS TITLES

(SEE ALSO GAMES)

- *Make an "O" into an 8-Ball.*
- *Replace an "I" or "L" with a Cue Stick.*

Back Spinner
The Balls Know When You're Broke
Cue-Ball Kissed
Behind The 8-Ball
Dirty Pool
Dusted 'Em All..."With Blue Chalk That Is!"
Feather Master
Fluke Shooter
Got Pool Cues?
King Of Scratch
Left In The Dust
Never Chalk Before Miscuing
Pocket Pool
Pool Duel
Pool Fools
Pool Fun
Pool Hall Fun
Pool Hall Junkies
Pool Is A Game Of Brains Not Brawn
Pool Players Do It With Stroke
Pool Players Enjoy Bustin' Balls
Pool Shark
Poolin' Around
Rack 'Em
Scratch King
Screw Ball
Stack 'Em & Rack 'Em
Straight Pool Is The Breakfast Of Champions
Straight To The "8"
Stunned
Undercut King/Queen

BINGO TITLES

(SEE ALSO GAMES)

- *Make the title on a Bingo card with the title letters circled or lightly daubed.*

Bingo Lingo
Dauber Queen/King
Diehard Dauber
G-3, Play Bingo With Me?
Garden Gates Win *(Eights)*
O-2 Have Too Much Fun
Was There Life B-4 Bingo?
Way To Go...Bingo!
When The Chips Are Down...Yell Bingo!
Won With Legs Eleven *(#11)*

____
____
____
____
____

BIRD TITLES

(SEE ALSO ANIMALS)

A Bird In The Hand
A Little Birdie Told Me...
As Light As A Feather
Bald As An Eagle
Bird Of Paradise
Bird Sanctuary
Birdie Barracks
Birds Eye View
Birds Of A Feather...
Bless Our Nest
Blue Bird On My Shoulder
Blue Birds Of Happiness
Bye Bye Birdie
Cheep-ish
Country Re-tweet
Don't Ruffle My Feathers
The Early Birds Catches The Worm
Eating Like A Bird
Everybirdy's Welcome Here
Featherbed Inn
Featherbeds For Wrent!!
Feathered Friends
Feed The Birdies...Please!
Flight School
Flights Of Fancy
Fly By Night Hotel
Fly Like An Eagle
As Free As A Bird
For Sale...Cheep!!
For Wrent
For Wrent...Cheep...Cheep!!
Home Tweet Home
How Tweet It Is!
Jailbird
Little Songbird
Lovebirds
SLOW!!!...Low Flying Hummingbirds!!!
Nest & Breakfast
Pigeon Toed
This Place Is For The Birds
Polly Wanna Cracker?
Private Bath...No Peeping
Proud As A Peacock
Sing Like A Bird
Sit Long, Chirp Much
Snow Birds Welcome
Something To Crow About
Songville....Bed & Breakfast
Sweetie Tweetie
Treetop Inn
Tweet Suite
Tweet, Tweet
Up, Up & Away
You're So Tweet

____
____
____
____
____

BIRTHDAY TITLES

(SEE ALSO AGE, PARTY & PRESENTS)

- *Use a Candle for an "I".*
- *Put a Candle on top of each letter.*

1 - A One-derful Party
Bearly 1
Fun Being 1
I'm 1-derful On My 1st Birthday
I'm 1 & My Story's Just Begun
I'm 1 & Tons Of Fun
I'm 1 After A Year Of Fun
It's The Big 1!
What Fun...I'm 1

2 - 2 Adorable
2 Hot 2 Handle
2-rrific Two's
Choo-Choo, *(Child's name)* Turned 2
Got The Clue *(Child's name)* 2
I'm 2-rrific
Look Who's 2 & So Much To Do
What To Do, Now That I'm 2!
What To Get Into Now That I'm 2!

B B B B B B B B B B B B B B B B B B B B B B B B B B B B B B

3 - I'm 3-mendous
It's Time To Be The Big 3!!!
Look At Me, Now I'm 3
This Is Me At 3
Thrilling 3
4 - Fantastic 4
I'm 4 & Growing More & More
I'm 4...Hear Me Roar
One Year More, Now I'm 4!
5 - Fine At 5 & That's No Jive
Ready To Dive Into 5!
5-Alarm Fire
6 - Finally 6 & Full Of Tricks
Now I'm 6 & Full Of Kicks
Silly 6's
What A Fix...I Just Turned 6
7 - 7 Is Heaven
Oh My Heaven, I'm Now 7
Simply 7
8 - It's Great To Be 8
On This Date...I Turned 8!
7 Was Heaven, But 8 Is Great!
9 - 9 Is Fine
9 & Feelin' Fine
No Time To Whine, Now I'm 9!
10 - Can You Believe Where I've Been?...
And Now I'm Moving On...I'm 10!!
Perfect 10
11 - It's Heaven To Be 11
13 - Lucky 13
16 - 16 Candles
16 Going On 17
Sweet Little 16
18 - Lean, Mean 18
Queen 18
Sweet 18
21 - 21 & Legal
21-derful
21's Totally Fun
It's The Big 21
29 - 29 & Holding
30 - 30 Is A Dirty Word
30 & Still Holding
My Next 30 Years...
Oh, No! It's The Big 3-0! *(Any age)*
39 - 39 Again!?
39 & Holding!
Forever 39
40 - 40 & Still Sporty
After 40, It's A Matter Of Maintenance
I'm Not 40...I'm 18 With 22 Years Experience
Lordy, Lordy Look Who's 40!
50 - 50 Is Nifty
50 = 5 Perfect 10's
After 50, It's Patch, Patch, Patch!!!
60 - 60 & Sexy
I'm 60 Of Age...That's 16 Celsius
Silly 60's
24, 34, 44, Hear Me Roar
A Ball Of A Birthday
Aged To Perfection
All Mine
...And Many More
Another Candle On Your Birthday Cake
Another Year Older & Better
Another Year Older...Another Year Cuter
At My Age, Happy Hour Is Nap Time!
Birthday Bash
Birthday Blitz
Birthday Blow Out *(Blowing out candles)*
Birthday Blues
Birthday Bonanza
Birthday Bounty *(Presents)*
Birthday Diva
Birthday Girl
Born In The USA...A Loooooong Time Ago
Born To Party
Cake Anyone?
Cake Decorating 101
The Celebration Is On!!!
Can I Have Another Birthday Tomorrow?
A Cause For A Celebration
Caution: Old Zone
Classified Antique
Clownin' Around
Cute As A Cupcake
Don't Fear, It's Just Another Year
Eating My Cake & Wearing It Too
For Me?!
Forever Young
Forty Isn't Old... If You're A Tree!
Fun Zone
My Golden Birthday
Growing Older
Hip, Hip Hooray...It's My Birthday Today!
Huffin' & Puffin'
I Wish For...
I'll Have My Cake & Eat It Too!
I'll Huff & I'll Puff & I'll Blow My Candles Out
I'm A Year Smarter
I'm Not Getting Older, I'm Getting Better!
I'm Not Old...I'm Chronologically Gifted
In Dog Years, I'm Dead!!!
It Took Me *(Age)* Years To Look This Good
It's MR. Old Fart To You
It's My Birthday!

It's My Party, & I'll Cry If I Want To!!!
It's Party Time
Just What I've Always Wanted
Kiss *(Age)* Good-bye
Kiss Me, I'm 20/30/40/50 etc.
Let Me Eat/Wear Cake
Let's Party
Life Begins At 50/60/70/80
Look Who's The Dinosaur Now!
Make A Wish
The More Candles...The Bigger The Cake
The More Candles...The Bigger The Wish
Oh Dear, Another Year
Older & Wiser
Once Over The Hill, You Pick Up Speed
One Year Older & Cuter Too
One Year Older...One Year Wiser
Over The Hill
Over The Hill, I Don't Remember Any Hill!?
Party Animals
Party Friends
Party Hardy
The Party Starts Here
Party Time
A Pinch To Grow An Inch
"Presents" Time
Put On Your Party Hat
Ready...Set...Blow!
A Royal Birthday
Scrappy Birthday
A Smile To Grow A Mile
So Many Candles, So Little Cake
A Spankin' Good Time
Still Young At Heart
There's No Time Like The Presents Time
Those Whom The Gods Love Grow Young
Time For Cake
Today Is Your Day
Truth Be Told...You're Growing Old
Under Wraps *(Surrounded by wrapping paper)*
I Wanna Eat My Cake & Wear It Too!
We Need More Candles...
We Are Always The Same Age Inside
We Mourn The Passing Of Your Youth
You Take The Cake

____
____
____
____
____

BLACK TITLES

(A great way accentuate the word Black in the title, is to create that word only in Black. Make Black larger and even in a different type style than the rest of the title)

All In Black
Angel In Black
Big Black Caddy
Black As Coal
Black As Pitch
Black As The Ace Of Spades
Black As The Night Sky
Black Beauty
Black Cloud Rain
Black Diamonds
Black Eyes
Black Friday
Black Gold
Black Hawk
Black Hole
The Black Hole Of Calcutta
Black Magic
Black Magic Woman
Black Monday
Black Orchid
Black Out
Black Pearl
Black Rose
Black Sheep
Black Star
Black Widow
Black Velvet
Black Is Beautiful
Black Tie Affair
Blue Days...Black Nights
Blue On Black
Dressed In Black
Goddess In Black
Hit The Black Top
In The Black
Lady In Black
Little Black Book
Little Black Dress
Men In Black
My Knight In Black Leather
That Old Black Magic

____
____
____
____
____

B B B B B B B B B B B B B B B B B B B B B B B B B B B B B B

BLOCKS TITLES

- *Use a Baby or Lego Block for an "O".*
- *Place letters inside connectable or stackable Blocks.*
- *Create the word Block out of Legos.*

Block Heads
Block Talk
Building Blocks
We Built This City...
A Chip Off The Old Block
Havin' A Block Party
Lego Land
Lego My Blocks
Lego My Legos
New Kid On The Block
Nobody Stacks Up Next To You
Stackable Fun

BLUE TITLES

(A great way accentuate the word Blue in the title, is to create that word only in Blue. Make the word Blue larger and in a different type style than the rest of the title)

Baby Blues
Baby Blue Eyes
Baby's Got Blue Eyes
Beyond The Blue
Black & Blue
Blue Afternoon
Blue Bayou
Blue Beard
Blue Boy
Blue Christmas
Blue Eyed Savior
Blue Eyed Soul
Blue Eyes
Blue Eyes Cryin' In The Rain
Blue Heat
Blue Hi-Heels
Blue In The Face
Blue Jean Baby
Blue Jean Beauty Queen
Blue Jeans & Barefeet
Blue Midnight Glow
Blue Monday
Blue Mood
Blue Moon
Blue Skies
Blue Skies Blue
Blue Skies Shinin' On Me
Blue Spanish Sky
Blue Suede Shoes
Blue Velvet
Bluebird On My Shoulder
These Blues Can't Loose
California Blue
Crystal Blue Persuasion
Devil With The Blue Dress On!
Feeling Blue Today
Forever In Blue Jeans
It's A Blue World
Little Boy Blue
Midnight Blue
Misty Blue
Moody Blues
My Baby Blue
New Blue Moon
Once In A Blue Moon
Out Of The Clear Blue
The Power Of Blues *(Blue Jeans)*
Sky Blue
Song Sung Blue
This Must Be His Blue Period
Tin Roof Blue
A Touch Of Blue
True Blue
Under Blue Skies
When The Sky Turned Blue

BOAT TITLES

(SEE ALSO CRUISE & SAILING)

- *Use a Life Ring or Ship's Steering Wheel for the "O".*

Ahoy Matey
All Aboard
Anchored With Love
Anchors Away
Banana Boat
Boat Bums
This Boat Floats...I Hope!
A Canoe For You
Captain At The Helm
Captain *(Child's name)*
Catch The Wind
Come Sail Away
Come Sail Away With Me!
Cruise Director
Cruisin'
Cruisin' Along

Don't Give Up The Ship
Don't Rock The Boat
Fantastic Voyage
First Mate
Fresh Off The Boat
Full Steam Ahead
Harbor Lights In Sight
Hello Sailor!
Krazy 'Bout Kayaking
Learnin' The Ropes
The Little Tugboat
Love Boat
Missed The Boat
My Ship Has Come In
On A Slow Boat To China
On The Ropes
Out To Sea
"Pull"
Rockin' The Boat
Row, Row, Row Your Boat
Sail Away With Me
Sailing The Open Seas
Sea Of Love
Set Sail
Ship Shape
Shippin' Out
Ship's Ahoy
Shiver Me Timbers
That Sinkin' Feeling
Sittin' On The Dock Of The Bay
Smooth Sailin'
Someday My Ship Will Come
Starboard Home
Steamboat *(Name)*
Up A Creek
Voyage To The Bottom Of The Sea *(Sub)*
Waiting For Your Ship To Come In
Whatever Floats Your Boat
Yo Ho Ho
You Float My Boat
(Name) Row The Boat Ashore

BOOK TITLES

(SEE ALSO EDUCATION, SCHOOL & TEACHER)

- *Replace "O" with Books having a bookworm crawling under books or peeking over top.*
- *Put each of the title letters inside a Book.*
- *Make an open Book with the title on pages.*
- *Place the title on the front of the Book as the Book's title.*

Adventure Is Just A Page Away
All Booked Up
Book Buddies
Book Of Dreams
Book Of Love
The Book Of My Life
Books Are Food For The Brain
Books Are My Bag
Bookworm
Bored? Read A Book!
By The Book
Easy Reader
Extra! Extra! Read All About It!
Favorite Stories
The Grim Reader
Hit The Books
I Can Read Now!
I Can Read Your Love
Just Read It!
Librarians Are Happy Bookers
Librarians Are Novel Lovers
My Life's Like An Open Book
Little Black Book
Little Bookworm
The Need To Read
New Reader
Once Upon A Page
Our Little Bookworm
Playing By The Book
The Power Of Reading
Power Reader
Read All About It
Read 'Em & Weep
Read Me A Story
Read With Me
Reader Of Many Books
Reading Dreams
Reading King
Reading Matters
Reading Rainbow
Reading Rocks
Reading Room
Reading Rules
Reading The Day Away
So Many Books...So Little Time
Soul Reader

Speed Reader
To Read In The Morning & At Night
Today, I Will Read
Twilight Reader
Weekly Reader
The Written Word
You Wrote The Book Of Love

BOWL/BOWLING TITLES

(SEE ALSO SPORTS)

- *Use a Bowling Ball for an "O".*
- *Replace an "I" or 'L" with a Bowling Pin.*
- *Run Wood-Grain paper (as the Lane) across top of page with Bowling Pins at left, title in middle & Ball rolling towards letters.*

300 Ring
Alley Cats
Alley Oops
Anchor Man
Applied Again
Bowled Over
Bowlers Have Time To Spare
Bowlers Love To Strike Out
Bowling Is A Ball
Bowling Is Right Up My/Your Alley
Five Bagger *(5 Strikes)*
Grip It & Rip It
Gutter Ball
Gutter Balls Stink
Havin' A Ball
Hit It With A Creeper *(Slow ball)*
In My Spare Time...
In The Gutter
In The Pocket
Just Call Me Scratch!
Just Pin It!
Keep That Ball A Rollin'
King Of The Pins
Kingpin
League Of Rollers
A League Of Their Own
Let 'Er Roll
Let The Good Times Bowl
Let's Bowl
Life Is A Bowl Of Strikes
Look Out Dick Weber
Pin Boys
Pin Busters
Pin Heads
Pin Setters
Pin Splitters
Poodle Player *(Gutter ball)*
Ready...Set...Bowl
Ready...Set...Roll
Right Up Your Alley
Rolled A Frozen Rope
Rolled Snake Eyes *(7-10 Split)*
Rollin' Rocks
Rollin', Rollin', Rollin'
Scratch Bowler
Six Pack Player *(6 Strikes)*
Spare Me!
Spare Play
Splits Happen
Stay Outta The Gutter
Strike It
Superbowler Star
Throwin' Rocks
Turkey Roller/Bowler *(3 Strikes)*
You Bowl Me Over

BOXING TITLES

(SEE ALSO SPORTS)

- *Create Boxing Gloves hanging from title.*

...And In This Corner
Are You Ready To Rumble?
Bash...Bang
Bobbin' & Weavin'
I Coulda Been A Contenda
Dance Like A Butterfly...
Dancing 'Round The Ring
Didn't Lay A Glove On Him!
Down For The Count
Dropped His Guard
Featherweight Champ
A Fighting Chance
First Blood
Gave 'Em The Ole 1..2..
The Great Contender
He Can Run, But He Can't Hide!
Heavyweight Champ
Hit The Mat
Hit With A Jab
The Hurricane
In The Ring
Just Jab Him
Kerpow!
Killer Instinct

Knock You Out
Left Hook 'Em
The Main Event
On The Ropes
Pound For Pound
Raging Bull
The Real McCoy
Saved By The Bell
Shadow Boxing
South Paw
Splat
Split Decision
Survived The Standing '8'
Threw An Uppercut
Threw In The Towel
TKO
We Wuz Robbed!
Welterweight Champ

____
____
____
____
____

BOY TITLES

(SEE ALSO BABY, BOY, CHILDREN & SON)

100% Boy
A Boy & His Trucks
A Boy Is A Boy
All American Boy
Angel Boy
Atta Boy
Baby Boy
Backyard Boyz
Baseball Diamonds Are A Boys Best Friend
Beach Boys
Beautiful Boy
Big Boy...
Big Boy Toys
Boogie Boy
Boogie Woogie Bugle Boy
Bouncing Boys
Boy: A Noise With Dirt On It!!!
Boy, It's Cold Out There!
Boy Genius
A Boy Like You
Boy Meets World
The Boy Next Door
Boy Of A 1,000 Faces
Boy Of Steel
Boy, Oh Boy
Boy Story
Boy Toy
The Boy Who Giggle So Sweet
Boys = Dirt
Boys & Their Toys
Boys Are Angels Too!
The Boys Are Back In Town
Boys Don't Cry
The Boy's Gone Home
Boys Just Wanna Have Fun
The Boys Of Summer
Boys 'R Us
Boys Rule
Boys Will Be Boys
Boyz Will Be Boyz
Bulldozer Boy
Busy Boy
Candy Boy
City's Boy Dream
Country Boy
Country Boy Can Survive
Cowabunga Dude
Crazy Boy
Cute Boy
Daddy's Little Buddy
Daddy's Little Helper
Danny Boy
Drummer Boy
Genuine Boy
Georgie Boy
Gimmie The Beat Boys
Golden Boy
GQ Boy
He's A Good Ole Boy
Here Comes The Son
Hot Boy
I Love Boys, Every Girl Should Own One
I Wanna Be Like You-o-o!
If I Were A Rich Boy
I'm A Big Boy Now!
I'm Just A Country Boy
It's A Boys/Boyz Life
It's A Girl's World...Boys Just Live In It!!
It's A Guy/Boy Thing
Lazin' Around
Let The "SON" Shine
Let's Hear It For The Boy
Like Father, Like Son
Lil' Mr. Sonshine
Little Big Man
Little Boy Blue
Little Boy Blue Jeans
Little Boys Are Angels Too!
Little Boys Do Cry
Little Buddy
Lonely Boy
Lord, Have Mercy On A Country Boy

Lover Boy
Macho, Macho Boy
Mama's Boy
Man Under Construction
Master Of Mischief
Me & My Boyfriend
Men Are Just Boyz Grown Tall
Mischief Maker
Mr. Mighty Might Man
Mr. Snips & Snails
Mr. Style
My Boy
My Boy, My Joy!
Nature Boy
Non-Stop Action
Oh Boy! Oh Joy!
Oh Boy...When You're With Me...
Our Lil' Cowboy
Out & About
Pretty Boy, I Love You
Puddle Jumper
Rough & Ready
See It In A Boys Eyes
Sexy Boy
She's In Love With The Boy
Silly Boy
Snakes & Snails & Puppy Dog Tails
Snips & Snails & ...
Snugly, Cuddly Baby Boy
So Handsome
Thank God I'm A Country Boy
Thank Heaven For Little Boys
That's What Little Boys Are Made Of...
The Joys Of Boys!
The Strongest Boy In The World
The "Y" Chromosome
They Call Me Trouble
Tiny Man
Tough As Nails
Tough Guy
Walking With My Boyfriend
Warning...Likes To Play In The Mud! *(Dirty child)*
What Are Little Boys Made Of?
What Little Boys Are Made Of...
What's A Boy To Do?
What's It Gonna Be Big Boy?
When Boy Meets Girl...
When I Was A Young Boy...
Where The Boys Are!
Wonder Boys
You've Got Male

BOYFRIEND TITLES
(SEE BOY, DATING & LOVE)

BOYSCOUT TITLES
All Knotted Up
Always Prepared
Bear Cubs On The Prowl
Cubcakes
Learning The Ropes
Natur-ally Gifted
On My Honor
On The Trail To Eagle
Scouts Honor
Scouting Rocks
Tiger Cubs On The Prowl
Tiger Cubs Roar
To Keep Myself Morally Straight, Physically Strong & Mentally Awake
Wolf Cubs On The Prowl

BREAK/BREAK-UP TITLES
(SEE ALSO HEART & LOVE)
Achy Breaky Heart
All Broke Up
Bend & Break
Break Away
Break Dancing Duo
Break 'Em Up
Break Even
Break It Off
Break It On Down
Break It Up
Break Me Down
Break My Fall
Break Of Dawn
Break Out
Break The Chain
Break The Ice

Break The Silence
Breakin' Bread
Breakin' Every Rule
Broke Every Rule
Broke The Bank
Broken Hearted
Can't Break Thru
A Change Of Heart
Commercial Break
Divorce Court Here I Come
Gimmie A Break
Give Me A Break
Go For Broke
Good Ridden's
Heart Breaker
How To Mend A Broken Heart
I Want To Break Free
If It Ain't Broke...
If We Break A Few Rules...
I'll Never Smile Again
Letting Go
Lonely With A Broken Heart
Love Hurts
Make A Break For It
Morning Has Broken
New Beginnings
Out With The Old & In With The New
Reunited
See Ya!
She Loves Me...She Loves Me Not...
There Will Never Be Another You
Time Heals All...

BROTHER TITLES

(SEE ALSO BOY)

Always My Brother
Am I My Brother's Keeper?
Back To Back...Brother To Brother
Being Brothers Is The Best
Being Brothers Is Something Special
Best Buddies
Best Buddies Are We...My Brother & Me!
Big Brother Blues
Big Brother Is Watchin' Over You
Birds Of A Feather
Blue Ribbon Brother
Bros & Buds
Brother, Can You Spare Me Some Time
A Brother Is A Forever Friend
A Brother Like No Other
Brother My Brother
Brother Of Mine
Brother To Brother
Brotherhood
Brotherly Love
Brotherly Ties
Brothers & Buddies
Brothers Are A Work Of Heart
Brothers Are As Close As Hands & Feet.
(Vietnamese Proverb)
Brothers Are Forever
Brothers Are Special...Especially Mine
Brothers Are Just Like Sisters, Only They Like Bugs
Brothers Are The Best Kind Of Friends
Brothers Are The Crab Grass In The Lawn Of Life
Brothers By Chance, Friends Because Mom Said So
Brothers By Chance...Friends By Choice
Brothers From The Start...Friends From The Heart
Brothers - Gotta Love 'Em!
Brothers In Arms
Brothers Make The Best Friends
Brothers Share A Love Tied With Heartstrings
Brothers Since The Beginning...Friends 'Til The End
My Brother's The Bomb
The Bruisin' Brothers
Celebrating Brotherhood
Celebration Of Brothers
Chance Made Us Brothers, Hearts Made Us Friends
Chuckles, Secrets & Sometimes Tears
Double Blessing
Double Trouble
Each Of Our Lives Will Always Be A Special Part Of The Other
First A Bother, Then A Brother, Now A Friend
First A Brother, Now A Friend
Forever My Brother, Always My Friend
God Made Us Brothers...Prozac Made Us Friends
He Ain't Heavy, He's My Brother
He's My Brother
He's Your Brother
Hey Big Brother
Just Like Big Brother

I Am My Brothers Keeper
I Love My Brother
Love Is Blind But Kid Brothers Are Not
Me & My Bro
My Brother, My Friend...
My Brothers Keeper
Near & Dear
Oh, Brother!
Oh Brother, He's My Brother
Peas In A Pod
Sibling Rivalry
Smile On Your Brother
Sometimes Enemies, Sometimes Friends, Always Brothers!
Soul Brother
There's No Buddy Like A Bro
There's No Other Like My Brother
Two Of A Kind
We Share A History
What A Pair!
What's Yours Is Mine & What's Mine Is Mine!
When A Child Is Born, So Is A Brother
When I Get Big, I'll Get Even!!!
Yo! Bro!
You Drive Me Nuts
(Name) Has Been Promoted To Big Brother

BROWN TITLES

(A great way accentuate the word Brown in the title, is to create that word only in Brown. Make the word Brown larger and in a different type style than the rest of the title)

Brown-Eyed Blues
My Brown-Eyed Girl
Brown Eyes
Brown Sugar
Charlie Brown
Chocolate Brown
Don't It Make My Brown Eyes Blue
Down Town Brown
Genie With The Light Brown Hair
Sweet Georgia Brown
Them Pretty Brown Eyes
These Brown Eyes

BUBBLES/BUBBLEBATH TITLES

(SEE ALSO BATH/BATHTIME)

- *Make the "O" into a Bubble.*
- *Make Bubbles out of Vellum & place letters inside of them.*

Blowing Bubbles
The Boy In The Bubble
Bubble Baby
Bubble, Bubble What's All The Trouble?
Bubble Buns
Bubble Do *(Hair full of bubbles)*
Bubble Head
Bubble Your Troubles Away
Bubble-ing Over With Fun
Bubblicious
A Bubbly Personality
Bursting Bubbles
Double The Bubbles, Double The Fun
Double Trouble...Boys/Girls In Bubbles
Doubly Bubbly
Living In A Bubble
Mr. Bubbles
My Bubble Gum Years
Ready, Set, Blow Bubbles
Shimmer, Sparkle & Shine
Soap Bubbles
Tiny Bubbles
Yummy Bubbles In My Tummy

BUGS TITLES

(SEE ALSO BEES, BUTTERFLY'S, FIREFLIES, LADY BUGS & SPIDERS)

- *Use a Spider in place of an "O".*
- *Have a Spider hanging from title.*
- *Have little Bugs crawling all over title.*
- *Make a trail of Ants weaving thru title letters.*
- *Have Ants carrying title letters.*

2-Legged Pests
Adam Ant
Along Came A Spider
Ant Attack
Ant Farm
Ant Invaders
Ants In My Pants
The Ants Were Marching One By One
Army Of Ants
Baby Bugs

Backyard Bugs
Be My "Love Bug"
Bitten By The Love Bug
Born To Catch Bugs
Bug-A-Boo
Bug Bug
Bug Catcher/Collectin'
Bug-Eyed Wild
Bug Eyes
Bug Hunting
Bug In A Box/Jar
Bug Juice
"Bug" Me Again & I'll Bite
Bugged Out
Bugging Out
A Bug's Life
Caution: Critter Crossing
Cootie Bug
Creepy Crawlers/Crawly
Cuddle Bug
Cute As A Bug
Cuter Than A Bug
Don't Bug Me
Don't Let The Little Things Bug You
Doodle Bug
Fashion Bug
The Flu Bug
Here's The Buzz
I'm Buggy For Bugs
I'm In "BUG" Trouble!
It's A Bug's Life
Itsy Bitsy Spider
Itty Bitty Bug Catcher
The Jitter Bug
June Bugs
Just Buggy
Just Buzzing Around
Lice Ain't Nice
Love Bug
Love Bugs & Crazy Daisies
Love Them Bugs
Mad As A Hornet
No Ifs, Ants Or Bugs About It
Our Little Love Bug
Quit Bugging Me
Shutter Bug
Slug Bug
Snug As A Bug In A Rug
Snuggle Bug
Stars In A Jar *(Fireflies)*
Stink Bug
Twilight Zone *(Firefly pics)*
Water Bugs
When Ants Attack...
Why Didn't Noah Swat Those 2 Mosquitoes?
Y2K Bugs
You "Bug" Me!

____
____
____
____
____

BULLDOZER TITLES

(SEE CONSTRUCTION)

BUS TITLES

(SEE ALSO SCHOOL)

- *Create a Bus and have title letters on the Bus or in its windows.*

Big Yellow School Bus
Bumpy Bus Ride
Bus Boy
Bus Buddies
Does This Bus Stop In *(City or State)*
Feelin' Yellow
Found Love A On A Bus
Get On The Bus
The Long Bus Ride Home
Just Call Me Yellow
The Magic School Bus
On A Bus To *(City or State)*
On The Backseat Of A Greyhound Bus
Rollin', Rollin', Rollin'
School Bus Drivers Are Big Wheels!
Skool Bus Ride
Slow Bus Movin'
Waitin' At The Bus Stop
Waiting For The Bus
The Wheels On The Bus Go 'Round & 'Round

____
____
____
____
____

BUTTERFLY TITLES

- *Put Wings on an "I".*

Butterflies...Flowers That Fly & All But Sing.
(Robert Frost)
Butterfly, Butterfly In The Sky So High
Butterfly Chasing
The Butterfly Collector
Butterfly Effects
Butterfly Fly, Fly Away
Butterfly Garden
Butterfly Kisses
Flights Of Fancy
Flutter By Butterfly
Flutter Like A Butterfly
God Bless The Butterflies
Little Butterfly Come Back
Madame Butterfly
She's A Butterfly
Social Butterfly
Wings Of A Butterfly
Your Love Gives Me Wings Like A Butterfly

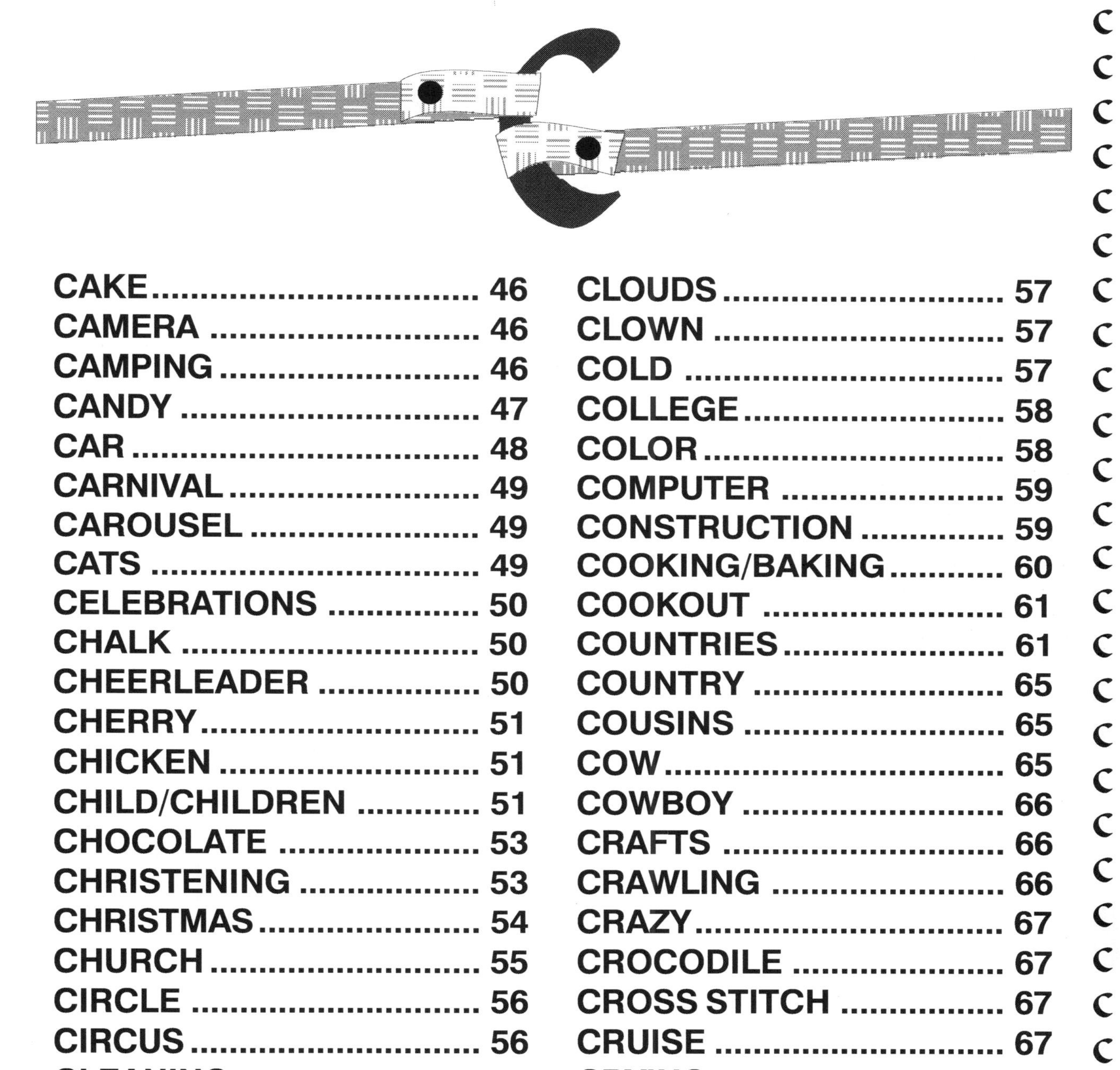

CAKE TITLES

(SEE ALSO FOOD)

Angel Cake
Another Piece Of Cake Please
Cake On My Face & Hands & Chest & Legs &....
Cup Cake Cutie
Devil's Food Cake
The Icing On The Cake
Icing Sweet Icing
I'll Have My Cake & Eat It Too!
It's A Cake Walk
Let 'Em Eat Cake
Patty Cake, Patty Cake
Piece Of Cake
Pound Cake Please
Smash Cake
That Takes The Cake...
Wearing My Cake Tastes Better
Your My Chocolate Cake

____
____
____
____
____

CAMERA & POSING TITLES

(SEE ALSO PHOTOGRAPHER/PHOTOGRAPHY)

Addicted To Pics
Ain't I Cute?
Big Shot
Budding Photographer
Camera Bug
A Candid Afternoon
A Candid Moment
Capture The Moments/Memories
Caught On Film
Feeling Snappy
Film At 11
Freeze Frame
A Golden Moment
Grin & Bear It
Guaranteed Grinable
Hammin' It Up
I Ought To Be In Pictures!
I'm A Star
In The Camera's Eye
In The Spot Light
I've Been Framed
Kodak Moment
Let's See What Develops
Lights, Camera, Action!
Miles Of Smiles
This Moment Caught Forever In Time
A Moment In Time
Mom's Got The Camera Again!
A Mug For The Camera
Mug Shots
My Camera Never Lies
My Focus Is Sharp
A Not-So-Kodak Moment
Okay! Take It Already!
Photogenic
Photo Phinish
A Picture's Worth A Thousand Words
Picture Perfect
Picture This
Pretty As A Picture
Processed To Perfection
Say "Cheese"
Show Us Those Pearly Whites
Shutter Bug
Smile For The Camera
Smile, You're On Digital Camera!
Snap Shots & Smiles
Strike A Pose Or Two Or Three!!!
Super Star
Take A Picture, It Lasts Longer!
Take Your Best Shot
Wide Angle Watcher
You Ought To Be In Pictures

____
____
____
____
____

CAMPING TITLES

(SEE ALSO COOKOUT, FOOD, HIKING, NATURE & OUTDOORS)

- *Make "O's" into Roasted Marshmallows.*
- *Create a small A-Frame Tent for an "A".*
- *Use tiny twigs or sticks to spell out title (twigs can be made from paper then chalked)*

Adventure Time
Ah, Wilderness
The Ants Go Marching One By One...
Around The Campfire
Back To Basics
Bad Boy Of Boot Camp
Barefoot In The Campsite
The Big Hike
A Bit Squirrelly
Ah! Wilderness
Back To Nature
Boy Meets Grill
Burnt Offerings
Cabin Fever

A Cabin In The Woods
Call Of The Wild
Calling All Campers
Camp More...Work Less!
Campers Have S'more Fun!
Campfire Cookin'
Camping Anyone?
Camping Beneath The Moon & Stars
Camping Capers
A Camping We'll Go
Candid Camping
A Canoe For You
Climb Every Mountain
Club Camp
Communing With Nature
Cuddly Campers
Don't Bug Me...
Eating Outside
Explorer Extraordinaire
Fantastic Campfires
Fireside Fun
Getting Back To Nature
Goin' Wild
Gone Campin'
The Great Outdoors
Happy Campers
Happy Tenters
Hardrocks Cafe
Home Away From Home
Home Sweet Motorhome
Home Sweet Tent
I/We Love Picnics
Lakeside Adventures
Let's Go Camping
Life At Its Best
Marshmallow Madness
Marshmallows Roasting On An Open Fire
Moonlight Madness
Nature Boy/Girl
Nature Center
Nature's Beauty
Not A Happy Camper
On The Trail
One With Nature
Our Neck Of The Woods
The Outback
Outdoor Adventures
Outdoor Fun
Outdoor Odyssey
Picnic Fun
Playing With Fire
Primetime Adventures
Primetime Fun
Roughin' It
Rugged Outdoorsman
Scaling New Heights
Setting Up Camp
Sleeping Under The Moon & Stars
Smoke Gets In Your Eyes
S'more Camping Fun
S'more Fun!
S'more Good Times
S'more Memories
S'more S'mores Anyone?
S'morelicious
S'mores & Snores
Space Camp
Star Light, Star Bright...
Survival Of The Fittest
Take A Hike
Tent Fever
A Tent In The Woods
Tent Sweet Tent
This Is The Life
Trading Spaces
Trailer Life
Trailer Life Is The Life For Me
Under The Stars
We're Nuts!
Where's My Real Bed?

____
____
____
____
____

CANDY TITLES

(SEE ALSO FOOD)

- *Make the "A" or "O" into different kinds of Candies like a Sucker or a Peppermint.*

Candied Kids
Candy By The Pound
Candy Coated
Candy Coated Lips
Candy Hearts
Candy Kisses
Candy Man
Candy Solves Everything
Candyland
Cotton Candy Crazy
Cotton Candy Land
Drippin' In Candy
Eye Candy
Give Me Some Sugar Baby!
How Sweet It Is!
I Want Candy
I'm Stuck On You
It's All About The Candy

A Kid In A Candy Store
Lollipop, Oh! Lolli Lolli, Lollipop!
Love Is Candy
Rockin' Rock Candy
A Sweet Deal
Sweet Kiss Of Candy
Sweet Like Me
Sweet Loot
Sweet On You
A Sweet Taste Of Heaven
Sweet Tooth
Sweeter Than Candy
Sweetheart
Sweets For A Sweet
You Are My Candy Girl/Boy
Your Love Is Like Candy To Me

CAR TITLES

(SEE ALSO DRIVING & RACING)

- *Make the "O" into a Tire or Steering Wheel.*
- *Make the "I" into a Stick Shift.*
- *Create the title to look like a License Plate.*

3 On The Tree
4-Banger For My Bucks
4 On The Floor
Accident Happens!!!
Accidents Happen!!!
Along For The Ride
At The Carwash
Automobile Adventure
Baby, You Can Drive My Car!!!
Backyard Mechanic
Beep-Beep, Beep-Beep The Car Went Beep, Beep, Beep
Benz Brat
Big Bad Cad
Box Car
Bucket Of Bolts
Buggin' Out
A Caddy Is Not A Car To Scorn
Car Crazy
A Car Of Her/His Own
Car Quest
Cars, Cars & More Cars
A Classic On Four Wheels
Crazy 'Bout A Mercury
Don't Tread On Me
Dreamin' Of Beamin'
Drivin' Along In My Automobile
Easy Ride
Endless Project
Enjoying The Ride
Feelin' Buggy
Fender Bender
First Set Of Wheels
Get In, Sit Down, Hold On & Shut Up!!!
Get Ready To Rumble
Get The Wheels Rolling
Going Places
Got Car...Will Drive
Got Trucked
Grease Monkey
Have Car Will Travel
Heavy Chevy
Hey Buddy, How Do I Get This Car Outta 2nd Gear?
The Horn Went Beep, Beep, Beep
Hot Rod
Hot Rod Ford
Hot Wheels
I Got Me A Car
I Love My Car
I Need A Faster Car
I'd Rather Ride Around With You
In My Car, I'll Be The Driver
It's A Gas Hog
'Jeep'ers Creepers
Junkyard Wars
Just Add Oil
Let's Cruise
Let's Roll
Little Nash Rambler
Little Red Corvette
Love Buggin'
Mustang Sally *(or Your name)*
My Other Car Is A Broom
My-Stang
Never Buy A Car You Can't Push
Ode To My Car
On A Roll
Pretty Pink Cadillac
PT Proud
RC Crazy
Rhythm From A Red Car
See The USA In A Chevrolet
She Stole My Heart In My Chevy
She's A Classic
She's An Automatic
Snappy Little Sports Car
Spinning Your Wheels
The Squeaky Wheel Gets The Grease
Super Souped Up Supra
Sweetie PT

A Truck Of Her/His Own
Ultimate Off-Road Vehicle
Uneasy Rider
USA Road Hog
Vroom! Vroom!
Wheels At Last
Workin' At The Car Wash
You "Auto" Be In Pictures
You Can't Tie A Mustang Down
You Gotta A Fast Car!

____
____
____
____
____

CARNIVAL TITLES
(SEE AMUSEMENT PARK & CAROUSEL)

CAROUSEL TITLES
(SEE ALSO AMUSEMENT PARK & DISNEY)
Giddy-Up
This Horsey Won't Go
I've Got A Ticket To Ride
Merry-Go-Round
Merry-Go-Round We Go
Up & Down, & 'Round & 'Round

____
____
____
____
____

CAT TITLES
Alley Cat
A"mews"ing Grace
Assistant To My Cat
Ball Of Fluff
Blessed Are The PURR At Heart
Cat Got Your Tongue
Cat In The Hat
Cat Scratch Fever
Cat Tails/Tales Here
Cat Walk Fever
Cat-astrophe
Cat-i-tude
Cat-napping
Catopia
Cats Get The Importance Of Naps
The Cats In The Bag
Cats In The Cradle
Cats Make Life Purr-fect
The Cat's Meow!
The Cat's Outta The Bag
The Cat's Whiskers
Caution: Attack Cat On Duty
The Cheshire Cat
Cleo"Cat"ra
Cold Nose...Warm Heart...Great Love
Cool Cat/Kitty
Copy Cat
Crazy Cat
Curious Kitty
Curiously Cute Kitty Cat
Every Life Should Have "9" Lives!!!
Faithful Friend
Family Felines
Fat Cat/Cats
Feline Groovy
Feline Lazy/Sleepy
Feline Sublime
Fluff Ball
Furr Ball
Furr-ever Friends
Fur-rocious Fun
Furr-purrrrrrson Residence
Furry Angel
Fuzzy Face
Fuzzy Memories
Hangin' Out For The Holidays
Home Is Where The Kitty Is
Honky Cat
How Much Is That Kitty In The Window?
I Don't Do Mouse Work
I'm The Cat's Meow
Im-PAWS-ible
It's Tough Being Purr-fect
I've Got Cat-itude
Kitten Kaboodle
My Kitty Sitting So Pretty!
Lap Warmer
Love That Cat
Lovable Ball Of Furr
M-E-O-W
A Meow Massages The Heart. - *(Stuart McMillan)*
Meow Spoken Here
Meowie Christmas
Meow-sousse
My Cat Kneads Me
My Cat Walks All Over Me
The Nine Lives Of *(Cat's name)*
Our Friendly Feline
Our Furry Child
Pampered Puss
Paw Lickin' Good
Paw Prints
Paws & Enjoy
Paws-itively Purr-fect

Pet Palace/Paradise
Pick Of The Litter
Pretty Kitty
Prima Dona
Purr-anoia - Mischievous Kitty's
Purr-ecious Cat/Kitty
Purr-fect
Purr-fect Angel
Purr-fect Pals
Purr-sonality
Pussy Cat, Pussy Cat...Where Have You Been
Pussy Footin' Around
Rugrat
Santa Claws/Paws
Scarredy Cat
Sitting Pretty With My Kitty
Sleep & Let Sleep
Static Kling Kitty
A Tail Of (#) Cats
Take Me To Your Litter
Tension Reliever
There's A Whole Lot Of Hissin' Goin' On
There's A Whole Lot Of Purrin' Goin' On
Thoughts, Prayers & Purrs To You
Time For A Cat Nap
The Truth About Cats
We Believe In Santa Paws
Welcome To My Domain
What's New Pussy Cat?
When Mom's Away, The Cat Will Play!
Will Purr For Tuna!
Wipe Your Paws
Year Of The Cat
(Cat's name) Is The Cat's Meow

____
____
____
____
____

CELEBRATION TITLES

(SEE BIRTHDAY, KWANZAA & PARTY)

CHALK TITLES

(SEE ALSO ART & COLORING)

- *Make title look like it was written with Chalk.*

Chalk It Up To Talent
Chalk It Up To Ya!
Chalk One Up For *(Name)*
Chalk Talk
Concrete King/Queen
Pavement Picasso
Sidewalk Chalk Artist

____
____
____
____
____

CHEERLEADER TITLES

- *Make the "O" into a Pom-pom.*
- *Have title words coming from a Megaphone*
- *Create Pom-poms hanging from title.*

Cheer All Out
Cheer Me Up
Competition Bound
Extend Yourself...Cheer!
Go! Fight! Win!
Go, Team, Go
Flying Is For Cheerleaders
Hold That Line
I Don't Just Cheer...I Inspire!
If You've Got Game, We've Got Cheer
Jump, Shout, Yell!
Just Nail It
Let's Go Look At Her Fly!
I Love To Fly
Nail It
Pep Rally
Pom Poms & Ponytails
Push 'Em Back, Push 'Em Back...Waaaay Back!
Ra! Ra! Girls!
Short Skirts & Attitudes
Stand Up & Cheer
We Got Spirit
We've Got Spirit, Yes We Do!
We've Got The Cheer
Wimps Lift Weights...Cheerleaders Lift People!
Yea! Team

CHEERLEADER

Cheerful
Happy
Energetic
Extreme
Radicle
Loud
Exuberant
Active
Delightful
Enthusiastic
Radiant

CHERRY TITLES

(SEE FOOD)

CHICKEN TITLES

(SEE ALSO BIRD)

Bucket Of Chicken
Chick-A-Dee
Chicken Little
Cock-A-Doodle-Do
C-O-C-K-Y
Cocky Locky
Don't Count Your Chickens Before They Hatch
Don't Ruffle My Feathers!
A Good Egg
Hen Pecked
Here Chicky, Chicky, Chicky
Just A Little Cracked
Our Little Chickadee
Roosters Crow, But Hens Deliver
Run Chicken Run
Slick Chick
Spring Chicken

CHILD/CHILDREN TITLES

(SEE ALSO BABY, BOY, DAUGHTER, GIRL, GRANDCHILDREN & SON)

100% Cute
24 Carrot Kid
About A Kid
Adventurer!
The Age Of Innocence
All American Star Spangled Kid
All By Myself
All My Children
All The Little Children Of The World
Always Be A Child
An Angel With A Crooked Halo
Angel Child
Apple Of Mom & Dad's Eyes
As Good As Gold
Backstreet Kids
Basically Bummin'
A Beam Of Sunlight From God
Beautiful Child
Behold The Children Are A Gift From The Lord
Bless The Children
Bless This/You Child
The Bold & The Beautiful
Boogie Child
Brat Pack
Busy As A Beaver
Busy, Busy Boy Child
Caught In The Act Of Being Cute
The Child In Us
A Child Is A Beam Of Sunlight From God
A Child Is The Root Of The Heart
A Child Of All Seasons
Child Of God
Child Of Innocence
Child Of Mine
Child Of The Night
Childish Fun
Children Are A Breath Of Fresh Air
Children Are Angels With Crooked Halos
Children Are God's Way Of Telling You Tomorrow Is Beautiful
Children Are Life's Breath
Children Are Jewels Dropped From Heaven
Children Are The Keys Of Paradise
Children In Bloom
Children Make A Family Complete
Children Make The World Go Around
Children Of The Morning
Children Of The World
Children...Sometimes A Handful, Always A Heartful
A Children's Lullaby/Story

Child's Play
A Chip Off The Old Block
Clean Cut Kid
A Completion Of Our Family
Cool Kids
December's Child
A Diamond In The Rough
A Dynomite Kid
Dream Child
Dreams Of Children
An Extension To The Family Tree
To Feel The Love Of A Child's Heart
Flower Child
For Unto Us A Child Is Born
Forget The Dog, Beware Of The Kids
Friday's Child Was Born To Give
Full Of Giggles & Wiggles
God Bless The Child
God's Most Beautiful Thought
The Golden Child
Good To The Last Drop
Hangin' Out *(Kids on jungle gym)*
Having A Child Is A Blessing From God
Heartbreak Kid
Heavy Metal Kids
My Home Grown Jewels
Hot Child In The City
I Am A Child Of God
I Am Your Child
I Do It Myself
I Think My Name Is No-No!
I Will Follow
I'm A Busy Little Boy/Girl
I'm Just A Kid
I'm Not Rich, But My Kids Are Jewels
I'm So Cool/Special
Imagination Station
In The Mind Of A Child...
Jesus Loves The Children Of The World
The Jewelry Of Our Family
Just Hangin' Out
The Key To Paradise
Kid Of A 1,000 Faces
Kids Just Wanna Have Fun
Kids On The Street
Kids 'R Us
Kids Will Be Kids
Kidz Zone
Kiss The Children
Kool Kid
The Laughter Of A Child Is The Light Of The House
Let The Children Play
Life As A Child
The Light Of Our Lives Is The Son In Our Eyes
Little Angels
Little Charmers
Little Child Full Of Love
Little Rascals
Live Dangerously...Have Kids
Look At Me
Look What I Can Do
Love Child
The Magic Of Childhood
The Many Faces Of *(Name)*
Miracle Child
Model Children
Mom's Passions
Mommy's Little Growing Experiences
Mommy's Little Mess Makers
Mommy's Little Monster
Mommy's Little Precious Treasures
Mommy's Little Squirt
More Precious Than Gold
The Most Beautiful Flowers
Mother & Child Union
My Favorite Things...
My Milestones
My Name Is Not No-No!
Nature's Child
Peek-A-Boo...I See You
Polka Dot Tot *(Chicken Pox, Rash, or Freckles)*
Poor Man's Riches
Oooooh Child, Things Are Gonna Get Easier
On The Go/Move
Our Pride & Joy
The Rainbow Children
Ready...Set...Run!!!
Rebel Child
Rock 'N Roll Kids
See What I Can Do
Shower Us With Love & Watch Us Grow
Small Child: House Wrecker, Inc.
Small Steps Make For Big Adventures
So Much To Do...So Little Time
So Peaceful Like A Child
The Soul Is Healed By Being With Children
Still My Child
Storybook Children
Street Kids
Sugar Pie, Honey Bunch
Sunshine On A Cloudy Day
Sweet Child Of Mine
Texas Tornado
There's A New Kid In Town
They Call Me Trouble
This Is What Love Looks Like...
Thou Shall Not Whine!!!
Thru The Eyes Of A Child

Trust With The Eyes Of A Child
A Unique & Unrepeated Miracle
U-R-A-Q-T
Us 'R Kids
Warning...Likes To Play In The Mud *(Pics of muddy kids)*
We Are The Children
What A Busy Little Body
What A Cutie Pie
When A Child Is Born
When The Children Cry
When The Sun Is Out, The Son Is Out
When You Were A Child...
Wild Child
With A Child's Heart/Love
With The Eye's Of A Child
The World's Best Kid
You Are My Destiny Child
You Light Up My Life
You Rock
The Young & The Restless
You're A Golden Child
You're One In A Million
You're Out Of This World

MONDAY'S CHILD
(Original Version)
Monday's Child Is Fair Of Face
Tuesday's Child Is Full Of Grace
Wednesday's Child Is Full Of Woe
Thursday's Child Has Far To Go
Friday's Child Is Loving & Giving
The Child That Is Born On The Sabbath Day
Is Fair & Wise & Good & Gay.

(Revised Version)
Monday's Child Is Fair Of Face
Tuesday's Child Is Full Of Grace
Wednesday's Child Is On The Go
Thursday's Child Is A Joy To Know
Friday's Child Is Loving & Giving
Saturday's Child Takes Joy In Living
The Child That Is Born On The Sabbath Day
Is Merry & Blithe & Bright & Gay.

CHOCOLATE TITLES
- *Make the "O" look like a Chocolate Kiss.*

A Basic Necessity Of Life
Chocoholic
Chocolate & You...What A Sweet Treat
Chocolate...My Essential Nutrient
Chocolate Is Proof That God Loves Us!
Chocolate Is The Best Medicine
Chocolate Melts Away The Blues
Chocolicious
Eat Now, Diet Later
Forget Love, I'd Rather Fall In Chocolate
Friends Are The Chocolate Chips Of Life
Hands Off The Chocolate & No One Gets Hurt!
Have Chocolate Will Travel
Hot Chocolate
I'd Give Up Chocolate, But I'm No Quitter
Indulge!!!!
If It's Not Chocolate, It's A Vegetable
Life, Liberty & The Pursuit Of Chocolate
Life's Too Short...Eat More Chocolate
A Little Taste Of Heaven
Money Talks...Chocolate Sings
On The Eighth Day, God Created Chocolate
So Much Chocolate...So Little Time
SOS...Need Chocolate
Sweet Like Chocolate
Things Are Bad!!!...Send Chocolate
White Chocolate Love

CHOCOLATE
Chocolicious
Heavenly
Oooh La La
Climaxing
Obsessive
Luscious
Ambrosial
Tantalizing
Enchanting

CHRISTENING TITLES
(SEE BAPTISM & RELIGIOUS)

CHRISTMAS TITLES

(SEE ALSO DEER/REINDEER, PRESENTS & SANTA CLAUS)

- *String Light Bulb die-cuts along top of page with string, ribbon or yarn with letters inside.*
- *Hang small Bulb Ornament die-cuts from top of page with string, yarn or ribbon & put letters inside them.*
- *Color title letters like Candy Canes.*

12 Days Of Christmas
All Hearts Come Home For Christmas
All I Want For Christmas Is...
All I Want For Christmas Is You
All Is Calm...All Is Bright
All The Trimmings
An Old Fashioned Christmas
...And The Stockings Were Hung!
...And To All A Good Night
As Stuffed As The Christmas Stockings
Away In The Manger
Babes In Toyland
Blue Sky Christmas
Candy Cane Kids
Children Put The Magic Back In Christmas
Christmas At Sea
Christmas Belles/Bells
Christmas Blues
A Christmas Carol
Christmas Cheer Reins Here
Christmas Cheer Welcome Here
Christmas Glow With Love
Christmas In Your Arms
Christmas Is A Claus For Celebration
Christmas Is A Very Santa-mental Time
Christmas Lullaby
Christmas Memories
Christmas Shimmer
Christmas Thru A Child's Eyes
A Christmas To Remember
A Christmas Tree Hunting We Will Go
Christmas Wishes
Christmas With My Baby
Cool Yule!!!
Countdown To Christmas
Dear Santa...I Want It All
Deck The Halls With Bells & Holly
Delights Of December
Desperately Seeking Santa
Do Reindeer Really Know How To Fly?
Down The Chimney He Came
Dreaming Of A White Christmas
Everything Christmas
Family & Friends Are True Christmas Gifts!
Feels Like Christmas
Festive Trimmings All Merry & Bright
Follow The Star...He Knows Where You Are
For Goodness Sake
Free The Elves
Gingerbread Boys/Girls/Kids
Glad Tidings We Bring
Hangin' Out For The Holidays
Happy Christmakkah
Happy Holly Days
Happy Yule Ya'll
Hark The Herald Angels Sing
Have A Maui Christmas
Having Ourselves A Merry Little Christmas
Here We Come A Caroling
Ho Ho Holiday
Holiday Goodies
Holiday Memories Warm Even The Coldest Days
Holiday Surprises Come In All Sizes
Holly-Day Hoopla
A Holly Jolly Christmas
Holly Leaves & Christmas Trees
Home For The Holidays
Hooked On The Holidays
Hope...Joy...Peace
I Believe In Santa Claus
I Have Christmas All Wrapped Up
I Still Believe
I'll Be Home For Christmas
In Love On Christmas
In Search Of The Perfect Tree
It's A Wonderful Life
It's All About The Presents
It's Beginning To Look A Lot Like Christmas
It's Christmas All Over!
It's The Most Wonderful Time Of The Year
Jesus Is The Reason For The Season
Jingle All The Way
Jingle Bell Rock
Jingle Belles
Jingle Bells
Jolly Holidays
Jolly Holly Days
Jolly Ole St. Nick
Joy...Noel
Joy To The World
Joys Of The Season
Just For Santa
Kandy Kane Kids
Kids Need A Stable Environment
Kiss Me Under The Mistletoe
Let It Glow, Let It Glow, Let It Glow!
Let's Leave Christ In Christmas
Lights Of Fun
Little Treasures

Look What I Got!
Lord, Bless This Wonderous Christmas
The Magic Of Christmas
Magical Holidays
Magical Holly Days
Making Merry Christmas Memories
Making Spirits Bright
May Your Days Be Merry & Bright
Meet Me Under The Mistletoe
Merry & Bright
Merry Christmas Baby
Merry Kiss-mas
Merry Kiss-Miss
A Merry Meal
Merry, Merry Christmas
Mistletoe Magic
Naughty Or Nice
No Sneakin' Or Peekin' 'Til Christmas
N-O-E-L
Not A Creature Was Stirring...
Oh, Christmas Tree
Oh, Come All Ye Faithful
Oh, Come Let Us Adore Him
Oh, Holy Night
Once Upon A Starry Night
Our Little Elves
Our Little Stocking Stuffer
Our Spirit Of Christmas
Our Tiny Tots With Eyes All Aglow
Pa-Rum-Pa-Pa-Pum
Peace On Earth
Precious Christmas Memories
Precious Moments
Preparing Hearts & Home For A Season Of Joy
Presents & Cards & Lights...Oh My!
Presents Galore
Rainy Day Christmas
Reindeer Crossing!
Rejoice!
Remembering The Reason For The Season
Ring The Bells...It's Christmas
Rockin' 'Round The Christmas Tree
Sancho Claus
Santa Claus Is Coming To Town
Santa Express *(Use a train)*
Santa Still Makes House Calls
Santa Stops Here
Santa's Helper
Santa's Workshop
The Season Of Goodwill
Silver Belles
Silver Bells
Sleigh Bells Ring
Snowy Christmas Day
So Many Toys, So Little Time
Sorry, No Humbugs Allowed
Storybook Christmas
Stringing The Lights
Sweets For Santa
This House Believes In Christmas
'Tis The Season For Love
'Tis The Season To Be Jolly
Too Precious For Coal
Tree Trimming Time
"Tree"mendous Trimmings
"Tree"mendous Wishes
Trimming The Tree Time
'Twas The Night Before Christmas
Twinkle, Twinkle Little Christmas Star
Under The Tree
Unto Us, A Child Is Born *(Pics of xmas baby)*
Unwrapping Christmas
Visions Of Sugar Plums
What Christmas Means...
White Christmas Wonder
Who Needs Santa When You Have Gramma!
Wow, Thanks Santa!
Yes, *(Child's name)* There Is A Santa!
You Are My Christmas Special
You "Light" Up My Life
Yuletide Carols
Yuletide Glow

Christmas Cheer
Holly Days
Reindeer
In The Spirit
Santa Claus
Tree
Mistletoe Kisses
All The Trimmings
Silver Bells

____
____
____
____
____

CHURCH TITLES

(SEE RELIGIOUS)

CIRCLE TITLES

As The Little Boy/Girl Goes 'Round
Circle Dance
Circle Of Friends
Circle Of Life
Circle Of Love
Circle Perfect
Don't Break The Circle
Endless Circles
Eternal...Circle
Going In Circles
Gone Full Circle
Here We Go 'Round & 'Round
I Keep My Mom Going In Circles
It's A Round Up
Kids Of The Round Table
Let's Go Another Round
Love's Shining Circle
Merry Go Round We Go
My Circle Of Friends
No Beginning...No End
Perfect Circle
Round About
'Round & 'Round
'Round & 'Round We Go/Spin
Round Up
Running In Circles
Something Going 'Round
Spinning In Circles
Walking In Circles
We're Going In Circles
We've Come Full Circle
You Make The World Go 'Round
You Turn Me Around

____
____
____
____
____

CIRCUS TITLES

(SEE AMUSEMENT PARK & CAROUSEL)

CLEANING TITLES

(SEE ALSO WORK)

- *Make the "I" or "L" into a Mop or Broom.*

All Washed Up
Bless This Mess
Born To Shop, Not To Mop
Clean As A Whistle
Clean-Cut Kid
Clean Sweep
Cleaned Out
Cleaned Your Clock
Cleaning Crew
Cleaning Gives You Warts
Cleaning Makes You Ugly
Cleaning Whiz
Coming Clean
A Couple Of Dishes *(Kids doing dishes)*
Don't Sweat The Small Stuff
Fresh & Clean
God Made Dirt & Dirt Don't Hurt
Good Clean Fun
Hey, Garbage Kid!
Housework Makes You Ugly
It's A Wash
Killer Dust Bunnies On The Loose
Lawn Mower Man
The Lawn Ranger
A Little Dirt Never Hurt
Little House Of Horrors
Little Sweeper
Love Me...Love My Messes!
Making A Clean Attempt
Mess? What Mess?
Mr. Clean
Mr. Clean Jeans
My Honey Do Crew
Pig Pen
A Princess Doesn't Clean
Scrub, Scrape & Wipe
Splish Splash, I'm Scrubbin' The Bath
Sponge Mom, Square Rag
Sponge *(Person's name)*, Square Pants
Squeaky Clean
Suck It Up *(Vacuuming)*
Sweep It Under The Rug
There's A Method In This Madness
This Is The Maid's Day Off
Wash It Away
Wash Me Clean

What A Dish!
What A Pig Sty!
Wiped The Slate Clean
Wishy Washy

CLIMBING TITLES

(SEE ALSO HIKING, MOUNTAINS, NATURE & OUTDOORS)

Ain't No Mountain High Enough
Climb Every Mountain
Climbing The Ladder Of Success
Climbing The Walls
Climbing To New Heights
Everybody's Got A Mountain To Climb
Friends In High Places
To Half Dome We Roam
High Hopes
Higher & Higher We Go
The Higher The Better
The Higher You Climb
King Of The Hill
Mile High Club
Only 4,737 Ft. Left Up To Half Dome We Go

CLOCK TITLES

(SEE TIME)

CLOTHING TITLES

(SEE DRESS-UP)

CLOUDS TITLES

(SEE ALSO HEAVEN)

- *Put title on a Cloud, cut small slits in clouds & slide bottom of letters down into slits to look like they are snuggled in the clouds)*

2 Clouds Above 9
Above The Clouds
As Sweet As The Clouds Are High
Behind The Clouds, The Sun Is Shining
Black Cloud Rain
Born On A Different Cloud
Chasing The Clouds Away
Clouds So Swift
Dreaming In The Clouds
Get Your Head Out Of The Clouds
High Hopes
I Saw Your Face In A Cloud
Like A Cloud In The Sky
Love In The Clouds
On Cloud Nine
Sky High
Watching The Clouds Roll By

CLOWN TITLES

(SEE AMUSEMENT PARK)

COLD/COOL TITLES

(SEE ALSO SNOW & WINTER)

- *Put small quote-like marks to sides of letters making them look as if Shivering.*
- *Wrap a piece of ribbon around one of the letters to look like Neck Scarf.*

3 Cool Cats
All Bundled Up
Arctic Blast
As Cool As Can Be
As Winter's Chill Caress's The Day
Baby, It's Cold Outside
Baby You're So Cool
Be Cool
Better Inside Than Out!
The Big Chill
The Big Freeze
Bone Chilling Cold
Brrrrr...It's Cold
Brrr Shiver Brrr
Children Of The Ice Age
The Chill Factor
Chill Out!

Chiller Nights
Chillin'
Chilly Weather
A Cold & Gray Day
Cold As Ice
Cold Blooded
Cold Blows The Wind
Cold Dark Night
Cold December Nights
Cold Feet
Cold Gray Light Of Dawn
Cold Hands, Warm Heart
Cold Hard Rain
The Cold Morning Light
Cold Northern Breeze
A Cold Winter's Day
Cool & Cute
Cool As A Cucumber
Cool Cats
Cool Is My Middle Name
Cool Jewel
Cool Kids
Cool Kiss
Cool Love
Cool Rider
Cool Rules
Cool Water
Cooler Than Cool
Coolin' Down
Crazy Cool
Cuddlin' With Cocoa
Dressed To Chill
Dressed Up Like Eskimos
Even When It's Cold Outside, Our Memories Keep Us Warm!
Fabulous February
The Fire Is So Delightful
For The Cool In You
Freeze Frame
Have Cool...Will Travel
How Cool Is That?I Put The "oo" In Cool
Ice, Ice Baby
I'm So Cool
I'm So Cool, I Gotta Wear Shades
I'm So Cool, I'm Hot
In The Chill Of The Night
In The Cold, Cold, Night
It's The Roll Of The Ice
Jack Frost Nippin' At Your Nose
Keeping Warm *(Bundled up or sitting by fireplace)*
Licensed To Chill
Lost My Cool
Mr. Freeze Has Struck
Oh, What Do You Do To Keep Cool???
The Polar Express
A Real Cool Time
Shake, Shutter & Shiver
Shakin' & Shiverin'
Shakin' Like A Leaf
Shiver Me Freezing
Shiver Me Timbers
So Cool, I Rule
Stone Cold
Sub-Zero
There's A Chill In The Air
Too Cool
We're So Cool

____
____
____
____
____

COLLEGE TITLES

(SEE EDUCATION & SCHOOL)

COLOR/COLORING TITLES

(SEE ALSO ART & CHALK)

- *Make "I" or "L" into a Crayon or Paintbrush.*
- *Write out title with Crayon in childlike style.*
- *Do each letter in a different color.*

All The Colors Of The Rainbow
Any Color You Like
The Art Of Color
Be Bold...Color Outside The Lines
Can You Paint With All The Colors Of The Wind?
Changing Colors
Child Of Many Colors
Color Blind
Color Me Brightly/Psychedelic
Color Me Crazy
Color Me Happy
Color Me Perfect
Color Me Silly
Color Me Wonderful
Color My Life
Color My World
The Color Of Freedom
Colorful Creations
Colors Everywhere
Colors Of Love
The Colors Of My Dream/Life
The Colors Of Nightfall
"Crayon" The Wall
Doodling
Dreams Of Color
Easy Breezy Colorful Girl

Every Color Under The Sun
Every Color You Are...
In Full Living Color
It's A Colorful World
It's Colortime
In Living Technicolor
The Magic Of Crayons
The Many Colors Of Fall/Autumn
The Many Colors Of *(Name)*
Rainbow Connection
Scribble, Scribble, Scribble
She Colored In Many Colors
Showing My True Colors
Surpassed With Flying Colors
True Colors Come Shining Thru
You Color The World With Love
(Name) Has Such A Colorful Imagination

COMPUTER TITLES

- *Use a Script-type style lettering, as if wiring, & put computer mouse at end of word.*
- *Create a Keyboard & put title on Keys.*

Blog Off/On
Boot Up!
A Chat Has Many Lives
Chat That!
Compute This...
Computer Blues
Computer Bug
Computer Nerd
Computer Whiz
Computers Byte!
Computie Cutie
Connecting...
C-R-A-S-H
Cyber Love
C:/DOS
C:/DOS RUN
C:/ Is The Root Of All Directories
Don't Byte Off More Than You Can View!!!
Fax Is Stranger Than Fiction
Floppy Fun
Gigabyte Goddess
Got The .com Bug!
Hard Driver
Just Blog It!
Keyboard Krazy
Kilobyte Kids/King/Queen
I Love My Mouse!
In Touch With The World
Love At First Byte
Mega Byte Mamma
Mousin' Around
On-Line Time
Processed To Perfection
RAM, ROM, DOS...Whatever!!!
RUN/DOS/RUN
Surfin' The Net
There's No Place Like http://www.home.com
User Friendly
Webmaster
What Boots Up Must Come Down
What Does "Formatting Drive 'C' Mean?"
Windows Never Cease
You're A Computie Cutie
You've Got Mail

CONSTRUCTION/CARPENTER TITLES

(SEE ALSO REMODELING & TOOLS)

- *Use different kinds of Construction Tools to replace; Hammer for "T", Nail or Screw for "I" or Bolt for an "O".*

Brick House
Building Loads Of Memories
Building Our Dream
Building The Future
Built For Comfort
Built To Last
Bulldozer Boys
Carpenters Are Just Plane Folks
The Carpenter's Son
Caution: Boys At Play
Construction Destruction
Destruction Delight
Destruction Zone
Dig It!
Drill Instructor
Drillin' Dude
Fortress Built By Love
Hammer Head
Hammer Man
Hammered
Hammerhead
Handy Man
The Helpful Hardware Man
The House That Our Love Built
The House That *(Name)* Built
If I Had A Hammer...

If I Were A Carpenter...
I've Built Us A Castle
Just Build It
Loads Of Love
Lumber Lover
Mr. Drill Man
Mr. Fix It
Mud Man *(Drywall mud)*
My Grandpa Is A Carpenter
My Tool Man Can!
Nail It Down
Nail It To Me!
Nail Man
Nailed It!
They Paved Paradise To Pour A Parking Lot
Rome Wasn't Built In A Day
Rusty Nailer
Stone By Stone
Studman
They Call Me Stud-ly
Tool Man
Tools Of Destruction
Total Destruction
Tough As Nails
Under Construction
Visions In Wood
When The Hammer Falls/Hits...
With Hammer & Nails...
Wood & Hammer & Nails...Oh My!
The Wood Cuter
Wood God
Wood Worker
Workin' The Wood Pile
Works Wonders With Wood!
(Name) The Builder

COOKING/BAKING TITLES

(SEE ALSO COOKOUT & FOOD)

- *Replace Cooking Utensils for some letters.*
- *Use a Cookie as an "O".*
- *Place a Chef's hat on a letter.*

A Very Kneady Baker
Baked With Love
Baker's Delight *(Child helping bake or cook)*
Baker's Dozen
Burnt Offerings
"C" Is For Cooking
Chef Au Jour *(Chef of the Day)*
Come Into My Kitchen
This Cook Loves To Be Kneaded
Cookie Cutter *(Person cutting cookies)*
Cookie Monsters
Cookin' Up A Storm
Cooking With Gas
Cutie Pie
Don't Mess With The Cook's Buns
Dough Boy *(Making cookies)*
Fast, Frozen, Canned & Microwaveable...
Feelin' Kneady
Feelin' The Knead To Bake
Flour Power
A Good Cook Beats All
Good Ole Home Cookin'
Gramma's Cookin' Rocks
Gramma's Kitchen...Kids Eat Free
Half Baked
Head Carver
Hell's Kitchen
Here's What's Cookin'
Hey Good Lookin' Whatcha Got Cookin'?
I Came...I Saw...I Decided To Order Take Out
I Don't Cook On Days That End In Y
I Hate 4-Letter Words Like: Cook & Bake
I Kiss Better Than I Cook
If Yer Lookin' For Home Cookin'...Go Home!
I'll Have My Cake & Eat It Too!
I'm Cookin' Now
Kiss The Cook
Kiss The Cook & Then Take Her Out To Dinner
Kissin' Don't Last...Good Cookin' Does
The Kitchen Is The Heart Of The Home
Look What's Cookin'
The Messy Gourmet
Mom's Kitchen...Tasters Welcome
My Favorite Recipe...Eat Out/Order In
Never Trust A Skinny Cook
No Accounting For Taste
The Pampered Chef
A Pinch Of This...
Recipe For Love

Shake & Bake
Someone's In The Kitchen With Mama...
Special Recipe
Sugar & Spice & Everything Nice
Sweet Tooth
Taste Test
This Kitchen Is Seasoned With Love
We Knead Gramma's Bakin'/Cookin'
We'll Be Jammin' *(Making jam)*
Well Look Who Came To Dinner
We're Cookin' Now!
What's Cookin' Good Lookin'?
What's For Dinner?
Whip It, Whip It Good

COOKOUT TITLES

(SEE ALSO CAMPING, COOKING & FOOD)

Backyard Bash/BBQ
BBQ For You
Boy Meets Grill
Burnt Offerings
Campfire Cookin'
Country Cookin'
The Grill Of Your Life
Grill King
Grillin' & Chillin'
Just Call Me, "Mr. Grill Man"
Licensed To Grill
Look Who's Doin' The Barbecuin'
Men Do It On The Grill
Smoke Out
Sunset Griller/Grillin'
Thrilling Grilling
Weenie Roast
We're Fired Up Now

COUNTRIES TITLES

AFRICA

Africa Bamba
Africa The Beautiful
African Angel
African Dawn
The African Dream
African Evening
African Moon
African Nights
African Storms
Blue Africa
Homeland Africa
The Marrakesh Express
Out Of Africa
Pride Of Africa
Storms Of Africa
Under African Skies
Wild On Africa

ASIA - MISC

The Cathedrals Of Russia
China Belle
China Doll
China Girl
From Russia With Love
Midnight In China
Midnight In Moscow
Moscow Nights
Mother Russia
On A Little Street In Singapore
On The Great Wall Of China
On The Road To Mandalay
Remember Russia
The Road To Hong Kong
Russian Autumn Heart
The Russian Paradise
A Russian Tale
A Russian Treasure
Tokyo Road
Tokyo Rose
Walkin' Thru Tokyo

AUSTRAILIA
Aussie Through & Through
Austrailia...The Place To Be
The Land Down Under

CANADA
Blue Skies Over Canada
Canada We Love You
Canadian Rose
Canadian Sunset
Crystal Cold Clear Canada
The Fall In Canada
God Bless Canada
Oh Canada
Rivers Of Canada

EUROPE - MISC.
Beautiful England
The Bells Of London
Crossing London Bridge
England Bound
English Summer Rains
English Sunset
The Ethereal Lights Of England's Spring
European Vacation
Hail To England
Havana Moon
In Old England Town
Last Train To London
London By Night
London Nights
London's Crown Jewels
London's Rains
Merry Old England
New England In The Summer
Oh, England
Oh England, My Lionheart
Oh To Be In England
Purple & Orange Sunsetting Skies Of England
Rainy Days In London
The Shining Lights Of Liverpool
Summertime In England
Swiss Miss
Swiss Mountain Rock 'N Roll
Tahitian Moon
Those New England Spring's
Towers Of London
Under London's Fog

GERMANY
Delightful Germany
Germany Calling
Germany - It's The Sauerkraut
Happy Days In Germany
Oktoberfest In Munich
South Of Germany
To Germany With Love

HOLLAND
Double Dutch
A Dutch Treat
In The Dutch Mountains
The Heavenly Hills Of Holland
The Lowlands Of Holland
A Nederlandse Rainy Day
The Shiny Streets Of Amsterdam
Tiptoe Thru The Tulips
This Watercolor Land
Windmills & Tulips

IRELAND/IRISH

Best O' Luck
Better Than A Pot Of Gold
Blarney Blast
Blarney Spoken Here
Clover Caper
Dance A Jig
The End Of The Rainbow
The Fair Hills Of Ireland
Feelin' Green
Feelin' Irish
Feelin' Lucky
For The Love Of Ireland
Forty Shades Of Green
Full 'O Charm
Green Eggs & Ham
The Green, Green Grass Of Home
Happy St. Paddy's/Patrick's Day
Hills Of Rolling Green
I Love Being Green
I'm Looking Over A Four-Leaf Clover
I'm The Lucky One
Ireland's Emerald Rainbows
Irish Blessings - For A Day - Lassie
Irish Cream
The Irish Cream Of The Crop
Irish Eyes Are Smilin'
It's Not That Easy Being Green
A Kiss For Luck
Kiss Me, I'm Irish
Kissably Irish
Land Of Enchantment & Mystery
Land Of The Emerald Isles
Leprechaun Kisses
Leprechauns & Shamrocks
Lil' Leprechaun
A Little Bit Of Blarney
Looking For Leprechauns
The Luck Of The Irish
Luck Of The Irish To Ya!
Luck Of The Leprechauns
Lucky Charmers
Lucky Charms
Lucky Four-Leaf Clover
Lucky Me, I'm Irish!
Lucky To Be Irish
Mom's Pot O' Gold
Mother Ireland
My End Of The Rainbow
My Favorite Leprechaun
My Four Leaf Clover
My Love Is Irish
No Blarney Allowed
Oh, Blarney!
Our Little Leprechaun
Our Little Lucky Charm
Our Little Pot O' Gold
The Rainbow Connection
The Rocky Road To Dublin
The Sacred Isle
Today, Everyone Is Irish
Top O' The Mornin' To Ya!
Under The Green Moon Of Ireland
The Wearin' Of The Green
When Irish Eyes Are Smilin'...
You Are Magically Adorable
You're My Lucky Charm

V.I.P. = **V**ery
Irish
Person

____
____
____
____

ITALY

All Roads Lead To Rome
Big Italian Rose
Italian Stallion
Little Italy
Mambo Italiano
On Italian Shores
To Italy We Rome
Viva La Difference
When In Rome, Do As The Romans Do!

____
____
____
____

JAPAN

Dreaming Of Japan
Full Moon Over Japan
In A Japanese Garden
Japanese Gardens
Japanese Lilies
On A Balmy Night In Japan
Pristine Gardens Under The Starlight

____
____
____
____

MEXICO
Acapulco Gold
Ballad Of Mexico
Down Mexico Way
Good To Go To Mexico
In Old Mexico
Mexico, O Mexico
On The Banks Of The Rio Grande
The Road To Ensenada
South Of The Border
Under The Mexican Moon
Viva La Mexico

PARIS
Adieu, Paris
An American In Paris
April In Paris
Bells Of Paris
Bon Jour, Paris!
A Country Girl In Paris
A Dream Of France
Evening In Paris
The French Connection
French Fantasy
Last Tango In Paris
I Love Paris
Moonlight Over Paris
Oh Star Of France
Oh Glorious France
Passport To Paris
Paris By Night
Paris In The Springtime
Paris Was Made For Lovers
A Rainy Night In Paris
Romance In France
Springtime In Paris
The Streets Of Paris
The Sun Rises Bright In France
Tour De France
Tricky French Connection
Under Paris Skies
A Walk Through Paris Streets
We'll Always Have Paris

SCOTLAND
Bonnie Scotland
Highland Cathedral
A Highland Fling
Misty Covered Mountains
Misty Morn
The Pipes Are Calling
Roamin' In The Gloamin'
Rolling Hills Of The Borders
Scotland The Brave
Scottish Dew
Scottish Fantasy
Scottish Highlands

SOUTH AMERICA - MISC.
Clear Pure Beauteous Skies Of Brazil
Down Argentina Way
The Peaceful Banks Of The Ipiranga
Rio Rocks
Samba Brazil
The Yellow Sun Of Equador

SPAIN
Blue Spanish Skies
Boots Of Spanish Leather
Castles In Spain
My Lady Of Spain
My Spanish Angel
Spanish Dancer
Spanish Eyes
Spanish Flea
Spanish Harlem
Spanish Is The Loving Tongue
Spanish Lullaby
Spanish Moon/Nights
Spanish Rose

COUNTRY TITLES

(SEE ALSO COWBOY, FARM & SOME SPECIFIC ANIMALS)

All American Country Boy/Girl
Angels In The Country
Born Country
Country Blessings
Country Boy Can Survive
This Country Boy's A Rockin'
Country Bumpkin
Country In My Heart
The Country Life
Country Livin' Is The Life For Me
Country Love
Country Music Warms The Heart
Country Roads Take Me Home
Countryfried
This Country's A Rockin'
Crazy Country Boys & Girls
Deep In The Heart Of The Country
Going To The Country
God Made The Country & Man Made The Town!
God's Country
Gone Country
I Was Country When Country Wasn't Cool
I'm A Little Bit Country
I'm Just A Country Boy/Girl
Kindly Keep It Country!
Livin' In The Country
Long-Haired Country Boy
Oh, Thank You Lord For The Country
Pure Country...Preserving The Past
Raised On Country Sunshine
Rock This Country
Tearin' Up The Country
Thank God I'm A Country Boy/Girl
Wild In The Country

COUSIN TITLES

(SEE ALSO FAMILY)

Branches Of The Family Tree
Christmas Cousins
Cool Cousins
Crazy About My Cousins
Crazy Cousins
Cute Cousins
Dozens Of Cousins
A Herd Of Cow-sins
Kissin' Kousins
Kooky Kousins
Lovin' Cousins
My Cousins...My Friends

COW TITLES

(SEE ALSO FARM)

- *Fill in title letters to look like Cow print.*

Cow'nt Your Blessings
Cow's It Goin'?
Don't Have A Cow!
Fat As A Cow
Got Milk?
A Herd Of Cow-sins
I'm Not In The Moo-d!
In The Moo-d
In The Moo-d For Love
Let's Get Moo-vin'
Lil' Cowpoke
Me Moo-oo-dy
Milkin' It For All It's Worth
Moo-ey Christmas
'Til The Cows Come Home
Udderly Adorable

COWBOY TITLES

(SEE ALSO COUNTRY, FARM & HORSE)

- *Use Hemp as a Rope to Lasso the title.*
- *Place a Cowboy Hat on some letters.*
- *Use a Horseshoe as a "U".*

At Home On The Range
At The End Of My Rope
Back In The Saddle Again
Boot Scoot Boogie
Buck-A-Roo
Casanova Cowboy
The Cowboy In Me...
Cowboy Love
The Cowboy Rides Away
Cowboy Take Me Away
Cowboys & Angels
Cowboys Just Got To Ride
Cowboys Know The Taste Of Dirt
Cowboys Love To Rope & Ride
Cowboys Rope
Cowtown Cuties
Cryin' Cowboy
Cutie Pie Cowboy
Diamond Cowboy
Don't Squat With Yer Spurs On
Giddy Up Cowboy
Happy Trails
"Hay" Good Lookin'
Hold Yer Horses
How The West Was Fun
Howdy Buck-A-Roo
I Wanna Be A Cowboy
It's Cool To Be A Cowboy
Just Rope It
Knows The Ropes
Lil' Buck-A-Roo
Lil' Cowboy/Cowgal/Cowpoke
Make Mine Western
Midnight Cowboy
Our Lil' Cowboy/Cowgirl
Park Yur Boots & Spurs & Sit A Spell!
Real Cowboys Don't Take Baths
Real Cowboys Don't Take Baths, They Just Dust Off
Remove Yur Spurs Before Getting In Bed
Rhinestone Cowboy/Cowgirl
Ride Cowboy Ride
Ride 'Em Cowboy/Cowgirl
Ridin', Ropin' & Ranglin'
Rock 'N Roll Cowboy
Rodeo Cowboy/Cowgirl
Rodeo King/Queen
Should've Been A Cowboy
Speak Your Mind...Then Ride A Fast Horse!
Thank God I'm A Cowboy
These Boots Are Made For Lookin' Like A Cowboy
WANTED...
A Well-Made Boot Is Work Of Art
Wild, Wild West Warriors

CRAFTS TITLES

(SEE ALSO CROSS STITCH, QUILTING, SCRAPBOOKING & SEWING)

Craft Crazy
The Craft Creator
Craft Queen
Crafters Are Bazaar
A Creative Mess
Creativity Runs In This Family
C-R-A-F-T-Y
Handmade With Love
Hearts & Crafts
Just Bead It
Just Kiln Time
Take It Or Weave It
Tole Painted
Under The Glue Gun
(Name) Get Your Glue Gun

CRAWLING TITLES

5-Finger Crawl
Crazy Crawler
I Get Around
Going, Going, Gone
The Little Baby That Could...And Did!
Look Out World, Here I Come
Look Out, He's/She's On The Crawl
Ready, Set, Crawl
To Small To Crawl
I Think I Can, I Think I Can...I Can!
Watermelon Crawl
You Gotta Crawl Before You Walk

CRAZY TITLES

8 Crazy Nights
Crazy Cool Over You
Crazy Cool With You
Crazy, Crazy Nights
A Crazy, Crazy World Like This
Crazy For You
Crazy In Love
Crazy Kooky Fun
Crazy Little Love Of Mine
Crazy Little Party Girl
Crazy Little Thing Called Love
Crazy Love
Crazy Over You
Crazy World
Fallin' For Your Crazy Love
I'm Crazy 'Bout You
Let's Get Crazy
Love Makes You Crazy
Miss You Like Crazy
Oh, You Crazy Boy
Still Crazy After All These Years
Stone Cold Crazy
Those Lazy, Hazy, Crazy, Days Of Summer
You Must Be Crazy For Me
Your Crazy Ways

CROCODILE TITLES

(SEE ALSO ANIMALS)

After A While Crocodile
Crocs Rock
Crocodile Dundee
Crocodile Hunter
Crocodile Rock
Crocodile Tears
Gator Country
It's A Lizard's Life
Leaping Lizards
Lounging Lizard
Pearly Chompers
Reptile House
Ruff, Tuff Reptile
See Ya' Later Alligator
What A Croc

CROSS STITCHING TITLES

(SEE ALSO SEWING)

Anytime's A Cross-Stitchin' Time
Born To Cross Stitch
Counting Is A Stitch!!!
Cross-Stitchers Are People Who Count!!!
Cross-Stitchers Are X-rated!!!
Cross-Stitchers...You Can Count On Us!!!
Hands To Work...Hearts To God
I'm A Cross-Stitchin' Girl
I Think...Cross Stitch
I Will Cross That Stitch When I Come To It!
Itchin' To Be Cross-Stitchin'!!
Memories Are Cross Stitched With Love
My Heart Sings Joyfully With Each Cross Stitch I Take!!
Ready...Set...Cross Stitch...
Real Cross-Stitchers Floss Every Day!
A Cross Stitch In Time...
A Cross Stitch In Time...Saves Nine
Stitchers Bear Their Crosses Each Day

CRUISE TITLES

(SEE ALSO BEACH, BOAT & SAILING)

- *Use a Ship's Steering Wheel or a Life Ring as an "O".*

Ahoy Mateys
All Aboard
All Aboard That's Comin' Aboard
All Hands On Deck
Anchors Away
Bon Voyage
Celestial Voyage
Come Sail Away
Come Sail Away With Me
Cruisin'
Cruisin' Along
Cruisin' Down The River
Cruisin' The Caribbean
Cruisin' The Deep Blue Seas
Cruisin' The Seas
Don't Rock The Boat
Fantastic Voyage
Full Steam Ahead
From Sea To Shining Sea
Goin' On A Sea Cruise
Island Paradise
Land Ho!
The Long Voyage Home

The Love Boat
On The High Seas
Our Maiden Voyage
Out To Sea
Room With A View
Sailin' The Winds
Sailing, Sailing Over The Ocean Blue
Sailing The South Pacific
Sea Cruise
My Ship Has Finally Come!
Ship Ahoy
Ship Mates
Ship Shape *(Pics of working out on ship)*
Steady As She Goes
Voyage Across The Sea

Cruising
Relaxing
Under the Sea
Islands
Spectacular
Incredible
Nautical
Grand Adventure

____
____
____
____
____

CRYING/POUTING TITLES

(SEE ALSO MAD & SAD)

- *Have Teardrops falling from letters in title.*

100 Tears More
After All These Tears
All Teary-Eyed
All The Tears That I Cry
As The Tears Fell...
As The Tears Go By...
Baby Don't Cry
Before The Next Teardrop Falls
Behind These Tears...
Big Boys/Girls Do Cry
Big Boys/Girls Don't Cry
Big Brother's/Sister's The Reason For The Screamin'
Blue Eyes Cryin' In The Rain
Bored To Tears
Boys Cry Tough
Crocodile Tears
Crocodile Tears On My Pillow
Cry Baby
Cry Baby Cry
A Cry For Help
A Cry In The Night
Cry Just A Little
Cry Myself To Sleep
Cryin' A River
Cryin' Buckets
A Cryin' Shame
Crying Eyes
Crying Tears On My Pillow
Don't Cry Baby
Don't Cry No Tears
Don't Cry Out Loud
Don't Let The Sun Catch You Cryin'
Don't Shed Tears
Drowning My Sorrows
Emotional Girl
Even Angels Cry
Every Little Tear You Cry...
Every Time I Cry...
Every Time You Cry...
A Flood Of Tears
For Cryin' Out Loud
Here Come Those Tears
Holding Back The Tears
How Many Tears...
Hush Little Baby Don't You Cry
I'm Drowning In My Tears
I'm Gonna Sit Right Down & Cry
I'm So Happy I Could Cry
I'm So Lonesome I Could Cry
It's All Over But The Cryin'
It's My Party & I'll Cry If I Want To
Kisses & Tears
Lonely Teardrops
Lonesome Tears In My Eyes
Mama Don't Allow No Poutin' Here
My Achy Breaky Heart
No Use Cryin' Over Spilled Milk/Juice
"NO WHINING" Zone!
Sea Of Tears
Sometimes You Just Gotta Cry
The Sound Of Your Cry...
Tear After Tear
A Tear & A Smile
Tear Drops Fall Like Rain Drops
Tear Drops On Your Cheeks
Tear Jerker
Tears From My Eyes
Tears In Your Blue Eyes
Tears Of Joy
Tears On My Pillow
The Tears Roll On Down
Tiny Little Teardrops
Too Many Tears
Tracks Of My/Your Tears

Trail Of Tears
Up To My Ears In Tears
Whaaaaaa!
When The Children Cry...
Where Teardrops Fall
With This Tear...
You Better Not Pout
You Can Cry On My Shoulder
You Would Cry Too If It Happened To You!
Your Tear-Soaked Pillow

CUT TITLES

(SEE ALSO KNIFE)

Clean Cut Cutie
Clear Cut
Cut & Dry
Cut & Run
Cut It Out
Cut Out
Cut The Cord
Cut The Crap
Cut To Fit
Cut To The Chase
Cut You In
Cuts Like A Knife
Cuttin' Up
The Final Cut
On The Cutting Edge
Prime Cut
(Name) Scissor Hands

CUTE TITLES

(SEE ALSO BEAUTY)

Absolutely Adorable
Ain't I Cute?
Babe In The Hood
Belle Of The *(Place)*
Cute As A Bug
Cute As A Button
Cute As Can Be
Cute But Dangerous
Cute, Cute, Cute
Cute Is My Middle Name
The Cute Little Things I Say & Do
Cute 'N Cuddly
Cutie Patootie
Cutie Pie
I Couldn't Be Cuter If I Tried!
Enchanting Presence
Foxy!
Hello Gorgeous!
I Feel Pretty
Just As Cute As Can Be
Kewpie Cutie
Little Charmer
Perfect '10'
Picture Perfect
Pretty As A Picture
Pretty In Pink
Pretty Is As Pretty Does
The Prince/Princess Of Cuteness
Short & Cute
Simply Irresistible
Snootie Little Cutie
Strike A Pose!
Too Cute!
Too Cute For Words!
Tutu Cutie
What A Doll!
With A Face Like This, Life Will Be Smooth Sailin'
You Are So Beautiful To Me
You Bet I'm Cute
You Look Maaaah-velous
You Ought To Be In Pictures
You've Got The Cutest Little Baby Face!

DADDY TITLES

(SEE FATHER)

DANCE TITLES

- *Make tiny Ballet Slippers to create an "A".*
- *Make little Ballet Slippers to hang from title.*

All Life's Problems Are Solved By Dancing
All She Wants To Do Is Dance
All That Jazz
Amazing Grace
Attitude Dancing
The Baby Boogie
Baby Take A Bow
Ballet Beauty
Ballet Dancers Always Have A Pointe!
Ballet...It's Gotta Be The Shoes
Ballet Keeps Me On My Toes
Ballet...The Few...The Proud...The Pink!!!
Ballet Togs
Beautiful Ballerina
Bee Bop
Been There, Danced That!!!
Belle Of The Ball
Best Of Show
Blame It On The Bossanova
Boogie Dancin' Feet
Boogie Down
Boogie Fever
Boogie Nights
Boogie Streets
Boogie Wonderland
Bop 'Til You Drop
Boppin' At The Hop
I Brake For Dancers
Bravo!! Encore!!
Break Dancin'
Catch A Rising Star
Caught The Rhythm Bug
Cloggin' King/Queen
Come Dance With Me
Come & Dance Into The Light
Could I Have This Dance?
Crazy Dancer
Crocodile Rock
D-A-N-C-E
Dance A Little Dance
Dance All Night
Dance Allows Your Dreams To Speak
Dance & Shout
Dance As Though No One Is Watching You
Dance Craze
Dance d'Amore Dance
DANCE - DANCE - DANCE
Dance Dreams
Dance Electric
Dance Fever
Dance For Me Baby
Dance Into The Light
Dance Is A Work Of Art
Dance Like Nobody's Watching
Dance Like The Angels
Dance, My Pretty, Across The Floor
Dance On Little Dancin' Queen
Dance The Night Away
I Dance Therefore I Am
Dance 'Til The Stars Come Down
Dance 'Til We Burn This Disco Out
Dance To Live, Or Live To Dance
Dance To The Music
Dance To The Stars
Dance Under The Stars
Dance With Me
Dance With Me Under The Moon
Dance With The Music In Your Heart!
Dance Your Life Away
Dance Your Tutu Off!
Dancer In A Daydream
Dancer With An Attitude
Dancers Are The Athletes Of God
Dancer's Attitudes Never Cease, Ever!
Dancers Have Attitude
Dancers Have The Best Buns!
Dancers "Turn" Out Better
Dances With Wolves
Dancin' Feet
Dancin' In The Streets
Dancin' On A Saturday Night
Dancin' Queen/King
Dancin' To A Different Beat
Dancing Cheek To Cheek
Dancing Duo
Dancing Dynamo
Dancing Girl
Dancing In My Dreams
Dancing In Paradise
Dancing In The Dark
Dancing In The Moonlight
Dancing In The Street
Dancing Is Like Dreaming With Your Feet!
Dancing Is The Poetry Of The Foot
Dancing Machine
Dancing Madly
Dancing The Night Away
Dancing Toes
Darlin' Remember This Is Our Dance
The Dipsy Doodle
Disco Baby
Disco Dancer

Disco Days
Disco Down
Disco Duck
Disco Inferno
Disco King/Queen
Disco Lady
Disco Stomp
Do A Little Dance
Do The Hustle
Do The Locomotion
Do The Mash Potato
Do You Love Me Now That I Can Dance?
Do You Wanna Dance?
Doin' A Jig
Doin' The Twist
Don't Stop Dancing
I Dream Of Dancing
Dreams Of Dancing
Dressed To Dance
Fancy Dancer
Fancy Footwork
Feel The Rhythm Flow
Feet Don't Fail Me Now!
The First Step Is The Two-Step
Flash Dancin'
Future Ballerina
G.I. Jive
God Gave You Toes, So Pointe Them
Gotta Boogie
Hip, Hip Hora!
Hip Hop
Hip Hoppin'
The Hippy, Hippy Shake
Hoof It
The Hop
This House/Hall/Place Is A Rockin'
Get Up & Dance
Go-Go Dancin'
Gotta Dance
Happy Feet
Having A Ball *(At a formal dance or Prom)*
Hey, Macarena!
I Hope You Dance
I Just Wanna Dance With You
I Wanna Dance All Night Long
I'm A Dancer, Watch Me Jete...
I'm Dancing As Fast As My Feet Will Go
I'm Happy Just To Dance With You
I'm Your Boogie Man
In The Spotlight
It Ain't What You Dance, It's The Way You Dance
It Takes Two To Tango!
I've Got Rhythm
Jazzing
Jinglebell Rock
Jitterbug Gal
Jitterbuggin'
Jukebox Saturday Night
Just Dance
Keep On Dancin'
Last Dance Tonight
The Last Waltz
Let Me/Us Entertain You
Let The Little Cowboy/Cowgirl Dance
Let's Boogie
Let's Dance...Let's Shout
Let's Dance Tonight
Let's Go To The Hop!
Let's Limbo Some More
Let's Twist Again
Life Is Simple...Eat, Sleep, Dance!
Life's A Dance
Lord, Keep Me On My Toes *(Ballerina)*
Lord Of The Dance
I Love To Dance
Magic Dance
May I Have This Dance?
Mexican Hat Dance
Monster Mash, It's A Graveyard Smash
Moonlight Dancing
Mr. Bojangles
The Music Makes Me Dance
My Baby Loves To Dance
Neutron Dance
Of Course I Have An Attitude, I'm A Dancer!
On Pointe! *(Ballet)*
Once A Dancer, Always A Dancer!
One Good Turn Deserves Another
One Last Dance
Our Hearts & Feet Dance Today
Pas De Deux *(Ballet)*
Peppermint Twist
Perfect Point *(Ballet)*
Practice Makes For Sore Muscles
Private Dancer
Put On Your Dancin' Shoes
Put On Your Red Shoes & Dance
Puttin' On The Ritz
Rhythm Of A Dancer
River Dance
Rock Around The Clock
Rock Your Body & Dance
Saturday Night Fever
Save The Last Dance For Me!
Shadow Dancer
Shake It, Shake It Wild Thang!
Shake It Up Baby Now...Twist & Shout
Shake That Bootie

Shake Your Body Down To The Ground
Shake Your Groove Thing
Shall We Dance?
She Likes To Lead When She Dances
Shimmy Shake
Shining Star
Sidekicks *(Ballet)*
Slow Dancing
Some Days You Just Gotta Dance
Something In The Way She Moves
A Song & A Dance
A Song & Dance Man
Step By Step
Steppin' Out
Stompin' Steps
Superstar
Swing Kids
Tappin' Toes
Gliding Thru The Tennessee Waltz
There's A Whole Lot Of Shakin' Goin' On
This Is Our Dance
Time To Tap
Tiny Dancer
Tiny Tapper
Toe Shoes & Tutu's
Touch Me When We're Dancing!
Tutu Beautiful
Tutu Cute
Tutu Dancer
Tutu Fun
Tutu Much
Twinkle Toes
Twistin' The Night Away
Two Left Feet
Up On Their Two's
Waltz On By
We Danced!
We're Dancin' In The Streets
We've Got Rhythm
Why Walk When You Can Dance?
Won't You Dance With Me?
Y-M-C-A
You Make Me Feel Like Dancing
You Are Tu-Tu Cute
You Should Be Dancin'
Your Mama Don't Dance!!!

DATE/DATING TITLES

(SEE ALSO HEART, KISS & LOVE)

- Use a Heart in place of an "A" or "O".

Afternoon Delight
Baby It's You
Bet Your Heart On Me
Building Special Memories
By The Light Of The Silvery Moon
A Cheap Date
Cute Couple
A Date Of/With Destiny
Dating Days
The Dating Game
The Do's & Don'ts Of Dating
Dream Date
First Date Jitters
For Me & My Gal/Guy
Goin' Steady
He Says, She Says
Heart Attacked
How Did I Get So Late, So Early?
I Have Found The One My Soul Loves
I Just Called To Say "I Love You"!
I Think She Likes Me
I Thought He'd Never Ask
I Wanna Be With You
I Want To Walk You Home
I'd Rather Ride Around With You
Inseparable
It's A Date
Just The Two of Us
Just You, Just Me, Just Right
Like Birds Of A Feather...
Lost In Love
Made For Each Other
A Match Made In Heaven
Moonstruck
A Night On The Town
The Odd Couple
Perfect Harmony
Perfect Together
Put 1 & 1 Together To Get...
Ready For Romance
Shadows In The Moonlight
So Happy Together
So This Is Love?!
Some Enchanted Evening
You Light Up My Life
Sweethearts
This Guy's In Love With You
Together Hand In Hand
Together Is A Wonderful Place To Be
Two Less Lonely People In The World
Until I Met You...

We Go Together Like A Wink & A Smile
We're In This Love Together
We've Got It Goin' On
We're Two Of A Kind
What A Wonderful, Wonderful Feeling
When I Look Into Your Eyes...
When I'm With You...
With All The World Around Us...I'm Glad We Found Us

DAUGHTER/IN-LAW TITLES

(SEE ALSO CHILDREN & GIRL)

Darlin' Daughter
Daughter Dear
Daughter = Flower
A Daughter Is A Mother's Best Friend
A Daughter Is A Reflection Of Her Mother's Heart
Daughter Of Mine
Daughters Are The Flowers Of Life
Dream Daughter
Like Mother...Like Daughter
Mirror, Mirror On The Wall...I Am My Mother After All!
Mothers & Daughters Are Closest When Daughters Become Mothers
My Darling Daughter
Woven Of The Same Thread

DAY/DAYS TITLES

A Day In The Life Of *(Name)*
All In A Day
An Eventful Day
And This Day...
Another Day In Paradise
Any Day Now
As Beautiful As The Day Is Long...
At The End Of The Day...
Back In The Day...
Beautiful Day Dreamer
Blue Sky Day
A Brand New Day
Carpe Diem *(Seize The Day)*
Cherish The Day...
The Dawning Of A New Day
Day After Day
Day By Day
A Day From The Lord
The Day Has Come
Day In...Day Out
A Day Not Wasted, Is A Day Wasted!
A Day On The Town
A Day Without Sunshine Is Like Night
Days Done By
Days Of Our Lives
Days Of Summer
Dog Days Of Summer
I Don't Do Mornings
A Dreamy Day
Each Dawn Is A New Beginning
Eight Days A Week
Every Day Is A New Day
Every Day Is A Winding Road
Every Day Of Your Life Is A Page Of Your History
First Light Of The Day
Forever & A Day
From This Day On...
The Glory Of Daybreak
Good Day Sunshine
Happy Days
Happy Days Are Here Again
Heavenly Day
Here Comes The Sun
Here Today...
In The Morning...
It's A Beautiful Day
It's A Lovely Day When...
It's A Wonderful Day
It's Been A Hard Days Night
Just A Day Away
Just Another Day In Paradise
Just Another Lazy Day Afternoon
Lazy Dayz

Let The New Day Begin
Like Night & Day
Live For The Day
Lonely Days...
The Longest Day
Make My Day
Mama Said There'd Be Days Like This
Midsummer Day
A Misty Morning Does Not Signify A Cloudy Day
The Morning After
Never Put Off 'Til Tomorrow What You Can Do Today
A New Day Is Dawning
Not A Day Goes By...
Nothing Is Worth More Than This Day
Oh Happy Day
On A Day Like Today...
On Any Given Day...
One Bright Day
One Day At A Time
One Fine Day
One Sweet Day
Our Day Will Come
The Promise Of A New Day
Remember A Day...
Seize The Day
Sing For The Day
Sunny Days & Cozy Nights
Sunny Days Are Here Again
Sunshiny Day
There's A Brand New Day On The Horizon
These Are The Days We Will Remember
This Is The Day That The Lord Has Made
Those Were The Days
Today's The Day
Today's The First Day...
Tomorrow Is Another Day
Tomorrow Never Knows
Under The Sun, Every Day Shines
What A Difference A Day Makes
When The Night Meets The Day
Yesterday Once More
Yesterday, Today & Tomorrow
You Deserve A Break Today
You Fill Our Days With Hugs & Kisses
You Make My Day

DAYS OF THE WEEK TITLES

SUNDAY

Barefoot On Sunday
Beautiful Sunday
Blue Sunday
Lazy Sunday Afternoon
Never On Sunday
On Any Given Sunday
On Any Sunday
Palm Sunday
Somethin' 'Bout A Sunday
Sunday Brunch
Sunday Comics/Funnies
Sunday Morning Sunshine
Sunday Sunshine
Super Sunday

MONDAY

Another Monday
Blame It On Monday
Blue Monday
Come Monday, It Will Be All Right
Hang-Over Monday
It Sure Is Monday
Just Another Manic Monday
Manic Monday
Monday, Monday!
Monday Morning Blues
Monday Morning Breakdown
Monday Morning Quarterback
Monday's Child Is Fair Of Face
Rainy Days & Mondays
Rainy Days & Mondays Always Get Me Down
Stormy Monday
Suddenly Monday

TUESDAY
Groovy Tuesday
If It's Tuesday, This Must Be Belgium!
Only On Tuesday
Ruby Tuesday
Terrific Tuesday
Totally Tuesday
Tuesday's Child Is Full Of Grace

WEDNESDAY
Any Wednesday
Wednesday's Child Is On The Go
Wild & Wacky Wednesday

THURSDAY
Jersey Thursday
Thankful Thursday
Thursday's Child Has Far To Go
Thursday's Child Is A Joy To Know

FRIDAY
Black Friday
Finally Friday
Freaky Friday
Friday...I'm In Love
Friday Night Fun
Friday On My Mind
Friday The 13th
Friday's Child Is Loving & Giving
Girl Friday
Good Friday
T-G-I-F
Thank Goodness It's Friday!
When The Week Ends, The Fun Begins

SATURDAY
Almost Saturday
Another Saturday Night
Dancing On A Saturday Night
Saturday In The Park
Saturday Matinee
Saturday Morning Cartoons
Saturday Night Divas
Saturday Night Fever
Saturday Night Live
Saturday Night Special
Saturday Night's Alright
Saturday's Child Takes Joy In Living
Sunrays On Saturday
Super Saturday

DEATH/PASSING (MEMORIAL) TITLES
(SEE ALSO ANGELS, HEAVEN & MEMORIES/ MEMORIAL)
Cherish The Memory Of You
A Gift From God For A Moment In Time
God's Littlest Angel
Gone But Not Forgotten
In Loving Memory...
Now An Angel Watches Over Us
Rest Peacefully
Some Only Dream Of Angels

DEDICATION TITLES
(SEE BAPTISM & RELIGIOUS)

DEER/REINDEER TITLES
(SEE ALSO CHRISTMAS)
Do You Recall The Most Famous Reindeer Of All?
My "Deer" Friends
Our "Deer" Neighbors
Reindeer Crossing
Reindeer Games

D D D D D D D D D D D D D D D D D D D D D D D D D D D D

DIET TITLES

(SEE ALSO EXERCISE & FOOD)

- *Create a Measuring Tape & place under title.*
- *Make a Tape Measurer look like it's squeezing the title thinner.*

Broken Cookies Don't Have Calories!
Calories Don't Count When You're On Vacation
To Diet Is To Know "Thigh"self
Diets Make Me Thick & Tired
Dieting Is Just Mind Over Platter
Dieting Is Wishful Shrinking
Eat Now, Diet Later
Every Inch Counts
Fit & Fabulous
Fit As A Fiddle
Fits Like A Glove
From Thick To Thin
Hello Cravings
If You Stuffeth, You Puffeth
The Incredible Shrinking Man/Woman
Life Is Full Of Ups & Pounds
Light As A Feather
No "Body" Is Perfect
No Salt, No Fat, No Fun
Slammin' Body
Slim & Trim
Survival Of The Fittest
Taste = Waist
Think Thin!
Through Thick & Thin
Tomorrow's Another Diet

____
____
____
____
____

DINOSAUR TITLES

An Extinct Adventure At La Brea
No Bones About It
"Dino"mite
"Dino"mite Fun
"Dino"mite Kid
Dragon Ranger
Dragon Slayer
Extinctly Old
Genealogists Live In The Past Lane!
The "Old" & The Beautiful
Old As Dirt
The Older The Better
Oldie But A Goodie
Reptile House

____
____
____
____
____

DIRT/DIRTY TITLES

(SEE ALSO MESSY & MUD)

- *Rub Brown Chalk around title to look like Dirt.*
- *Sprinkle Dirt splats around title.*

Angel With A Dirty Face
Completely Washable
Desert Dirt
Dig It!
Diggin' Dirt
Diggin' To China
Dirt Bag
Dirt Cheap
Dirt Demon
Dirt Dirty
Dirt Got Your Tongue
Dirt Poor
Dirt Rider
Dirt Squirt
Dirty Boys
Dirty Business
Dirty Deeds
Dirty, Dirty Boy/Girl
Dirty Dudes
Dishin' Dirt
Do The Dirt Walk
Down & Dirty
Downtown Dirt
Dr. Dirt
Eat My Dirt!
Filthy Dirty
Filthy Rich
From Grubbin' To Tubbin'
Gettin' Down & Dirty

Gettin' Grubby
God Made Dirt...And Dirt Don't Hurt!
Got Dirt?
Got Grunge!!!
The Grunge Factor
Happiness Is...Dirt
Head Dirt...Face Dirt...Arms Dirt...
Here's Dirt In Your Eye
Here's Dirt On Your Head
Here's The Dirt
Hit Pay Dirt
I Love Dirt
It's A Dirty Shame
It's Time To Get DIRTY!!!
Joe Dirt
Just Call Me, "Mr. Dirt!"
Kiss The Dirt
A Little Dirt Never Hurt
My Place Is In The Dirt
Old As Dirt
Old Dirt Road
Older Than Dirt
On An Old Dirt Road
Pig Sty!
Real Boys Know The Taste Of Dirt
Sweaty, Dirty & Havin' Fun
That's Not Dirt In My House, It's Angel Dust
They Call Me, "Mr. Dirt!"
This Little Piggy...
Warning...Likes To Play In The Mud! *(Dirty child)*
What's A Little Dirt Between Friends?

____
____
____
____
____

DIRTBIKE TITLES

(SEE ALSO BICYCLE, MOTORCYCLE & RIDING)

After A Hard Day At Work/School, I Like To Hit The Bars...
Biker Babe/Baby
Biker Buddy/Dude
Born To Be Wild...Fear Is Not An Option
Born To Bike/Ride
Breaking Away
Berm Banger/Burner
Diggin' Dirt *(Dirt bike riding)*
Dirt Bike Tyke
Dirt Bikers Love To Eat Dirt!!!
Dirt Demon
Dirt Dominator
Dirt Rider
Dirt Tracker
Dirty Rider
Do It In The Dirt
Does This Dirt Bike Make My Butt Look Fat?
Don't Tell Me I Can't Jump It!
Double Jumper
Doubles Delight
Dreamy Dirt Biker
Dust Maker
Dusty Rider
"E" Ticket Rider
Easy Rider
Full Throttle Fanatic/Freak
Go Big Or Go Home!
Go Speed Racer
Got Air!?!
Happiness Is...A New Knobby!
If It Has Two Wheels, I Love It
It Doesn't Matter What You Ride, As Long As You Ride
Jr. Jumper
Just Jump It!
Just Pin It!
Look Out...Here I Come!
Makin' Tracks
Over the Whoops & Through The Berms, To The Finish Line I Go!
Puttin' The Pedal To The Metal
Race It Or Chase It!
Radicle Rider
Rally Fun
Ready...Set...Go/Race/Ride!
Ride Like The Wind
Ride *(Blue / Red / Yellow / Green)!*
Ridin' The Rollers!
Riding On....
Riding Radicle
Rollin O'er The Rollers
Rollin', Rollin', Rollin'...Keep Those Wheels A Rollin'
Rough Rider
'Round & 'Round
Rowdy Rider
Rugged Rider
Sweet On Suzuki
Suzuki Sweety
Table Top Attempt/Triumph/Trouble
There's No Looking Back Now
Too Much Power Is Just Enough!!!
Trail & Error
Trail Blazer
Treadin' Dirt
Tricky Triple
Triple Triumph
Two Wheel Travelin'

Two Wheelin'
Uneasy Rider
Watch Me Go
The Wheels On My Bike Go 'Round & 'Round
Wheely Fun
When In Doubt...GAS IT!!!
White Knuckle Rider
Whoops There Goes Another Dirt Biker Down!
Why Do I Ride CR500's? Cause They Don't Make CR600's!
Wide Open Spaces
Wide Open Til You See God, Then Brake!!!
Yes It's Fast...No You Can't Ride it!

____
____
____
____
____

DISNEY TITLES

(SEE ALSO AMUSEMENT PARK, CAROUSEL & WINNIE THE POOH)

- *Use Cartoon die-cut Hands as Mickey's hands holding the title.*

101 Ways To Have Fun
A Day Of Disney
Animals...Animals...Animals
Argh, Matey!
The Bear Necessities
Belle Of The Ball
Bibbidy Bobbidy Boo
Blasting Off To Tomorrow Land
Bouncin's What Tiggers Do Best
Bump 'Em! Crash 'Em! Smash 'Em!!!
Bungle In The Jungle
Can You Feel The Love Tonight?
Celebrate The Magic Of Disney
Chim, Chim Cheree
Darlin' Dumbo
Deep In The 100 Acre Woods
Dining Disney Style
Disney Duo
Disney Friends
Disney Or Bust
Disneyfied
Disneyland Is The Happiest Place On Earth
Dizzyland
Do You Believe?
Doin' A Disney Dance
A Dream Is A Wish Your Heart Makes *(Cinderella)*
Drive Safely...No Bumping
Ducky Love
"E" Ticket Rides Rock!
Everyone Loves A Parade
A Fairy Tale Dream Come True
Fairy Tales Do Come True
Feel The Magic
Feelin' Mousey
Flying On A Magic Carpet Ride
Getting Goofy
Goofin' With Goofy
Goofy-in' Around
Goofy-in' 'Round With Disney
Gosh, This Is Swell! - *(Mickey Mouse)*
Hakuna Matata
The Happiest Place On Earth
Heffalumps & Woozles Are Very Confusal
Hey, Mickey You're So Fine
Hi Ho, Hi Ho, It's Off To Disney We Go
Hip, Hip Pooh-Ray
House Of Mouse
I Just Can't Wait To Be King
I See Spots...101 Of Them!
I Won't Grow Up!!
I'm Goofy For You
I'm Rumbly In My Tumbly. - *(Winnie the Pooh)*
In The Jungle, The Mighty Jungle
To Infinity & Beyond
It Started With A Mouse
It's A Jungle Out There!
It's A Small World After All
It's Mickey Time
It's Winnie & Tigger Too
Just Goofin' Around With Goofy
Just Like Sleeping Beauty
Just Mad About Disney The Mouse
Kids With Character
Let The Adventure Begin
Let The Magic Begin
Let's Go Bouncin'
Little Mermaids
Little Piglets
Look To The Future In Tomorrow Land
Lovely Little Mermaid
Mad As A Hatter
The Mad Hatter
Mad Hatters Tea Party
Magic Carpet Ride
Magical Moments
Main Street USA
Mickey & Me

Mickey Mouse March
Minnie-Me
Mirror, Mirror On The Wall...
A Mission To Space & Beyond
Monsters Inc.
Mouse Magic
Mouse Tracks
"Mouse"atively Fun
Mousin' Around
My Goofy Family
My Little Mermaid
Never, Never Land!!!
Oh, Bother!!!
Oh Bother! It's A Blustery Day!
On! The Right Track
Our Goofy Troop
Our Little Disney Darlins'
Our Mousekateers
A Parade Of Princesses
A Pirate's Life For Me
A Pirate's Voyage
Pooh Is Cool
A "Pooh"rrific Adventure
Pretty As A Princess
Quack Attack
So This Is Love
Someday My Prince Will Come
Spaced Out From Space Mountain
A Spoon Full Of Sugar...
Spots, Spots, Spots
Supercalifragilisticexpialidocious
The Thrill Of Disneyland/World
Tigger-rific
A Tigger-rific Time
Tons Of Toon Town Fun
Toon Town Fun
Tutt, Tutt...It Looks Like Rain!
Under The Sea
Vroom Vroom!!!
Walt's World
We Had A "Pooh"rrific Adventure
We Had A Tigger-rific Time
We Survived Space Mountain
We Survived Splash Mountain
We're All Ears
What A Bunch Of Characters
When You Wish Upon A Star...
Where Dreams Really Do Come True
Where The Wild Things Are!
Who Said Disneyland Is Just For Kids?
A Whole New World
The Wonderful World Of Disney
Woody's Round-up
You Quack Me Up
You've Got A Friend In Me
Zippity Doo Dah Zippity Aye!

____
____
____
____
____

DIVORCE TITLES
(SEE BREAKUP)

DOCTOR TITLES
(SEE ALSO ILLNESS, INJURY & NURSE)

- *Use a Thermometer, Band-aid or Needle die-cut as an "I".*

An Apple A Day Keeps The Doctor Away
Call The Doctor
A Clean Bill Of Health
Diagnosis: Homesick
Diagnosis: Lovesick
Diagnosis: Spoiledrottenitis
The Doc Stops Here
Doctor, Doctor Give Me The News...
Doctor For My Heart
Doctors Do It With Patience!
Doctor's Orders
Dr. Doolittle
Dr. Scary
Healthy, Not-So-Wealthy, But Wise!
I Love A Doctor
I'm The Doctor
Say, "Ahh!"
What's Up Doc?

____
____
____
____
____

D D D D D D D D D D D D D D D D D D D D D D D D D D D D D D

DOG TITLES

- *Use a Bone to replace an "I".*

All Dogs Go To Heaven
Bad To The Bone
Bark In The Park
Barking Up The Wrong Tree
Best Of Breed
Beauty & The Beast
Bird Dog
Bone Appetite
Bone Head
Bone Voyage
Bow-wowing The Night Away
Breed All About It
Canine Crazy
Canine Crime
Canine Cutie
Chow Chow Time
Cold Nose...Warm Heart
Dem Bones
Diggin' Out
Dog Day Afternoon
Dog Days
Dog Days Of Summer
Dog Daze
A Dog Has The Soul Of A Philosopher
A Dog Wags Its Tail With Its Heart
Doggone Adorable/Cute
Doggone Best Friends
Doggone Good Fun/Time
Doggone It!
Doggone Tired
Dogmatic
Don't Fence Me In!
Dogs Best Friend
Dogs Know Best
Dogs Make Tracks Across Our Hearts
Every Dog Has Its Day
Everyone Needs Their Own Spot
Fetchin' For Fun
Fine Canine
Furr-ever Friends
Fur-rocious Fun
Gone To The Dogs
Happiness Is A Warm Puppy
Hot Diggity Dog
Hot Dog
How Much Is That Doggy In The Window?
I Have A Leash On Life
I Ruff You
I'm Im-paws-ible
I'm Mutts Over You
In The Dog House
In The Ruff
It's A Dog Day World
It's A Doggy Dog World
It's A Dog's Life
It's A Ruff, Ruff Life
I've A Bone To Eat/Pick
Just Me & My Dog
K-9 King
King Of The Yard
Kiss Me...I'm "Fur"riendly
Lady & The Tramp
Let Sleeping Dogs Lie
Licked Clean
Licks Of Love
Life Has Gone To The Dogs
Make No Bones About It...I'm Cute!
Man's Best Friend
Me & My Shadow
My Little Dog, A Heartbeat At My Feet
My Little Pound Puppy
No Bones About It...We Love *(Pet's name)*
No Bones About It...You're Just Doggone Cute!
Nuts About My Mutt
Oh, That's Dog Wash
Old Yeller
Our Furry Child
Pampered Pooch
Paws & Enjoy
Pet Palace/Paradise
Pick Of The Litter
Pitter Patter Of Little Paws
Play It To The Bone
Puppy Love
Puppy Play/Power
Pur-fection
Real Dogs Carry Papers, They Don't Have Them
Romancing The Bone
Ruffin' Around
Santa Paws
See *(Pet's name)* Run!
Silly Dog
Sit *(Pet's name)* Sit
Smoochin' Pooch
Take A Bow-Wow
Take Me To Your Litter
They Call It Puppy Love
Too Cute & No Bones About It
Top Dog

Under Dog
We Believe In Santa Paws
Who Let The Dogs Out?
Woof!
You Lucky Dog
(Pet's name) Got A Leash On Life

____
____
____
____
____

DOLL TITLES
All Dolled Up
Baby Doll
China Doll
A Doll Among Her Toys
Dolly Play
Hello Dolly
Little Doll
Little Rag Doll
Living Doll
I Love Andy More Than Candy!!
Never Too Old To Play With Dolls
Oh, Baby Doll
Paper Doll Play
Valley Of The Dolls
What A Doll!

____
____
____
____
____

DRAWING TITLES
(SEE ART, CHALK & COLOR/COLORING)

DREAM TITLES
(SEE ALSO ASPIRATIONS, HOPES, SLEEPING & WISHES)
- *Create a Thought Cloud & put title inside.*

All I Can Do Is Dream Of You
All I Have Is A Dream
All I Have To Do Is Dream
American Dream
Are We Dreamin' The Same Dream?
As Long As I Can Dream...
Awake & Dreaming
Beautiful Dreamer
Believe In Miracles
The Building Of Dreams
California Dreamin'
Chase A Rainbow To Your Dreams
Chase Your Dreams, You Might Catch One
Close Your Eyes & Dream
Dare To Dream
Day Dreams
Day Dream Believer
Day Dreamin'
Daydreaming = Wishcraft
Don't Dream Your Life, Live Your Dreams
Dream A Little Dream
Dream A Little Dream Of Me
Dream Away
Dream Boy
Dream Catcher
Dream Chaser
A Dream Come True
Dream, Dream, Dream...
Dream Girl
A Dream Is A Key To A Locked Door
A Dream Is A Wish Your Heart Makes
The Dream Is Still Alive
Dream It, Be It!
Dream Love
Dream Lover
Dream Lover, Please Be Mine
Dream Lover, You Are The One I Love
Dream Magic
Dream Painter
To Dream Of Love
A Dream Of Scarlet Nights
I Dream Of You Again
Dream On!!!
Dream On Little Dreamer
Dream On Until Your Dreams Come True
Dream Sweet Dreams
Dream Team
Dream Time
Dream Time In Progress
I Dream, Therefore I Become. - *(Cheryl Grossman)*
Dream Weaver
Dream When Your Feeling Blue
Dreamin'
Dreaming Of You
Dreamland
Dreamland Express
Dreams Are Necessary To Life. - *(Anais Nin)*
Dreams Do Come True
Dreams In The Night
Dreams Make A Wish Come True
Dreams Of The Everyday Housewife
Dreams Within The Still Of The Night
A Dreamy Day
Dreamy Eyes
Everything I Ever Dreamed Of & More
Field Of Dreams
Follow Your Dreams

Follow Your Rainbow
A Girl Can Dream
He's A Dream
Hold On Tight To Your Dreams
Hold Onto Your Dreams
Hope Is A Waking Dream. - *(Aristotle)*
I Am The Dreamer, You Are The Dream
I Can Dream Can't I?
I Guess I'll Have To Dream The Rest
I Had/Have A Dream
I Had Too Much To Dream Last Night
I Hope You Dream
I Like Dreamin'
I Must Be Dreaming
If You Can Dream It, You Can Do It. - *(Walt Disney)*
I'm Only Dreaming
Impossible Dream
In Pursuit Of My Dreams
In Your Dreams...
Keep On Dreamin'
Keep On Pushing
Keeping The Dream Alive
A Kiss To Build A Dream On
Let Your Dreams Set Sail
Life Is But A Dream
Live As You Dream
Living In A Dream
Look To Your Dreams
Make A Wish
Meet Me In My Dreams
Meet Me Where We Can Dream
Men Of Action Are Dreamers
A Mid-Summer Night's Dream
Mr. Sandman Bring Me A Dream
Mr. Sandman Bring Mommy/Daddy/Baby A Dream
In My Dreams
My Elusive Dreams
My Wildest Dreams
Never Give Up On A Dream
No Sleep, No Dreams
Nothing Happens Unless First A Dream
Now I Lay Me Down To Dream...
One Summer Dream
Only In My Dreams
The Path Not Taken
The Path Taken
The Power Of Dreams
The Power To Be Your Best
The Prince Of Dreams
Put Your Dreams Into Action
Reach For The Stars
Reach High & Touch The Stars
Set Aside Some Time For Dreaming
Shhh...Baby Dreamin'
Simple Pleasures Are Life's Greatest Treasures
To Sleep...Perchance To Dream!
Spread Your Wings & Fly
Sweet Dream Baby
Sweet Dream Baby...I Love You
Sweet Dreams
Sweetly Dreamin'
These Dreams
Think Big
Twilight Time To Dream Awhile
What A Day For A Daydream
What A Dream/Dreamer
What If ...
When I Dream...
When You Wish Upon A Star, Your Dreams Come True
Where Do You Go When You Dream?
While You Were Dreamin'...
While You Were Sleeping...
Who Needs Sleep?
With My Eyes Wide Open, I'm Dreaming
Wrap Your Troubles In Dreams
You Are My Dream Come True
You Are My Dream Of Sweet Desire
You Are The Theme For My Dream
You Beat Any Dream I've Ever Had
You Can't Stop Me From Dreaming!
You Make My Dreams
You Tell Me Your Dreams & I'll Tell You Mine
You'll Always Be In My Dreams
You'll Always Be My Dream

DRESSING/DRESS-UP TITLES

Accessorize, Accessorize, Accessorize
All Dolled Up
All Dressed Up & No Place To Go
All Spiffed Up
Amelda Wanna Be *(Shoe fascination)*
Baby...You've Got Style
Baubles & Bangles
Bell Bottom Blues
Best Dressed
Bloomer Girl
Blue Jeans & Barefeet
Blue Suede Shoes
Bobby Sox To Stockings
Buttons & Bows
Dedicated Follower Of Fashion

Denim Darlin's
Denim Days
Denim Dolls
Denim Duo
Devil With A Blue *(Any color dress)* Dress On
Don't Hate Me Because I Can Accessorize
Don't You Love All The Patches!?
Dress For Success
Dressed To Kill
Dressed To The Nines
Dressed To Thrill
Fashion Bug
Fashion Diva
Fashion Fades...Style Is Eternity
Fashion Fanatic
Fashion Frenzy
Fly By The Seat Of Your Pants
Forever In Blue Jeans - *(Neil Diamond)*
Glamour Gal/Girl
Go-Go Girl
GQ Guy/Boy
I Have **PMS**...**P**urchase **M**ore **S**hoes Disease!!!
Hey Girl, I Like Your Style
Hip Huggin' Dayz
I Do It Myself!
If The Shoe Fits...Buy It In Every Color!!!
It's All In The Jeans
It's Gettin' Hot In Here...So I'm Takin' All My Clothes Off!!! *(Toddler undressing)*
It's The Shades
Just A Little Patchy
Leather & Lace
Lookin' Good...Good Lookin'
Make Up! What Make Up?
Peddle Pushers
Pink Suede Shoes
Pretty In Pink
Puttin' On The Ritz
Quick Change Artist
Ribbons & Bows
Ruffles & Lace
Simply Irresistible
Snappy Dresser
So Many Clothes, So Little Time
Some Days I Just Can't Decide What To Wear
Some Days I Just Can't Decide Which Color To Wear So...
Style Matters
Sweeter In A Sweater
Tailor Made
These Boots Are Made For Walkin'
Tight Fitting Jeans
Tuxedo Function
What Not To Wear
You Can Never Have Too Many Shoes!
You Wear It Well
Zoot Suited
(Name) Long Stockings

____
____
____
____
____

DRINK/DRINKING TITLES

(SEE BEVERAGES)

DRIVING TITLES

(SEE ALSO CAR & RACING)

- *Make "O" into a Tire or a Steering Wheel.*
- *Make the "I" into a Stick Shift.*
- *Create the title to look like a License Plate.*

1 Hour Drive
4-Wheelin' Fun
10-4 Good Buddy
Along For The Ride
Are We There Yet?
Asleep At The Wheel
At The End Of The Road
Automobile Adventure
Baby You Can Drive My Car
Back On The Road
Backseat Driver
Beep-Beep...Beep-Beep
Bucket Of Bolts
Bump Em!! Crash Em!! Smash Em!! *(Bumper Cars)*
But Officer...I Didn't See You!
The Call Of The Open Road
Can't Wait To Get On The Road Again
Caution: Driver Legally Blonde
Caution: Teen Driver
Checkered Flag Dreams
Crash Test Dummies *(Fender bender)*
Crazy Driver
Cruisin' Along In My Automobile
Dead End Street
Demolition Derby/Driver
Dirt Road Blues
Don't Drive Faster Than Your Guardian Angel Can Fly!!!
Drive In! Drive Out!
Drive Safely...No Bumping!!!
Driver Wanted
The Driver's Seat...Sweeeet!!!
Drivin' All Over Town
Driving Around In My Automobile

Driving Down A Country Road
Driving Force
Driving Me Crazy
Driving Miss Daisy
Driving Mom/Dad Crazy
Driving On An Endless Highway
Easy Rider
Eat My Dust!
Enjoying The Ride
First Set Of Wheels
Four-Wheelin' Fun
Get Ready To Rumble
Get In, Sit Down, Hold On & Shut Up
Go-Go-Go
Go Speed Racer
Going Places
Good To Go
Got Our Kicks On Route 66
Got The Ticket To Drive
Grand Prix Dreamer
Hang On For The Ride Of A Lifetime
Hit The Highway
Hit The Road *(Name)*
Hot Rod Dreamer/Dreams
I Wanna Drive You Home
I'd Rather Ride Around With You
If You Don't Like My Driving...Get Off The Sidewalk
I'll Do The Driving!
I'm In The Driver's Seat
In The Driver's Seat
In The Fast Lane!!!
It's The Journey, Not The Destination
In The Middle Of The Road
Just Can't Wait To Get On The Road Again
Just Drivin' Around
Keep On Truckin'
King Of The Highway
King Of The Road
Kruisin' Kid
Ladies & Gentlemen...START YOUR ENGINES
Let Me Drive
Let The Good Times Roll
Licensed To Drive!
Lead Foot *(Name)*
Life In The Fast Lane
Life's A Highway
Life's Highway
The Long & Winding Road
Long Lonely Highway
The Long Road Home
Look Out Road...Here I Come *(New license)*
Look Out World...Here Comes *(Name)*
Look Out World...Here I Come! *(New license)*
Makin' Tracks
Moonlight Drive
My Way Or The Highway
Not So Fast
Ocean Drive
Off The Beaten Path *(4-Wheelin')*
Oh, That Broken Road
On A Long & Winding Road
On A Roll
On The Go!
On The Move
On The Right Track
On The Road Again
On The Road Again & Again & Again!
On The Road To Recovery
Pass With Care
Pedal Power
Put The Pedal To The Metal
I Put The Pedal To The Metal, & All I Got Was A Lousy Ticket!!!
Racing Radicle
Red Hot Love
Red Light, Green Light
Road Adventures
The Road Goes Ever On
Road Hog
Road Rage
Road Rash
Road Rules!!!
Road Trip
Road Warrior
The Road Less Traveled
The Road You Leave Behind
Rockin' Down The Highway
Rocky Road Blues
Roll On
Roll On 18-Wheeler, Roll On
Rollin' Down The Highway
Rollin', Rollin', Rollin' Keep Those Wheels A Rollin'
Rough Roadin'
'Round & 'Round
Show Me The Road
Shut Up & Drive
Somewhere Down The Road
Spinning Your Wheels
Steering Clear
Take The Road Less Traveled...
There's A Road I'm Wanderin'
There's No Looking Back Now
True Love On The Love
Two On The Road
Two Wrong Turns Don't Make A Right

Uneasy Rider
The Wheels On My Car Go 'Round & 'Round
When I Drive...
Where The Blacktop Ends
Where The Road Leads
Where The Rubber Meets The Road
Who's In The Driver's Seat?
Wild Ride
With My Good Looks, I Could Stop Traffic!
You Drive Me Crazy
You Drive Me Nuts
Zoom, Zoom, Zoom!!!
(Name) Is On The Road Again

DRUMS TITLES

(SEE ALSO MUSIC)

- *Use Drum Sticks in place of an "I" or "L".*
- *Use a Drum in place of the entire word.*

Bang A Drum
Bang The Drum All Day
Banger Boy
Bang! Clash! Bang!
Beat That Drum
Dancin' To The Beat Of A Different Drum
Drum Solo
Drum Talk
Heavy Metal Drummer
I Wanna Bang On My Drum All Day
Jungle Drummer
Kiss The Drummer
Lil' Drummer Boy
Me & My Drum
The Sound Of Drumsticks
Wound Tight As A Drum

DUCK TITLES

All The Ducks In A Row
Be Kind To Your Web-Footed Friends
Birds Of A Feather
Disco Duck
Duck & Run
Duck, Duck *(Name)* *(Feeding ducks)*
Flights Of Fancy
Just Ducky
Lucky Ducky
Quack Attack
Quackin' Up
Rubber Ducky
Sitting Duck
Waddle I Do For Food/Love?!
What's Good For The Goose, Is Good For The Gander
What's Up Duck?
You Quack Me Up
You're Just Ducky

D

D

D

D

D

D

D

D

D

D

D

D

D

D

D

D

D

D

D

D

D

D

D

D

D

D

D

D

D

D

EARS/EARRINGS/HEARING TITLES

All Ears
An Official Set Of Ears
Bobbles & Bangles
Can You Hear It/That?
Can You Hear Me Now?
Can You Hear My Heart Beating?
Do You Hear What I Hear?
Ears Looking At You Babe/Baby
Ears To Hear With
Ears To You
Fears, Tears, Beautiful Ears *(Ear piercing)*
Got An Earful
Green Behind The Ears
Grinning Ear To Ear
Hear Me Cry
Hear No Evil
Heard It Thru The Grapevine
Holes In The Head
Holey, Holey, Holey
I Can Almost Hear Her Wings
I Can Hear The Laughter
I Can Hear Your Heart Beat
I Can't Hear You
I Hear A Symphony
I Hear The Rain
I'm All Ears
I Just Had To Hear Your Voice
Just To Hear You Say That You Love Me
My Ears Are Burning
Piercing A Hole In The Situation
Piercing Situation
Piercing Screams
Play It By Ear
Put Your Ear Into It
Selective Hearing
Sparkling Stones
Stick It In Your Ear
The Walls Have Ears
Up To My Ears
The Walls Have Ears
I Wanna Hear You're Heart Beat
We're All Ears
Wet Behind The Ears
Whisper In My Ear

EARTH & EARTH DAY TITLES

(SEE WORLD)

EASTER TITLES

(SEE ALSO RABBIT)

- *Use an Egg or Jelly Bean as an "O".*
- *Make larger Eggs or Jelly Beans for mats to put each title letter on.*

24-Karrat Kids
All My Eggs Are In One Basket
Another Egg-scuse To Eat Chocolate
Art To The Egg-streme
A Basket Full Of Precious Eggs
Basket Of Love
Basketful Of Goodies
Basketful Of Love
Baskets & Bunnies
Bunny Crossing
Bunny Love
Bunny Treats
Carrot Patch
Carrot You Find Any Eggs?
Celebrating One Lord
Chick Me Out!!!
Christ Is Risen Today!
Color Me Eggs-tra Special
Color Me Happy
Colorful Creations By *(Child's name)*
Cute Chicks
Cute & Fuzzy
Cute & Fuzzy As A Bunny
Don't Put All Your Eggs In One Basket
Easter Art
Easter Blessings
Easter Brunch
Easter Egg Dips
Easter Egg-cellent
Easter Egg-cellent Art
Easter Egg-citement
Easter Hoppenings
Easter "Pooh"rade
Easter-rific
An Egg Hunting We Will Go
Egg Painting Zone
Eggs To "Dye" For
An Egg-citing Resurrection Story
Egg-specially Cute
Egg-sposed
An Egg-stra Big Mess
An Egg-stra Special Easter

Egg-stravaganza
Everyone Is Entitled To A Bad "Hare" Day
Everyone Needs A Friend Who Is All Ears
For Peeps Sake
I Found My Easter Basket
Funny Bunny
Get Crackin'
The Glory Of Easter
A Good Hare
The Greatest Story Ever Told
Had A Great Hare Day
Hare Comes Peter Cottontail
Hippity, Hoppity
Hippity, Hoppity...Happy Easter
Hippity, Hoppity *(Child's name)* Is On The Hunt
Hopping Down The Bunny Trail
Hoppy Easter
Hot Chicks
The Hunt Is On!
A Hunting We Will Go
I'm So Egg-cited
In My Easter Bonnet With All The Trimmings On It!
Jelly Bean Baby
Jelly Bean Boys
Jelly Bean Time
Jelly Belly Baby
Lil' Chicks
Loads Of Eggs
My Little Chick
Oh, Hoppy Day
One Cute Easter Chick
Our Little Chick-A-Dee
Painting Eggs...Done Cheep
Peep-Peep
Rotten Eggs
Scramblin' For Eggs
Some Body Parts Should Be Floppy
Some Bunny Loves Me
Some Bunny's Having An Easter Egg Hunt
A Sp"Egg"tacular Easter
Sp"Egg"tacular Picasso's
You're Some Bunny Special
Spring Flings & Easter Things
Sunrise Service
There's No Bunny Like You
The Thrill Of The Hunt
A Tisket, A Tasket, A Green & Yellow Basket
A Very Bunny Day
Walk Softly & Carry A Big Carrot
What An Egg-cellent Egg
You Crack Me Up
You're A Special Egg
You're Full Of Jelly Beans
You're No Bunny 'Til Some Bunny Loves You

____
____
____
____
____

EAT/EATING TITLES

(SEE DIET & FOOD)

ENGAGEMENT TITLES

(SEE ALSO LOVE & MARRIAGE)

Always & Forever
...And She Said, "Yes"
A Beginning For Us
The Beginning Of A Great Adventure
Beginning Today...
Engaged At Last
Engaged...Finally
The First Sunbeams Of The New Beginning
From The Beginning...
From This Day Forward...
In The Beginning...
It's Only The Beginning
Just The Beginning
Let The Love Begin
Let's Start With Forever
Our Journey's Just Begun
This Magic Moment
A Real Good Place To Start
The Rules Of Engagement
Shall We Begin
Starting Today...
Starting With You...
The Start Of Something Good
I Thought He Would Never Ask
We've Only Just Begun
What A Wonderful Beginning
Where It All Began

____
____
____
____
____

EXERCISE TITLES

(SEE ALSO DIET)

1, 2, 3, 4...1, 2, 3, 4 Up & Down I Go!
...And Breathe, 2, 3, 4...
Body Builder/Building
Body Machine
Breathe Easy
Buffed
Burnin' Calories
Commit To Be Fit
Eat Now, Exercise Later
Exercising My Right Not To
Fat Burning...
Feel The Burn
Feelin' Fit
Firm, Fit & Fab
Fit As A Fiddle
Fit 'N Firm
Hardbody
Hardbody In Training
House Of Pain...My Gym!
Huff...Puff...Huff!!!
Huffin' & Puffin'
In A Sweat
Lean Mean Machine
Never Let 'Em See You Sweat
New Body In The Works
No Pain...No Gain!
The Pain Game
Pump, Pump, Pump It Up
Pumped Up
Sweatin' Bullets
Sweatin' It Out
Sweatin' With The Oldies
The Way I See It Is...No Pain, No Pain!
This Can't Be An Exercise!!!
Tight Body In Training
Workin' It Out
Workin' Up A Sweat

____
____
____
____
____

EYES TITLES

- *Use an Eye in place of the word Eye.*

3-2-1 Contacts
5' 2"...Eyes Of Blue
20-20 Vision
All Eyes On Me
Angel Eyes
Apple Of My Eyes
As Far As The Eyes Can See
At First Sight
Baby Blues
Baby's Blue Eyes
Baby's Got Blue Eyes
Beautiful Eyes
Beautiful In My Eyes
Before My Very Eyes
Be"Spec"kled
Better Watch Out
Big Eyes
Blind As A Bat
Blue-Eyed Beauty
Bright Eyes
Brown-Eyed Blues
Brown-Eyed Girl
Brown-Eyed Handsome Man
Bug Eyes/Eyed
Cat Eyes
I Can See Clearly Now!
Can't Take My Eyes Off You
Can't You See The Love In My Eyes?
Close Your Eyes & Dream
Close Your Sleepy Little Eyes
Crying Eyes
Crystal Eyes
Daddy's Eyes
Don't Make My Brown *(Any color)* Eyes Blue
Double Vision
Dreamy Eyes
Emerald Eyes
Everytime I Close My Eyes
Everytime I See Your Face
Eye In The Sky
The Eye Is The Jewel Of The Body.
(Henry David Thoreau)
My Eyes Adore You
The Eyes Are The Windows To The Soul
The Eyes Have It
The Eyes Have One Language Everywhere.
(George Herbert)
Eyes Like Diamond
Eyes Of A Girl
Eyes Of A Thousand Eyes
Eyes Of A Woman
Eyes Of An Angel

Eyes Of Blue
Eyes Of Innocence
Eyes Of Love
Eyes That Shine Like Blue Diamonds
Eyes That Sparkle
With Eyes Wide Open
For Your Eyes Only
Forever In Your Eyes
Gorgeous In Glasses
Got A New Per"spec"tive *(Glasses on wrong)*
Great Big Beautiful Eyes
Green Are Your Eyes
Green-Eyed Girl/Guy
Green Eyes
Heaven In Your Eyes
He's Makin' Eyes At Me
Her Eyes Are Homes Of Silent Prayers.
(Lord Alfred Tennyson)
Here's Lookin' At You
Honesty Shines Like A Light Thru Your Eyes
I Can't Take My Eyes Off You
I Must Be Seeing Things
I Only Have Eyes For You
I'll Always Look Up To You
I'm Too Sexy For My Glasses
In My Daughter's Eyes
In The Eye Of The Beholder
In The Eye Of The Storm
In Your Eyes...
Innocent Eyes
Irish Eyes
Irish Eyes A Smilin'
It's In Your Eyes
It's The Shades
I've Got My Eyes On You
Jeepers Creepers...What Cute Peepers
Just Seeing Your Eyes
The Light In Your Eyes...
Little Brown-Eyed Girl
Long Time No See
Lookie, Lookie At Me!
Lookin' At My Baby
Looking At The Eyes Of An Angel
Lost In Your Eyes
Love At First Sight
I Love What I See
The Lovelight In Your Eyes...
Love's In Your Eyes
Makin' A "Spec"tacle Of Myself/Yourself
Mesmer"Eyes"
Mommy's Eyes
My Brown-Eyed Girl
My Eyes Adore You
My Eyes Are Beautiful Because They Are Looking At You
Not A Dry Eye In The House
One's Eyes Are What One Is. - *(John Galsworthy)*
Pretty Little Angel Eyes
I See God In Your Eyes
See Me...Love Me
See That Girl
See The Ball
Seeing Double
Seeing Eye To Eye
Seeing Is Believing
Seeing Life Thru Rose Colored Glasses
Seeing The Lights Shine
Set Your Sights Farsighted
Snake Eyes
Someone To Watch Over Me
Spanish Eyes
"Spec"tacular
Starlight Eyes
Starry Eyes
Stars In My Eyes
Stay Focused
Teardrops From My Eyes
Teardrops In My Eyes
Them Pretty Brown Eyes
These Brown Eyes
These Eyes
These Eyes Adore You
Thru My Eyes
Thru The Eyes Of Love
Trust With Eyes Of A Child
Two Eyes Are Better Than One!
Visions Of Love
Wanderin' Eyes
Watch Me Shine
Watching The Day Go By
Watching The Rain
Watching The Sun Set
Watching You Makes My Heart Beat
Watching You Shine...
What You Get Is What You See
When I Close My Eyes...
When I Look Into Your Eyes...
When I See You Smile...
When You Smile...
You Can Close Your Eyes
You Light Up My Eyes
You Opened My Eyes

FAIR TITLES
(SEE AMUSEMENT PARK & CAROUSEL)

FAIRYTALE TITLES
As You Wish...
At The Stroke Of Midnight...
Day Dream Believer
Fairytale Hero
Fairytale King
Fairytale Love
A Fairytale Love Story
Fairytale Princess
Happily Ever After
Hear Ye, Hear Ye!
I Dub Thee...
Jester Fun
Joust For Fun
The King & His Castle
Magic Kingdom
Mid-Evil Times
My Fair Lady
My Fairy God Mother
My Knight In Shining Armor
My Royal Jester
Once Upon A Time...
Our Little Prince/Princess
Queen For A Day
Royalty
Sir *(Name)*

FAITH TITLES
Act Of Faith
Baby...I Believe In You
Believe In Dreams
Believe In Me
Believe In Miracles
Believe In You & Me
Believe In Yourself
Believe It Or Not
Believing With Faith
Blind Faith
Dare To Believe
Do You Believe In Love
Do You Believe In Magic
Face Of Faith
Faith By Faith
Faith Full
Faith...Hope...Love
Faith Is A Journey
Faith Is The Key
Faith's Touch...Faith's Wonder
Full Of Faith
I Can Hardly Believe You Are Mine
I Can't Believe It's True!!!
I Can't Believe My Eyes
I Do Believe
I Have Faith In You
If You Believe...
If You Believe In Dreams...
In You...I Believe
It's Only Make Believe
Just Believe
Keeping The Faith
Leap Of Faith
Miracles Happen When You Believe
On The Wings Of Faith
Only Believe
Promise To Believe
Seeing Is Believing
She Believes In Me
Test Of Faith
This I Believe
To Achieve...You Must Believe
Unshakable Faith
You Are My Reason To Believe

FALL/LEAVES TITLES
(SEE ALSO AUTUMN & HARVEST)
- *Have the "L" falling from the title.*
- *Use a Leaf as an "A".*

All For Fall
...And The Leaves Came Tumbling Down
As The Leaves Turn
Back In Gear For Fall
I Be"Leaf" In You
Buried Treasure *(Kids under leaf piles)*
A Bushel Of Fun
Changing Leaves
Changing Seasons
Chasing The Winds Of Fall
A Child Of All Seasons
The Chill Of Fall
Colors Of Fall
Cozy Cuddle Days Of Fall
Crisp Days Of Fall
Crisp Fall Air
C-R-U-N-C-H
Dancing Leaves Fall Down

Dive In!
Don't Leaf Me!!
Drifting Into Fall
Fabulous Fall
Fall Announces Itself Very Bold With Leaves Of Red & Gold
Fall Ball
Fall Extravaganza
Fall, Falling...Fallen Leaves
Fall Family Fun
Fall Festival
Fall Festival Of Colors
Fall Fiesta
Fall Foliage
Fall Frenzy
Fall Fun
Fall Fun For All
Fall Getaway
Fall Guys
Fall Happenings
Fall Harvest
Fall Has Came That Is For Sure
Fall In Love With Autumn Falling
Fall Into Autumn
Fall Into The Fall Season
Fall Into...*(Your City or State)*
Fall "Leaves" Me Happy
Fall Leaves You Breathless
Fall Memories
The Fall Of Shame
Fall Splendor
Fall...The Season Of Changes
Fall...The Season Of Fun
Fall Ushers In The Winter Fun
Fall vs. Winter
Fall-bulous
Fall-errific
Fallin' Leaves
Falling Behind
Falling For You
Falling In Love Again
Falling Into You
Falling Leaves
Fall's Coloring Book
Fall's Harvest
"Fall"tastic
Family Fun In The Gold & Red Season Of Fall
Fantastic Fall
The Feeling Of Fall
Feels Like Fall
A Festival Of Fall Colors'
Finally Fall
Fire Up For Fall!
Forever Fall
Free "Fall"in'
Frolic In The Fall Leaves
Frolicking In The Fall
Frolicking In The Fun Colors Of Fall
Fun Colours Of Fall
Golden Days Of Fall
A Golden Fall
Golden Fall Days
Have A Nice Trip...See Ya Next Fall
Hay Rides & Pumpkin Pie
Hello Fall!!!
Hi Ho, Hi Ho...It's Off To Rake I Go
Horn Of Plenty
The Hunt For Red October
I'll "Fall" For You Anytime
Into Our Lives A Little Fall Must Rein
It Leaves You Breathless
It's Time To Fall Into Autumn!
I've "Fall"en & I Can't Get Up
I've "Fall"en For You!
Jack Frost Painted The Leaves!
Jump Into Fall!
Kaleidoscope Of Colors
This Kid Is "Oak"ay
"Leaf" It Up To me
"Leaf" Me Alone
Leaf Wars
"Leaf"ing Summer Behind
Leapin' Leaves
Leaves Abound From All Around
The Leaves Are Changing
Leaves Are Falling
Leaves Come Tumbling Down
Leaves Fall...God Doesn't
Leaves Of Time
The Leaves Of Time Fall
Legends Of The Fall
Like A Graceful Ballet Dancer, The Leaves Flutter About
Magical Colours Of Fall
October Fall
October Sky
Phenomenal Fall
Piles Of Smiles
Piling Up Memories
Playing In The Leaves
Raining Leaves
Rake...Dump...Jump!!!
Rake It Up Baby!
Rakin' Up Some Fall Fun
Raking The Days 'Til Christmas
Rolling In The Leaves
Scenes Of Fall
The Season Has Changed, Fall Now Reins

Season Of Change
Season Of My Life
September Leaves
September Mornings
September Splendor
September To Remember
A Sign Of The New Season
Silly As A Scarecrow
Snuggle Days Of Fall
Something To Crow About
Starry Nights Of Fall
Summer "Leaves"...Fall Begins!
Summer vs. Fall
Sweatshirt Season
Sweet September
Taking A Fall
Thankful Days Of Fall
Time For Fall Fun
Turning Over A New Leaf
We All Fall Down
We Rake...We Pile...We Jump!!!
When Fall Falls
Who You Gonna Call...Leaf Busters!

____
____
____
____
____

FAMILY TITLES

(SEE ALSO COUSINS & FAMILY TREE)

All American Family
All In The Family
All Things Grow With Love
Blessed Be Our Nest
Blessed With A Crowded Nest
Branching From Generation To Generation
Cherish Your Family, For They Are Your Treasure
A Chip Off The Old Block
Circles Of Love
"Crazy" Is A Relative Term In My Family!
Deep Rooted Heritage
Families Are Forever
Families Are Tied Together With Heart Strings
Families Bloom With Love
A Family Affair
Family Business
Family Faces...Are Like Magic Mirrors
Family Faces Thru Time
Family Feud
Family Folk
Family Frenzy
Family Fun
A Family Grows One Smile At A Time
A Family Is A Gift That Lasts Forever
A Family Is A Great Thing To Love
A Family Is A Little World Created By Love
A Family Is A Packaged Deal
A Family Is A Patchwork Of Love
Our Family Is A Work Of Heart
A Family Is Like A Warm Quilt Wrapped Around Your Heart
The Family Is One Of Nature's Masterpieces. *(George Santayana)*
Family Life
Family Man
Family Matters/Ties
Family Of Love
Family Snapshot
A Family That Plays Together, Stays Together
A Family That Prays Together, Stays Together
Family...The We Of Me!!!
Family Ties
Full House
Gang's All Here
Genealogists Are Time Unravelors
Genealogists Live In The Past Lane
Genealogy: Chasing Your Own Tale!
Generations Of Love
Generation To Generation
God Chooses Our Families
The Good Life
Happiness Is Homemade
A Happy Family Is But An Early Heaven
I Think My Ancestors Had Several "Bad Heir" Days
I'm Not Stuck, I'm Ancestrally Challenged!
In-Laws & Out-Laws
Individually We Are Special, Together We Are Family
It Runs In The Family
It's A Family Tradition
It's All In The Genes
It's All Relative
Keepin' It In The Family
Kindred Spirits Linked By Love *(Charm bracelet)*
Love Is A Circle Of Family
Love Is...Family Togetherness
Love Is Spoken Here
The Love Of A Family Makes Life Beautiful
The Luckiest People In The World
Lucky To Have Each Other
Many A Family Tree Needs Pruning
My Family, My Life
Near & Dear
The Newest Branch On The Family Tree
Next Of Kin

Obviously Good Looks Run In The Family!
Ode To My Family
One Big Happy Family
One More Makes Four
Our Family Is A Circle Of Love
Our Family Tree Blooms With Love
Our Family Tree Is Blessed With Thee!
Our Family Tree Is Chocked Full Of Nuts
Our Legacy Lives On With Family
Our Nest Is Blessed
Out On A Limb With Our Family Tree
Party Of *(# of family members)*
Prime Time Family
Relative Bliss
Remember Your Roots
So Many Ancestors...So Little Time!
The Ties That Bind...
There's Something About The Name
To A Genealogist, Everything Is Relative!
Together Again
Together Again - At Last
Traditions Begin With Family
We Are A Happy Family!
We Are F-A-M-I-L-Y
We Are Blessed
We Begin & End With Family
As We Gather Together
We're A Wacky Bunch
We're All In This Together
Wild & Wacky Family
You Can Go Home Again
You Have Our Family Face
Yours, Mine & Ours
The *(Surname)* Family Stays Busy
The *(Surname)* Clan

Father
And
Mother
I
Love
You

____
____
____
____
____

FARM/FARMERS TITLES

(SEE ALSO ANIMALS, COUNTRY, COWBOYS, HORSE & SOME SPECIFIC ANIMALS)

Ah, Shucks!
Animal Farm/House
Barnyard Animals
B'gosh That's My Baby Boy/Girl
Bless This Barn/Farm
Bought The Farm
Bull Dozer *(Bull sleeping)*
Cattle Call
Chicken Run
The Corn On This Farm Has Ears!
Counting Sheep
Cows & Chickens & Ducks Oh My!
Cowtown Cuties
Daddy's Deere
Down On The Farm
Down On The Funny Farm
E-I-E-I-O
Ewe Are Loved
Farm Fresh
Farm Livin' Is The Life For Me!
The Farmer In The Dell
Farmer *(Name)*
Farmers Are The Best In Their Fields
Free Hay Rides
Future World Champion Bull Rider
Get Along Little *(Name)*
Going Hog Wild
Going Whole Hog
Green Acres
The Green, Green, Grass Of My Home
Greener Pastures
Happy As A Pig In Mud
Having A "Hay" Day
"Hay" Fever
"Hay" Good Lookin'
"Hay" Is For Horses
"Hay" There
Herd The Call
High On The Hog
Hog Heaven
Hog Wash
Hog Wild
Hogs & Kisses
Home On The Range
How The West Was Fun
Howdy Pardner
Howdy Ya'll
I Love Ewe
The Lady Takes The Cowboy Everytime!
Land Spreadin' Out So Far & Wide
Lil' Buckaroo

Lil' Cowpoke
Lil' Farmer Boy
This Little Piggy
This Little Piggy Went Night, Night
My Little Piggies
The Okay Corral
On The Funny Farm
Pig Out
Piggin' Out
Piggy Back Riders
Piggy Back Rides Here
Pretty In Pink *(Pigs)*
She Thinks My Tractor's Sexy
She Wants To Marry A Cowboy
This Little Piggy
Ye Old Homestead/Farm
Wanted...
Welcome To Our Funny Farm
Welcome To Our Ranch
Were You Raised In A Barn?
What A Pig Sty!
When Pigs Fly...
Where The Buffalo Roam!
Wild, Wild West
____
____
____
____
____

FATHER TITLES

(SEE ALSO FATHER-IN-LAW)
#1 Father/Dad
Beary Best Dad
The "Bear"y Best Pa In The Land
Best Dad Award
Big Daddy
Celebrating Fatherhood
A Chip Off The Old Block
"Dad"itude
Dad's #1 Fan
Dad's Best Buddy
Dad's Grrrrrrreat!
Daddy Dear
Daddy Did It!
Daddy-O
Daddy's Angel
Daddy's Buddy
Daddy's Eyes
Daddy's Girl
Daddy's Hands
Daddy's Little Girl/Guy
Daddy's Little Helper
Daddy's Princess
Dear Ol' Dad
Father Knows Best
My Father...My Guiding Light
Father Of Mine
Father Of The Year
Father On The Go
Father To Son
Father's Day Fun With His Sons
Fearless Leader
Following In Daddy's Footsteps
The Gleam In Father's Eyes
He Calls Me Daddy
He's The Man
His Father's Son
Hop On Pop
I Am Dad...Hear Me Roar/Snore
I'm Glad You're My Dad
Just Like Dad
Just Me & My Dad/Pa
King Of Hearts
King Of The Hill
Life With Daddy/Father
Like Father, Like Son/Daughter
The Mama & The Papa
Man Of The Hour
A Man's Home Is His Castle
My Dad
My Dad Rules!
My Daddy Hung The Moon
My Daddy...My Hero
My Dad's A Hero
My Dad's A Star
My Heart Belongs To Daddy
No Lion, Dad Is Grrrreat
No One Can Fill Dad's Shoes
Not A Shirt & Tie Kind Of Guy
Our Dad Has A Heart Of Gold
Our Dad's The Greatest
Papa Loves Mama
Papa Was A Rolling Stone
Patio Daddio
Proud Papa
She Calls Me Daddy
Sugar Daddy
Suit Yourself
Super Dad
The Tie That Binds Me
A Toast For Dad
What A Dad
World's Best Daddy

World's Greatest Father
You Can't Scare Me...I Have Kids

Dandy
And
Delightful

FATHER-IN-LAW TITLES

(SEE ALSO FATHER)
Father By Marriage...Friend By Choice
Her/His Father...My Friend
My Other Father

FEET/FOOT TITLES

(SEE ALSO WALKING)

- *Place Foot Prints under title or even have them walking over the top of it.*
- *Make a large Foot & put title inside it.*

The Agony Of De"Feet"
Alive & Kicking
Baby Steps
Back On My Feet
Barefoot & Fancy Free
Barefoot In The Park
Barefootin'
Big Foot
I Can Walk The Line
Careful Where You Step
Cold Feet
Dancin' Barefoot
Dancin' Feet
Every Step Of The Way
Fall Head Over Heels
These Feet Are Gonna Walk All Over You!
Feet Don't Fail Me Now!
Filthy Foots
First Steps
Following In *(Name)* Footsteps
Foot Stompin' Fun
Footloose
Footloose & Fancy Free
These Foots Are Made For Eatin'
These Foots Were Made For Dancin'
Head To Toe
The Ground Beneath My/Your Feet
Happy Feet
Head Over Heals
High-Heel Sneakers
If You're Gonna Walk The Walk...
The Journey Begins With A Single Step
Jump In With Both Feet
Just A Step From Heaven
Kick Up Your Heels
Kick Your Feet Up
Kiss My Feet
Knocked Off My Feet
This Little Piggy
These Little Piggy's
Makin' Tracks
Next Step
On Your Toes
One Step Ahead
One Step At A Time
Pitter Patter
Playing Footsie
Pound The Pavement
Pretty In Polish
Put Your Best Foot Forward
Put Your Left Foot In
Shoe Business
Step By Step
Step By Tiny Step
A Step Too Far
Stinky Feet
Sweet Feet
Sweet Little Feet
Swept Off My Feet
Tasty Toes
Ten Feet Tall
Ten Tiny Fingers & Ten Tiny Toes
There's Nothing More Sweet Than The Pitter Patter Of Little Feet
This Little Piggy Went Night Night
Twinkle Toes
Two Left Feet
With Both Feet On The Ground
Yep, Ten Yummy Toes!
You Knock My Socks Off

FIGHT/FIGHTING TITLES

(SEE ALSO WRESTLING)

- *Make little Boxing Gloves hanging from title.*

Are You Ready To Rumble???
The Battle Cry
Battle Of Wills
Brow Beatin'
The Bruisin' Brothers
Can't Fight This Feeling
Caught In The Act
Cleaned His Opponents Clock
Come Out Fighting
Crimes & Misdemeanors
Cruisin' For A Bruisin'
Dark Horse Winner
A David vs. Goliath Fight
Don't Fight It
Down For The Count
Family Feud
Fight Night
Fight The Feeling
A Fight 'Til The End
Fighting Back The Tears
Fighting For Love
Foolish Feud
Fought Pound For Pound
Got Beat Like A Drum
Got His Bell Rung
Got His Clock Cleaned
Grudge Match
Hit Below The Belt
Hit Between The Numbers
Hit By A Bolt Of Fives
Hit The Spot
I'll Fight For You
It Takes Two To Tangle
It's Not The Size Of The Dog In The Fight, It's The Size Of The Fight In The Dog
Keep Your Eye On The Prize
Kids For Sale...Dirt Cheap!
A Knock-Out Blow
Kung Fu Fighting
Oh, That Had To Hurt
On The Ropes
Pick Your Battles
Put 'Em Up
Rang His Bell
Rasslin'
A Real Knock Out
Rock 'Em Sock 'Em Guys/Kids *(Boxing/fighting)*
Saturday Night Fights
Those Are Fightin' Words
Time Out Tangle *(2 kids face to face in time out)*
Time Out Time
TKO
Your Worth Fighting For

FIRE/FIREMAN TITLES

(SEE ALSO HOT)

- *Use Thermometers with the mercury at real Hot to create the "H".*
- *Make Water Drops dripping from the letters as if they were sweating.*
- *Draw Flames coming from tops of letters.*
- *Put title in Puffs of Smoke.*

Ad Serviendum Dedicatus *(Latin - Dedicated To Serving)*
After The Fire...
All Fired Up
Always Ready
Baby...You Caught My Heart On Fire
The Best That Never Rest
Blowin' Smoke
Burnin' For Your Love
Burnin' Love
Burning Rubber
Burnt Offerings
Bustin' Ours...Savin' Yours
C'mon Baby Light My Fire
Cool It Down
Does Anyone Have A Light?
Don't You Wish Your Boy/Girl Friend Was Hot Like Me?
Earth...Wind...Fire
Emotional Fire
Extinguish My Burnin' Love
Eyes On Fire
I Feel A Burnin' Inside My Bones
I Feel You Burnin' Inside Of Me
The Few Dedicated To The Many
Find 'Em Hot...Leave 'Em Wet
Fight Fire With Fire
I Fight What You Fear
Fire & Ice
Fire Dance
Fire In The Rings
Fire In The Sky
The Fire Is So Delightful *(Campfire)*
Fire It Up
Fired Up & Ready To Rumble
Firefighter = Special Person
Firefighters Are Cool When It Gets Hot!

Firefighters Do It Hotter
Firefighters Like It Hot!
Firefighters Save Hearts & Homes
Firemen Are Always In Heat
Firemen Have Long Hoses
Fire's Reflection
The Flame Of Love's Burnin' Hot
Flames Of Desire
Flames Of Happiness
Flamin'
Flaming Youth
Four-Alarm Fire
Four-Alarm Kid
Friendly Fire
Fun At The Firehouse
Got A Fire Burnin' In My Soul
Great Balls Of Fire
My Heart Burns For You
My Heart's A Burnin'
My Heart's Affire For You
Hearts-Afire *(Couple in front of firehouse or trucks)*
The Heat Has Got Me Burnin'
To Hell & Back
Ho'oikai'ka *(Hawaiian - Together Strong)*
Hose Me With Your Happiness/Love
Hot Like Fire
Hot, Hot, Hot!
Hot Stuff
Hottie
Hug A Firefighter...Feel Warm All Over!
Hunk Of Burnin' Love
I'll Walk Thru Fire For You
It's A Burnin' Love
I've Got A Burnin' Feeling
I've Got A Burnin' Hunger For You
Ladies Love Me...Flames Fear Me
Let's Set The Night On Fire
Light My Fire
Light The Fire Again
The Little Fire Engine That Could
Love Is A Burnin' Thing
Love Set Afire
Love's Fire
My Soul's On Fire
Not For One, But For All
On Top Of Old Smokey
Onair Do Na Mairbh *(Gaelic - Honour The Fallen)*
Playing With Fire
Pride...Committment...Service
Protection & Assistance
Ready, Willing & Able
Red Hot!
Rescue Me
Ring Of Fire
To Save Lives & Protect Property
See Spot *(Dalmatian)*
To Serve & Protect
Service For Others
Service With Compassion & Integrity
Serving The Community
Serving To Prevent, Protect & Preserve
She's Burnin' Hot
Sizzlin' Hot
Sizzlin' Sweet Love
Smoke Gets In Your Eyes
Some Like It Hot!
Smokin' Hot
Smokey Mountain Boy
The Stars Shine Like Fire
Takin' Care Of Business
The Thing To Do Since 1902
There's Desire Burnin' Deep Down In Inside Me
This Is Not Darth Vadar...This Is A Hero! *(Photo of firefighter in full gear including face mask)*
To The Rescue
Too Hot To Handle!
Two Hearts Burnin'
Two Hearts On Fire
Up In Flames/Smoke
Ut Ali Vivant *(Latin - That Others May Live)*
Veni-Vidi-Vice *(Latin - We Came, We Saw, We Conquered)*
Walking Where The Devil Dances
We Came, We Saw, We Conquered!
We Hold Thee Safe
We Strive For The Good Of All
We Strive To Save In Time Of Need
We're Always Ready When You Want Us
We're There When You Need Us
We've Got You Under Our Wings
What We Do, We Do For You!
Where Duty Calls - There You'll Find Us!
Where's Smokey When You Need Him!
Where's The Fire?
You Are My Burning Desire
You Keep Our Love Sizzlin'
You Set My Heart On Fire
Your Fire Burns Bright
You're Smokin'
You've Got Me Burnin', Yearnin', Turnin'...
You've Got My Heart Sizzlin'

FIRSTS TITLES

Be First To Believe
First born
First Comes Love...Then Comes Marriage
First Grade Rules
First In Line
First Kiss
First Light Of The Day
First Love
First Rule Is...
First Steps
First Things First
First Time
First Time In Love
Girls/Ladies First
I Made It After All
In The Beginning
Just The Beginning
Life Is Full Of Firsts
Love In The First Degree
My First Oreo
There's A First Time For Everything
Today Is The 1st Day Of The Rest Of Your Life

FISH/FISHING TITLES

- *Create title with worms*
- *Use a Fish as an "I".*
- *Have title hanging from a Fishing Pole.*

Angel Fish
Angler's Heaven
Any Fishies In There?
Baiting Is The Hard Part
Best Catch Of The Day
Big Eyed Fish
The Big One Got Away
Born To Fish...Forced To Work
Carpe Diem *(Seize the Fish)*
The Cast, The Cadence, The Catch
Casting 101
Catch A Fishy & You're Sittin' On Top Of The World
Catch Of The Day
I Caught A Fish This Big...
Caught Our Limit
Caughtcha...Hook, Line & Sinker
Down At The Ol' Fishin' Hole
Field & Stream
Finding Nemo
Fish Come To Those Who Bait/Wade!
Fish For Dinner
Fish Heads
Fish More...Work Less
Fish On!
Fish On A Line
Fish Out Of Water
A Fish Story
Fish Tales Told Here!
The Fish That Got Away
Fish Tremble When They Hear My Name
The Fisher King
Fisherman's Delight
Fisherman's Ruler...1, 2, 3, 7, 15, 20
Fishermen Can
Fishermen's Blues
Fishin' & Swishin'
Fishin' Is My Mission
Fishing Fun
Fishing From Dawn To Dusk
Fishing In The Dark
Fishing Is Easy...Catching Is Hard
Fishing Is My Life
Fly Fishin' Fun
Get "Reel"
Go Fish...Get Reel?
Gone Fishin'
Gone Fishin' Again!
Gone Fishin'...Be Back At Dark Thirty
Gone Fishing...Be Back Someday
Got Fish?
Got Reel...Get Fish!
I Had A "Reel" Good Time
Here Fishy, Fishy, Fishy
Hook, Line & Sinker
Hooked On Fishin'
Hooked On You
I Don't Exaggerate...I Remember Big!!!
I Fish Just For The Halibut
I Fish, Therefore I Lie!
I Left The Fish There For Someone Else!
I Only Fish On Days That End In "Y"
Ice Fishing
If The Hat Is Missing, I've Gone Fishing!
I'm A Reel Catch!
I'm On A Fishin' Mission
It Was This Big...Honest!
Just For The Halibut Of It!!!
Let's Go Fishing
Life's Like A Fish Bowl
Look What I Caught!
Look Who Caught The Big One!
Lure The Best
The Lure's The Thing
My Goal: Fish More...Work Less

Nothing But Net
The Old Man & The Sea
On Golden Pond
One Fish, Two Fish, Red Fish, Blue Fish
Pain In The Bass!!!
Plenty Of Fish In The Sea
Reel By Reel
Reel-axed & Havin' Fun
Rise 'N Shine...It's Fishin' Time
A River Runs Thru It
Rod & Reel
Something's Fishy
Sounds A Bit Fishy!
Stranger Than Fishin'
Taking The Bait
There Are Plenty Of Fish In The Sea
There's Something Fishy Goin' On 'Round Here
This Takes Guts
What A Catch
When In Doubt, Exaggerate
Wish I'd Gone Fishin'
My Wish...To Catch A Fat Fish!
If Wishes Were Fishes...
Wishin' Good Fishin'
Wishin' We Were Fishin'
Women Love Me, Fish Fear Me
You Catch...You Clean
(Name) Is A "Reel" Good Fisher

FLAG TITLES

(SEE ALSO PATRIOTIC)

American Flag
Carry Your Flag Proud
Checkered Flag Dreams
Flag Day
Flag Of Courage
Flag Of Love
Flag Of Patriotism
Flag Of Truce
Fly Your Flag Proudly
Flying Flags
Freedom Flag
High Flyin' Flag
To Hold The Flag
Let Freedom Wave
Littlest Flag Bearer
Old Glory...The Flag
Raise The Flag Of Red, White & Blue
Raise Up Your Flag
Raising The Flag
Six Flags
Solute The Flag

FLOWER TITLES

(SEE ALSO GARDEN)

- *Replace an "O" with a Flower.*
- *Make letters into Flowers with a Stem & Leaf under each letter.*

All Things Grow With Love
American Beauty Rose
An Annual Event
April Showers Bring May Flowers
Aroma Therapy: Dirt, Flowers & Gardening
Backyard Beauty
Basketful Of Love
Beautiful Rose
Bed Of Roses
Best Buds
Beware Of Snap Dragons!
Bless The Flowers
Bloom Where You Are Planted
Bloomin' Babe
Bloomin' Beauties
That Bloomin' Kid
Blossoming Love
Bluebonnet Beauty
Bright As Flowers...Be Thy Life's Hours
A Budding Beauty

Budding Friendship
Bunches Of Love
Butterflies & Blooms
Children In Bloom
Children Of The Flowers/Garden
Coming Up Roses
Covered In Roses
Crazy Daisy
Cream Of The Crop
Daisy Days
Daisy Summer Days
"Dandelion" Darlin/Dude *(Child with a Dandelion)*
Desert Blossom/Flower
Diamonds & Roses...
The Earth Laughs In Flowers
Everything's Coming Up Roses
Families Bloom With Love
Feelin' Snappy
Field Of Dreams
A Flower Amongst Weeds
Flower Child/Children *(Kids in fields of flowers)*
Flower Girl
Flower Hour
Flower In The Sun
The Flower Of One's Youth
Flower Power
Flowers After The Rain
Flowers Are God's Way Of Smiling
Flowers Are The Stars Of The Earth
Flowers Bring Smiles
Flowers Feed The Soul
For Thee Earth Puts Forth Sweet Flowers
Freshest Of The Bunch
Freshly Picked With You In Mind
Friendship Is In Bloom
Gather Ye Rosebuds While Ye May
Get Growing
Gods Most Beautiful Thoughts Bloom Into Children
Growing Love
He Loves Me...He Loves Me Not!
Heard It Thru The Grapevine
Here Mommy...You Left This In The Ground!
In Full Bloom
In Search Of The Perfect Rose
Innocence Blooms
Kiss From The Rose
Lady In The Flowers
Late Bloomer
Let Love Bloom
Like A Wild Rose
Lilies Of The Field
Little Girls Are Heaven's Flowers
Little Sun Flowers
Lone Star Splendor *(Bluebonnets)*
Look Who's Blooming
Love Blooms
Love Bugs & Crazy Daisies
Love Grows Here
Love In Full Bloom
Love Is A Rose To Me
Love Is In Bloom
Loving Love's Bloom
May All Your Weeds Be Wild Flowers
A Meeting Of Mums
Mighty Like A Rose
My Flower
My Little Flower Princess
Passion Flower
Passionate Flower
Petal Power
Pickin' The Daisies
Plant Your Own Garden!
Poppy Fields Forever
Red Roses For A Blue Lady
Red Roses For My Love
Roses Are Red...
Roses Of Red...
Say It With Flowers
Scarlet Rose
Scents Of Love/Romance
Seize The Daisies
She Blooms Like A Flower
Sleeping In The Flowers
So Many Weeds...So Little Time
Something Wonderful Has Sprouted Here
Sow Seeds Of Kindness
Spring Has Sprung
Stop & Smell The Roses/Flowers
Sweet As A Rose
Take Time To Smell The Roses/Flowers
Texas Treasure *(Bluebonnets)*
Tip Toe Thru The Tulips *(Or any flowers)*
True Love Turns Weeds Into Flowers
Weeds Are Pretty Too!
Where The Lilies's Bloom
Where The Wild Roses Grow
Wild About Wildflowers
Wild Little Flower
A Wish In The Wind *(Child blowing Dandelion)*
You Are My Flower
You Are The Flower Of Love

FLOWERS

Fragrant
Lovely
Ornamental
Wondrous
Elegance
Remarkable
Serenity

ROSES

Remarkable
Outstanding
Surreal Beauty
Extraordinary
Splendor

____
____
____
____
____

FLY/FLYING TITLES

(SEE AIRPLANE)

FOOD TITLES

(SEE ALSO BERRY, BEVERAGES, CHOCOLATE, COOKING, COOKOUT, DIET, SOME SPECIFIC FOODS & WATERMELON)

- *Use food items in place certain letters.*
- *Spatter Food Splats around title.*

"A" Is For Apple
Adams Apple
All I Want To Do Is Chew, Chew, Chew!
American Pie
Any Time Is Cookie Time
An Apple A Day
An Apple A Day Keeps The Doctor Away
An Apple For The Teacher
Apple Days
Apple Days Are Delicious
Apple Of My Eye
Apples Away
As American As Apple Pie
Banana Republic
Batter Up!
Beans, Beans, The Magical Fruit
Beginner's Muck
Berry, Berry Yummy!
Berry Best Buddies/Friends
Berry Bunch
Berry Christmas
Berry Cute
Berry Fun
A Berry Good Girl/Boy
Berry Much Alike
Berry Precious
Berry Scary
Berry Special
Berry Special Friends
Berry Sweet Smile
Better Latte Than Never
The Big Apple
The Big Slurp Out *(Popsicles, ice cream, etc.)*
Bit Off More Than I/You Can Chew
Black Cherry Crush
Blowing Raspberries
Blue Plate Special
Bottomless Pit *(Eating)*
Bowl Of Yum
Brain Freeze
Breakfast Club
Breakfast Of Champions
Broken Cookies Don't Have Calories!?!?
Burger King
Burnt Offerings!!!
Bushels Of Fun *(Apples)*
Caffeine Is My Gift...I Shall Not Doze
Candy Kisses
Caught With A Hand In The Cookie Jar
Chef's Inspiration
Cherry Blossom Girl
Cherry Lips
Cherry Picker
Cherry Pickin'
Cherry Pie
Cherry Top *(Police car)*
I "Cherry"sh You So Much
Chow Time
"C" Is For Cookie *(Helping make cookies)*
Coffee, Tea Or Me?
A Coke & A Smile
Conspicuous Consumption
Cookie Monster
Cookies Solve Everything
Cool As A Cucumber
Corn In The USA
Cornivore *(Eating corn-on-the-cob)*
Cream Of The Crop
A Cup Of Kindness
Cutie Pie *(Arrange pictures to look like a pie)*
Days Filled With Cherry Red Wine
Death Before Decaf!!!
Dig In
Dining Delights
Do The Mashed Potato
Dominoes To The Rescue
Don't Cry Over Spilled Milk
Don't Sit Under The Apple Tree

Drinkin' Ice Cold Cherry Coke
Easy As Pie
Eat, Drink & Be Merry
Eat It?
Eat It!...I Can't Even Pronounce It!
Eat Now, Diet Later
Eating Again!?
Eating Bait *(Sushi)*
Eating My Cake & Wearin' It Too!
"Egg"stra Special
Everything's Peaches 'N Cream
Expresso Yourself
A Feast Fit For A King
Feed Me I'm Yours
Feeding Frenzy
Feeding The Animals
Finger Food
Finger-Lickin' Good
A Fishy Story
Flour Power
Food Fight
Food Fight & Baby/Mommy Lost
Food Frenzy
Forbidden Fruit
From The Vine To The Mouth
That Frosty Mug Sensation
Full Of Beans
Gerber Baby/Gal/Guy
Gimmie Something Good To Eat
God Bless My Microwave
Going Bananas
Good To The Last Drop
Got A Strawberry *(A rash or scrape)*
Got Cookies?
Got Milk?
Green Eggs & Ham
Guess Who's Coming To Dinner?
Had A Peach Of A Day
Happiness Is A Berry Big Hug
Happiness Is Licking The Spoon
Have A Berry Happy Day
Have It Your Way
Here's The Dish...
Here's The Scoop
Hey Kool-aid
Home Is Where The Cookies Are
Home Made Lovin' From The Oven
Honey Bunch
Hot Diggity Dogs
Hot Potato
How'd You Like Them Apples?
Huckleberry Hound
I Ate The Whole Thing
I Ate Tooooooo Much!
I Can't Believe I Ate The Whole Thing!
I Heard It Thru The Grapevine
I Put Veggies In My Tummy
I Yam What I Yam
Ice Creamilicious
If You Knew Sushi...
I'm A Little Teapot
I'm Feelin' Just Peachy
I'm In A Jam *(Making jam/canning)*
I'm In A Pickle *(Eating a pickle)*
In The Raw
It's A Piece Of Cake
Juicy As A Watermelon
Just A Little Bit Corny
Just For The Taste Of It!
Just Peachy
Kibbles & Bits
Let's Eat
Let's Roll
Licking The Bowl
Life Is Berry Precious
Life Is Uncertain...Eat Dessert First!
Life Would Be The "Pits" Without You
Life's A Bowl Of Cherries
Life's A Peach
Life's Too Short...Eat More Chocolate
A Little Dab'll Do Ya
Loafin' Time
Lotsa Lobsta
Love At First Bite
Love Me...Love My Messes!!!
I Love You A Munch
I Love You Berry Much
I Love You With A Cherry On Top
The Lunch Bunch
Make Like A Banana & Split
Mama Mia, Thatsa Spicy Meatball
Man Shall Not Live By Bread Alone *(Child eating sandwich)*
Melts In Your Mouth...Not In Your Hands
Messy Eater
Milk...It Does A Body Good
Mmm, Mmm Good!
Mommy's Little Mess Maker
Moms Give Loving Spoonfuls
More Please!?
The More You Eat, The More You Want
Mug Shots *(Put pics in mugs)*
Munch-A-Bunch
Munch Madness
Munch Time
My Balanced Diet...A Cookie In Each Hand!
My Main Squeeze *(Lemons)*
My Own Apple Dumpling Gang

Name That Food
Noodling Around *(Eating spaghetti)*
Not My Cup Of Tea
Nothin' Says Lovin' Like Fresh Pie From The Oven
Nuts To That Idea
Nuttier Than A Fruitcake
Nutty As A Fruitcake
Oink, Oink, I'm A Little Piggy
On A Roll
On Top Of Ole Spaghetti
One Bad Apple In The Bunch
One In A Melon
Ooooey, Goooooey!
Out Of His Gourd
Peach Fuzz
A Peach Of A...
Peachy Keen
Pear-Shaped
Peas In A Pod
Peas Pass The Peas!
That Person Is Nuts
The Pick Of The Crop
Pickin 'N Grinnin'
Pig Out
Pigging Out
Plop, Plop...Fizz, Fizz...
Plum Crazy
Plum Out Of Ideas
Pop-Pop Popcorn, Fun To Eat
Poppin' For Popcorn
Popsicle Paradise
Popsicle Smiles
Porking Out
Pretty As A Peach
Pretty Please With A Cherry On Top
The Princess & Her Peas
Raw Passion *(Sushi)*
The Rind Is A Terrible Thing To Waste
A Royal Tea
A Rumbly In My Tumbly
Sandwich Artist
Say Cheese
I Scream, You Scream, We All Scream For Ice Cream!
Scrumpdillyumscious
She's My Cherry Pie
Shriveled Like A Raisen
Simply Delicious
A Sittin' & A Slurpin' & A Spittin' & A Thinkin'
A Slice Of Life
A Slice Of Summer
Slimmy, Yet Satisfying *(Feeding baby)*
A Slurpin' Good Time *(Popsicle/ice cream)*
S'more Great Moments
Snack Time
Snap, Crackle, Popcorn
So, Eat Already!
So Yummy For My Tummy
Some Cherries Are The Pits
Some Like It Hot
Soup Is Good Food
Sour Apples
Sour As A Green Apple
Sour Grapes
Spaghetti, Spaghetti, All Over My Face
Spot Of Tea?
A Strawberry Blonde
Strawberry Fields Forever
Strawberry Hill
Strawberry Jammin' *(Making jam)*
Strawberry Lips
Strawberry Love
Strawberry Shortcake
Strawberry Wine
Sugar & Spice
Sugar Pie Honey Bunch
Summer Sweets *(Popsicles)*
Sushi /n./ - Known To Most Of The World As 'Bait'
A Sushi Situation
Sweet As A Peach
Sweet As Apple Pie
Sweet As Cherry Pie
Sweet As Sugar
Sweet Georgia Peach
Sweet Pea
Sweet To Eat & Lots Of Fun Too!!!
Sweet To Eat & Sticky Too!
Sweets For A Sweet
Taking The Bait
A Taste Of Summer
A Taste Of Tradition
Taste Test In Progress
Tasty...Tasty
A Tasty Tradition
Tea For Two
Tea Time
Tender Vittles
That's A Peach
That's Brisk Baby
This Eating Stuff Is Hard Work
Too Corny
Top Banana
Trix Are For Kids
Two Peas In A Pod
Two Scoops *(Ice Cream)*
Uh Oh, Spaghetti-Ohs
The Un-Cola

Use Your Coconut
Use Your Melon
What A Peach!
When Do We Eat?
When Life Gives You Lemons, Make Lemonade!
Where's The Beef
Who Needs A Fork?
With Food & Friends Life Is Good
The Wonder Of A Watermelon
Wonderful Watermelon
Working For Peanuts
Yes We Have No Bananas
You Are The Apple Of My Eye
You Are The Top Banana
You Are What You Eat
You Bake Me Happy
You Bowl Me Over
You Can't Get Blood From A Turnip
You Drive Me Nuts
You Take The Cake
You're A Peach
You're A Real Piece Of...
You're My Huckleberry
You're One In A Melon!
You're Tea-rrific
Yum, Yum, Give Me Some!
Yummy, Yummy, I've Got Veggies In My Tummy
Yummy, Yummy So Good In My Tummy!

FOOTBALL TITLES

(SEE ALSO SPORTS)

- *Use Footballs in place of an "O".*

...And It's Good!!!
Are You Ready For Some Football?
Backfield In Motion
Backyard Blitz
Big Win
Blitzed
Blue 52, Set, Hike
Cleaned Their Clocks
Clutch Player
Couldn't Buy A Goal
Dark Horse Winner
A David vs. Goliath Game
Fight...Fight...Fight
First & 10
Flea Flicker Finale
Flew To The 1st Down
Football Fanatic/Freaks
Football Fever
Football Fun
Football Is A Kick
Football Wisdom
A Game Of Two Halves
Go For The Goal
Go For The Whole 9 Yards
Goals Happen
Golden Arm
Got Beat Like A Drum
Got His Clock Cleaned
Got Pigskin
Got Trucked
Half Time
Hang Time
Hard Nose...Smash Mouth...Football !!!!!
Have Ball...Will Travel
Hut, Hut, Hike!
Interception Connection
It's A Kick For Some
It's Football Time In *(Your town/home)*

A Knock-Out Blow
The Lonesome Kicker
Monday Night Madness
MVP In Training
A Nip & Tuck Game
Oh! That Had To Hurt
On Any Given Sunday
Penalty
Picked Off
Pickin' The Pigskin
Pigskin Party
Played Good "D"
Playin' The Pigskin
Punky QB
Punt, Pass & Run...Football's Lot's Of Fun
Quarter Back Sneak
A Rifle Arm Passer
Sacked Out
Sports Spectacular
Streakin' For The Zone
Super Sacker!
Superbowl Here We Come
Superbowl Shuffle
Tackle King
Tackle Time
Tacklin' Tykes
Ten Yard Tackle
Thru The Yellow Bars
Throwin' A Bomb
Time To Tackle Another Year
Touch Down!
Touchdown Boy
Two-Minute Warning
Varsity Blues
West Coast Offense
The Whole Ten Yards
Wish Bonin' For The Touch Down

FOOTBALL
Forward pass
Offense
Overtime
Touchdown
Blocking
Astroturf
Linemen
Lateral

FOOTBALL
Flea flicker
Out of bounds
Offsides
Tackle
Blitz
Audible
Line of scrimmage
Loose ball

____
____
____
____
____

FRECKLES TITLES
- *Sprinkle dots on title to look like freckles.*

A Face Without Freckles Is Like A Night Without Stars!
Freckle Face
Freckles Are Sun Kisses
Polka Dot Tot
These Aren't Freckles, They're Tiny Little Tans
You've Got The Cutest Little Freckle Face!

____
____
____
____
____

FRIEND/FRIENDSHIP TITLES

All My Friends
Anytime You Need A Friend...
A Beautiful Friendship
A Best Friend To Take Your Hand
Best Friends Always Remember
Best Friends Never Let You Down
Best Friends 'Til The End
The Best Of Friends, The Best Of Times
The Best Ships Are Friendships
Bestest Buddies/Friends
Big Time Friends
My Circle Of Friends
Dear Friends
Devoted Friends
Double The Fun
Faithful Friends
A Feast Of Friends
Forever My Friend
A Friend Can Hug Your Heart
A Friend Is A Friend
A Friend Is A Gift You Give Yourself
A Friend Is Someone...
Friend Of Mine
A Friend Of My Many Years
A Friend Spreads Sunshine In Our Path
Friend To Friend...Heart To Heart
A Friend To Me You'll Always Be
A Friend To You I'll Always Be
A Friend You'll Always Be
Friend...You'll Be Forever Close To Me
Friends Are Angels With Wings
Friends Are Kept Forever In The Heart
Friends Are Kisses Blown To Us By Angels
Friends Are Made In Heaven
Friends Are Never Far Behind
Friends Are Our Chosen Family
Friends Are Special Hugs From God
Friends Are The Best Collectibles!
Friends Are The Best Presents
Friends Are The Essence Of Life
Friends Forever
Friends Have A Way Of Speaking Without Words. - *(Alice Daigliesh)*
A Friends House Is Never Far
Friends In Sunshine & In Shade
Friends Know The Art Of Giving The Heart
Friends Like You...Make Life Sparkle
Friends Love All The Time
Friends Make Happiness Happen
Friends Make Life A Little Sweeter
Friends Never Say Good-bye
Friends...One Soul...Two Bodies
Friends Shop Together
Friends That Play Together, Stay Together
Friends Thru Thick & Thin
Friends 'Til The End
Friends Warm The Heart
Friends We Are...
Friends We'll Always Beeeeee...
If Friends Were Flowers, I'd Pick You
Friendship Buttons Us Together
Friendship In Bloom
A Friendship Is A Blessing Of Times
Friendship Is A Gift With Strings Attached... Heartstrings!
Friendship Is A Rainbow Between Two People
Friendship Is Everything
Friendship Is One Mind In Two Bodies
Friendship Keeps Our Hearts In Touch
Friendship Never Melts Away
Friendship...The Older It Grows, The Stronger It Is
Friendship Warms The Heart
Forever Friends
Giggles, Secrets & Sometimes Tears
Good Friends Are Angels On Earth
Gossip, Gossip, Gossip
Great Minds Think Alike
Greatest Of Friends
Hangin' Out Together
The Harmony Between Friends Is Sweeter Than Any Choir
Hold An Old Friends Hand
Hold True Friends With Both Hands
I Love My Friend
I Needed A Friend & God Sent Me You
In My Friend, I Find A Second Self. *(Isabel Norton)*
It Takes A Long Time To Grow An Old Friend
Just You...Just Me...Just Right!
Kindred Spirits
Kitchen Friends
Lean On Me
Life Long Friends
Life Would Be The Pits Without You
Long Live Friendship
Lovers & Friends
Many Joys Come & Go, But Friendship Is Forever
Me & My Friends
Me & My Shadow
More Precious Than Gold
More Than Friends
My Circle Of Friends
My Friends Near & Dear
My Funny Friend
My Pal, My Friend!

My True Friend
Neighborhood Pals
Ode To A Friend
Old Friends Are The Best Antiques
Our Gang
Partners...Brothers...Friends
Partners In Crime
People Let Me Tell Ya 'Bout My Best Friend
Planting Seeds Of Friendship
Power To All Us Friends
Priceless Treasure Of The Heart...
Real Deal Friends
Real Friends Listen With Their Hearts
Seeds Of Friendship Bring Flowers Of Joy
Sidekicks
Sowing The Seeds Of Friendship
Special Friends Bring Special Memories
Stand By Me
That's What Friends Are For
The Three Stooges
There Is No Gift So Precious As A True Friend
Thoughts Of You Make Me Smile
Three Muskateers
Three's Company
Together Again...Together Forever
True Blue Friends
True Friends Remain In Our Hearts Forever
True Friends Will Never Part
Tweedledee & Tweedledum
Two Friends...One Heart
Two Heads Are Better Than One
Two Of A Kind
Two Peas In A Pod
Two's Company
We Stick Together...
What A Difference You've Made In My Life
What A Friend I've Found In You
What Are Friends For...
What Makes A Friend...
When Friends Meet, Hearts Warm
Whenever I Call You Friend...
Whenever I Think Of You, I Smile Inside
With A Little Help From My Friends...
You & Me...Buds Forever!
You Can Count On Me
You Make My Heart Sing
You're One In A Million
You've Got A Friend
You've Got A Friend In Me

FROG TITLES

Be"Leap" Me, I'm Froggy
Croak
Don't Worry...Be Hoppy
Fat & Hoppy Froggy
Feelin' Froggy!
Feelin' Froggy? Jump!
Feelin' Hoppy
Frog Days Of Summer
Frog Prince
Frogs Eat What Bugs Them
Happy Hopper
High Jumper
Hoppin' Mad
A Hoppy Froggy
I Have A Frog In My Throat
I May Be A Prince, You Never Know!
I Toad You So!
If You Feel Froggy...Just Leap!!
I'm All Croaked Up
Is This Leap Year?
It's Not Easy Being Green
Jump Frog Jump
Kiss Me...
Leapin' Into The Fun Patch
Little Froggy In The Pond
My Favorite Color Is Green
My Heart Leaps For You
Oh, Hoppy Day!!!
Polly Woggy's
Ribbit...Ribbit!
Times Fun When You're Having Flies
Toad To Toad
Toad-al Trouble
Toad-ally Awesome
Toad-ally Cute
Toad-ally Terrific
Un-FROG-ettable
You Make My Heart Leap

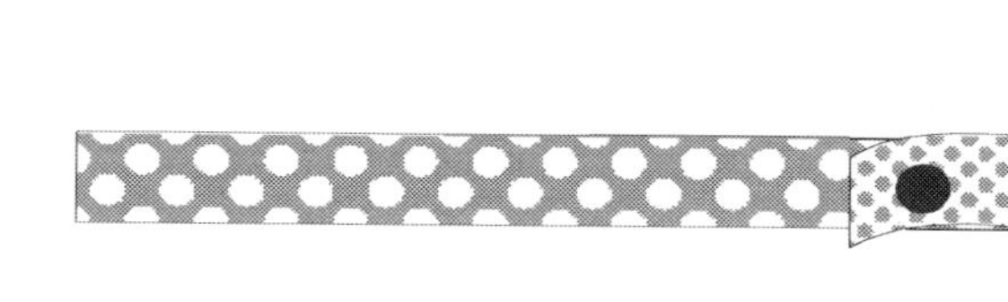

G G G G G G G G G G G G G G G G G G G G G G G G G G G G G G G G G

GAMBLING TITLES

(SEE ALSO GAMES)

G 21's So Fun!
Ace Of Spades
G Ace Up His Sleeve
All Bets Are Off
G Ante Up!
Beating The Odds
G Bet The House
Bettin' On The Flats
G Bingo
Black Jack
G The Buck Stopped Here
Bucked The Odds!
G Call Me Lucky
Card Sharks
G Cha-Ching
Deuces Are Wild
G Draw Of The Cards
The First Rule Of Poker Is...
G Full House
Fun & Games
G Gambler's Choice
Gambler's Roll
G The Games People Play
Got Your Game Face?
G Gotta Know When To Hold 'Em
High Roller
G Holding All The Cards
House Of Cards
G House Of Luck
I'll Betcha
G It's In The Cards
It's Only A Game
G It's Only A Game Until You Lose!
Jack Of Hearts
G Jacks Are Better
Keeper Of The Cards
G King Of Hearts
Know When To Hold 'Em...Know When To
G Fold 'Em
Let It Ride
G Let The Cards Fall
Let The Good Times Roll
G Let's Make A Deal
Life's A Gamble
G Lost Not At The Penny Slot
Lost Wages
G Luck Is A Full House
Luck Of The Draw
G Lucky Me
Midnight Rambler
G Oh, Craps! ! !
Ooh La! La! Got The Moolah!
Playing Your Cards Right
Poker Face
Poker's A Game Of Chance
Queen Of Hearts
Ramblin' Man
Rambling Gambler
Roll Of The Dice
Roulette Mama
Slot Machine King/Queen
Snake Eyes
Squares Abound
The Sweet Smell Of Victory
Tower Of Cards
Tumbling Dice
Video Poker Joker
Viva Las Vegas
Wanted To Be A Millionaire!
What A Deal
You're My Ace

____
____
____
____
____

GAMES TITLES

(SEE ALSO BILLIARDS, BINGO & PLAYING)

- *Make Games Pieces that coordinate with your layout to spell out title.*
- *Use Puzzle pieces as letter mats for title.*

All Fun & Games
Are You Game?
Around & Around & Around *(Hula Hoop)*
Beginner's Luck
Between Games
Board Games
Card Sharks
Crazy Game
Do Not Pass Go
Don't Play That Game With Me
Deuces Are Wild
Fair Game
Follow The Leader
Foolish Games
For The Love Of The Game
Fun & Games
Game Boy, Boy
Game Boy Girl
Game Of Chance
A Game Of Inches
The Game Of Love!
Game Over
The Games People/We Play
Get Your Game On!

Got Game?!
Got Game...Will Win
Guessing Game
Have Game...Will Play!
Head Games
He's Got Game
Hide 'N Seek
Home Game
Hula Hoopla
I'm So Far Behind, I Thought I Was Ahead
In The Game Of Love...
It's All In The Game
It's How You Play The Game
Jokers Wild
Slap Jacks
Let The Fun Begin
Let The Games Begin
Let The Good Times Roll
Let's Get Twisted
Let's Pretend
Master Of The Game
Mind Games
Name Game
Nintendo Maniacs
On Your Mark...Get Set...Go!!!
Patty Cake, Patty Cake
Ping Pogs
Playground Games
Playin' Marbles
Playing For Keeps
Playing Games
Power Game
Puttin' On My Game Face
She's Got Game
Simon Says...
Sooooory!
Tag, You're It!
Twistin' The Night Away
Two Can Play That Games
What's Your Game
Word Games
X That BOX
XBOX Addict
XBOX Rox
You Sank My Battleship

____
____
____
____
____

GARDEN TITLES

(SEE ALSO FLOWERS)

- *Replace specific letters with Gardening tools.*
- *Spell title with green ribbon or yarn as a hose.*

A 24-Carrot Day
A 24-Carrot Garden
Adventures In Gardening
All Things Grow With Love
Aroma Therapy: Dirt, Flowers, Gardening
As Delicate As A Flower
A Bed Of Roses
A Berry Good Day
Beware Of Snapdragons
Bless My Bloomers
Bloom Where You're Planted
Blooming Beauties
The Changing Of The Garden
A Country Garden
A Crazy Daisy Day
Darlin' Daisies
A Day In The Garden
Dig It
Every Flower Is A Soul Blossoming In Nature
Everything's Coming Up Roses
Fanciful Garden
For Thee, The Earth Puts Forth Sweet Flowers!
I Fought The Lawn & The Lawn Won
Fresh As A Daisy
In Full Bloom
Garden Angel
Garden Bug
My Garden Faire
Garden Fairies Come At Dawn
Garden Folks Have The Sunniest Smiles
Garden Goddess
Garden Goddess...Hard At Work!!!
Garden Guy
Garden Harmony
Garden Harvest Time
The Garden Is A Mirror Of The Heart
Garden Miracle
Garden Of Delight
Garden Of Delights
Garden Of Dreams
Garden Of Earthly Delights
The Garden Of Eatin'
Garden Of Eden
Garden Of Love
Garden Of Many Scents
Garden Of Serenity
Garden Of Weedin'
Garden Party
Gardener In Training
Gardeners Know All The Dirt

Gardening...Exterior Decorating
Gardening Grows The Spirit
Gardening Is A Work Of Heart
Gardening...Just Another Day At The Plant
Gardening Tills My Soul
A Gardening We Grow...
Gettin' Down & Dirty
The Glory Of A Garden
The Glory Of The Gardener
Gone To Pot!
Got Mulch?
Gramma's Garden
Green Thumb Gardener
Groomin' For A Bloomin'
Happiness Grows In My Garden
Herbs Make Good Scents
Hi Hoe, Hi Hoe A Gardening I Go!
How Does Your Garden Grow?
I Dig Gardening
I Dig My Garden
I'm Diggin' It!
I'm Happiest In My Garden
In My Garden...
In The Garden
In The Garden, My Soul Is Sunshine
It's Not Easy Being Green
A Jewel In God's Garden
Keeper Of The Garden
The Lawn Ranger
Learning To Mow
Let's Get Down & Dirty
Life Began In A Garden
Life Begins In A Garden
Lil Gardener
A Little Dirt Doesn't Hurt
Little Flower Gardener
Love Grows Here
Love In Bloom
Loving Hearts Bloom
Mom's Garden...Dad's Weeds
My Garden Angel
My Garden Grows With Love
My Little Blossoms
My Secret Garden
Nature Is The Art Of God
Oh, How My Garden Grows
On The Garden Path
Our Little Garden
Our Little Gardener
Our Little Sprout
The Pick Of The Crop
Pickin' & Grinnin'
Plant A Little Love...Watch A Miracle Grow
Plant Kindness, Gather Love
Plant Manager
Planting Seeds Of Friendship
Putting Down Roots
Rainbow Garden
A Rose Is A Rose Is A Rose
Scatter Seeds Of Happiness
Seedin' 'N Weedin'
Seeds Are A Link To The Past
She Who Plants A Garden, Plants Happiness!
Spring Thyme Season
Stop & Smell The Roses
Sunflowers Shine
The Sunlight On The Garden
Sweet As A Rose
Those Who Plant Kindness, Harvest Love
Thru The Garden Gate...
Tip Toe Thru The Tulips
A Tough Row To Hoe
Twilight Garden Delight
Twilight In The Garden
Veggie Tales
Weed 'Em & Reap
A Weed Is Just An Unloved Flower
Weeds Are Our Specialty
Welcome To My Garden
What You Sow Is What You Grow
(Name, Name) Quite Contrary, How Does Your Garden Grow?

GENTLE TITLES

As The Sun Crept Up Gently Upon Us
Break It To Me Gently
Gentle Beauty
Gentle Breezes
Gentle Child
Gentle Dreams
Gentle Kisses
Gentle Love
Gentle Man
Gentle On My Mind
Gentle Peace
The Gentle Raindrops Kissed Your Face
Gentle Spirit
Gentle Upon My Ears
Gentle Winds
Gentleness Is Your Soul
The Gentleness Of The Heaven's Glow
The Gentleness Of The Rain
Gently Sentimental

The Gently Whispering Winds
Go Gently
Her Gentle Gaze
Her Gentle Hands
His Gentle Touch
In The Gentle Night
In Your Gentle Arms
The Light Of Your Gentle Smile
Like Clouds Dancing Across Gentle Skies
Like Clouds Of Loves Gentle Touch
Love & The Gentle Heart
Love Me Gently
Rock Me Gently
Sleep Gentle
Tell It To Me Gently
There's A Gentleness To All You Do
You Have Touched Us With Your Gentleness

GINGERBREAD TITLES
Gingerbread Blessings
Gingerbread Girls Are The Sweetest By Far
I Don't Pop & I'm Not Fresh, That's My Cousin
Lovin From The Oven
My Favorite Kind Of Man Is A Gingerbread Man

GIRL TITLES
(SEE ALSO BABY, CHILDREN, DAUGHTER & WOMAN)
100% Girl
A Tender Heart Who Needs A Star To Wish Upon
Ain't She Cute/Sweet?
All American Girl
All Dressed Up
All Girl
American Beauty
Angel Girl
Atta Girl!
Ballerina Girl
Barbie Girl
Be My Girl
Be Your Own Girl
Big Girls Do/Don't Cry
Blooming Beauty
Blue-Eyed Girl
Brown-Eyed Girl
Buttons & Bows
Buttons & Bows Down To Her/My Toes
California Girl
Calendar Girl
Candy Girl
China Girl
Complicated Girl
Country Girl
Cover Girl
Crazy Little Party Girl
Curly Girl
Daddy's Little Girl/Princess
Diamond Girl
Diva
A Doll Among Her Toys
Don't Take The Girl
Dream Girl
Easy Breezy Colorful Girl
Emotional Girl
Everything Nice
Fairy Princess
Forever My Girl
Funny Girl
Genuine Girl
A Girl Can Dream
Girl Crazy
Girl Friday
A Girl Is A Pearl
Girl, My Heart Is In Your Hands
Girl Next Door
Girl Of A 1,000 Faces/Tears
Girl Of Mine
Girl Of My Dreams
Girl Power
Girl Talk
Girl Vision
Girl, You Shine
Girl, You'll Be A Woman Soon
Girls & Curlz
Girls Are A Little Piece Of Heaven
A Girls Gotta Do What A Girls Gotta Do
Girls Just Wanna Have Fun
Girl's Night Out
Girls Of Summer
Girls Rule
Girls Will Be Girls
Girly Girl
Glamour Girl
Green-Eyed Girl
Hair We "Bow" Again
Happy Girl
Has Anybody Seen My Gal?
Hello Pretty Girl

Hey, Did You Happen To See The Most Beautiful Girl In The World?
Her Majesty
Hey Little Girl
Hey Pretty Girl
I Have Found My Girl
I'm A Barbie Girl
I'm A Big Girl Now
Isn't She Great?
Isn't She Lovely?
It Takes Time To Look This Good!
It's A Girl Thing
It's A Girl's World, Boys Just Live In It!!!
It's Not Easy Being A Princess
Just An Old Fashioned Girl
Just The Girls
Kiss The Girl
Like Mother...Like Daughter
Lil' "Lady" Bug
Little Dolls
A Little Girl Is Only A Little Girl For So Long!
Little Girls Are Heaven's Flowers
Little Girls Are Like Angels Without Wings
Little Girls Are So Very Special
Little Girls Do Cry
Little Lady
Little Miss
Little Miss Sunshine
Little Princess
Little Surfer Girl
Little Sweetness
Little Woman/Women
Lucky Girl
Make-Up Artist
Material Girl
Maybe She's Born With It
Miss Smarty Pants
Mommy's Little Angel
More & More Like Mommy
More Spice Than Sugar
More Sugar Than Spice
My Bonnie Lassie
My Girl
My Girl, A Walkin', Talkin' Angel
My Girl Awaits For Me In Tender Time
My Heart Belongs To Daddy
My Kind Of Girl
Mysterious Girl
Not A Girl...Not A Woman Yet
One Polished Little Lady
Our Little Princess Of Quite A Lot
Our Sweet Angel
Pretty As A Picture
Pretty Girl
Pretty In Pink
Pretty Little Ladies
Pretty Little Ladies All In A Row
Pretty Maidens All In A Row
Pretty Young Thing
Princess In Training
Roller Girl
Sassy Lassy
She's A Lady Now!
She's A Mystery To Me
She's A Special Girl
She's My Girl
She's My Kind Of Girl
She's My Lady
Silly Girl
A Story About A Girl
Sugar & Spice & Everything Nice
Sweetie Pie
Sweetness
Thank God I'm A Country Girl
Thank Heaven For Little Girls
That Girl!
The Girl Most Likely...
Think Like A Girl
This Little Girl Is A Country Girl
Uptown Girl
Valley Girl
What A Girl Needs...
What A Girl Wants...
What Are Little Girls Made Of
When A Boy Meets A Girl...
When Boy Meets Girl...
Where The Girls Are...
Who's That Girl
You Go Girl
You "Grow" Girl

GIRL SCOUTS TITLES

Be Prepared
Bridging
Brownie Basics
Brownie Bridged To Junior
Burnt Offerings
Cadet Bridged To Senior
Cookies Anyone?
Experience Wildlife...Be A Scout Leader
Founder's Day
Golden Girl
Got Milk? We've Got Cookies!

I Love Cookies
Junior Bridged To Cadet
Make New Friends
On My Honor I Will Try...
Scouts Honor
Terrific Try Its
World Thinking Day

GIRLFRIEND TITLES

(SEE DATING, GIRL & LOVE)

GLASSES TITLES

(SEE EYES)

GOALS TITLES

Become Who You Are
Chasing Your Goals
Cherish Your Dreams
Dream Your Goals
Goal Driven
Goal Oriented
Goals Are Dreams With Deadlines
Heavenly Goals
Heaven's Our Goal
High Goals
Honor Your Aspirations
Impossible Goal
Living My Goal
My Goal & Mission
Reaching For My Goal
Seeking Life's Highest Goal
Set Achievable Goals
Tending My/Your Goal
You Goal Girl

GOLD TITLES

(A great way accentuate the word Gold in the title, is to create that word only in Gold. Make Gold larger and even in a different type style than the rest of the title)

All In The Golden Afternoon
All That Glitters/Shimmers Is Not Gold
Black Gold
California Gold
Days Of Golden Sunshine
Diggin' For Gold
Dusk In The Golden West
Fool's Gold
Glistening Gold
Go For The Gold
The Gold Coast
Gold Digger
Gold Dust
The Gold Standard
Golden Anniversary
Golden Beaches/Shores
Golden Chain Of Memories
The Golden Child
A Golden Day
The Golden Gate Stretched Far & Wide
A Golden Moment
A Golden Oldie
Golden Opportunities
Golden Rules
Golden Sunset
The Golden Touch
A Golden Tribute
Golden Years
Good As Gold
Hair Of Gold
Harvest's Golden Moon
Hazy Shades Of Gold
Heart Of Gold
Made Of Gold
More Precious Than Gold
On Friendship's Golden Wings
On Golden Pond
Over The Golden Horizon
Rolled Gold
Silence Is Golden
Silver & Gold
Sister Golden Hair
Solid Gold
Sunset's Golden Glow
There's Gold In Them Mountains

GOLF TITLES

(SEE ALSO SPORTS)

- *Use a Golf Ball for an "O".*
- *Replace an "I" or "L" with a Club or Golf Tee.*

Air Club
Any Time Is "Tee" Time
Birdie
Bogey
Caddy Shack
Daddy's Caddy
The Doc Says To Take My Irons Every Day
Drove A Worm Burner
Eagle
F-O-R-E
"Fore"ever Golfing
Future Tiger Woods
Golf "Fore" Ever
Golf Guru
To Golf Or Not To Golf? Silly Question!
Golf Suits Me To A "Tee"
Golf Yesterday...Golf Today...Golf Tomorrow!!!
Golfer's Diet: Greens Everyday
Golfing "Fore" Fun
Grip It & Rip It
I Hate Golf...NICE SHOT!! I Love Golf!
Hole In One
Hooked On Golf
Hunting For Birdies
I Take My Irons Everyday
I'm Happy When I'm Teed Off
I'm Over The Hill...On The Back Nine
Iron Man On The Green
Just Drive It
I Love My Greens
Par For The Course
Par Pro
Playing Through
The Pursuit Of Golfing
Putt, Putt, Par
Sliced In The "Right" Direction
Strokes Of Genius
The "Swinger"
"Tee" For Two
Tee'd Off
"Tee"ing Off
"Tee"rrific
There's No Time Like "Tee" Time
I Think I'm Ready For The Pro Circuit!
Tiger In Training?
To A Tee
When's "Tee" Time?
Worm Burner King

Greens Great
Off His "Tee"
Left Hook
FORE!
Eagle
Right Slice

GOODBYE TITLES

Adieu
Adios
Aloha
Beautiful Goodbye
Before The Goodbye
Before We Say Goodbye
Bye Bye
Don't Say Goodbye
Farewell
Good Riddens
Goodbye For Now
Goodbye Girl
Goodbye...Goodbye
Goodbye Heartbreak
Goodbye Is Not Forever
Goodbye Is Not The Final Word
Goodbye My Baby
Goodbye My Brother
Goodbye Old Friend
Goodbye Summer
Goodbye Tears
Goodbye To A Cold Winter
Goodbye To Innocence
I'll Never Say Goodbye
It's So Hard To Say Goodbye
A Kiss Goodbye
A Long Goodbye
Memories Never Say Goodbye
Our Last Goodbye
P.S. Goodbye
Saluto
Saying Goodbye
See Ya Later
So Long
So Long, Farewell, Auf Wiedersehen, Adieu, Adieu, Adieu, To Yieu & Yieu & Yieu
So This Is Goodbye
A Sunrise Goodbye

Sweetest Goodbye
When It's Time To Say Goodbye...

GRACE TITLES

Amazed By His Grace
Amazed By Your Grace
Amazing Grace
An Angel Of Grace
Beauty Grows Of Golden Grace
Beyond The Grace Of God
Budding Grace
But For The Grace Of God
By His Grace
By The Grace Of God
Charm & Grace...
Content In Her Own Gracefulness
Eternal Grace
Full Of Grace
Glorious Grace
God Of Mercy...God Of Grace
Goodness Gracious...
Grace...A Charming Sound
Grace By Which She Stands
Grace Like Rain
Graceful Steps Of Love
In Your Heart Is The Presence Of Grace
It's The Gracefulness Of Your Hands
Love & Grace
Of Beauty & Gracefulness
Precious Grace
Reflections Of Your Grace
Saving Grace
State Of Grace
The Sun's Last Grace
Sweet Days Of Grace
Sweetness & Grace
That Of A Child's Grace
Upon Graceful Wings
Vision Of Gracefulness
With Grace & Elegance
With Loving Grace
You Are Of Gracefulness & Love
Your Every Graceful Touch
Your Gracefulness Takes My Breath Away

GRADUATION TITLES

(SEE ALSO EDUCATION & SCHOOL)

- *Place a Grad Cap on letter in title.*
- *Use a rolled Diploma as an "I".*

C-E-L-E-B-R-A-T-E
Coming To An End & A Beginning
Congradurations
Congrats Grad!
A Darling With A Diploma
Diploma Dazzler
Finally Done At Last
The Finish Line
Free As We Always Wanted
Glad To Be A Grad
Goodbye Dorm, Goodbye School
Grad Night
A Grad With Honors
The Graduate
Graduation Day Is The Climax Of A Dream
A Happy Sad Day!
A Hard Goal Earned
Hard Work Pays Off
Hats Off!
Hats Off To You
Hi Skool Gradjuit!
I Did It!
I'm On My Way
I'm Phinished
It's Hard To Say Good-bye
Let The Adventure Begin
Let Your Night Shine
Looks Like We Made It After All
Make The Most Of Yourself
May All Your Dreams Come True
Next Step: College
Next Step: Real Life
No More Books
Now Willing To Consider CEO Position
On The Road To Success
Pomp & Circumstance
Reach For The Stars
Ready To Take On The World
Red Letter Day
Released Me!
So Long...Farewell
So Long Professors!!!
A Tassel Worth The Hassle
That's All Folks!
This Is The 1st Day Of The Rest Of Our Life
This Is The Day I've Worked So Hard For
This Paper Says I Have Brains
Three Cheers For Me
A Time We'll Treasure Thru The Years
We Be Glad To Grad

We/You Did It!
We'll Always Remember Grad Day
We've Only Just Begun
You Did It With Flying Colors
You Made It

GRANDCHILDREN TITLES

(SEE ALSO CHILDREN)

The Future Of The World
Garden Of Grandchildren
Generation To Generation
God Gives Us Grandkids To Keep Us Young At Heart
Gramma's Flower Garden
A Grandchild Is A Gift From Above
Grand Grandchildren
Grandchildren Are So Dear
Grandchildren Are The Crowns Of The Aged. *(Proverbs 17:16)*
Grandchildren Are The Light In My Eyes
Grandchildren Beautify The World
Grandchildren Make Life Grand!
Grandchildren Make Time Pleasurable
Grandchildren Put The Magic Back Into Life
Grandkids Are Grandparents Strength
Grandkids Are Great!
Grandkids Keep Hearts Young
Grandma's Delight
The Joy Of Grandchildren Is Measured In The Heart
Just Me & My Grandma/Grandpa
My Name Is No No, But Grandma Calls Me Precious
One To Cherish & To Love
Thank You Lord For Grandchildren
They Don't Call 'Em Grand For Nothing

GRANDPARENTS TITLES

(SEE ALSO FATHER & MOTHER)

Aged To Perfection
Ain't Life Grand?
All These Years & Still Young At Heart
Aren't They Grand?
Best Of Both Worlds
Blessed Be The Ties That Bind Generations
Call Grandma At: 1-800-I-Want-It!
Call Grandpa At: 1-800-Spoil-Me
A Day With Grandma Is A Priceless Day
For A Good Time Call: 1-800-Grandpa
Forever Young
Generation Gap
Generations Of Love
God Couldn't Be Everywhere So He Created Grandparents
Going To Grandma's & Grandpa's House
Golden Gal
Grandma, You Put The Grand In Grandma
Grandmas/pas...Angels in training
Grandmas Are Antique Little Girls
Grandma's Attic Memories
Grandmas Are Moms With Lots Of Frosting
Grandmas Are Mommies With Lots Of Practice
Grandma's/pa's = Earth Angels
Grandmas/pas Got That Magic Touch
Grandmas/pas = Great
Grandma's/pa's Little Heart Throb
Grandmas/pas = Special
Grandma's/pa's Shadow
To Grandmother's House We Go
This Grandpa Is An "Automatic Spoilin' Machine"
Grandpas Are Antique Little Boys
Grandpa's My Name...Spoilin's My Game
Grandparents = Angels In Disguise
Grandparents Are Oldies But Goodies
Grandparents Are Someone With Silver In Their Hair & Gold In Their Hearts
Grandparents Are The Child's Link To The Past
Grandparents Are The Footsteps To The Future
Grandparents Fill The World With Love
Grandparents = God's Gift To Children
Grandparents = Grand
Great Fathers Get Promoted To Grandfathers
Great Grandmas/pas Are Really Great
Great Mothers Get Promoted To Grandmothers
Grins & Grandpa
Groovy Grandma/Grandpa
Hangin' Out At Grandma's
It's A Grand World To Behold
Just Grandpa/Grandma & Me
Just Me & My Grandma/Grandpa
The Lap Of Loving
The Mamas & The Papas
Member Of The XOXOXOXOX Club
My Hero

No Spanking Zone
Off Her/His Rocker
Okay, That's It! I'm Calling Grandma!
Oldie But Goodie
Our Loving Legacies
Over The River & Thru The Woods To Gramma's House We Go
Priceless Wisdom
Saw It, Wanted It, Told Grandma, Got It!
Silver Fox
Snacks Taste Better At Grandma's House
The Best Thing At Grandpa's House Is Grandma!
There's No Place Like Home, Except Grandma's
They Don't Call 'Em Grand For Nothing
When A Child Is Born, So Is A Grandmother. *(Judith Levy)*
When Dad Says, "No" Ask Grandpa
When Mom Says, "No" Ask Grandma
Who's Spoilin' Who???
With Age Comes Wisdom
A Woman Of Wisdom
You Put The Grand In Grandma/pa
Young At Heart

TGIF
This
Grandma/**G**randpa
Is
Fantastic

GRASS TITLES
Don't Let The Grass Grow Under Your Feet
The Grass Is Always Greener On The Other Side
Grassy Fields Of Green
I'm Livin' Where The Green Grass Grows
It's Good To Lie In The Green Green Grass Of Home
I Lay In The Grass Watching The Clouds...
Lying In The Grass
Running Thru The Whispering Grass
September Grass, As Soft As A Featherbed
Splendor In The Grass
Walk On The Grass & Have Fun With Life
Walking Thru The Grass
When The Sky Is Blue & The Is Green...
Where The Green Grass Grows
With The Grass Tickling Your Toes...

GREEN TITLES
(A great way accentuate the word Green in the title, is to create that word only in Green. Make Green larger and even in a different type style than the rest of the title)
3 Shades Of Green
All In Green
The Color Green
Emerald Green
Everything's Gone Green
Feelin' Green
Fields Of Green
Gorgeous In Green
The Grass Is Always Greener On The Other Side
Grassy Fields Of Green
Green Are Her Eyes
Green As Green
Green Behind The Ears
Green Eggs & Ham
Green-Eyed Girl
Green-Eyed Lady, Lovely Lady
Green-Eyed Monster
Green Fields
Green, Green Grass Of Home
Green Tambourine
Green Thumb
Green With Envy
Greener Pastures
It's Not Easy Being Green
Little Green Men
Pretty In Green
Sea Of Green
Turning Green *(Sick)*
Waves Of Green
The Wearing Of The Green
Where The Green Grass Grows

GROW/GROWING UP TITLES

- *Create a Ruler under title & mark child's height.*

Absence Makes The Heart Grow Fonder
All Grown Up
All Things Grow With Love
As Tall As The Trees
As The Children Grow...
Don't Go Thru Life, Grow Thru Life
Get Growing
Getting Bigger Inch By Inch
Grow Old With Me
Grow Up
Growing Bigger, Inch By Inch
Growing By Leaps & Bounds
Growing, Growing, Grown
Growing High
Growing Like A Weed
Growing Pains
Growing To New Heights
Growing Up Lovely
Growing Up So Fast
Growing Younger
Growth Is The Only Evidence Of Life
Here I/We Grow
Home Grown
How I Measure Up *(Growth chart)*
I Blinked And...
I Don't Wanna Grow Up...
If I Could Save Time In A Bottle...
I'm A Big Kid Now!!!
I'm This Big
In Love We Grow
Keep On Growing
Knee High To A Grasshopper
Let It Grow
Look Who's Sproutin' Up
Measuring Up
The Miracle Of Growing Up
A Pinch To Grow An Inch
Ready Or Not, Here I Grow!
Ready Set Grow!
Room To Grow
Scaling New Heights
Short Stuff
Someone Wonderful Has Sprouted Here
Time To Grow
Together We Will Grow
Up, Up & Away
Vertically Challenged
Watch & See How I Grow
Watch Me Grow
Watch Out, Here I Grow
Way To Grow
When I Grow Up...
You "Grow" Girl

GYMNASTICS TITLES

Angel Come Tumbling Down
Balancing Act
"Beam"ing Beauty
Execution Is The Key
Freestyle Finale
Flip Flopped
Flipped Out
Flipped Over You
Flippin' Fun
Flipping Beans
Flipping Flop
A Flipping Vision
Going For The Gold
Hang Time
Have Balance In Your Life
I'd Bend Over Backwards For You
I'll Flip/Tumble For You
I'm Head Over Heels For You
It's All In The Landing
Lord Of The Rings
Nothing But Air
Olympics 2022, Here I Come
On A Roll
Perfect Balance
Ribbon Dance
Ride 'Em Cowgirl *(Vaulting Horse)*
Rollin' & Tumblin'
Rollin', Rollin', Rollin'...
Rollin' Over
Ruff & Tumble Boys
She Moves In Mysterious Ways
She's/He's On The Roll
Somersault Specialist
Tumblin' Time
"Tumblina"
Tumbling Act
Tumbling Tot
Tumbling Tumbler
Up In The Air
Zero Gravity

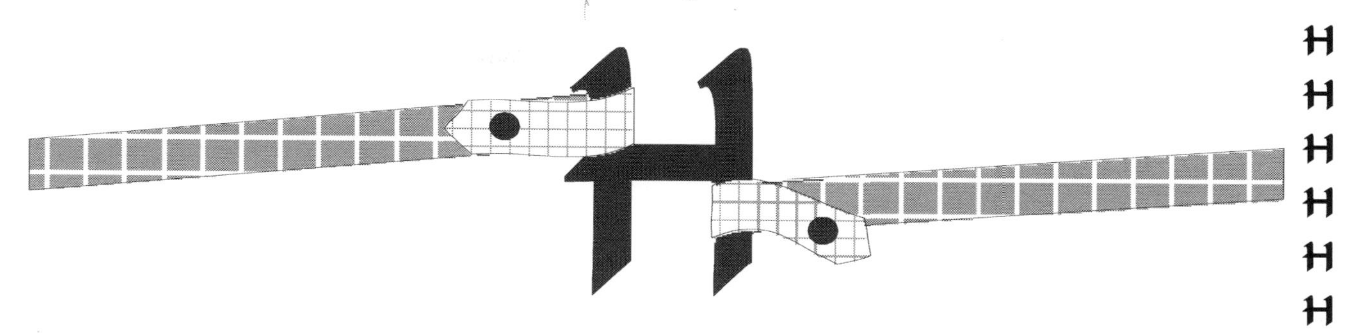

HAIR TITLES

- *Draw Hair coming from top of title letters.*
- *Place Barber Shop Poles on each side of title.*
- *Use different Hair Styling Tools as some letters.*

A Fro For Me...A Fro For You
Afro King/Queen
Bad Hair Day
The Bald & The Beautiful
Bald As An Eagle
Bald Is Beautiful
Barber Shop Buddies *(Father & son haircut)*
Barber Shop Quartet
Bed Head
Big Hair Day
Big Hairy Deal
A Bit Of A Do
Blonde Ambitions
Blonde Bombshell
Bodaciously Blonde Do!
A Brand New Me
Brill Creamin'
Buzzzzzy Cut
Carrot Top
Celebrate What Makes You Different *(Crazy or colorful hair)*
Chrome Dome
Classic Cut
Color Me Crazy
Crazy Curls
Crazy Hair Day
Curl Crazy
Curls & Cowlicks
Curly Locks
Custom Cut
A Cut Above
Cuts & Curls
The Cutting Edge
Dippity Do Doll!
Do It Myself Haircut
A Do To Dye For
Even On A Bad Hair Day, I'm Still The Cutest!
Fair-Haired One
Flat Top Frenzy
Flat Topped
The Fonz Would Be Proud
Future Hairstylist
Fuzzy Rug
Gettin' A New Do!
Getting To The Root Of Things
Girlz & Curlz
Givin' "Rodman" Some Competition
Going Blonde
Going To Great Lengths
Golden Hair
Goldy Locks
Got Bobbed Again
Got Buzzed
Gray Hair Is God's Graffiti. - *(Bill Cosby)*
Gray Is Great
Great Do
Hair Affair
Hair Art *(Kids own hair do)*
Hair Comes The Buzz
Hair Flair
Hair Of Gold...Eyes Of Blue
A Hair Raising Experience
Hair Stylists Are A Cut Above
Hair To Dye For
Hair Today...Gone Tomorrow
Hair We "Bow" Again
Hair? What Hair?
Hairlarious
Hair's To You
Happy To Be Nappy
Head Trip
Heads Up
Heavenly Hair
Holiday Hair
I Have A Brand New Hair Do
I Have A Comb, Not A Magic Wand
I Said, "Just A Trim!"
It Takes A Lot Of Pain To Be Beautiful
Knot Head
Knotty, But Nice!
Letting Our Hair Down
A Little Dab'll Do Ya
The Long & Short Of It *(Cut long hair short)*
Look Out "Don King"!
Look Out "Fonz"
Kewpie Do
Kids, Kuts & Kurls
The Maine Event
Major Bed Head
Miss Style
Mommy Scissor Hands
Mop Chopper
Mop Top
Mr. Style
My Favorite Blonde/Brunette/Red Head
Nappy Days
I Need A Hat *(Bad hair do)*
New Do
Now That's A Hat!
Off The Cutting Room Floor
On The Cutting Edge
Peach Fuzz

Pony Tail
Queen Of Braids
Raga Muffin
Rapunzel, Rapunzel!
Shear Bliss
Shear Delight
Shear Determination
Shear Do
Shear Happiness & Hair Cuts
Shear Like A Sheep
Shear Magic
Shear Pleasure
Shear Precision
Shear Torture
Shirley Temple Would Be Jealous
Simply To Dye For
Sister Golden Hair
Snip, Snip, Snip
A Spikey Do Dude
A Streaking Experience
Super Cut
Tress Obsessed
Up Do
Vanity Hair
What A Do!
What's The Buzz?
Where's My Hair?
Wiggin' Out
Wish You Were Hair
Wooley, Wooley
(Name) Gets A Buzzzz
(Name) Scissors Hands *(Cutting their own hair)*

____
____
____
____
____

HALLOWEEN TITLES

(SEE ALSO PUMPKINS)

- *Use a Pumpkin as "O" & a Ghost as an "A".*
- *Have Blood dripping from title for Vampire page.*
- *Replace letters with Candies or a Broom.*
- *Put a Witches Hat on top of some letters.*

All Dressed Up
Along Came A Spider
Are You A Good Witch Or A Bad Witch?
Are You A Scaredy-Cat?
Are You Afraid Of The Dark?
Bat Mom
Bat You Loved Halloween!?
I'm Bats About You
Bats All Folks
Bats In His Belfry
Bats 'R Us
Batty Cake
Batty Over Halloween
BBBB-BOO
Be Afraid, Be Very Afraid
Be My Treat
Be The Ghostess With The Mostess
Be "Witching" Halloween
Beary Scary
Beary Scary Halloween
Best Witches
Beware! Beauty & The Beast Lives Here
Be"Witch"ing
Bewitching Brew
Be"Witch"ing Halloween
Best Witches
Bibbidy Bobbidy Boo
A Big BOOO To You
Blood Curddling Screams
Blood Donors Needed...See The Count!
Bobbin' For Apples
Bone Voyage
Boo Bash
Boo Boulevard
Boo Brothers
Boo Crew
Boo From The Crew
Boo Time
Boo To You!
Boo Who?
Boo's A Brewin'
Bootiful Boo!
A Bootiful Night
Bootylicious
Brace Yourself For The Ex-FEAR-ience
Broom Parking .5 Cents
Broom Rides .25 Cents
Bubble, Bubble, Toil & Trouble
Bugs & Hisses
Buzzin' Thru Halloween
Candied Kids
Candy Corn Kids
Carvin' Out Some Good Times
Carving Out Good Times
Carving Out Memories
Carving The Pumpkin
Cast A Spell
Casting A Spell
Caught In The "Web" Of Friends
Caution! Black Cat Crossing
Caution! Ghost Crossing
Caution! Goblin Crossing
Caution! Monster Crossing
Caution! Skeleton Crossing

Caution! Witch Crossing
Chamber Of Horrors
Chills & Thrills
Coffin Break
Come As You Aren't
Cookin' Cauldron
Cool Ghouls
Costume Crazies
Costume Cutie
Costume Drama
Costumes & Pumpkins & Candy, Oh My!
Costumes On Parade
Count Down To Candy
Crazy Creatures
Creature Feature
Creatures Of The Night
C-R-E-E-P-Y
Creepy Characters
Creepy Crawly
Cute Little Spooks
Cutest Little Pumpkin In The Patch
Cuttin' Up
Deader Than A Door Nail
Deadly Intentions
Dem Bones
Demons Are A Ghouls Best Friend
Dental Nightmare
Ding Dong, The Witch Isn't Dead!
Don't Be A Scaredy Cat
Don't Be Scared…It's Just Us
Double Bubble Toil & Trouble...
Dressed To Scare
Drive Me Batty
Eat, Drink & Be Scary
Eeeeek
Eeerie & Spooky
Enter At Your Own RISK
Even Dogs Like Halloween
Every-batty Had A Great Halloween
Every Witch Way
Extreme Make-over
Fangs For The Memories & Nightmares
"Fang"tastic Fun
"Fang"tastic Halloween
Fear Factor
Feelin' Batty
Feeling Ghostly
Feeling Ghouly
Feeling Groovy
Forget The Ghosts, Beware Of Me
Forget The Ghost, Beware Of The Sugar Bugs
Found The Great Pumpkin
Fraidy Cats
Fraidy Cats Welcome
Franken-tastic
Frankie & Friends
Frankly! Halloween Doesn't Scare Me!
Freakie Frankie
Free Broom Rides
Freaky Fright Day
Friends Of Frankenstein
Fright Night
Frightfully Delightful
Funky Frankenstein
Funny Bones
Getting Into The "Spirit" Of Halloween
Ghastly Ghosts
Ghost Crossing
Ghost Of Good Cheer
Ghost Post
Ghost Town
Ghostbusters
Ghosties
Ghostly Gathering/Group
Ghostly Greetings
Ghosts Have Real Spirit
The Ghosts Of Halloween Past
Ghoul Friends
Ghoulish Gathering
Ghoulish Goodies
Ghoulish Guests
Ghouls Just Wanna Have Fun
Ghouls Rule
Gloomy Ghosts
Goblin Gatherin'
Goblin' It Up
Goblins On The Loose
Goin' Batty
Golden Pumpkins
Gone Haunting, Back At Midnight
Good Evening
Goose Bumps
The Great Pumpkin
The Great Pumpkin Caper
Gruesome Twosome
Hair Raising
Hallo-Scream!!
Halloween Haunt
Halloween Horror Nights
Halloween Howls
Halloween Hunk
Halloween Is A Real Treat
Halloween Is Brewing With Fun
Halloween Kids Are Such A Treat
Hand Carved Pumpkins .25 Cents
Hang Around For A Spell
Happy Boo Day
Happy Fright Night

Happy Frightful Halloween
Happy Halloween...Whatever You Are!
Happy Haunting
Happy Pumpkin Day
Happy Spook Day
Happy Trick Or Treating
H-A-U-N-T-E-D
The Haunted
Haunted House
Haunting Fun
Haunting Homes
A Haunting I Will Go
A Haunting We Go
A Hauntingly Delightful Halloween
Hauntingly Fun
A Hauntingly Happy Halloween
Havin' A Happenin' Halloween
Havin' A Rootin' Tootin' Halloween
Having A Booooo-tiful Halloween
Having A Boo-tiful Halloween
Heroes & Villains
Hip, Hip Hooray! Today Is Candy Day!
Honey Of A Halloween
The Horrors of Halloween
How Boo You Boo?
How Boo-tiful
How To Carve A Pumpkin
A Howlin' Good Time
I Am Boo-tiful
I Do Believe In Ghosts, I Do! I Do! I Do!
I Dream Of Jeannie
I Love Being Witchy
I Love My Mummy
I See Dead People
I Vant To Bite Your Neck
I Want Candy
I Want My Mummy
I Want To Drink Your Blood
If The Broom Fits...Fly It
If You've Got It, Haunt It
I'm A Ghastly Ghost
I'm A Pleasing Pumpkin
I'm A Scream
I'm Bats About You
In Search Of The Perfect Pumpkin
Interview With A Vampire
It's A Spooktacular Party
It's All About The Candy
It's Candy Day
It's Hallo-Scream
It's Pumpkin Time
It's Witchcraft
I've Put A Spell On You
Jack-O-Lanterns
Jack-O-Lanterns Are On The Cutting Edge
Jack-O-Lanterns Light The Night
Jazzy Jack-O-Lantern
Jeepers Creepers
Jolly Jack-O-Lanterns
The Joy Of Hex
Just Hanging Out With My Ghoul Friends
Just Say Boo
King Of The Pumpkins
Let's Go Out For A Bite…
A Little Batty
Look At Dem Bones
Look Out! Their Lurking About
Look What's Brewin'
Lookin' For The Great Pumpkin
Lots Of Creatures Were Stirring
Magic Spells While You Wait
Magic Wand
Make No Bones About It
Makes My Skin Crawl
Making "Spirits" Bright
Master Of Disguise
Me & My GHOUL-Friends
Meet My Mummy
Mind Your Mummy
Mischief & Mayhem
Mommy's Little Pumpkins
Mom's Little Monsters
Mom's Little Pumpkins
Monster Mash
Monster Mash - It Was A Graveyard Smash
Monster's Ball
Monsters For Sale
Monster's Holiday
Monster's Inc.
Monsters On Parade
Monsters, Spooks & Ghouls Oh My
Mummy Deadest
Mummy Dearest
Mummy Madness
The Mummy's Curse
Mummy's Little Monsters
Mummy's The Word
My Other Car Is A Broom
Near Death Ex-FEAR-ience
Night Crawlers
The Night Of The Living Dead
Night Of The Living Ghouls/Monsters
Night Stalkers
Nightmare On *(Your street)*
No Bones About It
No Tricks, Just Treats
No Tricks, Only Treats
Oh, What A Tangled Web...

October Fest/Fun
Off We Go A-Haunting
The Old Ball & Chain
One Scary Night...
Only Friendly Ghosts & Goblins Welcome
O-O-O-O-O-O-H!
Oooozz & Goooo
Our Lil' Pumpkin
Our Little Pirate Is All The Treasure We Need
Out For The Count
Out Of The Broom Closet
The Perfect Pumpkin
The Pick Of The Patch
Picking Pumpkins
Picking The Pumpkin
Please Come In For A Bite
Please Park All Brooms At The Door
Positively Defrightful
Practice Safe Hex
Pumpkin Faces & You
Pumpkin Pondering *(Trying to choose the perfect pumpkin)*
Queen Of The Pumpkin's
Raising Howl
Ready, Set, GLOW!
A Real Cut Up *(Pumpkin)*
Remember The Ghoul Times
R.I.P.
Scare Central
Scare Factory
A Scare Is Born
Scared Your Pants Off
Scaredy Cat
Scaring Up Some Fun
S-C-A-R-Y
Scream-Fest
Scream Seekers
Scramblin' Spiders
Shivers Up & Down Your Spine
Shivers Down Your Spine
Shout A Scary Greeting
Silly As A Scarecrow
Simply Bewitching Halloween
Slime Time
Something Wicked
Speak Of The Devil
Spell-Binding
Spell Checker
Spell-ectible
Spider Cider
Spookable
Spookable Spooktacular Halloween
Spookables
Spookiest Spooks Around
A Spooktacular Halloween
Spooktacular Kids
Spooky Greetings
A Spooky Halloween
Spooky Night
The Spooky Ones
Spooky Snacks
Spooky Style
Spoooooooooked
Spoooooooooky
Stop For A Spell
Stop In For A Bite
Sugar Fix
Sugar High
Sweets For The Sweet
The Terror Zone
Terror-ific
That's The Spirit
Things That Go "Bump" In The Night
I Vant You
The Walking Zombies
There's Mischief A Brewing
There's No Such Thing As Too Much Candy
Things That Go Bump In The Night
Tickled To My Bones
Time For A Coffin Break
Tis' The Witching Hour
Tomb It May Concern
Too Cute To Spook
Trick Or Treat
Trick-Or-Treat & Something Sweet
Trick Or Treat, Have A Sweet
Trick Or Treat, Sweets For The Sweet
Trick Or Tweet
Vamp It Up
Vamp Tramp
A Very Scary Halloween
Warning! An Alien Is Coming
A Way Spooky Boo Day
Weave A Wicked Web
Welcome, The Witch Is In
What A Feat For Just A Treat
What A Great Night For A Fright
What A Night...What A Fright!
Where My Witches At?
Where's My Treat?
Which Witch Are You?
Which Witch Is Which?
Who Said "Boo?"
The Wicked Witch Lives Here - Beware
Wicked Witches
Wicked Witches Convention Tonight
Wild Fang
Wild Thang/Things

Will Spook For Treats
Witch For Hire
Witch Hunt
Witch Way Is The Candy?
Witch You Were Here
Witches Brew
Witches, Goblins & Ghosts, Oh My
Witches Rest Stop - Prop Up Your Brooms Here
Witchful Thinking
The Witching Hour
Witchy Woman
You Drive Me Batty
You Give Me The Creeps
You Little Monster You
You Look So Boo-tiful
You're Boo-tiful
You're So Bootiful To Me
Yum, Yum Give Me Some

HALLOWEEN TOMBSTONE EPITAPHS

START THESE NAMES WITH: HERE LIES

Barry D. Live
Barry Dirty
Barry M. Deep
Bea A. Frade
Bea A. Good
Ben Better
Betty Will-Rott
C. U. Later
Dawn Under
Dedd N. Gonn
Doobie Ghoulish
Dr. Izzy Gone
Etsa Vacant
Etsa B. Darke
Fester N. Rott
Frank N. Stein
Gil A. Teene
Hal O. Weene
I. B. Brooke
I. B. Chunks
I. B. Gone
I. B. Krispy
I. B. Moldy
I. B. Nappin
I. Emma Goste
I. Emma Spook
I. M. Black
I. M. Gawn
I. M. Nekid
I. M. Slick
I Wilby Back
Ima Dedman
Ima Duste
Ima Gonner
Ima Live
Ima Smelly
Itwuz Kwik
Ivan O. Aire
Ivy Smokin
Jess Gough
Justin Angel
Justin Pieces
Justin Time
Kerry Meoff
Left B. Hynde
Les N. Moore
M. T. Box
M. T. Tomb
Mann E. Bones
Miss N. Cranium
N. A. Coffin
Nitta Shovel
O. I. Hurt
Otto B. Alive
Pearl E. Gates
Rattle M. Bones
Reid N. Weep
Rig O. Mortis
Ron D. Voo
S. Teenky
Shirley B. Gone
Sixfee Deep
Stone Coled
Sue D. Bum
Ted N. Barried
U. R. Gonn
Will B. Late
Will I. Rott
Yule B. Next

HAND TITLES

- *Have a Hand holding title.*

10 Tiny Fingers & Toes
All Thumbs
Busy Little Hands
Caught Red-Handed
Daddy's Hands
Gimmie Five
Go Together Hand In Hand
Hand In Hand Forever
Hand Jive
Hand Me Down
Hand On My Heart
Hand On Our Hearts For America
Hand Over Fist
The Hand That Feeds Me...
The Hand That Rocks The Cradle
A Hand To Hold Onto
Handle With Care
Hands Are For Grabbing *(Holding hands)*
Hands Down, You're The Cutest
Hands Of Love
Helping Hands
Hold On!
I Gotta Hand It To You
I Wanna Hold Your Hand
I'm A Handful...Hands Down
I'm Thumbody Special *(Sucking thumb)*
It's Outta My Hands
Jewel In The Hand
Life At Hand
Look Mom...No Hands!
Love & Life Go Hand In Hand
Loving Hands
Magical Hands
My Hands My Be Small, But I Can Still Wrap Daddy Around Them
One Hand...One Heart
Peace At Hand
Put Your Hand In My Hand
Slight Of Hand
So Hand-some
Talk To The Hand
Ten Tiny Fingers & Toes
Thumbody Loves Me
To Have & To Hold
Touched By The Hand Of God
Walking Hand In Hand
With Heart In Hand...
With The Wave Of Your Hand
Your Hand In Mine

HANUKKAH TITLES

(SEE JEWISH)

HAPPINESS/HAPPY TITLES

- *Make an "O" into a Happy Face.*
- *Put a Happy Face inside a "P".*

Are You Happy Now?
Be Forever Happy
"Bee" Happy
Blessed & Happy
C'mon Get Happy
Don't Worry, Be Happy
The Ethereal Glow Of Happiness
Everyone Is Happy When She Smiles
Everything About You Resonates Happiness
Feeling Happy
"H" Is For Happiness
Hakuna Matata
Happily Ever After
Happily In Love
Happily We Go Along
Happiness Hit Me The First Day We Met
Happiness Is...
Happiness Is Easy
Happiness Is Like A Rainbow To The Stars
Happiness Is The Best Face Lift
Happy & Free
Happy As A Clam
Happy As A Duck In Water
Happy As The Day Is Long
Happy Days
Happy Ending
Happy Eyes & Smiling Thoughts
Happy Faces
Happy Feet
Happy Go Lucky Me
Happy Hour
Happy Is...
Happy Moments
Happy Trails
Happyluyah
Her Laughter Is As Happiness Is
Hooked On A Happy Feeling

I Will Be Happy...
If Your Happy & You Know It, Clap Your Hands
I'm A Happy Girl
I'm So Excited
I've Been Blessed With Love & Happiness
Let The Happiness In
Lost In Happiness
Love & Happiness
Lovely & Happy
May Sunshine & Happiness Surround You
May You Be Happy Everyday
My Happy Place
Oh! Happy Day
Oh, How Happy You Have Made Me
A Place Where The Sun Keeps Shining Is Where Your Happiness Begins
Put On A Happy Face
She's Of Heavenly Happiness
Show Me The Funny
Show Me The Happy
So Happy Together
Sometime We Catch A Glimpse Of Perfect Happiness
There Smiles The Happy Child
Thinking Happy Thoughts
This Way To Happiness
True, True Happiness
What A Feeling Of Happiness
Where Love & Happiness Lives
I Wish You Happiness
You Are My Happiness
You Brighten Up The Darkness With Happiness
You Make Me Happy

HARVEST TITLES

(SEE ALSO AUTUMN, FALL & MONTHS OF THE YEAR)

- *Wrap Raffia around title mat.*
- *Have Raffia coming out from under ends of title mat to represent Straw.*

Autumn Harvest
Bales Of Fun
Bushel...Basket...Harvest
Bushel Of Blessings
Bushels Of Fun
Carol For The Harvest
Carving Out Good Times
Corn Husks
Corn Roast
Crazy For Corn
A "Crop" Of Good Food
A "Crop" Of Good Friends
A "Crop" Of Good Fun
A "Crop" Of Good Kids
A "Crop" Of Good Times
Fall Harvest
Fall's Harvest
A Harvest Day Today
Harvest Delight
Harvest Fields
Harvest Glory
Harvest Happenings
Harvest Hymns
Harvest Moon
A Harvest Of Memories
The Harvest Of The Earth
The Harvest Of The Sea
Harvest Party
Harvest Prayers
A Harvest Scene
Harvest Season
Harvest Time
Hay Day
Holiday Harvest
Hurrah For Harvest
It's Apple Time
The Lord's Harvest Of Plenty
Oktoberfest
Our Harvest
Pick Of The Patch
Pickin' Apples
Plowing Time
Preserving Our Harvest
Reap The Harvest
Reap What You Sow
Red Delicious
Season Of Harvest
Shine On Harvest Moon
Silly As A Scarecrow
Summer's Sweet Harvest
Under The Harvest Moon
When The Harvest Comes...

HAT TITLES

- *Put different kinds Hats on the title letters.*

All Wigged Out
All You Need Is The Right Hat
At The Drop Of A Hat
The Cat & My Hat
Cat In The Hat
Gone Cone Head
Gone Wiggy
Hang On To Your Hat
Hat Attack
Hat Dance
Hat Hair
Hat Head
Hat In The Wind
Hat Tricks
Hatlarious
Hatrageous
Hats All Folks
Hats Off To You
Hats Off To *(Name)*
Hats On To You
Hats 'R Us
Hattitude
Hiding A Bad Hair Day
I Keep It Under My Hat
I Tip My Hat To You
I Told You I Love Hats
I've Just The Right Hat For Every Occasion
I've/We've Got 'Hat'itude
Jack Of Hats
I Love My Hats
The Mad Hatter
Mexican Hat Dance/Dancer
A Mom Wears A Lot Of Different Hats
Now That's A Hat!
Oh, What Hat To Wear
Sacred Hat
So Many Hats...So Little Time
This Cowboy's Hat...
Top Hat Trip
Top Hat-titude
Wearin' My Hat Proud

____
____
____
____
____

HEART TITLES

(SEE ALSO KISS & LOVE)

- *Use a Heart in place of the word Heart.*
- *Replace an "A" or "O" with a Heart.*

Absence Makes The Heart Grow Fonder
Ace Of Hearts
Achy Breaky Heart
Affair From The Heart
After My Own Heart
All Of My/Your Heart
Always In My Heart
Angel Heart
Angel Of My Heart
As Tender As A Mother's Heart
At The Heart Of It
Be Still My Heart
The Beat Goes On
Beauty Is In The Heart Of The Beholder
The Best Gifts Are Tied With Heart Strings...
Bright Heart
Can't Get You Out Of My Heart
Can't Stop My Heart From Loving You
Careless Heart
Chains About My Heart
Change Of Heart
Close To My Heart
Constellation Of The Heart
Convictions Of The Heart
Country At Heart
Crazy Heart
Crazy Little Heart Of Mine
Cross My Heart
Cross My Heart & Soul
Door To My Heart
A Dream Is A Wish Your Heart Makes.
(Cinderella)
Each Word's A Beat Of My Heart
Eat Your Heart Out
Enter With A Happy Heart
Every Little Beat Of My Heat
Find A Way To My Heart
Flaming Heart
Follow My/Your Heart
Forever In Your Heart
From My Head To My Heart
From One Heart To Another
From The Heart
A Gift Of The Heart
Give Me Your Heart Tonight
I Give You My Heart
Given From The Heart Now & Forever
Giving You My Heart Forever
Golden Heart
Great Thoughts Come From The Heart...

Heart & Soul
Heart Attacked
Heart Beat
Heart Break Kid
Heart Breaker
A Heart Full Of Love
The Heart Never Forgets
Heart Of A Woman
Heart Of An Angel
Heart Of Gold
Heart Of Hearts
Heart Of Innocence
Heart Throb
Heart To Heart
Hearts & Kisses
Hearts Afire
Heart's Desire
Hearts On Fire
A Helping Hand Is Showing A Loving Heart
I Hold You In My Heart
Home Is Where The Heart Is
I Have You Hidden In My Heart
I'm A Heart Breaker
I'm Having A "Heart" Attack
In A Heart Beat
It Is Wisdom To Believe The Heart.
(George Santayana)
I've Got A Burning Heart
Jack Of Hearts
A Joyful Heart Is Good Medicine
Joys Of The Heart Are The Treasures Of Life
Keeper Of My Heart
Kind Hearted
King Of Hearts
I Know You By Heart
Let Your Heart Bloom
Life Is A Gift Tied With Heart Strings
Listen With Your Heart
Lock Me In Your Heart
Look Into Your Heart...
Love Makes A Heart Smile
Love Me With All Your Heart
Love Needs A Heart
I Love You With All My Heart
Love's Got A Hold On My Heart
Man Of My Heart
Matters Of The Heart
May Your Heart Be As Light As A Song
Miles Can't Separate Hearts That Care
Music To My Heart
My Heart & Soul
My Heart Beats For You
My Heart Beats So...That I Can Hardly Speak
My Heart Belongs To You
My Heart Stays With You
My Heart To Yours
My Heart's Delight
Near & Dear To My Heart
One Heart...One Mind
Only One Man In My Heart
Our Two Hearts Make One
A Piece Of My Heart
Queen Of Hearts
Rhythm Of My Heart
Rock My Heart
Sacred Heart
Schmoozing With You
Shot Thru The Heart
A Smile In Your Heart
State Of The Heart
Straight From The Heart
Sweetest Heart
Sweetheart
Tender-Hearted
A Thankful Heart
A Thankful Heart Is A Happy Heart
The Thunder In My Heart...
Two Hearts Beat As One
The Way To My Heart...
What The Heart Wants...
When The Heart Rules The Mind...
Wild At Heart
With A Song In My Heart...
With Every Beat Of My Heart
With Loving Hearts
A Work Of Heart
You Are A Work Of Heart
You Are My Heart
You Are My Sweet Heart
You Make My Heart Flutter
You Make My Heart Fly
You Make My Heart Sing
You Own The Key To My Heart
You Own The Most Special Place In My Heart
You Stole My Heart
Young At Heart
Your Words Are Poetry To My Heart
You're In My Heart
You're My Heart
You've Captured My Heart
You've A Hold On My Heart
You've Got The Key To My Heart

HEAVEN TITLES

(SEE ALSO ANGELS & CLOUDS)

- *Place a Halo on a few of the title letters.*
- *Put title on a Cloud, cut small slits in clouds & slide bottom of letters down into slits to look like they are snuggled in the clouds)*

All This & Heaven Too!
Almost Heaven
Breath Of Heaven
Can't Get Too Much Heaven
Child Of Heaven
Feels Like Heaven
For Me This Is Heaven
A Gift From Above
Heaven Bound
Heaven Can Wait
Heaven Help My Heart
Heaven Help Us
Heaven, I'm In Heaven
Heaven In Her/His Eyes
Heaven In Your Eyes
Heaven In Your Heart
Heaven Is In My Heart
Heaven Is The Whole Of The Heart
Heaven Is Waiting
Heaven Is You
Heaven Knows
Heaven Must Be Missing An Angel
Heaven On Earth
Heaven Or Bust
Heaven Sent
Heaven Sent Me To You
Heaven's Delight
Heaven's Golden Gates
Heaven's Little Angels
Heaven's What I Feel When I'm With You
I Feel Heaven In You
I Found Heaven
I Found Heaven On The Wings Of Love
It's Heaven To Be With You
A Little Slice Of Heaven
To Love Is To Receive A Glimpse Of Heaven
Made In Heaven
A Match Made In Heaven
One Night In Heaven
A Star In Heaven
Take Me To Your Heaven
This Is My Heaven
Together Were 1/2 Way To Heaven
Touch Of Heaven
A Wee Bit Of Heaven
I Wish You Heaven
With Hands To Heaven
You Are My Heaven
You Fell From Heaven
You Make Heaven A Place On Earth
You Make Me Feel Like Heaven
You Take Me To Heaven
You Wear Your Heart Like Heaven

____
____
____
____
____

HERITAGE TITLES

(SEE ALSO MEMORIAL/MEMORIES)

- *Use Fleur De Lis' as accents on title mats.*

All American Family
Ancestors...Hidden Treasures
Back In Grandmas/pas Day...
Beauty From The Past
Bits Of Yesteryear
A Blast From The Past
A Book Of Our Heritage
Branching Out From Generation To Generation
A Chip Off The Ole Block
A Classic
Days Of Our Lives
Deep Rooted Heritage
Fabulous Forties
Faces From The Past
Family Archives
Family Faces Are Magic Mirrors
Family Heritage
Family Traits
From Days Gone By
From Past To Present
Generation Gap
Generation To Generation
Generations Of Love
Golden Oldies
The Good Old Days
Heirlooms
Honor The Past...Imagine The Future
How Time Flies
In A Simpler Time
In Days Of Olde...
In The Good Ol' Days
Lasting Legacy
A Legacy Of Love
A Lifetime Of Memories
Long Ago & Far Away...
Looking At People Who Belong To Us
I Love Remembering...
Making History
Memories & Love Tie Our Hearts Together
Memories Of Years Gone By

A Moment Of Time Gone By
Moments In Time
My Ancestors
Nostalgia
Old Things Are More Beautiful With Time
An Oldie But Goodie
Once Upon A Lifetime...
Once Upon A Time
Our Ancestors...Our Greatest Treasures
Our Family Tree
Our Legacy
Past...Present...Future
Picture Perfect Memories
Pieces Of The Past
Piecing Together A Family Heritage
Precious Memories/Moments
Precious Treasures
Priceless Moments
Priceless Treasures
Remember When...
Remembering...
Remembering The Past...
Roaring 20's
Seems Like Yesterday
Simple Pleasures...
A Simpler Time...
Step Back In Time
A Stitch In Time Saves Nine
Sweet Connections
I Thank God For Every Remembrance Of You
The Way We Were
Then & Now
There Once Was A Little Boy/Girl...
Those Were The Days
Thru The Years
As Time Goes By...
Time Never Changes The Memories
A Time To Remember
Time Travel
Timeless Treasures
Trail Blazer
A Travel Thru Time *(Old cars)*
Travel Thru The Pages Of Time
Treasured Heirlooms Are Family Memories
Treasures Of Yesterday
A Walk Down Memory Lane
We Don't Remember Days, But Moments...
We Live As Long As We Are Remembered
Yesteryear

___
___
___
___
___

HIKING TITLES

(SEE ALSO CLIMBING, MOUNTAINS, NATURE & OUTDOORS)

- *Make title letters from Dirt or Rock paper.*
- *Put Hiking Boots in the corner of title mat.*

Ain't No Mountain High Enough
Altitude Adjustment
Backpacked The Peak
The Big Hike
Blazing Your Own Trail
These Boots Were Made For Hikin'
B-L-I-S-T-E-R-S
Bush Whacking
Climb Every Mountain
The End Of The Trail
Follow The Rocky Mountain Trail
Gaper Caper
Got Rocked On The Way
Happy Hikers
Happy Hikin'
Happy Trails To You
Hard Rock Cafe
Hard Rock Climber
Headed Down The Wrong Path!!!
Heigh Ho, Heigh Ho, It's A Hikin' We Go
High On The Mountain Top
Hike Every Mountain
Hike It Up
A Hike To The Brush
Hiker Haven/Heaven
Hiker's Paradise
Hikin' High
Hikin' The Rocks
Hikin' The Rocky Road
Hittin' The Trails
A Hiking We Will Go
Hittin' The Trails
I Dream To Roam
Just Hike It
Let's Get Rocked
Livin' On The Edge
The Lone Trail
The Long & Winding Road
The Long Trail
Lovers Trails
Many Trails
Nature Hike
Natur-ally Gifted
Oh! The Fresh Air!
On The Dusty Dirty Trail
On The Trail Again
On The Way To The Top
On Top Of Old Smokey
On Top Of The World

Over The River & Thru The Woods
Paths Of Glory
Roamin' Half Dome
Roamin' Up To Half Dome
Rockin' Out
Rocky Mountain High
Scaling New Heights
Slap Shot King
Slippin' & Slidin'
Take A Hike
Tall Trails
Trail & Error
Trail Blazers
The Trail Of No Return
A Trail Remembered
Trail To Freedom
The Trail We Blaze
A Walk On The Wild Side
Walkin' The Rocks
Welcome To Our Neck Of The Woods

HOCKEY TITLES

(SEE ALSO SPORTS)

- *Use a Hockey Puck for an "O".*
- *Replace an "I" or "L" with a Hockey Stick.*
- *Create a Hockey Net as background for title.*

At The Good Ole Hockey Game
Blade Runner
Blue Line Crew
Board Checked
Bump & Grind
Butt-Ended
Chicks With Sticks
Cold On Ice
Crashing The Boards
Double-Decked
Eat, Sleep, Breathe...Hockey!
Face Off
Fast Breaker
Fighting First...Hockey Second
Fighting Frenzy
Give Blood...Play Hockey
Gliding Light
Goalie Dude
Hat Trick Happy
He Shoots! He Scores!
Hitting The Ice
Hockey Hurts
Hockey Is My Goal
Hockey Is My Life
Hockey Players Stick Together
Holy Hat Trick
Ice Wars
Icing On The Season
I'm A Stick Man
In The Crease
Jumpin' Goalie
Know Hockey...No Life
Miracle On Ice
My "Goal" Is To Play Hockey
Our Goal Is More Goals
Pass The Puck Please!
Pouting Penalty
Power Play
The Puck Drops Here
The Puck Is In...SCORE!!!
The Puck Plopped
The Puck Stops Here
S-C-O-R-E!
Scored On The Fly
Skate To Be Great!
Slam The Puck
Slapshot
Slide The Puck Inside
Slippin' & Slidin'
Smooth As Ice
Smooth As Glass
Stormed The Crease
Too Cool!
Took The Final Flick Of The Stick
Two Minutes In The Pouting Box
We Get Our Kicks In Hockey
We Got Iced!
What A Slam
The Whistle Blows & The Puck Flies

HOCKEY

Honest
Obedient
Courteous
Kind
Elegant
Yeah Right!

HOME/HOUSE TITLES

- *Border the title mat with paper that is cut & chalked to look like planks of Wood.*
- *Create an A-Frame Roof spanning across top of page & place title on top or under roof.*

2 Of A Kind Working On A Full House
500 Milles Away From Home
All The Way Home
Almost Home
Animal House
Apartment Sweet Apartment
Around The House
Baby, Let Me Take You Home
Back Home Again
Be It Ever So Humble...
Bigger House...Bigger Debt
Bless This House
Building Our Nest
Casa Sweet Casa
City Home
Close To Home
Feels Like Home
Finally Found A Home
Fingerprints Make A House A Home
Fixer Upper
Forever Home
Gramma's Home
Green, Green Grass Of Home
Happiness Is...Homemade!!!
Home & Heart Will Never Depart
Home & Paradise
Home Again In My Heart
Home Alone
Home At Last
Home Away From Home
Home By The Sea
Home For The Holidays
The Home Front
Home In My Heart
Home In The Heartland
Home Of The Brave
Home On The Range
Home Sick
Home Sweet Home
Home...The Heart Of Life
Home...The Heart's Haven
Home...The Starting Place Of Love & Dreams
Home...Where My Heart Is
Home...Where One Starts From
Home...Where The Bills Are
Home...Where The Mortgage Is
Home...Where You Hang Your Heart
Home...Where Your Heart Is
Home...Where Your Story Begins
Homecoming
Homeward Bound
Honey, We're Home
A House Is A Home With A Heart Inside
The House Is A Rockin'
A House Is Not A Home
House Of Cards
House Of Fun
House Of Gold
House Of Joy
House Of Love
The House Of The Rising Sun

House On The Hill
The House That Love Built
The House That *(Name)* Built
House + Love = HOME
I Wanna Walk You Home
It's Good To Be Home
It's The Heart That Makes The Home
The Last Mile Home
Life At The *(Surname)* Home
Little House In The Big Woods
Little House On The Prairie
Lookin' Out My Back Door
Lord, Bless Our New Home
Love Makes A House A Home
Love Shack
Love's The Only House
Mad House
Makin' This House A Home
A Man's Home Is His Castle
My Castle Faire
My Childhood Home
My Heart Will Always Be At Home *(Child leaving home)*
My Old Kentucky Home
My Own Home
No Place Like Home
Oh Give Me A Home
On The Home Front
On The Road Home...
On The Street Where You Live...
Our Castle
Our Dream Home/House
Our First Home...The American Dream
Our House
Our House...In The Middle Of The Street...
Our Little Mansion
Our Neck Of The Woods
Our Nest Is Blessed
Our Tax Write-Off!
Peace In Our Home

A Place To Call Home
Rock The House
Room To Breathe Now!
Room With A View
Shakin' The House
Small, But Ours
So Glad To Be In Our First Pad!
Sweet Home Alabama
Take Me Home Country Roads
There's No Place Like Home...
This Is My Home, My Castle Faire
This Old House!
Thoughts Of Home Are Always Dear
Two Old Crows Live Here
Welcome Home
Welcome To Our Coop
You Can Go Home Again
You Can't Go Home Again

HOPE TITLES

Brave New Hope
Breathtaking New Hope
Dare To Hope
Faith...Hope...Love
Flame Of Hope
Full Of Hopes & Dreams
Garden Of Hopes & Dreams
Glimmer Of Hope
Heartbeat Of Hope
High Hopes
Hope For Love
Hope Is The Key
Hope Is The Thing With Feathers
The Hope Of My Heart
Hope Of The Future
Hope Springs Eternal
I Hope You Dance
Hopes & Dreams
Hopes Set High
I Can Only Hope
In Faith, In Hope, In Love!!!
Keep Hope Alive
Land Of Hope & Glory
Land Of Hopes & Dreams
My Hopes & Dreams
Never Lose Hope
A New Hope
Ray Of Hope
A Single Hope Believed
A Star Filled With Hope

HORSE TITLES

(SEE ALSO COUNTRY, COWBOY & FARM)

- *Make an "S" with 2 Horseshoes turned on sides in opposite directions.*
- *Run Horseshoes around title to create border.*
- *Use Hemp string to Lasso the title.*

Airs Above The Ground
All The Pretty Horses
As I Sit Upon My Horse...
Back In The Saddle Again
Between My Horses Wings...
Black Beauty
Blazing Saddles
The Bond Between Horse & Rider
Galloping Gal
Giddy Up
Gone Ridin'
The Grandest Horse
Happiness Is...Being A Cowboy/Cowgirl
Happy Trails
"Hay" Fever
"Hay" Good Lookin'
"Hay" Is For Horses
High Up On A Horse
Hit The Hay
Hitchin' Post .10 Cents...The Reins Stop Here!
Hold Your Horses
Horse Lovers Are Stable People
Horse Play
Horse Sense
Horse Sense Is Only Stable Thinking
The Horse Whisperer
Horsin' Around
I Need A "Stable" Environment
I'm A Stable Person
I'm Riding, Therefore I Am
I'm Too Sexy For My Saddle
In Riding A Horse, We Borrow Freedom.
(Helen Thomson)
In The Saddle Again
It's A Dressage Thing

Learning The Ropes
Our Little Buckaroo!
A Little Dapple Do Ya!
Love Me...Love My Horse
The Love Of A Horse
The "Mane" Attraction/Event
Mr. Ed Said There'd Be Days Like This!
My Little Pony
My Pretty Pony
My Wild Mane
On A High Horse
One "Stick" Pony
My Place Is On A Horse
Phony Pony
Pony Boy
Pony Express
My Pony Pal
Pony Tale
To Ride Or Not To Ride...Stupid Question!
My Rocking Horse
Round 'Em Up
Running Wild
Saddle-Up
A "Stable" Place
Straight From The Horses Mouth
Thoroughbred
I Think I'm Getting Horsey Sick!
Wild Horses
A Woman's Place Is On Her Horse
Yipee-I-O! Off We Go
You Are "Mare"velous

HORSE RACING TITLES

Around The Turn
At The Post/Track
Blazing Saddles
Breakneck Speed
By A Length
By A Neck/Nose
By The Rail
Call To The Post
Center Field
Daily Double
Derby Bash/Day
Down The Backstretch
Down To The Wire
Go Baby Go
In The Gate
In The Paddock
Jockey's On Parade
Makin' A Move
On The Turn
On Track
Photo Finish
Placin' A Bet
Race To The Finish
Run For The Roses
Splendor In The Bluegrass
The Sport Of Kings
The Starting Gate
Thoroughbred
Triple Crown
Win...Place...Show
The Winner's Circle

HOT TITLES

(SEE ALSO SUMMER & SUN)

- *Use Thermometers to create an "H".*
- *Makes Water Drops dripping from the letters as if they were sweating.*

The Big Heat
Body Heat
That Burning Feeling
A Burning Love
Feelin' Hot! Hot! Hot!
Feel The Burn
Full Of Hot Air
Get It While It's Hot
The Heat Is On
Hot & Bothered
Hot Blooded
Hot Boys
Hot Child In The City
Hot Dog
Hot Enough To Fry An Egg On!
Hot For You
Hot Fudge
Hot Fun In The Summertime
Hot Head
Hot In The City
Hot Lips
Hot Love
Hot On The Heels Of Love
Hot Pants
Hot Shot
Hot Stuff
Hot Summer Nights
Hot Time In The City
Hot Wheels
Hotline To Heaven
In Hot Water
In The Heat Of The Night
In The Hot Seat
It's A Desert Heat Wave
It's HOT! HOT! HOT!
It's Like A Heat Wave...
Lickin' The Heat *(Popsicles)*
Like A Heat Wave
Oh, What Do You Do To Keep Cool???
Red Hot
Red Hot Summer
Sizzzzzzlin' Fun
Sizzlin' Summer
Some Like It Hot
That's Hot
Too Hot To Handle
Triple Digits
We're Havin' A Heat Wave
When You're Hot, You're Hot!!!
You Sizzle!

____
____
____
____
____

HUGS/CUDDLES TITLES

(SEE ALSO KISS & LOVE)

- *Puckered Lips are great to replace the word Kiss.*
- *Surround the title with a border of X's & O's.*

100% Huggable
An Angel's Embrace
Bear Hug
Beautiful Embrace
Canoodling Fun
Cheek To Cheek
Come On & Squeeze Me
Cuddle A Little Closer
Cuddle Alert
Cuddle Angel
Cuddle Buddies
Cuddle Bug
Cuddles & Hugs
As Cuddly As A Teddy Bear
Cute 'N Cuddly
Embrace Life!
Everyone Needs Hugs
Gimmie All Your Hugs
Got A Lot Of Huggin' To Do
Happy Hugger
Happy Hugs
Hold Me, Hug Me, Rock Me
Hold Me, Hug Me, Squeeze Me Tight
How Sweet It Is To Be Hugged By You
Hug & Squeeze
A Hug A Day Keeps The Meanies Away
Hug Department Always Open
Hug, Hug, Hooray!
A Hug Is A Handshake From The Heart
Hug Me!
Hug 'O War
Huggable

Huggy Bear
Hugs & Cuddles
Hugs & Kisses
Hugs & Kisses & Stars For Wishes
Hugs Are The Universal Medicine
Hugs Are To Squeeze The Pain Out Of You
Hugs Enclosed
Hugs From The Heart
Hugs Grease The Wheels Of The World
Hugs Handed Out Here
Hugs Of Sweetness
I'm An Equal-Opportunity Hugger
In Love's Sweet Embrace
It's A Cuddle Night
Just Hug Me
Kisses & Cuddles
Lovable, Snuggable, Huggable
Lovable, Snuggable Hugs To You
Love Is A Hug
Love's Hugs
My Main Squeeze
I Saved All My Hugs For You
Smothered In Hugs
Snuggle Bug
Squeezably Soft
Squeeze Box
Squeeze Me Tight
Sweet Embrace
Walk Into My Hug
XOXOXOXOXOX
You Can't Give A Hug Without Getting A Hug
You Fill Our Days With Hugs & Kisses
You Put The Squeeze On Me

HUNTING TITLES

- *Use Eyelets or Buttons speckled around & thru the title words to look like Bullet Holes.*

22 Sharpshooter
Annie Oakley
Big Shot
The Buck Stops Here
Bug Hunter
Bug Hunting
Bullseye
Call Of The Wild
Croc Hunter
Daddy's Gone A Huntin'
The Dear Hunter
Did You Hear That?
Dream Hunter
Go Ahead, Make My Day!
Goin' On A Scavenger Hunt
Goin' On A Treasure Hunt
Gone Huntin'
Gone Huntin'...Be Back At Dark Thirty!!!
Gone Huntin'...In Pursuit Of Old Tom
Happy Hunting
The Happy Hunting Grounds
Have Gun, Will Hunt
Hunt To Live...Live To Hunt
Hunter Of The Heart
The Hunter's Delight
Hunters Will Do Anything For A Buck
Huntin' Buddies
Hunting High & Low
A Hunting We Will Go
I'd Rather Be Deer Hunting
The Jolly Hunter
Lone Hunter
A Long Shot
Love Hunter
Marksmanship Counts
The Mighty Hunter
Mystery Hunt
Oh Deer!!!
On The Hunt
Perfect Aim
Pistol Packin' Mama
Practice Makes Perfect
Ready, Aim, Fire!
Right On Target
Quick Draw McGraw
Sharpshooter
Straight Shooter
Sure Shot
Survival Of The Fittest
Tag 'Em & Bag 'Em
Target Practice

The Thrill Of The Hunt
Top Gun
Trail Blazers
Treasure Hunter
Under The Hunter's Moon
The Wild Hunt
Will Hunt For Food

____
____
____
____
____

HUSBAND TITLES

As You Become My Husband...
Beloved Husband Of Mine
The Greatest Man I Ever Knew
Husband & Lover
Husband Of Mine
A Husband's Love
Main Man
Main Squeeze
My Beloved Husband
My Dear & Loving Husband
My Dearest Husband
My Dream Come True
My Gorgeous Husband
My Guy
My Husband...Desire Of Thy Heart
My Husband, My Forever
My Husband, My Heart
My Husband, My Love
My Husband, My Pride
My Husbands Hands
My Life's Partner
My Love Grows For You With Every Passing Day
My Love...My Husband
My Loving Husband
My Man
My Success Is My Husband
A Loving Heart To Rely On
One Good Man
The One I'll Always Love
The Perfect Husband
Real Good Man
Sharer Of Hopes & Dreams
Soul Mate
A Strong Arm To Lean Upon
You Are My Man

____
____
____
____
____

ICE CREAM TITLES

(SEE ALSO FOOD & MESSY)

- *Make Single-Scoop Cones & place title letters inside each Scoop.*
- *Make each letter look like a Popsicle.*
- *Have some letters dripping.*

The Big Freeze
The Big Slurp
Double Decker Delight
Drip, Droppin' Away
Good Lickin'
Good To The Last Lick
Here's The Scoop
Hey, Good Lickin'
I Scream, You Scream, We All Scream For Ice Cream
Ice Creamilicious
It Takes A Lickin' & Keeps On Drippin'
I've Been Slimmed
Lickin' The Heat
Lickity Licks
Popsicle Face, Hands, Knees, Toes...
Popsicle Smiles/Paradise
Romancing The Ice Cream Cone
Scooped Just For You
Slurpin' & Drippin'
Takin' My Licks

____
____
____
____
____

ILLNESS TITLES

(SEE ALSO DOCTOR & INJURY)

- *Use Bandages, Thermometers, or Needle to create letters.*
- *Sprinkle Red Dots on letters as Rash or Pox title.*

A Bug Got Your Tongue?
An Apple A Day Keeps The Doctor Away
Bad Medicine
I Can Play Connect The Dots With My Dots
Caught A Bug
Chicken Pops/Pox
Connect The Dots *(Pox, Rash or Hives)*
Cranky Critter
A Cute Flu Bug
Doctor, Doctor, Give Me The News...
Doctors Orders
Emotion Sickness
ER Or Bust
Feelin' Funky
Feelin' Stronger Everyday
General Hospital
"Hay" Fever
Healing Hands
Home Sick
How Do You Spell Relief...Rolaids
In Bed With A Bug
In Sickness & In Health
Itch By Itch
I've Got A Rumbly In My Tumbly
I've Got A Sick Feeling
I've Got What?
Just What The Doctor Ordered
Laughter Is The Best Medicine
Life Is Fragile...Handle With Prayer
Love Sick
Maloxx Moment
Mamma Called The Doctor & The Doctor Said...
Miserable...Even On Medication
Moanin' & A Groanin'
Morning Sickness
My Doze Is All Tuffed Up, Bobby!
My Sick Bed
Oh, My Aching...
A Picture Of Health
Polka Dot Tot *(Pox, Rash or Hives)*
Prescription: TLC
Rest, Keep Warm & Drink Liquids...
Road To Recovery
Saturday Night Fever
Say Ahh!
Sea Sickness
I See Spots
Sick & Sad
Sick & Tired
Sick As A Dog
Sick Chick
Sick To My Stomach
So Sexy In My Gown
So, So Sick
S-T-U-F-F-Y
Take 2 Aspirin & Call Me In The Morning
Temperatures A Risen'
There's A Pill For Every Ill, & A Bill For Every Pill
Tissue Time
Under The Weather
When Mommy's Sick...
Worried Sick

____
____
____
____
____

IMAGINATION TITLES

Active Imagination
An Idea Is Salvation By Imagination.
(Frank Lloyd Wright)
Armed With Imagination
Beyond The Walls Of Imagination
Can You Imagine...
Chasing Your Imagination
Devoured By Your Imagination
Figments Of My Imagination
If You Can Imagine It, You Can Achieve It...
(William Arthur Ward)
Imagination & Ambition
Imagination Is Limitless
Imagination Is The Eye Of The Soul.
(Joseph Joubert)
Imagination Is The Highest Kite One Can Fly.
(Lauren Bacall)
Imagination Station
Imagination Will Take You Everywhere.
(Albert Einstein)
Imagine & Believe
To Imagine Is Everything. - *(Anatole France Thibault)*
Imagine That...
The Joy Of Imagination
Just Imagine...
Just My Imagination
Just My Imagination Running Away With Me
Live Out Of Your Imagination. - *(Les Brown)*
The Princess Of Imagination
Pure Imagination
Vivid Imagination
World Of Imagination

INDEPENDENCE DAY TITLES

(SEE FLAG, JULY 4th & PATRIOTIC)

INJURY TITLES

(SEE ALSO DOCTOR, ILLNESS & NURSE)

- *Replace an "I" or "L" with a Bone.*
- *Create letters out of Crutches or Bones.*
- *Make a Doctor's Bag & put title on Bag.*

9-1-1
911 Emergency
Accidents Happen
Against All Odds
The Agony Of De"feet"
Ahh! No More Tonsils
All Bent Out Of Shape *(Broken bones)*
All Broken/Stitched Up
All Thumbs *(Thumb wrapped)*
Bee Patient
Boo Boo Baby
Break It To Me Gently
Broken & Bent/Bruised
Broken Angel
Broken, Confused & Hurt
Bullseye *(Black eye)*
Bumps & Bruises
The "Cast"ing Couch
Cracked Up
Crash & Burn
Emergency Room Or Bust
Fat-Lipped
Feelin' The Pain
General Hospital
Gimmie A Break
Handful Of Pain
Healing Hands
The Healing Touch
Hurt 'N Pain
I Am Stuck On Bandaids, Cause Bandaids Stuck On Me
I Can't See Clearly Now *(Eye Patch)*
I Did A Big Oops!
I Haven't Got Time For The Pain
Insult & Injury
It's A Pain
Just A Pain In The Neck
Knot Head *(Bump on head)*
The Arm *(Any Bone)* Bone Was Connected...
The Leg Bone's Connected To The Hip Bone. *(X-ray)*
Life Is Fragile...Handle With Care!
Major Repair Job
Medical Miracle
Moanin' & Groanin'
Mommy Cried More Than Me
My Boo-Boo
My First Scar
My Guardian Angel Works Overtime

Not Sticks Nor Stones Broke *(Name)* Bones!
Nurses Call The Shots
Nurses Love Me
Oh, My Aching Back
Oh, That Had To Hurt!
On The Mend
On The Road To Recovery
Ooops! I Did It Again *(Injured Again)*
Oopsie Daisy
Operation Ouch
Ouch!
Pain Hurts...But Only For A Minute
Pain In The Neck
The Pain Of Pain
Pain, Pain Go Away
Patched Up *(Eye patch)*
Prescription: Tender Loving Care
Scars Are Tatoo's With Better Stories
Send The Pain Away
Somebody Take The Pain Away
Star Patient
Sticks & Stones Didn't Break My Bones...
Stitch By Stitch
Stitches & Itches
A Stitchin' Time
Super Shiner
Tested The Law Of Gravity & Gravity Won
Them's The Breaks
They Told Me, "Break A Leg" & I Did!
Time Heals All Wounds
Totally Broken
Tough Break
What A Nose Job *(Broken nose)*
Wipe Out
A "Wreck"reational Day
You Didn't Deserve & Break Today
You Got A Break Today
You Keep Me In Stitches

____
____
____
____
____

INSPIRATIONAL TITLES

(SEE ALSO RELIGIOUS)

Ahh! Perfection
Ain't Life Grand?
All That We Have...
All The Wonders You Seek Are Within Yourself. *(Sir Thomas Brown)*
Amazing Grace
Cherish The Moment
Cherish Yesterday...Dream Tomorrow...Live Today
Couldn't Be Prouder
Delight Yourself In The Surprise Of Today
Do Not Wish Upon A Star, Reach For One!
Enchanted Presence
God Closes One Door To Open Another
Good Advice Has No Presence
I Knew You Could Do It
If At First You Don't Succeed...
If You Believe It, You Can Achieve It!
It's Only Me, But I Can Change A Life
Inspirational Insight
Lean On Me
Live In The Moment
Moments Of Discovery
On The Wings Of A Dove
Only The Strong Survive!
Pure & Simple
Reach For The Stars
Splendor In The Grass
Stop & Smell The Roses
Sweet Inspiration
Time Of Inspiration
The Unexamined Life Is Not Worth Living. *(Socrates)*
Way To Go
We Only Have One Life To Live
We're Not Meant To Fit In, We're Meant To Stand Out. - *(Sarah Ban Breathnach)*
When I Count My Blessings, You're Always On My List
Wisdom Begins In Wonder. - *(Socrates)*
Where There's A Will There's A Way
Whispers Of Inspiration
The Wind Beneath My Wings
You Are My Guiding Light
You Light Up My Life
You're Our Inspiration

____
____
____
____
____

INSTRUMENTS TITLES

(SEE DRUMS & MUSIC)

IRISH TITLES

(SEE COUNTRIES-IRELAND/IRISH)

ISLAND TITLES

(SEE ALSO CRUISE, STATES & TRAVEL)

An Island To Ourselves
Blue Island
Deserted Island
Devil's Island
Easter Island
Fantasy Island
Heaven's Island
Island Dreams
Island Gems
Island Girl
Island In A Stream
Island In The Rain
Island In The Sun
Island Memories
Island Of Love
Island Pleasure
Islands Golden Radiance
The Island's Shores
Lonely Island
Love Island
My Sunny Island
No Man's An Island
Oh, This Island In The Sea
On An Island With You...
Peaceful Islands
Perfect Islands
Rocky Island
Sailing The Islands
Summertime Islands
Thunder Island
Treasure Island
Wintering On Coney Island

JEWISH/HANUKKAH/PASSOVER TITLES

(SEE ALSO PRESENTS)

- *Use a Dreidel as an "A" or "O".*
- *Create Menorah use letters as Candle Flames.*
- *Put a Yamaka on a few of the letters.*

100% Kosher
Cantor Can Sing
The Charm Of Chanukkah
Charming Chanukkah
Cuttin' The Challah
Days Of Awe!
I Dream Of A Bright Menorah
Dreidel Days
Dreidel Dee, Dreidel Dah!
Dreidel Do Dah!
Dreidel, Dreidel, I Made It Of Clay
Different From All Other Nights
A Different Night
Eat Your Gelt Wisely
Eight Crazy Days/Nights
Eight Little Candles All In A Row
Eight Little Candles Glitter & Shine
Eight Nights Of Lights
Exodus
Feast Of History
Festival Of Lights
Finding The Afikomen
First Day At Yeshiva
Flicker, Flicker, Little Candles
Gelt Fired Up
Geltalicious
Got Gelt?
Hanukkah Funukkah
Hanukkah Happiness/Happenings
Happy Chanukkah
Happy Christmakkah
Happy Hanukkah
Happiness Is...A Lot Of Gelt
Hava Nagila
I Have A Little Dreidel
Have Kiddish Will Drink
Hip, Hip, Hora!
Holly Jolly Hanukkah
Holy Lights
Hugs & Kisses...Latkes & Knishes
It's A Spin Off *(Dreidel game)*
Joy & Light
Latke's A Sizzlin'
Latkes, Latkes, Good To Eat
Let It Glow, Let It Glow, Let It Glow
The Light Show
Light Up My/Your Life
Lighten Up
These Lights Are Holy
The Lights Of Hanukkah
A Little Gelt Never Hurt
Lotsa Latkes
Magnificent Menorah
May Love & Light Fill Your Home & Heart At Hanukkah.
May The Lights Of Hanukkah Usher In A Better World
Menorah Magic
Menorah Midnight Madness
The Menorah The Merrier
Mozel Tov
Munchin' On Challah
Night Of Sukkot
Nun, Gimel, Heh & Shin, See The Dreidel Spin
Oh, Dreidel, Dreidel, Dreidel
One Candle More
Oh, Light The Candles Bright
One More Candle
Oy Vay!!!
Pasach
Passover Seder
Rejoice In The Festival
See The Dreidel Spin
Shalom
Shine Menorah Shine
Shining Brightly
Spin, Spin, Spin
Star Of David
Star Of David In Heart
Superstar Of David
Tashlich
That Is Psalm Cantor!
Tiny Lights Shining Bright
A Tree Of Life
Yakkin' In Yiddish *(Older generation pics)*
Yakkin' Yiddish
Yamaka, Yamaka...Look Who's Got One Now!
You Light Up My Life *(Lit Menorah)*

JOY TITLES

Bundle Of Joy
Child Of Joy
Fields Of Joy
First Joy
I Got The Joy
House Of Joy
Joy & Peace In Believing
Joy & Wonder
Joy In The Journey
Joy In The Presence Of Angels
Joy Is A Flower That Blooms When You Do
Joy Is Beauty Forever
Joy Is Not In Things, It Is In Us. - *(Richard Wagner)*
Joy Is The Feeling Of Grinning On The Inside. - *(Dr. Melba Colgrove)*
Joy Is The Grace We Say To God. - *(Jean Ingelow)*
The Joy Of A Spirit Is The Measure Of Its Power. - *(Ninon de Lenclos)*
Joy Of Innocence
Joy Labor
Joy Of Loving
Joy Of My Soul
A Joy That's Shared Is A Joy Made Double
Joy To The World
Joyful Girl
Joyful Life
The Joyful Sounds Of You
The Joys Of Love
The Joys Of Youth
Jump For Joy
Let Joy & Innocence Prevail
Moments Of Joy
My Secret Joy
Pride & Joy
Release The Joy
Sea Of Joy
Song Of Joy
Surprised By Joy
I Wish You All The Joy That You Can Wish. *(William Shakespeare)*
I Wish You Joy
You Are My Joy
You Bring Me Joy

JUMP/JUMPING/HOP TITLES

- *Make a dotted Hopping Trail under title words with a Frog at the end.*

By Leaps & Bounds
C'mon & Jump
Crazy Country Hop
Do The Bunny Hop
Don't Worry, Be Hoppy
Free Falling
Get Up & Jump
Go Jump In A Lake
High Jumper
Hip Hop
A Hop, Skip & A Jump Away
Is This Leap Year?
Jump Back
Jump In With Both Feet
Jump Master Says, Go! Go! Go!
Jump Start
Jump To The Beat...
Jump Up...Jump Back
Jumpin' For Joy
Jumpin' Jive
Jumpin' Junipers
Jumping Beans
Jumping Jaxs
Jumping Out Of The Fire & Into The Frying Pan
A Leap Of Faith
Let's Go To The Hop
Look Before You Leap
Puddle Jumper
Soc Hop

JUNGLE TITLES

(SEE ANIMALS, ZOO & SOME SPECIFIC ANIMALS)

K K K K K K K K K K K K K K K K K K K K K K K K K K K K K K

KARATE TITLES

(SEE MARTIAL ARTS)

KIDS TITLES

(SEE CHILDREN)

KING TITLES

(SEE ROYALTY)

KISS TITLES

(SEE ALSO HEART, HUGS & LOVE)

- *Use Puckered Lips to replace word Kiss.*
- *Surround title with a border of X's & O's.*

Angel Kisses
At First Kiss...
Baby Kisses
Butterfly Kisses
Candy Kisses
Caught Smoochin'
Could I Have This Kiss Forever?
Cuddles & Kisses
Eskimo Kisses
Everytime I Kiss You...
First Kiss
Friends Are Kisses Blown To Us By Angels
Gimmie A Kiss
Gimmie Some Sugar
Give Me Some Lip
Give Me Some Sugar Baby
Hello Sweet Lips
Hold Me, Thrill Me, Kiss Me
Hold You, Love You, Kiss You
Hot Lips
Housework Can Wait, My Kids Need Kisses
How About A Kiss
Hugs & Kisses
Hugs & Kisses & A Star For Wishes
Innocent Kiss
Is Not A Kiss The Very Autograph Of Love. *(Henry Finck)*
It's In His/Her Kiss
Just How Many Toads Do I Have To Kiss?
Just Kiss Me
Just One Kiss
Just One Little Kiss
Kiss & Make Up
Kiss & Tell
I Kiss Better Than I Cook
A Kiss Can Beautify Souls, Hearts & Thoughts
A Kiss For Luck
A Kiss Is A Jumper Cable To The Heart
A Kiss Is Just A Kiss
Kiss Me At Midnight
Kiss Me Baby
Kiss Me Crazy
Kiss Me Quick
Kiss Me Softly
Kiss Me Tender
Kiss Me Under The Mistletoe
Kiss Me You Fool
Kiss My Grits
The Kiss Of A Lifetime
Kiss Of Love
Kiss The Bride
Kiss The Girl
A Kiss To Build A Dream On
A Kiss To Remember
A Kiss Worth A 1,000 Words
Kissable
Kisses & Hugs
Kisses $1.00
Kisses From An Angel
Kisses Sweeter Than Wine
Kissing Cousins
Let's Kiss Like Angels Do
Like A Kiss From A Rose
Lipstick Kisses
One Kiss For Old Time's Sake
Our First Kiss
Perfect Kiss
Planting Two Lips
Prelude To A Kiss
Pucker Power
Pucker Up
Pucker Up & Kiss Me
Sealed With A Kiss
Smack Attack
Smooches Gracias
Smoochin'
So Kissable
Soul Meets Soul On Lovers Lips. - *(Percy Shelley)*
It Started With A Kiss
Sucking Face
Sun-Kissed
S-W-A-K!!!
Sweet Smooches
This Kiss...
I Wanna Kiss You All Over
When We Kiss...
When You Kiss Me...
World's Best Kisser
You Fill Our Days With Hugs & Kisses

Your Kiss I Can't Resist. - *(Faith Hill)*
Your Kiss Is Not Just A Kiss
Yuck, Cooties!
(Name & Name) Sittin' In A Tree, K-I-S-S-I-N-G!

KITCHEN TITLES

(SEE ALSO COOKING, COOKOUT & FOOD)
A Clean Kitchen Is The Sign Of A Wasted Life
Keep This Kitchen Clean...Eat Out!
I Love A Man With Dishpan Hands!
Make Yourself At Home; Clean My Kitchen!
A Messy Kitchen Is A Sign Of A Good Meal
Mom's Cafe...Open 24 hours!
The Dishes Are Done So Please Go Away!

KITE TITLES

- *Make a Kite & put the title inside of it.*
- *Use titles letters to create the Kite Tail.*

Aim High
The Art Of Kite Flying...
A Boy & His Kite
Come Fly A Kite & Watch It Sail
Flyin' High
Flying In The Wind
Go Fly A Kite
Gone With The Wind
Have Kite & String...Will Fly
High As A Kite
High Hopes
High In The Sky
Higher & Higher
I Flew A Kite Up In The Sky!
If At First You Don't Succeed, Fly, Fly Again!
Kite Dreams
Kite Flying Crazy
Kite Flying Fun
Kite, Kite Soaring High
Mile High Club
My New Kite
Sail Away
Sky Bound
Soaring Above The Trees
Swooping & Swirling & 'Round You Go
Up, Up & Away
The Wind Took The Sail Out Of The Kite

KNITTING TITLES

(SEE ALSO CROCHETING, QUILTING & SEWING)

- *Use Knitting Needles as "I", "L", or "T".*
- *Spell out title using a Ball of Yarn.*

All Tied Up At The Moment
Blanket Statement
Close Knit Family/Friends
Got The Knitty Gritty
Happy Hooker
Hook, Yarn & Knitter
I Sits & I Knits
I Think Knit
I'll Be Yarned! *(Cat playing with yarn)*
I'm Sittin' & Knittin'
Knit Head!
Knit Me!
Knit One, Pearl Two
Knit Wit
Knitty But Nice!
Memories Knitted In Love

KNOT TITLES

All In Knots
All Knotted Up
All Tied Up At The Moment
Connecting The Knots
Fit To Be Tied
I Think Knot!
Knot Head *(Bump on head)*
Knot Me!
Knots Of Love
Knots On My Noggin
The Knots That Bind Us
Knotty But Nice!
Love Knots
My Hands Are Tied
Tied Up In Knots
The Ties That Bind Us
Tying The Knot
With One Hand Tied Behind My Back...

KWANZAA TITLES

7 Days...7 Principles...7 Symbols
Celebrate For Seven Days
Celebrating Family, Community & Culture
First Kwanzaa
Got The Kwanzaa Spirit
Habari Gani - "What's The News?"
In Union There Is Strength
Kwanzaa Fest
Kwanzaa Karamu
Kwanzaa, Kwanzaa Time For Good Cheer
Let's Let The Holiday Shine
Light A Glowing Candle Every Night
Lighting The Kinara
Many Hands Make Light Work
Merry Kwanzanukamas
Red, Green & Black...Kwanzaa Is Here
Spirit Of Kwanzaa
The Story Of Kwanzaa
Strive For Discipline, Dedication & Achievement
The Time Is Always Right To Do What Is Right
A Time To Reflect On The Past
Zawadi For Everyone

FLAG COLOR'S MEANINGS

BLACK...for the People
RED...for the Struggle
GREEN...for the Future & Hope that comes from their struggle

KWANZAA CELEBRATION INFO:

KWANZAA PRINCIPLES - NGUZO SABA

Kwanzaa is based on the Nguzo Saba *(7 guiding principles)*, one for each day of the observance & is celebrated from December 26th to January 1st.

- Umoja - (OO-MO-JAH) - *Dec. 26* - Unity
- Kujichagulia - (KOO-GEE-CHA-GOO-LEE-YAH) *Dec. 27* - Self Determination
- Ujima - (OO-GEE-MAH) - *Dec. 28* Collective Work & Responsibility
- Ujamaa - (OO-JAH-MAH) - *Dec. 29* Cooperative Economics
- Nia - (NEE-YAH) - *Dec. 30* - Purpose
- Kuumba - (KOO-OOM-BAH) - *Dec. 31* Creativity
- Imani - (EE-MAH-NEE) - *Jan. 1* - Faith

KWANZAA'S SEVEN SYMBOLS

Mishumaa - 7 candles (3 red, 3 green, 1 black), standing for Kwanzaa's seven principles.
Kinara - a candle holder, representing the stalk of corn from which the family grows.
Mkeka - a straw placemat, recalling tradition & history.
Mazao - a variety of fruit, symbolizing the harvest.
Vibunzi - an ear of corn for each child, celebrating the child's potential.
Kikombe Cha umoja - a cup of unity, commemorating one's ancestors.
Zawadi - modest gifts, encouraging creativity, achievement & success.

KARAMU PROGRAM *(CELEBRATION)*

Kukaribisha - *Welcoming*
Kuumba - *Remembering*
Kuchunguza Tena Na Kutoa Ahadi Tena *Reassessment and Recommitment*
Kushangilla - *Rejoicing*

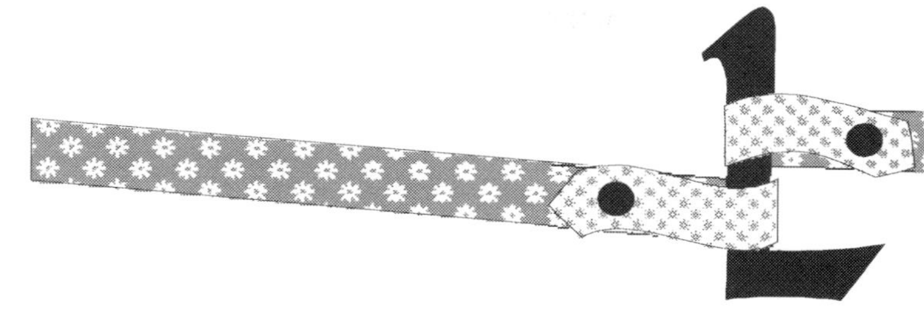

L L L L L L L L L L L L L L L L L L L L L L L L L L L L L L L L

LABOR DAY TITLES

A Laborless Day
All Play & No Work Today
Celebrating A Workless Day
The End Of Labor Is To Gain Leisure
No Work On This Labor Day

LADY BUG TITLES

(SEE ALSO BUGS)
I'm The Lady Of This Garden
Lady Bug, Lady Bug Fly Away Home
Lady Bug Lane
Lady Bug Of The Garden
Lady Bugs Welcome Here
Little Lady
Little Lady Bug
Pretty Little Ladies

LAUGH/LAUGHING TITLES

(SEE ALSO SMILE)
A Baby's Laughter Is Music To A Mother's Heart
Between A Laugh & A Tear
A Child's Laughter...
C'mon Get Happy
Color Me Happy
A Day Is Lost If One Has Not Laughed
Falling Into A Giggle
Funny Business
A Giggle A Day, Keeps The Gloomies Away!
Giggle Box
Giggle If You Want To
Giggles Down To Your Tummy
Giggles 'N Grins
Gigglin' Girls
A Glad Heart Makes A Cheerful Countenance. *(Proverbs 15:13)*
He Who Laughs Last, Laughs Best
Here's Laughin' At You Kid!
I Only Wanna Laugh
It Was Not A Laugh But Merely A Loud Smile
I've Never Seen A Smiling Face That Was Not Beautiful
Laugh & The World Laughs With You
A Laugh A Day Makes Everything Okay!
Laugh A Little
Laugh At Life
A Laugh A Minute
A Laugh Is A Smile That Bursts. - *(Mary H. Waldrip)*
Laugh Loudly & Often
Laugh Often...Love Much
Laugh Out Loud
Laugh It Up
Laughing All The Way...
Laughter Enriches Our Souls
Laughter Is An Instant Vacation. - *(Milton Berle)*
Laughter Is The Best Medicine
Let Laughter Dance Across Your Face
Live Well...Laugh Often...Love Much
I Love To Laugh
I Love Your Laugh
Major Belly Laugh
Sharing Laughs & Giggles
Should I Laugh Or Cry?
A Smile Is Just A Whisper Of A Laugh
Tickled Pink
Tickles & Giggles
We Love To Laugh
What A Great Laugh
When I Hear You Laugh...
With Laughing Eyes...
You Make Me Laugh

LAW TITLES

- *Create a title mat in the shape of a Badge & put title on it.*
- *Put a Cop's Hat on a few of the letters.*

Above The Law
Adam 12
Always Ready
Angel In Blue
Anything You Say Can & Will Be Used Against You...
Bad Boys
Bad Boys, Bad Boys, Whatcha Gonna Do When They Come For You?
Backyard Bandit
The Best Never Rest
Book 'Em
Boys In Blue
Breaking The Law Of Love
Car *(54)* Where Are You?
Committed To Excellence

Committed To Our Community
Copper
Cops
Divine Law
Down By The Station
Dragnet
Faithful Unto Death
The Few Dedicated To The Many
Fearless Of Danger
Fighting The Las
I Fought The Law...
Got A Badge!
Here Comes The Fuzz
Hey! Mr. Police Man
I Am The Law!!!
I Know My/Your Rights
It's The Law
Law & Grace
Law & Order
The Law Maker
Law Of Gravity
Law Of Nature
Law Of Opposites
Law Of The Land
Layin' Down The Law
Let None Live In Fear
License & Registration Please?
Long Arm Of The Law
Love & Law
The Man/Woman Behind The Shield
Martial Law
Men In Blue
The Men In Uniform
Miami Vice
The Mod Squad
Murphy's Law
NYPD Blue *(Use any city)*
Officer *(Child's name)*
Our Community, Our Commitment
Police Line - Do Not Cross
Pride, Commitment, & Service
Protection & Assistance
Public Safety, It's What We Do
Put Your Hands In The Air
The Rookies
Service For Others
Serving The Community
Sheriff Of Everything
Spiritual Law
Step Away From The Vehicle
SWAT
To Serve & Protect
Today's In Uniform
Top Cop
The Untouchables
We Aim To Please
We Hold Thee Safe
We're Only A Phone Call Away
We're There When You Need Us
What You Call A Hero, I Call Just Doing My Job
You Have The Right To Remain Silent...
You Make My Heart Beat
(City initials) PD Blue
(Your town or Surname) Street Blues

______

______

______

______

______

LEADERSHIP TITLES

All Roads Lead Me To You
Born Leader
Fearsome Leader
The Flickering Stars Will Lead The Way
Follow The Leader
I Will Lead You
I'll Follow Your Lead
In The Life Of Which I Lead
Lead Her/Him Lord
Lead Me, Guide Me
Lead Me On
To Lead The People, Walk Behind Them. *(Lao-Tzu)*
Leader By Choice
A Leader Is A Dealer In Hope
A Leader Leads By Example
Leader Of Love
Leader Of Men
Leader Of The Band
Leader Of The Pack
Leadership Is Action, Not Position
Leading The Way
Let God Lead The Way
Let Me Lead
Let Your Heart Lead Your Mind
The Life You Lead
The Lost Leader
Love Will Lead You Back
There Are Leaders & There Are Followers
This Life I Lead
Your Heart Will Lead You Home

______

______

______

______

______

LIFE/LIVE TITLES

Ain't Life Grand?
Ain't Life Sweet?
All American Life
All My Life...
And So Is Life
And This Is Life
At The Speed Of Life
Beautiful Life
Believe In Life
Best Of My Life
The Best Things In Life Are Free...
The Best Things In Life Are Not Free, But Priceless. - *(Benjamin Lichtenburg)*
Big As Life
The Bright Side Of Life...
Can't Live Without Your Love
Celebrate The Moments Of Your Life
Celebrate Your Life
Change Of Life
Cherish Yesterday, Dream Of Tomorrow, Live For Today!
Circle Of Life
City Life
Color My Life
Colors Of My Life
The Country Life
Crazy Life
A Day In The Life Of...
Days Of Our Lives
A Design For Life
Don't Dream Your Life, Live Your Dreams
Downtown Life
Embrace The Mystery Of All You Can Be
Enjoy A Slice Of Life
Enjoy Life...It's Delicious
Everyday Life
Face Your Life Head On
The Facts Of Life
Fantastic Life
For Once In My Life...
Get A Life
The Good Life
Got A New Lease On Life
High On Life
In The High Life
It Is Not The Length Of Life, But Depth Of Life
It's A Hard Knock Life
It's A Wonderful Life
It's Just Life...Just Live It. - *(Terri Guillemets)*
It's The Little Things In Life That Matter
Joyful Life
Just Once In My Life...
Kiss Of Life
Larger Than Life
Let The Sun Set On Our Lives
Let's Live For Today
Life Can Be So Sweet
Life In The City
Life In The Fast Lane
Life Is A Collection Of Moments
Life Is A Great Bundle Of Little Things. *(Oliver Wendell Holmes)*
Life Is A Journey
Life Is A Journey, Not A Destination
Life Is A Party
Life Is A Roller Coaster
Life Is A Song...So Sing Along
Life Is A Work Of Art & We Are Its Artists
Life Is Now...This Day, This Hour. *(Charles Macomb Flandrau)*
Life Is Sweet
Life Is The Game That Must Be Played. *(Edwin Arlington Robinson)*
Life Isn't A Matter Of Milestones, But Of Moments. - *(Rose Fitzgerald Kennedy)*
Life Of Leisure
A Life Of Our Own
Life On My Own
Life's A Dream
Life's A Picnic
Light Of My Life
Live & Learn
Live & Let Live
Live A Life Of Love
Live As Though There Is No Tomorrow
Live Every Moment
I Live For You
I Live For Your Love
Live Free
Live It Up
Live Life As Though Heaven Is On Earth
Live Life To The Fullest
Live Well...Laugh Often...Love Much!
Live Your Dreams
Livin' On The Bright Side Of Life
Livin' The High Life
Look On The Bright Side Of Life
Lover Of Life
Lovin' The Finer Things In Life
Lovin' The Night Life
Lust For Life
May You Live All The Days Of Your Life *(Jonathon Swift)*
Maybe She's Born With It
My Life...My Love
My Mission In Life...
A New Life Begins...

An Ordinary Life
Prism Of Life
Reflections Of My Life
Rhythm Of Life
A Sailor's Life
The Secret Of Life
The Simple Life
The Story Of My Life
Storybook Life
There Is No Wealth But Life. - *(John Ruskin)*
The Time Of My Life
This Is The Life
This Is Your Life
The Unexamined Life Is Not Worth Living. *(Socrates)*
Variety Is The Spice Of Life
The Way We Live
Where There Is Love, There is Life. *(Mahatma Ghandi)*
Wild Side Of Life
You Are The Author Of Your Own Life Story
You Are The Sunshine Of My Life
You Light Up My Life
You Light Up My Way

LIGHTHOUSE TITLES

- *Put a small Lighthouse off to the side, make glow from Lighthouse of vellum spreading across page & put title in light's glow.*

Beacon Of Safety
Coast On In
Eye Of The Seas
The Flickering Light On The Sea
Follow The Light
A Friendly Light
From Far Away...A Friendly Light
A Glow In The Night
Guiding Light
A Guiding Star In The Night
Keep The Light Shining
Let The Lighthouse Shine
Let Us Walk In The Light Of The Lord. *(Isaiah 2:5)*
A Light In The Night
The Lighthouse Beacon Of Safety
The Lighthouse Down By The Sea
Lighthouse In The Night
The Lighthouse Of The Lord
A Lighthouse Tale
Lighthouses Blow No Horns; They Only Shine. *(D. L. Moody)*
Lighthouses...Guides To Friendly Harbors
The Lighthouses Promise To See
Lightin' Up The Night So Bright
Long Point Light
The Lord Is My Light & Salvation. - *(Psalm 27:1)*
The Lord My God Will Enlighten My Darkness. *(Psalm: 18-28)*
A Nighttime Glow
Oh, Little Lighthouse
The Old Lighthouse
The Path Of The Just Is As The Shining Light. *(Proverbs 4:18)*
Safe Harbor
Shining Brightly
Shining On Midnight Shores
Signal In The Sea
The Watchman In The Lighthouse

LOVE TITLES

(SEE ALSO ANNIVERSARY, DATING, ENGAGEMENT, HEART, HUGS, KISS & WEDDING)

- *Use a Heart in place of an "O" or in place of entire word Heart.*
- *Loop together 2 Heart frames to show hearts are connected.*
- *Make a Heart with an Arrow thru it & Cupid off to the side.*

A Love Story
A Piece Of My Heart
A Time For Love
ABC...123...Baby You & Me
Addicted To Love
Afternoon Delight
Always
Always & Forever
Always On My Mind
All I Ever Need Is You
All I Have To Give...
All My Love
All You Need Is Love
Amor or Amour
...And They Called It Puppy Love
Anticipation *(Waiting or getting ready for 1st date)*
April Love
As Long As You Love Me...
At Last My Love Has Come
Babe

Basketful Of Love
Be Still My Heart
Beautiful In My Eyes
Beauty & The Beast
Because You Loved Me
Best Of My Love
The Best Thing To Hold Onto In The World Is...Each Other
Bit By The Love Bug
The Bonds Of Love
Born To Give My Love To You
Boy Meets Girl
By Your Side
Can You Feel The Love Tonight?
Can't Buy Me Love
Can't Fight This Feeling
Can't Help Falling In Love With You
Can't Take My Eyes Off You
Carryin' Your Love With Me
The Circle Of Love Is Never Ending
Close Enough To Perfect For Me
Close To My Heart
Close To You
Color The World With Love
Crazy For You
I Cross My Heart
C-R-U-S-H
Cupid's Bullseye
A Diamond Is Forever
Do You Believe In Magic?
I Don't Need Anything But You
A Dream Come True
Dream Lover
A Dream That Is Dreamed By Two Will Always Come True
In Dreams & In Love, There Are No Impossibilities. - *(Janos Arnay)*
Each Sunrise Is Another To Love You
Easy Love
Endless Love
Eternal Flame
Ever After
Ever Lasting Love
Every Beat Of My Heart
Every Day I Fall More In Love With You
Every Heart Beats True
Faith...Hope...Love...
Faithfully
Fallin'
Falling For You
Falling In Love Again
Filled To The Brim With Love
First Love
First Love...Last Love
First Time Ever I Saw Your Face
For All Eternity
For The Love Of You
Forever Your Girl/Guy
Forever Yours
I Found My Prince Charming
Funny Face I Love You
The Gift Of Love
Girl Meets Boy
The Glory Of Love
God Blessed Me With You
God Must Have Spent A Little More Time On You
The Greatest Of These Is Love
A Groovy Kind Of Love
Grow Old Along With Me, The Best Is Yet To Be. - *(Robert Browning)*
Happy Hearts
Have I Told You Lately That I Love You?
He Loves Me...He Loves Me!
He Loves Me A Lot...So We Tied The Knot
Head Over Heals For You
Head Over Heals In Love
Heart Attacked
Heart-Felt Love
A Heart Full Of Love
The Heart That Loves Is Always Young
Hearts Afire
Heart's Desire
He's Making Eyes at Me
Home Is Where My Honey Is
Hopelessly Devoted To You
How Beautiful Is The Day That Is Touched By Love!
How Deep Is Your Love
How Do I Love Thee, Let Me Count The Ways
How Right It Is To Love You
How Sweet It Is To Be Loved By You
Hug Me
Hugs & Kisses
Hugs & Kisses, Please
Hugs & Kisses, Stars For Wishes
Hugs Handed Out Here
I Can't Give You Anything But Love
I Can't See Me Lovin' Anyone But You
I Can't See Me Lovin' Nobody But You
I Do It For You, {Everything I Do}
I Do Love You
I Don't Mind The Thorns If You're The Rose
I Don't Want To Miss A Thing
I Feel For You
I Got You Babe
I Honestly Love You
I Just Called To Say, "I Love You"

I Just Fall In Love Again
I Just Want To Be Your Everything
I Love The Way You Love Me
I Love To See You Smile
I Love You For Sentimental Reasons
I Love You More Today Than Yesterday...
I Love You This Big
I Love You To The Moon & Back
I Love You With All My Heart & Soul
I Love Your Way
I Loved You The First Moment I Saw You
I Melt With You
I Need Love
I Only Have Eyes For You
I Think I Love You
I Wanna Hold Your Hand
I Want To Know What Love Is
I Want You To Want Me
I Will Always Love You
I Wish You Love
I Would Die 4 U
I'd Do Anything For Love
If That Isn't Love...
If This Isn't Love...
I'll Be There
I'll Be There For You
I'll Go One Loving You For Always
I'll Make Love To You
I'll Stand By You
I'm All Yours
I'm Gonna Be Warm This Winter With Your Love
I'm Having A "Heart" Attack
I'm My Beloveds & He's/She's Mine
I'm Stuck On You
I'm Walkin' On Sunshine
I'm Yours
In A Heartbeat
In A Tender Moment Like This
In The Mood For Love
In This Life I Was Loved By You
In Your Eyes
Is This Love
Islands In The Stream
Isn't She Lovely?!
It Had To Be You...
It Must Have Been Love
It's Gotta Be You
It's In The Kiss
I've Been Waiting For A Girl/Guy Like You
Just For You My Heart Beats
Just The Two Of Us
Keep On Loving You
Keep True To The Dreams Of Thy Youth.
(J. F. von Schiller)
Key To My Heart
Kiss Me
Laugh Often...Love Much
Let Love Bloom
Let Love Guide Your Heart
Let Me Call You Sweetheart
Let There Be Love
Let's Get It On
Let's Stay Together
Life Is Sweeter Because Of You
Life Is The Song...Love Is The Music
A Life Of Love
Light My Fire
Live Well, Laugh Often, Love Much
Loads Of Love
Lookin' For Love
Looks Like We Made It
Lost In Love
Lost In Love's Embrace
Lovable, Snuggable Hugs To You
Love & The Whole World Loves With You
Love As Though You've Never Been Hurt
Love At First Sight
Love Bears All Things
Love Birds
Love Blooms Here
The Love Bug
Love Can Build A Bridge Between Your Heart & Mine
Love Can't Ever Get Better Than This
Love Comforts Like Sunshine After Rain
Love Conquers All
Love Each Day That You Live
Love 'Em Anyway
Love Hurts
Love In Bloom
Love In The Afternoon
Love Is...
Love Is A Dream For Two Lives To Share
Love Is...A Friendship Caught On Fire
Love Is...A Friendship Set To Music
Love Is...A Gift We Can Give Every Day
Love Is...A Wonderful Thing
Love Is...A Work Of Heart
Love Is, Above All, The Gift Of Oneself
Love Is...All You Need
Love Is...Everlasting
Love Is...Heaven-Sent
Love Is In The Air
Love Is Like A Violin
Love Is Love's Reward
Love Is...Nature's Second Sun

Love Is Not A Word; It's The World. - *(Dev Kishore)*
Love Is On Its Way
Love Is...One Heart, One Soul, One Life
Love Is...Patient, Love Is Kind
Love Is...Pulling Together Against All Odds
Love Is Spoken Here
Love Supreme
Love Is...The Celebration Of A Miracle
Love Is...The Key That Opens The Heart
Love Is...The Open Door To The Fullness Of Life
Love Is...The Poetry Of The Senses. *(Honoré de Balzac)*
Love Is...The Power That Gives Us Wings To Soar
Love Is...The Purpose For Living!
Love Is...The Secret Ingredient In The Recipe Of Life
Love Is...The Thread Of Life
Love Is...The Thread That Ties Us All Together
Love Is...The Work Of The Heart
Love Is...What The Heart Wants
Love Isn't Love 'Til You Give It Away
Love Letters
Love Lights The Hearts Of Those Who Share It
Love Makes Life Complete
Love Makes Life Richer
Love Makes The World Go 'Round
Love Makes The Whole World Wonderful
Love Me & The World Is Mine. - *(David Reed)*
Love Me Tender
Love Me True
Love Notes
The Love Of My Life
Love On A Hot Afternoon
Love One Another
Love Sealed With A Kiss
Love Sick
Love So Fine
Love Story
Love Struck
Love Ties Our Hearts Together
Love To Love You Baby
Love Via AOL
Love Will Find A Way
Love Will Keep Us Alive
Love Will Keep Us Together
Love Ya
I'll Love You For All Of Time
I'll Love You For Always
I'll Love You Forever
Lover's Lane
Lover's Leap
Love's Got A Hold On Me
Mad About You
Magic Moments
Magic Moon
Man Of My Dreams
Marriage Is A School Of Love
A Match Made In Heaven
Matters Of The Heart
May Love Be Your Angel
Maybe I'm Amazed
Mi' Amor
Moonlight Madness
Moonlight Serenade
More Than A Feeling
More Than Wonderful
More Than Words
Music Of The Heart
Must Be Love
My Best Friend...My Love
My Eyes Adore You
My Girl/Guy
My Favorite Place Is Inside Your Hug
My Heart Belongs To Mommy/Daddy
My Heart Explodes For You
My Heart Flutters For You
My Heart Is Full Of Love For You
My Knight In Shining Armor
My One & Only
My Love For You Is Like A Circle, It Has No End
My Love Is A River Running Soul Deep
No Words Are Necessary Between Two Loving Hearts
Nobody But You For Me
Nobody Loves Me Like...
Nothing Compares Two You
Oh How We Love
Old Flames Don't Hold A Candle To You
I Only Have Eyes For You
Only You
Opposites Attract
Our Love Goes Forward On The Wings Of Love
Our Love Grow More Each Day
Our Love Is Here To Stay
Our Love Is Poetry To My Heart
Our Love Is Tied With Heartstrings
Our Love Lights Up My Life
Playing For Keeps
The Power Of Love
Prisoner Of Love
P. S. - I Love You
Puppy Love
Ready For Romance
Respect Is Love In Plain Clothes
Romance 101

Safe In The Arms Of Love
Save The Best For Last
Sealed With A Kiss
Seasons Of Love
Share A Little Love
Sharing My Love
She Loves Me A Lot...So We Tied The Knot
She's Got A Way
Signed, Sealed, Delivered, I'm Yours
Simply Irresistible
So In Love
So Much In Love
So This Is Love
Soaring On The Wings Of Love
Some Like It Hot
Somebody Loves You
Someone To Love
State Of The Heart
Sweetheart
Sweetie Pie
That's The Way Love Goes
There Will Never Be Another You
There's Just Something About You I Love
Thief Of Hearts
This I Promise You
This Is What Love Looks Like...
This Love Will Shine
This Thing Called Love
Thou Art To Me A Delicious Torment.
(Ralph Waldo Emerson)
Thoughts Of You Always Make Me Smile
Thru The Eyes Of Love
Thumbody Loves Me/You
Time Cannot Touch Two Hearts That Truly Love
Time Stands Still With Your Love
Time That Is Not Spent Loving Is Waisted
To Be In Love Is To Surpass One's Self
To Be With You
To Know Him Is To Love Him
Together Forever
Together Is A Wonderful Place To Be
Together Times
Tons Of Love
Too Much Of A Good Thing Is Wonderful
Total Eclipse Of The Heart
Touched By love
Traces Of Love
True Love
True Love Doesn't End!
True Love Is A Treasure
True Love Never Grows Old
Two Hearts Become One
Unconditional Love
Undying Love
Unforgettable
Vision Of Love
We Belong
We Fit Together Perfectly
We Go Together Like A Wink & A Smile
We Got An "A" In Chemistry
What The World Needs Now...Is Love Sweet Love!
When A Man Loves A Woman
When I Count My Blessings I Count You Twice
When I Fall In Love...It Will Be Forever
When I Look Into Your Eyes...
When I See You Smile...
When I'm With You...
Where Is The Love?
Where There Is Love, There Is Life.
(Mahatma Ghandi)
Whole Lotta Love
Wild Thing, I Think I Love You
Wild Thing, You Make My Heart Sing
Will Always Love You
With Loving Hearts!
With You I'm Born Again
With You Is Where I Like To Be
The Woman Of My Dreams
Wonderful Tonight
Wonderland Of Love
Words Spoken In Love Live Forever In Memory
A World Of Our Own
www.iloveyou.com
XOXOXOXOX
You & Me & Me & You...
You & Me...So Happy Together
You & You Alone Are So Beautiful
You Are My Destiny
You Are My Favorite Pastime
You Are So Beautiful To Me
You Are The Light Of My Life
You Are The Sunshine Of My Life
You Are The Sunshine That Starts My Day
You Are The Wind Beneath My Wings
You Beat Any Dream I've Ever Had
You Belong To Me
You Complete Me
You Complete My Heart
You Decorate My Life
You Fill My Day With Sunshine
You Fill Our Days With Hugs & Kisses
You Had Me From Hello
You Have A Smile That Lights Up The World
You Have My Heart In Your Hand
You Hold The Key To My Heart
You Light Up My Life
You Look So Good In Love

You Make My Heart Leap
You Make My Heart Sing
You Mean The World To Me
You Say It Best When You Say Nothing At All
You Stole My Heart
You Take My Breath Away
You Taught Me The Meaning Of Love
Young Love
Your Love Hits The Bull's Eye
Your Love Is Magic
Your Love Is The Music Of My Heart
Your Love Keeps Lifting Me Higher
Your Love's So Bright, I Have To Wear Shades
You're Always In My Heart
You're An Angel In My Eyes
You're Close Enough To Perfect For Me
You're In My Heart
You're My Best Friend
You're My Soul & Inspiration
You're Still The One
You're The First, The Last, My Everything
You're The Million Reasons Love's Reflecting
In My Eyes. - *(Faith Hill)*
You're The One That I Want
You've Captured My Heart
You've Got A Way With Me
You've Made Life A Song

LUCK TITLES

All The Luck In The World
As Luck Would Have It...
Beginner's Luck
Better Luck Next Time
Blessed Or Lucky?
Blind Luck
Born To Be Lucky
Down On My/Your Luck
I Feel Lucky
Feeling Lucky
Good Luck
Good Luck Charm
Happy Go Lucky
Hard Luck Story
How Lucky I Am
Irish Luck
Just My Luck
Lady Luck
Love & Luck
Luck Be A Lady
Luck Be With You
Luck O' The Irish
Luck Of The Draw
Lucky Charm
A Lucky Day
Lucky Duck
Lucky In Love
Lucky Me
The Lucky Ones
Lucky You
My Lucky Day
Out Of Luck
Sheer Luck
Some Have All The Luck
Stroked Of Luck
Thank Your Lucky Stars...
With A Little Luck...
You're My Lucky Star

MAD TITLES

(SEE CRYING & SAD)

C'mon Get Happy
Fit To Be Tied
I Just Wanna Be Mad
I'm Going Mad
Love You Madly
Mad About You
Mad As A Hornet
Mad Dog
Mad House
Mad, Mad Little Man
Mad Man
Madder Than A Wet Hen
Madly In Love
Please Don't Cry
So Crabby
Sour Puss
Truly, Madly, Deeper

MAGIC TITLES

- *Create a Black Hat with a Rabbit peeking out of the top of it & put the title on the hat.*
- *Create a Magicians Wand tapping the top of the title with sparkles around it.*

Abra Kadabra
All I Want Is Magic
...And For My Next Trick!
As If By Magic...
Black Magic
Black Magic Woman
Caught Up In The Magic
Could It Be Magic
Do You Believe In Magic?
Every Little Thing She Does Is Magic
Games Of Magic
He's A Magic Man
He's Got Magic
I Was Made To Love Magic
In The Hand Of A Magic Man...
Is This Magic?
It's Magic!
Let's Make Some Magic
Little Miss Magic
A Little Thing Called Magic
Magic Hands
The Magic I Wish...
The Magic In My Hands
There's Magic In The Air
Magic In The Night
Magic Man
This Magic Moment
The Magic Of A Heart Beat
Magic Of Love
The Magic That You Do
The Magic Touch
Magical Hands
The Magical Hour
Magical Kind Of Love
Magical Moments
Magical Mystery
Magical Nights
Magical Touch
Make A Little Magic
Oh, What Sweet Magic You Make
That Old Black Magic
Once Upon A Magic Show
This Only Looks Easy!
Simply Magic
Spell Bound
Strange Magic
Teenie Houdini
Under Your Magic Spell
What Are The Magic Words?
You've Got Us Spell Bound

MARDI GRAS TITLES

- *Create a string of Green, Gold, or Purple beads to encircle the title.*
- *Create title words with a string of beads.*
- *Use colored coins in place of an "O".*

Beaded Babes
The Beaded One
Beaded Wonder
Beads, Bangles & Bobbles
Beads, Cups, Doubloons & Coins, Oh My!
Been Bejeweled
Bit The Baby
Bouef Gras
Bourbon Street Treat
Deplumed
Donned By Doubloons
Epiphany Season
Fas Do Do Fun
Fat Tuesday *(French for Mardi Gras)*
The Feast Of The Three Holy Kings
Flogged By Favors
In The Land Of Dixie

It's All About The Plumes
Jester Fun
Jambalaya Hoopla
Jumbo Gumbo
Just Bead Me
King Cake For A Queen
King's Day
Little Christmas Day
Lundi Gras *(Fat Monday)*
Mardi Gras Madness
Masked Maiden
Masked Man
Masquerade Parade
Masquerade Charade
N'awlins Mardi Gras
New Orleans Fantasy Land
Partied From Lundi Gras Thru Mardi Gras
Sweets On St. Charles
Throw Me Somethin' Mistah

____
____
____
____
____

MARRIAGE TITLES

(SEE ALSO ANNIVERSARY, HEART, KISS, LOVE & WEDDING)

After All These Years
As We Became One...
Ball & Chain
Endless Love
From This Moment
From You I'll Never Part
Given In Marriage Unto Thee
The Golden Hook
The Heart Of Marriage Is Memories. - *(Bill Cosby)*
Honor The Ocean Of Love. - *(George de Benneville)*
Hooked On You
Hooked To You
Husband & Wife Team
The Key To A Blissful Marriage...
Let's Stick Together
Looks Like We Made It
Love & Marriage
Love Birds
Love Is The Dawn Of Marriage & Marriage Is The Sunset Of Love. - *(De Finod)*
Love Of A Lifetime
The Love You Gavest Me...
Love You To Death
Marital Bliss
Marriage...A Fortress Of Love
The Marriage Bells
Marriage Bound
A Marriage Experience
Marriage Is Forever
Marriage Is The Blending Of Two Hearts
A Marriage Made In Heaven
A Marriage Proposal
Marriage Vows
Never Ending Marriage
One Good Turn Got Me You
The Perfect Marriage
Right Beside You Is Where I Belong
Rock Solid
Rules For A Perfect Marriage
So Many Years...So Much Love
Still Going Strong
Stuck Together Forever
Sweet Success
Thru The Years...
To Have...To Hold...To Love
Together Forever
Two Hearts...One Soul
Two Hearts That Beat As One. - *(Fredrich Halm)*
Two Souls & One Thought, Two Hearts & One Pulse - *(Halen)*
Walking The Marriage March
We Beat The Odds
Your Love Keeps Lifting Me Higher
You're Still The One...
You've Brought So Much To This Marriage
You've Decorated My Life
You've Got Me Always

____
____
____
____
____

MARTIAL ARTS TITLES

- *Create a tied Belt that spans the width of the page & place on the belt.*

1,000 Memories
24 Karate Kid
Above The Belt
Alive & Kicking
Art Of The Knife Hand
Caution: I Know Karate & 6 Other Karate Words
Chop Chop
Chumbee
Discipline...Integrity...Loyalty...Respect
Dojo
Getting Our Kicks
Hi Karate!
I Get A Kick Out Of This

The Inside Kick
It's A Kick
Judo Kudo's
Just Kick It
Karate Chop
Karate Is A Kick
Karate Kid
Kiai!
Kick Back
Kick Freak
Kick It
Kick It Out
Kick-Off
Kick The Habit
Kick Your Game
Kickin' Up My Heels
Kung Fu Fighting
Kung Fu Hustle
Kung Pow
The Next Karate Kid
No Retreat...No Surrender
A Passion For The Arts
Sensei Says...
Sparring To The End
What A Kick!!!

MEMORIAL/MEMORIES TITLES

(SEE ALSO DEATH, HEAVEN & HERITAGE)

All My Memories
...And All The Heaven's Smiled
...And Still The Memories Cling
Angels Watching Over Me/You
Attics & Memories
Beyond Of The Mist Of Memories
Building Special Memories
Cherished Memories
A Collection Of Memories
Dancing On The Memories
A Day To Remember
Everyday Moments Become Cherished Memories
Faded Memories Of The Past
Farewell My Friend
Fondest Of Memories
For Old Time Sake
Forget Me Not
Forgotten Pasts & Present Memories
A Golden Chain Of Memories
Golden Memories
Gone...But Not Forgotten
Gone From Our Lives...Not From Our Hearts
The Good Ole Days
He Will Hold You In The Palm Of His Hands
Home Is Where The Memories Live
I Love Remembering
Just Making Memories
Keeping The Memories Alive With Love
A Lifetime Of Memories
Magical Memories
Making Memories
Memories...A Melody Of Love
Memories Are For A Lifetime
Memories Are Heartbeats Sounding Thru The Years
Memories Are Keepsakes
Memories Are Lights Burning To Keep The Heart Alive
Memories Are Made Of Love
Memories Are Made Of...
Memories Are Precious Treasures
Memories Are Roses Blooming Evermore
Memories Are Stitched With Love
Memories In The Making
Memories In The Wind
Memories Never Say Goodbye
Memories Of Days Gone By
Memories Of Love
Memories Of The Heart
Memories To Cherish
Memories With Thoughts Of You
Memory Lane
Memory Making Night
Misty Memories
Moments & Memories
Moments In Time
Of Memories We Share
Only A Memory Away
Only In My Memories
Photographs & Memories
Picture Perfect Memories
Precious Memories
Precious Memories With...
Priceless Memories
I Remember When...
Special Friends Bring Special Memories
Such Are The Memories Of The Days Of My/Your Youth
Sunkissed Memories
Sweet Dreams & Happy Memories
Sweetest Memories
Tender Memories Of...
Thank God For All My Remembrances Of You
Thanks For The Memories

These Are The Times To Remember
Those Were The Days
Through The Years
Time Never Changes The Memories
Time Stood Still In My Heart
A Time To Remember
Timeless Memories
Touchstone Of Memories
Treasured Memories
A Walk Down Memory Lane
The Way It Used To Be
The Way It Was
The Way We Were
We Don't Remember Days...We Remember Moments
We Live As Long As We're Remembered
Where Did The Time Go?
Whispering Memories
With Loving Memories...
Those Wonderful Memories
www.memories.com

____
____
____
____
____

MEN TITLES
(SEE ALSO BOY & FATHER)
21st Century Man
All The Man That I Need
Any Man Of Mine...
Baby Man
Big Boy Toys
Big Daddy
Big Man In Town
The Bigger The Boy, The Bigger The Toy
Blues Man
Boogie Man
Boss Man
The Boy Inside The Man
Boy, Oh Boy!
The Boys Are Back In Town
Boys Just Wanna Have Fun!
Boys Night Out
Boys To Men
Brown-Eyed Handsome Man
Candy Man
Demolition Man
Fall Guys
Family Guy
Family Man
Fire Inside The Man
From A Prince To A King
God Fearing Man
A Good Man Is Hard To Find
The Greatest Man I Ever Knew
Guys Will Be Guys
A Guy Is A Guy
Handy Man
Hard Workin' Man
I Am Man...Hear Me Roar
An Innocent Man
Iron Man
It's A Guy Thing
It Takes A Woman's Love To Make A Man
Just One Of The Guys
Ladies Man
Little Big Man
Little Boys Grow Up To Be Bigger Little Boys
Macho Man
Magic Man
The Male Animal
A Man & His Truck
Man In The Middle
Man Of Action
Man Of God
Man Of Miracles
Man Of My Dreams
Man Of Steel
Man Of The Hour
Man Oh Man!
Man To Man
The Man With A Child In His Eyes
Manly Man
The Measure Of A Man
Medicine Man
Men Are Just Little Boys Grown Tall
Men At Play
Men At Work
Men In Black/Blue/Red etc.
Motorcycle Man
Mr. Fix-it
Mr. Style
Mr. Tambourine Man
My Guy
Mystery Man
One Good Man
One Woman Man
The Quiet Man
Quite The Stud
Ramblin' Man
Real Good Man
Remote Control King
Rocket Man
Secret Agent Man
Self-Made Man
Sharp-Dressed Man

Solitary Man
Soul Man
Stand By My/Your Man
The Strongest Man In The World
The "Y" Chromosome
Totally Testosterone
Travelin' Man
Walk Like A Man...
Where The Guys Are...
Who's The Man?
Wise Guy
The Woman Behind The Man
You Are My Man
You've Got Male

MERRY-GO-ROUND TITLES

(SEE AMUSEMENT PARK & CAROUSEL)

MESS/MESSY TITLES

(SEE ALSO DIRT & MUD)

- *Place Dirt Splats around on the title mat.*
- *Smudge the title mat with brown chalk for a messy look.*

Beautiful Mess
Beauty & The Mess
Don't Mess With Me
Filthy, Dirty...But Oh So Cute
God...Please Bless This Mess
Have You Ever Seen Such A Mess?
I'm A Mess
Makin' Messes
Messy Little Man/Missy
Miss Messy
Mr. Messy
Oh What A Tangled Mess We Make
Panic Room *(Child's room)*
A Pretty Mess
This Little Piggy
This Room Is Trashed
The Slob
Those Filthy Hands
Tornado Alley *(Child's room)*
What A Mess!

MICKEY MOUSE TITLES

(SEE DISNEY & WINNIE THE POOH)

MEDIEVAL TITLES

(SEE FAIRYTALE, MARDI GRAS & RENAISSANCE)

MILITARY TITLES

(SEE ALSO PATRIOTIC)

- *Replace an "A" or "O" with Stars.*
- *For Navy, use a Ship's Steering Wheel for an "O".*
- *Make Dog Tags large enough to place title on.*

Above & Beyond *(U.S. Air Force)*
Above & Beyond The Call Of Duty
Air Force "1"
Air Force Brat
Air Man
All Aboard
All American Hero
All Ashore
Always Ready *(Coast Guard motto)*
America, We Salute You
America...Where Liberty Dwells
American Bravery
American Brotherhood
American Champions
American Hero
American Patrol
American Pride, American Strength & America's Heroes
An American Spirit
America's 911 Service. - *(USMC)*
America's Airforce...No One Else Comes Close
America's Finest
An Army Corps Is On The March
An Army Guy Am I
An Officer & A Gentleman
Anchors Away/Aweigh
Another American For Peach
Army Brat
As You Were!
Ask Not What Your Country Can Do For You...
At Ease!
At Sea & On Shore
Attention!
Aviation Adventures
Aye, Coast Guard, We Fight For You
The Battle Of *(Place or Country)*
Be All You Can Be
Bell Bottom Sailor
Blessed Are The Peacemakers
Blue Angel
Blue Navy Blue...I'm As Blue As Can Be
Bombs Away
Boot Camp

Born To Fly
Bound By Honor
Bravery - *(noun)*: 1. Brave Spirit Or Conduct 2. Courage, Valor
Bravery On The Seas
Brothers In Arms
By Land Or By Sea
Can Do! *(Seabee motto)*
Captain At The Helm
Celebrate Freedom
Clear The Decks
Come Sail Away
Damn The Torpedoes - Full Speed Ahead! *(Admiral David Farragut - 1864)*
De Oppresso Liber - *(To Free The Oppressed)* *(US Army Special Forces)*
Defenders Of The Skies
Defenders Of Our Constitution
Devil Dogs
Don't Give Up The Ship! - *(Cpt. James Lawrence)*
Down By The Sea
A Few Good Men
The Few, The Proud, The Marines
Fire When Ready
Fly Boys
A Force To Be Reckoned With
Fortune Favors The Brave
Forward...March
Freedom Fighter
Freedom For All
Gettin' In Gear
G. I. Jive
G. I. *(Child's name)*
Glory! Glory! Hallelujah! His Truth Is Marching On
God Bless America
Got Gear...Will Serve
Grant Us Peace
The Greatest American Hero
Hair Today...Gone Tomorrow
He Wears A Pair Of Silver Wings
I Hear An Army Charging Upon The Land
Heavenly Force
Heroes Get Remembered, Legends Live Forever
Heroes Of The Sea
Hey Ricky You're So Fine
Hip, Hip Hooray For The USA
Hit The Decks
Home Is Where The Army/Uncle Sam Sends You
Home Of The Brave
Honor, Courage & Commitment *(Navy motto)*
Honoring The Military In All Its Forms
Hooah!! Airborne!!
I Came, I Saw, I Conquered. - *(Julius Ceasar)*
I Have Not Yet Begun To Fight. *(Cpt. John Paul Jones)*
I Smell P-Day
I Volunteered For This?!?!
If A Country Is Worth Living In, It's Worth Fighting For. - *(Manning Coles)*
If It Waves, Salute It!
Improvise, Adapt, Overcome. - *(USMC)*
In Honor Of Those Who Serve
In The Army Now!
In The Army Reserves
In The Navy, You Can Sail The Seven Seas
Intense Training
It Came From Beneath The Sea
It's A Navy Life For Me
It's An Army Life For Me!
Join The Navy!
Jump Master Says...Go! Go! Go!
Keeping America Safe/Proud
King Of The Air
Kiss The Boys Goodbye
Land Of The Free
Land That I Love
Land's End
Lead, Follow, Or Get Out Of The Way
Leather Neck
Lest We Forget
Let Freedom Ring
Life At Sea
Lo Que Sea, Cuando Sea, Donde Sea *(Anything, Anytime, Anywhere)* - *(7th Special Forces Group - Airborne)*
The Long Voyage Home
I Love A Man In Uniform
Love In The Air Force
Loving Private *(Soldiers name)*
Made In The USA
Magnificent Marines
Making America Proud
The Making Of A Soldier
March On!
Marine Life...Hair Today, Gone Tomorrow
Marine Men 'R Us
A Marine Officer
The Marines Have Landed
Men Of Honor
Men Of Valour
Mighty Soldiers Prepare For Battle *(Kids dressed & playing as soldiers)*
Military Brat
Military Issue
Military Man
A Military Man I Am
Military Men Are We...Helping Keep America Free

Military Strong Man
More Sweat In Peace, Less Blood In War
My American Hero
My Brother, America's Hero
My Brother, My Hero
My Daddy's A Ruff & Tuff Marine
My Hero
My Knight With Shining Armor
Navy Blue
Navy Boys/Guys 'R Us
Navy Brat
Navy Life
Navy Man
Navy Men Walk The Talk
Navy Seal
No Pain, No Gain
No Promises, No Shortcuts. - *(USMC)*
Nobody Ever Drowned In Sweat. - *(USMC)*
That Noise You Hear Is The Sound Of Freedom
Not Self, But Country *(Navy motto)*
Ocean Adventures
Off We Go Into The Wild Blue Yonder
An Officer & A Gentleman
On Deck
On My Honor
On The Waterfront
One Of Uncle Sam's Toughest
Once A Marine, Always A Marine
Our American Protectors
Our Army Guy
Our Boys In Blue
Our Brave Soldier
Our Heroes
Out To Sea
P-Day Stinks
Pain Is Only Temporary, Pride Is Forever
Pain Is Weakness Leaving The Body
The Patriot
Patriot - *(noun)*: 1. One Who Loves, Supports & Defends Ones Own Country
Peace In Our Time
Peace Is Our Only Product
A Prayer & A Wing
The Price Of Freedom Is Eternal Vigilance. *(Thomas Jefferson)*
Proud To Serve *(U.S. Navy)*
Quarters Sweet Quarters
Rank & File
Red, White & Blue Thru & Thru
Ready, Willing & Able *(U.S. Army)*
The Real American Idols
Reporting For Duty
Riding The Waves
Sailing, Sailing Over The Ocean Blue
A Sailor Went To Sea
Seabees Can Do
Semper Fidelis
To Serve God & My Country
Serving His/Her Country
Serving Uncle Sam
Ship Mates
Ship Shape
Shipping Out!
Shore Leave
Sir, Yes Sir!
Soldier Boy/Girl
The Spirit Of A Warrior
Stand At Ease
Steady As She Goes
Still Waters Run Deep
The Story Of A Patriot
Such Is The Life Of A Military Wife
Swaby
Take Her Down! - *(Cdr. Howard Walter Gilmore)*
Take To The Skies
Their Finest Hour
There Was Once A Sailor
These Colors Don't Run
Those Magnificent Men In Their Flying Machines
Thunder Bird
To Liberate The Oppressed *(Special Forces motto)*
Top Gun
True Americans
Uncle Sam Wants Me
Under The Sea
Unsung Hero
U.S. Navy Seals 'R Us
USA...This Is My Way
USA's Finest
USMC...America's 911 service
USMC...Improvise, Adapt, Overcome
USMC Is Part Of The Navy - The Men's Department
USMC...No Promises, No Shortcuts
Victory Belongs To The Most Persevering. *(Napolean Bonaparte)*
Visualize World Peace. - *(Marine Sniper)*
Walking Proudly...The Airborne Walk
War & Peace
War Heroes
Warriors Of The Sea
We Build, We Fight *(Seabee motto)*
We Don't Care How You Do It In The Navy

We Love America
We Salute You
We Will Either Find A Way Or Make One!
Welcome Home Sailor Man
We're In The Army Now!
What Kind Of Training?...Army Training Sir!
What Part Of Marine Don't You Understand?
What You Call Being A Hero, I Call Just Doing My Job
When In Doubt Empty The Magazine
A Wing & A Prayer
Wings Of Victory *(U.S. Air Force)*
Wings Over The Navy
You Are The Wind Beneath My Wings
You Can Run But You Can't Hide
You're In The Army Now!
You're Our Hero
You've Earned Your Stripes

____
____
____
____
____

WW2 "SONG TITLES"

Across The Alley From The Alamo
American Patrol
Any Bonds Today?
Blue Moon
Boogie Woogie
Candy
I Can't Get Started
It Can't Be Wrong
Cow Cow Boogie
Daddy
Day By Day
Deep In The Heart Of Texas
Don't Sit Under The Apple Tree
I Don't Want To Walk Without You, Baby
Dream
Falling In Love Again
Friendship
G.I. Jive
Gotta Be This Or That
Happy Times
He Wears A Pair Of Silver Wings
He's Home For A Little While
Hit That Jive, Jack
Homesick, That's All
Homeward
I Left My Heart At The Stagedoor Canteen
I'll Be Home For Christmas
I'll Never Smile Again
Imagination
In The Mood
Is You Is Or Is You Ain't My Baby?
It Could Happen To You
It Had To Be You
It Started All Over Again
Juke Box Saturday Night
Kiss The Boys Goodbye
Let's Dance
Let's Get Away From It All
Lili Marlene
Love On A Greyhound Bus
Mademoiselle De Paris
Mr. Five By Five
My Shining Hour
Over The Rainbow
Rhumboogie
Rosie The Riveter
Rum & Coco-Cola
Sentimental Journey
Shoo, Shoo Baby
Smiles
Something To Remember You By
South Of The Border
Swingin' On A Star
Tangerine
Tico Tico
There Will Never Be Another You
When The Lights Go On Again - *All Over The World*
Wings Over The Navy
Yes, Indeed!
You Can't Say No To A Soldier

____
____
____
____
____

MILK TITLES

Drink Milk & Be Merry
Good Mornings Get Better With Milk
Got Milk?
Got Oreos & Milk!!!
It's Always Time For Milk
Milk Is Proof That God Loves Us
Milk...It Does A Body Good
Milk...It's The Real Thing
Milk Mustache
Milk Starts The Day Off Right
Milkin' It For All It's Worth

Milky Way
"Moo"re Milk Please
No Milk Today
Obey Your Thirst...Drink Milk
Passed Out On Milk
Udderly Adorable/Delicious
Where's The Milk?
White Lightning

MILLENNIUM PAGE TITLES

(SEE ALSO NEW YEARS)

12:01...And The Lights Still Work
1999 + 1 = 1900
2000 + 1 = 2002
2000 & Still Going Strong
2000 Remembrances Of The Past
2000 - Too Grand
Admit One To The 21st Century
An End Of An Era
Another Day, Another Century; So What's New?
Apocalypse? Not!
Blast Into A New Future/New Age
Bridging Two Centuries
Bridging Two Decades
Bridging Two Millennia
The Bug That Didn't Bite
Dawning Of A New Age
For Sale: Bottled Water & Canned Goods
Goodbye To A Century
Goodbye To A Millennium
Happy New Century
Happy New Millennium
Happy Y2K
Hooray For The New Millennium
Kiss Of The Century
Kiss Of The Millennium
Life Goes On
Lookin' Pretty Good For 2000
Made It Into The New Millennium
Magical Millennium
Millennium Madness
Much Adieu About Nothing
A New Beginning
A New Millennium & More
No End Of The World
Not The End Of The World As We Know It
Once In A Blue Moon
Once In A Lifetime
Party Like It's 1999
Party Of The Century
Party Of The Millennium
Putting The 1900's To Bed
Ringing In The New Millennium
Saying Goodbye...
This Scrapbook Page Is Y2K Compliant
Special Millennium Edition
The End Of Another 100 Years
To Boldly Go Where No Man Has Gone Before
Turn Of The Century/Millennium
Waiting For The Lights To Go Out...
We Survived The Millennium!
Welcome 21st Century
The World Didn't End
World Without End
Y2K A-OK
Y2K Bug
The Y2K Bug Is Dead
Y2K Compliant
Y2K Disaster...Not!!!
Y2K...Not!
Y2K This, Y2K That
Y2Zzzzzz

MIRROR TITLES

- *Use Foil as the matting for the title.*
- *Make the "O" into a Hand Mirror.*

An Angel's Reflection
The Beauty In The Mirror
My Eye's Reflect Your Love
The Girl In The Mirror
Here's Lookin' At You Kid!!!
Mirror, Mirror On The Wall...I'm My Mom After All!
Mirror, Mirror On The Wall...Who's The Prettiest Of Them All?
Mirror, Mirror On The Wall...Who's The Most Handsome Face Of All?
The Mirror's Reflection...
My Eye's Reflection...
My Own Reflection...
The Reflection In Her Eyes...
Reflections...
Reflections Of Then & Now

Reflections Of You
Reflections Of Your Grace
True Reflections
Whatcha Lookin' At Baby?

MISC. TITLES
A Cozy Place To Sit
All's Well That Ends Well
Altitude Adjustment
Are You Ready For This?
Born Free
Born To Be Wild
Break Away
Different Worlds
Don't Bring Me Down
Don't Cut Off Your Nose To Spite Your Face
Drownin' My Sorrows
Easier Said Than Done
Enjoy Yourself
Every Step Of The Way
Every Which Way But Loose
Extra! Extra! Read All About It!
Face In A Crowd
Follow That Dream
Follow You...Follow Me
Free Your Mind
Fun, Fun, Fun
Get Ready For This
Go Ahead...Make My Day
Groovin'
Hangin' Out With You Is My Favorite Thing To Do
Hangin' Tough
Hard Knock Life
Have I Told You Lately...
Have You Ever?
Hooked On A Feeling
I Don't Want To Miss A Thing
Isn't That Special
Just Do It
Just Hanging Out
Keep It Together
Leave No Stone Unturned
Let's Get Serious
Make Your Mark
Make Yourself Comfortable
Middle Of The Road
Missed Opportunity
Moving On Up
Never Let Me Down
No Easy Way Out
Off The Wall
Oh, What A Feeling
One More Time
One More Try
Ours Is Not To Question Why
Out Of The Blue
Over The Edge
Part Of The Plan
Peace Of Mind
Peaceful Easy Feeling
Picture Perfect
Please Remember Me
Practice Makes Perfect
Roll With It
Second Chance
Sharp As A Tack
Sitting On Top Of The World
Smart As A Whip
Snapshots!
Splendid Surprise
Take It To The Limit One More Time
Takes A Lickin' & Keeps On Tickin'
The Finer Things
These Are A Few Of My Favorite Things
Ups & Downs
What A Feeling!
Whip It...Whip It Good
We Can Work It Out
When You Wish Upon A Star
Whose Idea Was This?
Whose Idea Was This Anyway?
Wild Thang/Thing
Wild Thing...You Make My Heart Sing
Yipeeeee!

MONEY TITLES

- *Use Coins in place of an "O".*
- *Replace an "S" with a $ sign.*

$$$$$$$$$$$
All About Money
All That Glitters Is Not Gold
Another Day...Another Dollar/$
Because You're Worth It
The Best Things In Life Are Free
Bet Your Bottom $
Big Spender
Break The Bank
Brother Can You Spare A Dime?
Buck Naked
The Buck $tops Here
Cash Is A Girls Best Friend
Can't Buy Me Love
Cha-Ching
Charge It!!!
Cheap Thrills
Cheaper By The Dozen
Common Cents
A Dime A Dozen
Dirt Cheap
Don't Bank On It
Easy Money
Every Cloud Has A Silver Lining
Every Man Has His Price
Fame Or Fortune...Gimmie Fortune
Filthy Rich
Fool's Gold
For A Few Dollars More
For Richer...For Poorer
Free For All
Funny Money
Give A Little Bit
Gold Digger
Gold Rush
I Gotta $low Cash Flow
I Need A Money Tree
I Owe, I Owe...It's Off To Work I Go!
I Want To Be A Millionaire
If I Were A Rich Man...
I'm In The Money
I'm So Broke, I Can't Even Pay Attention
In The Money
A King's Ransom
Made Of Money
Million Dollar Baby
The Million Dollar Question
Mo Money...
Money Bags
Money Burns A Whole In My Pocket
Money Can't Buy Me Love
Money Doesn't Grow On Trees
Money For Nothin'
Money Honey
Money Maniac
Money, Money, Money
Money Monger
Money On My Mind
Money Talks
Money Talks...Mine Always Says Goodbye
Money...That's What I Want
Money Well $pent
Moolah
No Price To High
One For The Money
Ooh La La Moolah!
Pass The Buck
Pennies From Heaven
A Penny For Your Thoughts
Penny Lane
Penny Lover
Penny Pincher
A Penny $aved
A Penny Saved Is A Penny Earned
Penny Smart...Dollar Foolish
A Pretty Penny
The Price Is Right
Put Your Money Where Your Mouth Is
Rags To Riches
Rakin' It In
Raking In The Dough
Right On The Money
The Road To Riches
Rolling In The Dough
$aving For A Rainy Day
Shop 'Til You Drop
Show Me The Money
$ilver-Tongued
Spending Time...
Sugar Daddy
A Sweet Deal
Take The Money & Run
Thanks A Million
There Are Some Things Money Can Buy
I Thought Money Grew On Trees!
Tight Wad
Time Is Money
We're In The Money
Wheel Of Fortune

Who Wants To Be A Millionaire?
Worth A King's Ransom
Worth The Wait
Worth Your Weight In Gold
You Can Bank On It
You Can Bank On My Love
You're One In a Million
Zip, Zilch, Nada!!!

MONKEY TITLES

(SEE ALSO ZOO)

- *Use a Monkey holding the title as a sign.*
- *Have the title hanging by Monkey's Tail.*
- *Monkey See, Monkey Do are a great title.*

Funky Monkey
Goin' Bananas
Getting Into The Swing Of Things
Got Good Hang Time...
Hangin' Around/Out
Hear No Evil...See No Evil...Speak No Evil
Hey! Hey! We're The Monkeys!
I'll Be A Monkey's Uncle
In The Swing Of Things
Just Monkeyin' Around
Monkey Boogie
Monkey Boy
Monkey Business
Monkey Man
Monkey Mania
Monkey On My Back
Monkey See...Monkey Do
Monkey Time
Monkey Wrench
Monkeyin' Around
More Fun Than A Tree Full Of Monkeys
Our Little Monkeys
A Real Swinger
Swing My/This Way
Wild & Crazy Monkeys
You Can Fly...You Can Fly
You've Got The Cutest Little Monkey Face

MONTHS TITLES

January

Beautiful Snow Fell Under The January Sky
Chilly January Morning
A Cold Day In January
January...A Fresh New Beginning
A January Blast
January Blues
January Is Here With Eyes That Keenly Glow
A January Snow
January's Resolution
January's Snow Is Our Beauty
January's Thaw Is Long Awaited
Slow As Molasses In January
Summer In January
Sweet January

February

Fabulous February
February Brings Hopes Of Freshness
February Brings Love
February Fever
February 14th...The Day Of Love
February Moon
February...Smooth With Newly Laid Snow
February Stars
February Twilight
February's Cold Winds Blow
February's Rains
Freezing February
Foggy February
For The Love In February
Golden Flowers Shine Thru On February Days
Romantic February

March

As The March Winds Roar
A Full Moon In March
Green, Green March
March Is A Green All-Over Promise
March Is The Month Of Expectations
March Is The Promise Of Spring
March Madness
March Of Hope
March Promises The Four-Leaf Clovers
A March Snow
The March Winds Are The Morning Yawning
March Winds Blowing The Winter Away
A Mild March Afternoon
The Month Of Rainbows & Leprechauns
Moon On A March Night
Oh, March In Spring
Winds Of March

April

April Bright With Golden Daffodils
April Fool
April Fool's Day
April Hath Put A Spirit Of Youth In Everything.
(William Shakespeare)
April Lady
April Love
April Moon
April Rain
April Scatters Daisies At Our Feet
April Serenades In Spring
April Showers
I'll Remember April
The Kiss Of April Showers
Paris In April
Rainbows Of April
Rainy April Days
Soft Rains Of April
Sweet April Showers
The Sweet Scent Of April's Easter Lilies
Twilight Hours Of April Showers
Under The April Snow

May

Birds Sing In Tune To The Flowers Of May
Come What May
A Day In May
Fragrant, Lovely, Merry May
In The Merry, Merry Month Of May
Last Days Of May
Let All Thy Joys Be As The Month Of May
May Calls Forth The Violets
May Day
May Day Merriment
May Flowers
May Mornings
May Sunshine & Rain
May...The Month Of Birds & Flowers
May's Blue Skies & Sunbeams
May's Bouquets
May's Happy Sounds & Flowers
Rain In May

June

An Afternoon In June
Balmy Breezes Of June
Dusk In June
Everything's New In June
June Bride
June Bug
June Bursts Out In Flowers
June Days Of Gardening
June Gloom
June Night's Boast Of Romance
June...The Time Of Perfect Young Summer
June's Summer Moon
My Blooming June
The Rose Moon Of June
Showers & Sunshine Bring June's Roses

July

4th Of July's Sparkling Night
Celebrating Freedom This 4th Of July
A Cold Day In July
Fireflies Of July
Fourth Of July
Freedom On July 4th
July...When We Remember Patriotism
Hot July Nights
Hot July's Cooling Showers
Hot, Sunny Skies Of July
A July Afternoon
July Fireworks & Fun
July's Summer Rains
The Month Of Independence
One July Summer
The Summer Skies Of July

August

August Monsoons
August Rain
August Thunderstorms
Hot August Nights
Long Hot Days Of August
New Moon In August
Remember August
Sweet August

September

30 Days Hath September
Hot Days & Cool Nights Of September
See You In September
September Bells
September By The Shore
September Dreamer
September In The Rain
September Love
September School Bells Sing
September School Days
September Skies
September Splendor
A September To Remember
September's A Time For Harvesting
September's Leaves
September's Summers End
September's Winds
Sublime September
Sweet September

October

Autumn's October Colors
Crisp Clear Days Of October
Haunting October
The Hunt For Red October
Lovely October Leaves
Red October
October Brings Showers Of Leaves
October Brings The Turning Leaf
An October Evening
October Fun
October Is Red & Gold & Brown
October Leaves
October Pumpkin Picking
October Rain
October Sees The Harvest
October Gives Us Showers Of Autumn Leaves
October Skies
October's Autumn
October's Fall
Oktoberfest
Red, Brown & Golden October

November

Cold November Nights
Days Of Thanks In November
Kissed By The November Chill
Leaf-ing November
Love In November
November Blues
A November Chill
November Rain
November Reminds Us To Thank The Lord For All He Gives
November's Child
November's Here & So's The Snow
Remember November
Sweet November
Thanks To November's Giving

December

The Beauty Of December
Days Of December
December Brings Us Christmas
December Dreams
December Nights
December Rose
December Sees Miracles
December's Cold, Clear, Wintry Breath
A Drenching December
Eight Crazy December Days & Nights
Freezing December Days
Magical December
Miracles Of December Days
Summer In December

MONTHS MEANINGS

January - New Beginnings
February - Love
March - Uncertain weather, uncertainties of life
April - Risen Lord *(though sometimes Easter is in March...)*
May - Mother's love
June - Father's love
July - Freedom
August - Leisure time
September - Wisdom, Education
October - Harvest
November - Thanks be to God
December - Nativity

MONTHS RELIGIOUS PASSAGES

January - "Rejoice in the Lord always, again I say Rejoice!" - *(Philippians 4:4)*
February - "May the Lord make your love increase and overflow for each other." *(1 Thessalonians 3:12)*
February - "Now these three remain: faith, hope and love. But the greatest of these is love." - *(I Corinthians 13:13)*
March - "Sing to Him a new song, play skillfully and shout for joy!" - *(Psalm 33:3)*
April - "Behold, the former things have come to pass, now I declare new things." *(Isaiah 42:9)*
May - "How lovely is your dwelling place, oh Lord Almighty." - *(Psalm 84:1)*
May - "Like mother, like daughter." *(Ezekiel 16:44)*
May - "Her children arise and call her blessed; her husband also, and he praises her."- *(Proverbs 31:28)*
June - "The grass withers and the flowers fall, but the Word of our god stands forever." *(Isaiah 40:8)*
July - "And you shall know the truth, and the truth shall set you FREE!" - *(John 8:32)*
August - "The Lord God is a sun and a shield..." - *(Psalm 84:11)*
September - "Blessed is the man who finds wisdom, the man who gains understanding, for it is more profitable than silver and yields better returns than gold." *(Proverbs 3:13)*

September - "Make your ear attentive to wisdom, Incline your heart to understanding." - *(Proverbs 2:2)*
September - "The fear of the Lord is the beginning of knowledge." - *(Proverbs 1:7)*
October - ...You will reap a harvest if you do not give up." - *(Galatians 6:9)*
November - "Enter his gates with thanksgiving, his courts with praise." *(Psalm 100:4)*
November - "Give thanks to the Lord, for He is good; For His loving kindness is everlasting" - *(1 Chronicles 16:34)*
December - "GLORY to God in the highest and on earth PEACE among men." *(Luke 2:14)*

____
____
____
____
____

MOON TITLES

(SEE ALSO NIGHT, SPACE, STARS & SUNRISE/SUNSET)

- *Hang Title from a Half Moon.*

African Moon
The Beauty Of The Moon Over The Sea
Blue Moon
Bright As The Full Moon
By The Light Of The Silvery Moon
The Cow Jumped Over The Moon
Crying Under The Moon
Dancing In The Moonlight
Fly Me To The Moon
A Full Moon Night
Full Moon Rising
Galaxy Quest
The Golden Moon
Good Night Moon
He Hung The Moon
In The Light Of The Moon
In The Misty Moonlight
A Lover's Moon
The Magic Of Love In The Moonlight
Magic Moon
The Man In The Moon
Mississippi Moon
A Misty Moon Rises
Moon Beauty
Moon In The Autumn Dawn
Moon Ramadan
Moon Over Bourbon Street
Moon Over *(Your City/State)*
Moon River
Moon Shadow
Moonglow
Moonlight By The River/Sea
Moonlight Is Sculpture. - *(Nathaniel Hawthorne)*
Moonlight Madness
Moonlight Sonata/Serenade
Moonlit Night
Moon's Splendor
Moonshine Time
Moonstruck
My Daddy Hung The Moon
Neon Moon
New Moon On Monday
Once In A Blue Moon
Once Upon A Blue Moon
Paper Moon
Promise You The Moon
Reach For The Moon
The Rising Of The Moon
Sail Along The Silvery Moon
I See The Moon
Shadows In The Moonlight
She Hung The Moon
She Thinks I Can Rope The Moon
Shine On The Harvest Moon
Shooting For The Moon
Silvery Moon
Summer Moon
Sunset Moon
Under The Harvest Moon
When The Blue Moon Turns Gold
When The Moon Kisses The Sky
Where The Moon Kisses Town
Yellow Moon Rising
You Hang The Moon

____
____
____
____
____

MORNING/WAKING UP TITLES

(SEE ALSO SUNRISE)

Angel Of The Morning
Another Good Morning
The Awakening
Bathed By Morning's Light
A Beautiful Morning In The City
Bright Yellow Sunshiny Morning
The Brilliant Blue Of Morning
By Morning's Light
Cold Autumn Morning
The Crack Of Dawn

M M M M M M M M M M M M M M M M M M M M M M M M M M M M M M

Crisp Spring Morning
Each Dawn Is A New Beginning
Early Morning Dawn
Early Morning Starshine
The Early Show
Gentle Morning Rain
The Glory Of Daybreak
Good Morning, Merry Sunshine
Good Morning Nature
Good Morning Starshine
Good Morning Sunshine
Majestic Morning
Midsummer Morning
Misty Morning Sunshine
A Monet Moon
The Morning After
Morning Breeze
Morning...Fresh & Clear
Morning Has Broken
The Morning Light Came & Painted Whispers Of Joy
Morning Rain
Morning's Awakening
Morning's Beauty
Morning's Enlightenment
Morning's Glory
In Morning's Mist...
Morning's Warm Caress
A New Day Is Dawning
A New World In The Morning
Oh, Glorious Morning
Oh, What A Beautiful Morning!
The Red Blaze Of Morning
A Snowy Morning
A Summer Morning's Sunshine
The Sun Is But A Morning Star. - *(Henry David Thoreau)*
Sunday Morning Sunshine
Sunshiny Morning
This Is The Day That The Lord Has Made
'Til The Morning Light
Wintry Crimson Morning Sky

MOTHER TITLES

(SEE ALSO GRANDPARENTS & MOTHER-IN-LAW)

#1 Mom
3 Kisses For Mom
All I Am, I Owe To My Mother. - *(George Washington)*
Basket Case
Because I'm The Mom, That's Why!!!
The Best Academy...A Mother's Knee. *(James Russel Lowell)*
The Bestest Mommy
Big Mama
Calgon...Take Me Away
Caution: Mom Is Stressed
Dearest Mother
Every Mother Is A Working Mother
A Family Blossoms With A Mom's Love
Fast Food Queen
Following In My Mother's Footsteps
Gentleness...Mom
I Am Mom, Here Me Roar!
I Dig Being A Mother. - *(Whoopi Goldberg)*
I'm So Busy, Mom's Head Is Spinning
Laundry Queen
Like Mother...Like Daughter
Magical Mommy Moments
The Mama & The Papa
Mama Don't Allow No Poutin' Here!!!
Mama Mia
Mama...The Great Enabler
Mama's Arms
Mama's Boy
Me & My Mommie
A Meeting Of The Mom's
Mighty Is The Force Of Motherhood!
Mirror, Mirror On The Wall...I'm Like My Mom After All
Mom...Another Word For Love
The Mom In Me...
A Mom Is Her Son's 1st True Love
A Mom Is...Love...Hope...Joy
MOM Is WOW Upside Down
A Mom Of All Trades
Mom...The Wind Beneath My Wings
To Mom With Love
Mom's Day Off
Mom's The Word
Mommy & Me
Mommy Dearest
Mommy's Angel
Mommy's Eyes
Mommy's Kisses
The Momster
Most Beautiful Mom
Mother & Child Reunion

A Mother Is A Girl's Best Friend
A Mother Is A Mother Still, The Holiest Thing Alive. - *(Samuel Taylor Coleridge)*
Mother Is Another Word For Love
Mother Knows Best
A Mother Like No Other
Mother, May I...
Mother Of Gold
Mother Of Mine...Classic Through Time
Mother: The Most Beautiful Word On The Lips Of Mankind. - *(Kahlil Gibran)*
Motherhood: All Love Begins & Ends There. *(Robert Browning)*
Mothers...Always Caring, Always Giving, Always Loving
Mothers Are Special...Especially Mine!!!
A Mother's Arms Are Made Of Tenderness
A Mother's Children Are Portraits Of Herself
A Mother's Heart Is A Patchwork Of Love
A Mother's Heart Is As Big As The World
A Mother's Love Blooms Year 'Round
A Mother's Love Is The Heart Of The Home
A Mother's Love Perceives No Impossibilities. *(Paddock)*
Mothers Make The World Go 'Round
Mother Of Mother
A Mother's Touch
If Mothers Were Flowers, I'd Pick You!
If Mothers Were Flowers, Ours Would Be A Perfect Rose
A Mother's Work Is Never Done
Motorcycle Mama
Mum's The Word
My Greatest Blessings Call Me Mommy
My Mama Said...
My Mom...My Angel
My Mom...My Friend
My Mom...My Hero
My Mom Rocks!!!
My Mom's LOOK...
My Other Name Is...Chauffeur
No Influence Is So Powerful As That Of The Mother. - *(Sarah Josepha Hale)*
Nobody Cares Like A Mom
Nobody Does It Better Than Mom
Only A Mommy...
Papa Loves Mama
The Phrase *'Working Mother'* Is Redundant
Queen Of The House
Rock 'N Roll Mama
Safe In Mommy's Arms
Shhhhh! Mom Is In Time-out
Shine On Mama
Soccer Mom
Sugar Mama
Super Mom!
Sweet Mama
This Is What A Great Mom Looks Like...
When It Comes To Love, Mom's The Word
Woven Of The Same Thread *(With child)*
You Can't Scare Me...I Have Kids

MOM
Marvelous
Outstanding
Magnificent
MOM
Mother
Of
Mine

MOTHER
Marvelous
Original
True Blue
Heaven Sent
Encouraging
Ray Of Sunshine

____
____
____
____
____

MOTHER-IN-LAW TITLES
(SEE ALSO MOTHER)
His Mother, My Friend
Mother By Marriage, Friend By Choice
My Other Mother
Your The Mother That I Didn't Have

____
____
____
____
____

MOTORCYCLE TITLES

(SEE ALSO BICYCLE, DIRT BIKE & RIDING)

- *Use Motorcycle Wheels as an "O".*

Born To Be Wild
Born To Ride My Harley...Forced To Work
Brother Of The Wind
Chopper Rider
Easy Rider
Harley Angel
Harley Hog Heaven
Harley Honey/Hunk
Harley Rock Inn/Cafe
Hog Rider
Honda Honey
Iron Horse Rider
It's Not The Destination, It's The Journey
It's The Call Of The Road
Leather & Lace
Lil' Harley Chick
Live To Ride...Ride To Live
The Man Loves Motorcycles
Motorcycle Granny
Motorcycle Mama
Motorcycle Man
Motorcycle Mania
My Favorite Color Is Chrome
Quad-ruple Fun
Ride A Hog
Ride A HOG...Forever Free
To Ride Or Not To Ride...Stupid Question!
Road Hog
Rolling Thunder
Spirit In The Wind
Treadin' Asphalt
Two-Wheelin'
Wild Harley Man
Wild Hogs
Work To Ride...Ride To Work
Yes, It's Fast, No, You Can't Have A Ride

MOUNTAIN TITLES

(SEE ALSO CLIMBING, HIKING, NATURE & OUTDOORS)

Ain't No Mountain High Enough
Altitude Adjustment
As The Mountains Drip With Sunset...
Autumn Is Singing In The Mountains
Climb Every Mountain
Climb That Mountain High
Dawn In The Mountains
Everybody's Got A Mountain To Climb
Faith Can Move A Mountain
For Every Mountain There Is A Miracle. *(Robert H. Schuller)*
From The Mountain To The Sea
Go Tell It To The Mountain
God Gave Us Mountains To Climb
Going To The Mountains Is Going Home. - *(John Muir)*
High On The Mountain Top
How Glorious A Greeting The Sun Gives The Mountains! - *(John Muir)*
King Of The Mountain
Majestic Mountain Views
Mist Covered Mountain
Misty Mountain Morning
Moonshine On The Mountain
Mountain Dew
Mountain High
Mountain Mama
Mountain Man
Mountain Of Love
Mountain Views
Mountains Of Delight
Mountains Of Gold
My Side Of The Mountain
Mystic Mountain
On A Mountain High
On Top Of The Mountain
One More Mountain To Climb
Rocky Mountain High
Snow-Capped Mountains
Summer In The Mountains
The Sweet Mountain Air
There Is An Eminence Of These Mountains
When The Sun Says Good Night To The Mountains...
Whose Sun-Bright Summit Mingles With The Sky. - *(Thomas Campbell)*

MOVIES TITLES

- *Have a Reel-to-Reel Camera spinning off Film & put title in Filmstrip.*
- *Create a large Ticket Stub for title.*

Afternoon At The Matinee
Chick Flick
Dreams Of Being A Reel Star
A Freaky Flick
Get Reel
Going To The Movies
Lights, Camera, Popcorn!
The Magic Of The Movies
Matinee Fun
Matinee Idol
Movie Queen
Movie Star
Popcorn & Flicks Are "Reel" Fun
Reel By Reel
Reel Fun Movies
Reel Kids
Reel Star
A Short Flick
Snap, Crackle, Popcorn
We Saw A "Reel" Good Movie

MOVE/MOVING TITLES

- *Create a House on Wheels or Moving Truck with title on the side.*
- *Make stacked squares as Moving boxes & put title letters in the boxes.*

Again I Move
All The Right Moves
Born To Move
Bounce...Shake...Move...Swing
Building Memories
Bust A Move
Can't Move On
Faith Can Move Mountains
I Feel The Earth Move...
Get A Move On
Go With The Flow
God Moves In Mysterious Ways
Good Move
Growing Up & Moving On
Hit The Road
I Was Moved
I'm Moving On
I'm Ready To Move
Keep It Moving
Keep On Moving
I Like The Way She Moves
Look Out *(New Town)* The *(Surname)* Are Comin' To Town
Love Can Move Mountains
Love Can Move You
Make Room For The *(Surname)*
Make Your Move
Move A Little Closer
Move It
Move Me On Down The Line
Move Over
Move To The Music
Move Your Body
Move Your Feet
Movin' Along
Movin' Away
Movin' Forward
Movin' On
Movin' On Out
Moving Day
A Moving Experience
Moving In Day
Moving Mountains
Moving On Up
Moving Out
A Moving Tale
Moving Target
My First Move
New Address, New Attitude
New Digs
New Kid In Town
New Kid On The Block
New Move
A New Place To Call Home
Night Moves
On The Move Again
One Wrong Move...
Out With The Old & In With The New
Ready To Make A Move
Rental Sweet Rental
Smart Move
Sold!
Something In The Way She Moves...
Things That Move Me
Under Construction
The Way You Move
We're Movin' On Up
When The Spirit Moves...
When You've Gotta Move

You Move Me
(New Town) Or Bust

MUD TITLES

(SEE ALSO DIRT & MESSY)

- *Place Mud Splats on the title mat.*
- *Smudge brown chalk on title for a muddy look.*

Beyond The Mud
Cake Of Mud
Caked In Mud
Floaters In The Mud
Fun In The Mud
Have You Ever Seen Such A Mess?
Here's Mud In Your Eye!
Here's Mud In Your Eye & On Your Head & On Your Arms & ....
Just Call Me Mud
Little Man In The Mud
Little Mud Man
Makin' Mud Pies
Mighty Mud Mania
Mommy's Little Mud Puppy
Mud Bath
Mud Bath .5 cents
Mud Buddies
The Mud Called My Name...
Mud Flood
Mud Mess
Mud Pies .10 cents
Mud Pies 101
Mud Puddler
Mud Soup
Mud Wars
Muddy Buddies
Mud-licious Puddle Fun
My Name Is Mud!
Nothing Like A Wallow In The Mud
Oh, The Muddy Puddles
Oops!! My Name Is Mud
Return Of The Mud Man
Stick In The Mud
Stuck In The Mud
Warning...Likes To Play In The Mud! *(Muddy child)*

MUD
Mucky
Ucky
Dirt

MUSIC/SING/SONG TITLES

(SEE ALSO DRUMS)

- *Replace letters with Music Symbols.*
- *A Tambourine makes a cute "O".*
- *Create a mat with Staff lines on it & place title on the lines like a song.*

76 Trombones Lead The Big Parade
A Capella
Ain't Life Grand?
All That Jazz
All The Little Children Sing
...And All The Children Sang
...And The Band Played On
...And The Beat Goes On
Angel Of Music
As The Music Plays
Baby Grand
Baby I'm Grand
Baby Mozart
A Band Of Gold
Band On The Run
The Beat Goes On
Bee Bop
The Blessing Of Music
Boogie Woogie Bugle Boy
Broadway Here I Come!
Can You Hear The Music?
Can't You Just Hear The Music?
A Choir Of Angels
A Chorus Line *(Kids singing)*
Clef-hangers
Crazy Music
Dance To The Music
Diva
The Drum Major Is...The Leader Of The Pack
Earobics
Ebony & Ivory
Encore
Escape Into The Music
Face The Music
Familiar Refrain
Feel The Rhythm
Fiddlin' Around
Fit As A Fiddle

Foot Stompin' Music
For The Love Of Music
Garage Band
The Gift Of Music/Song
Gimmie The Beat Boys...
Good Vibrations
Got The Pitch
The Grandest Piano Player
Guitar Man...That's What I Am!
Halftime Belongs To The Band
A Harp Is Just A Nude Piano
To Hear An Angel Sing...
Heart Strings *(Guitar)*
High Fidelity
High Notes
I Believe In Music
I Believe In Rock 'N Roll
I Hear A Symphony
I'd Like To Teach The World To Sing
If Music Be The Food Of Love, Play On!
I'm Just A Singer In A Rock & Roll Band
I'm The Spotlight
In My Heart There Rings A Melody
It's Still Rock & Roll To Me
I've Got Music/Rhythm
I've Got The Music In Me
This House Is A Rockin'
Jam Session
Jazz Man
The Jazz Singer
A Joyful Noise
Just A Note
Just Sing, Sing, Sing
Jute Box Saturday Night
Karaoke King/Queen
Keep On Strummin'
Keys To You
La La La La La!
Leader Of The Pack
Let The Music Heal Your Soul
Let The Music Play
Let The Music Speak To You
Let's Hear It For The Band
Life Is A Musical
Life Is Music
Life Is The Song...Love Is The Music
Lift Up Your Voice & Sing
A Little Bit Country, A Little Bit Rock & Roll
Listen To The Music
Live & In Concert
Live For The Music
Look At Those Ivories
Lost In The Music
Make A Joyful Noise
Make A Joyful Noise Unto The Lord.
(Psalm 98:4)
Make Your Own Kind Of Music
Making Beautiful Music
Maestro
Makin' Sweet Music
Master Of Music
Mountain Music
Move To The Music
Mr. Tambourine Man
Music & Passion & Music
Music Blues
Music For The Masses
Music From The Heart
Music...Heart...Soul
Music Is An Outburst Of The Soul.
(Frederick Deluis)
Music Is Love In Search Of A Word.
(Sidney Lanier)
Music Is The Art Of Thinking With Sounds.
(Jules Combarieu)
Music Is The Food Of Love
Music Is The Poetry Of The Air. - *(Richter)*
Music Is The Voice Of Angels
Music Is Well Said To Be The Speech Of Angels. - *(Thomas Carlyle)*
Music Is What Feelings Sound Like
Music Makes Me High
Music Makes The Heart Sing
The Music Man
Music Notes
Music Of My Heart
Music Soothes The Soul
Music Teachers Are Really #Sharp#
Music To My/Our Ears
Musical Memories
Musically Inclined
Musicians Duet Better
My Shining Hour
Name That Tune
Note This...
Note-able
A Notable Moment
On A Different Note
Out Of Tune
Perfect Pitch/Harmony
The Piano Man
Piano Plunker
Piano Prodigy
Pickin' & Grinnin'
Playing By Ear
Play It Again Sam
Play It & They Will Leave
Play That Beat

Play That Funky Music
I Play To The Beat Of A Different Drum
Practice Makes Perfect
Remember The Music
Right On Cue
Rock Around The Clock
Rock In The USA
Rock-N-Roll
Rock-N-Roll Music
Rock Star In Progress
Roll Over Beethoven
Romancing The Trombone/Saxophone/
Xylophone
Saved By The Music
Say It With Music
Shake, Rattle & Roll
Sing Aloud
Sing As Though No One Can Hear You
Sing Baby Sing
Sing, Sing A Song
Sing Song, A Song I Sing
Singin' In The Rain
Singin' Love's Tune
Singin' The Blues
I Sing To The Beat Of A Different Drum
Singing Like An Angel
Slave To The Music
Song & Music
The Songbird Of The Opera
The Sound Of Music
Sounds Of Music
Strike A Chord
Strike It Up
Strike Up The Band
Striking The Right Note
Stringin' Along
Sweet Strings Of Music
Sweet Sweet Music
Swing To The Music
Symphony
Take A Bow
Thank You For The Music
There's Music In The Air
It's Time To Play The Music
Tone Deaf
Tuned Out
You Make My Heart Sing
Unchained Melody
Up Tempo
The Wedding Singer
We Make Sweet Music Together
We've Got The Beat
When Angels Sing...
When Words Leave Off, Music Begins.
(Heinrich Heine)
Where Words Fail, Music Speaks.
(Hans Christian Anderson)
Whistle While You Work
Wild Thing...You Make My Heart Sing
The Wonderment Of Music
You & The Night & The Music
You Are My Music
You Make Beautiful Music
You're My Song

MUSIC
Making
Unique
Sounds
Instead Of
Chaos

MYSELF TITLES
A Brand New Me
All About Me From A to Z!
All By Myself
Aren't You Glad You're You?
Be Good To Yourself
Enjoy Yourself
Got To Be Real
Got To Get Myself Together
I Still Haven't Found What I Am Looking For
Look At Me
The Same Old Me

NATURE TITLES

(SEE ALSO CAMPING, MOUNTAINS & OUTDOORS)

Act Naturally
America The Beautiful
Artistic Nature
Back To Nature
Barefoot In The Woods
Be One With Nature
The Beauties Of Nature
The Beauty Of Nature
Beauty...That Is Nature
Big Adventure
Come On A Safari With Me
Communing With Nature
Down By The Lazy River
Down To Earth
Enjoying Nature's Lullaby
Force Of Nature
Freak Of Nature
Fresh Air
Getting Back To Nature
Go Jump In A Lake
God's Gift...Nature
God's Tapestry
Great Oaks From Little Acorns Grow
The Great Outdoors
Hard Rock Hill
Hard Rock Mountain
Hurt Not The Earth
Itchin' & Scratchin' & Scratchin' & Itchin' *(Poison Ivy)*
Mother Nature
Natural Treasures
Nature At Work
Nature Boy/Girl
Nature: God's Art
Nature High
Nature Is The Art Of God. - *(Thomas Browne)*
The Nature Of Nature
Nature Sings
Nature Teaches More Than She Preaches. *(John Burroughs)*
Nature Walk
Nature-ally Beautiful
Nature's Bounty
Nature's Embrace
Nature's Glory
Nature's Gold
Nature's Music In The Hills
Nature's Perfection
Nature's The Child Of God
One With Nature
Our Neck Of The Woods
Out In The Country
Poison Ivy Scratches!!
Rebirth Of Nature
The River Is Wide
Seasons In The Sun
The Simplest Beauty In Nature Is A Sign Of Divinity
The Sky Is The Daily Bread Of The Eyes. *(Ralph Waldo Emerson)*
Sleeping Beneath The Moon & Stars
Smoke In The Water
Speak To The Earth & It Shall Teach Thee. *(Job 12:8)*
Splendor In The Wild
Vivid Shades Of Nature
When Nature Speaks
Where The Green Grass Grows
Whisperings Of Nature
Wide Open Spaces
The Wonders Of Nature

NEWSPAPER TITLES

Breaking News
Extra! Extra!
Extra, Extra, Read All About It!
Front Page News
Good News To Share
Have You Heard The News?
I Got The News Today
In The News
Making The Headlines
News Flash
Read All About It!
A Walk In The Woods
A Wonderful News
Yesterday's News

NEW YEARS/EVE TITLES

(SEE ALSO MILLENNIUM)

- *Make Ice Cubes from vellum, put title on them.*
- *Make Champagne Bubbles from vellum & put title in bubbles.*

2002...Just Me & You
10,9,8,7,6,5,4,3,2,1...A Toast To The New Year
All's New For 2002
...And Here Comes Another New Year
...And Now Let Us Welcome The New Year
...And The Ball Dropped
An Annual Celebration/Party
As The Clock Strikes Midnight...
As The Confetti Falls...
At Midnight...
At The Midnight Hour...
Auld Lang Syne
Beautiful Midnight
A Big End To A Big Year
Bridging Two Decades *(1999 - 2000)*
Bring On The New Year
Celebrate With Glee Into 2003
Celebrate The Good Times Of Days Past
Celebration In The Streets
Champagne, Confetti & Horns...Ring In 2004
Cheers *(Year)*
Cheers To The New Year
Cheers To *(Year)* Years
The Chimes At Midnight
Closed The Door On 2004...To Dive Into 2005!
Confetti Rain
Cork-Poppin' Chaos
Countdown To A Celebration
Countdown To A New Year
Dateline *(New Year)*
Embrace Sweet Memories Of Times Past
Father Time
The Flash At Midnight
The Future Looks Bright
Goodbye *(Year)*
Goodbye *(Year)*...Hello *(Year)*
Had Fun Ringing In *(Year)*
Hats...Confetti...Noise Makers, Must Be A New Year
In The Midnight Hour
In With A Bang
It's Time For A New Year!
Kiss Me At Midnight
Kiss Of The Decade
Magical Midnight
A Midnight Gathering
Midnight Kiss
Midnight Madness
Midnight Magic
Midnight Memories
Midnight Ponderings
Midnight Resolutions
A Midnight Sight
Midnight Special
The Morning After
A New Beginning
My New Year's Resolution Is...
A New Year...A New Beginning
New Year...New Love
A New Year With Old Friends
New Year's Day Is Every Man's Birthday. *(Charles Lamb)*
New Year's Cheers
New Year's Eve In Time Square
New Year's Eve In *(Your Town or State)*
A Night To Remember
Oh, What A Night
Our Midnight Wish...
Out With The Old...In With The New
Painted The Town Red
Party Like It's 1999
Party Of The Decade
Party Poopers *(Sleeping through it)*
Party'd Hardy
Pop The Cork
Psychedelic Midnight
I Resolve To...
Ring Out The Old & Ring In The New
Ringing In The New Year
Roared Into 2004!
Rockin' At Midnight
'Round Midnight
Saw The First Sun Of 2001
Snored Thru To 2004
Tell Me At Midnight
A Time To Celebrate
A Toast To The New Year
A Toast To Us
Tonight's The Night
Until Midnight
Up 'Til Midnight
Welcome *(Year)*
Zzzzzz's To 2003

____
____
____
____
____

NIGHT TITLES

(SEE ALSO MOON & SUNRISE/SUNSET)

- *Hang title from a Half Moon.*
- *Replace an "A" with a Star.*

1:00 a.m...My Crib...Be There!
All Night Long
All Tucked In
...And The Night Said Goodnight To The Mountains
...And The Night Stood Still
...And To All A Good Night
Are You Afraid Of The Dark?
Are You Lonesome Tonight?
As Day Dwindles Into Dusk...
As Evening Falls...
An Evening Reflection
At The Setting Of The Sun!
A Beautiful Evening
The Beauty At Dusk
Beauty Of A Moonlit Night
Before The Night Is Over...
The Calm Of The Evening
Children Of The Night *(Up late)*
Dance The Night Away
Dusk In The Golden West
Enchanted Night
An Evening At The Seashore
As Evening Blankets Us...
Evening Delight
An Evening Scene
Evening Tides
Evening's Enchanting Melody
Evening's Glorious Colors
Evening's Harmony
Evening's Love Song
Evening's Solace
From Dawn 'Til Dusk
Full Moon Night
Gloriously Blazed The Dusk
Good Night...Sleep Tight
It Happened One Night
Happy Days & Lonely Nights
Harbor Night
Hard Day's Night
The Heart Of The Night
Hello Darkness My Old Friend
Here Comes The Night
I'll Meet You At Midnight
In The Air Tonight...
In The Blue Of The Evening
In The Cool Of The Evening
In The Heat Of The Night
In The Midnight Hour
In The Night Air
In The Still Of The Night
In Walks The Night...
Into The Night The Evening Goes
It's Been A Hard Day's Night
Just Another Saturday Night
Kiss Me At Midnight
Kissed By Evenings Soft Breath
Like Night & Day
Lonely Is The Night
Lonely Nights!
I Love The Night Life
A Lovely Way To Spend An Evening
The Majesty Of The Night Sky...
Midnight Cinderella
Midnight Confessions
Midnight Fantasy
Midnight Flyer
Midnight Lady
Mine Is The Night, With All Her Stars. *(Edward Young)*
The Music Of Night...
The Mysteriad Sea At Dusk
The Night Belongs To You
Night Crawlers
Night Dreamer
Night Hawk
Night Is A World Lit By Itself. - *(Antonio Porchia)*
The Night Is Young
The Night Is Yours...The Night Is Mine
On A Night Like This
A Night On The Town
Night Owl
Night Rider
Night Shift
A Night To Remember
The Night We Met
Night, When Words Fade & Things Come Alive. - *(Antoine De Saint-Exupery)*
Nights In/Under White Satin
Nighty-Night
Oh, What A Night
On A Night Like This...
Once Upon A Summer Night...
One More Night...
Only The Nighttime Knows
Rhythms Of The Night
The Right Time Of The Night
Rise Of The Evening Stars
Rock The Night
Saturday Night Live
Saturday Night Special
Saturday Nights Alright...
Silent Night
Sleepless In Seattle *(Your town)*

So Long, Farewell, Auf Wiedersehen, Good Night.
Southern Nights
Spirit In The Night
Starlit Night Skies
Strange Bedfellows *(Child with comfort pal)*
Strangers In The Night
Sweet As The Evening Goes
Sweet Evening Breezes
Sweet Summer's Evening
Tender Is The Night
There's Magic In The Night
Things That Go Bump In The Night
Tonight Could Be The Night
Tonight My Love, Tonight
The Tonight Show
'Twas An Enchanting Evening
Twilight Of Evening
Twilight Time
Under Night's Sky...
Under The Evening Stars
Visions & Moonlight In The Night
Walking After Midnight
We've Got Tonight
When Night Falls...
When That Evening Sun Goes Down...
You & Me & The Night Sky

____
____
____
____
____

NOAH'S ARK TITLES

All Aboard
Flooded With Blessings
The Good Lord Made Them All
Two By Two

____
____
____
____
____

NUDE TITLES

- *Create title, then place ripped-edged vellum over top of title, (which will give it the essence of bare or nude) & fasten down with eyelets.*

Bare Faced
The Bare Facts
Bare Necessities
Barely Dressed
Barely Legal
Barely Naked
Barely There
Barely Two/2
Barin' To Go
Bottoms Up
Buck Naked
Butt Naked
No Butts About It
Centerfold Material
Cheek To Cheek
I Don't Have A Thing To Wear
Exposed
Feelin' Free
Flashin' Zone
As Free As A Bird
I'm Too Sexy For My Clothes/Diaper
In My Birthday Suit
Lady Godiva
Little Streaker
Me & Only Me
Naked As A Jaybird
Natural Beauty
Nature Is Beautiful
No Butts About It
Not A Material Girl
Over-Exposed
Pose Nude?...You Bet!
Running Bare
Showing My Assets
Sweet Cheeks

____
____
____
____
____

NURSE TITLES

(SEE ALSO DOCTOR, ILLNESS & INJURY)

After Two Days In The Hospital, I Took A Turn For The Nurse
Angel Dressed In White
Angel In Scrubs
Angels Are Nurses That Have Earned Their Wings
Caring Is The Essence Of Nursing
CCU Nurses Give Heartfelt Care
ICU Nurses Care Intensly
The Hospitality Of The Hospital
If Love Can't Cure It, Nurses Can
I've Been Scrubbed
LPN: Loving Person Near
LPN: Low Paid Nurse
Looking Scrubby
Night Shift Nurses Keep The Beat All Night
Night Walker
A Nurse Is Compassion In Scrubs
Nurse...Kind Of Like A Doctor But Nicer
Nurses Are Angels In Comfortable Shoes
Nurses Are Everyday Heroes
Nurses Are I.V. Leaguers
Nurses Are Medical Chicks
Nurses Are Patient People
Nurses Are The Cure-all!
Nurses Are The Heartbeat Of Health Care
Nurses Call The SHOTS!
Nurses Can Take The Pressure
Nurses Cover The Doctor's Butt
Nurses Give Intensive Care
Nurses Have A Lot Of Patients
Nurses Have The Touch Of Angel Wings
Nurses Heal Us With Love & Care
Nurses Hold The Key To Recovery
Nurses...One Of The Few Blessings Of Being Sick
Nurses Rate A 98.6!
Nurses Stick Butt
Nursing Is The Gentle Art Of Caring
Nursing Is A Work Of Heart!
Nursing Isn't A Job, It's An Adventure
Making A Difference Everyday
OR Nurses Are A Cut Above
RN Means...Real Nice !
You Make My Heart Beat

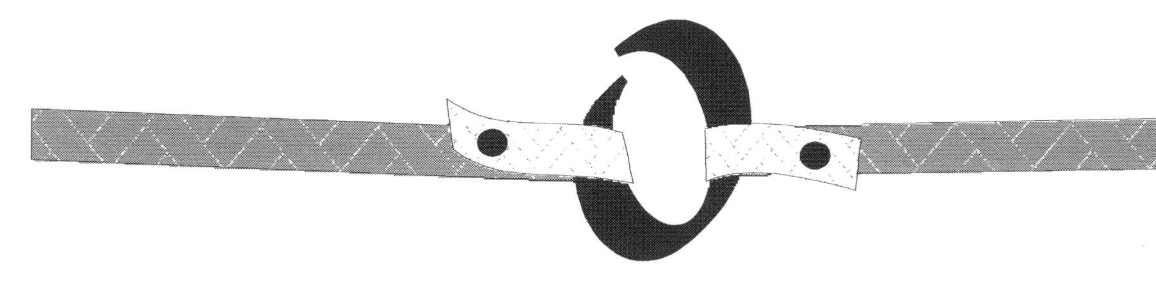

OCCUPATION TITLES
(SEE ALSO SOME INDIVIDUAL OCCUPATIONS)

ACCOUNTANT
Accountants Are Top Dollar!
Accountants Work Their Assets Off!
C.P.A. - Certified Pain In The A** !!!
I'm An Accountant...Not A Magician!

BANKER
Cash Me Quick
Full Of Interest
I Lost My Interest
Just Call Me Money Bags
Man Of Money
Mr. Banker

BOSSES
Big Boss Man
I Love My Boss
I Wanna Be The Boss
Who's The Boss?
You're The Boss

BRICK LAYER
Brick Babe
Brick By Brick
Brick House
Like It Level
Masonry Man
Mortar Man

CASHIER
Keyed Out
Keyed Up

DENTIST
The Boss Of The Floss
Mr. Drill Man
Open Wide
The Tooth Man

DIVER
Doin' It Underwater!!
In Deep Water!
In Over My Head

DOCTOR
(SEE DOCTOR)

ELECTRICIAN
All Wrapped Up
Sparky *(Electrical/Electronics)*
Totally Wired
Wire Man *(Electrician)*
Wire Tapped Out
Wired For Sound

ENGINEER
Doin' It Logically
Engineer *(Name)*
Logically Thinking
More Data *(Name)*
Need More Data

GARDENER
(SEE FLOWERS & GARDEN)

HOUSEWIFE
Domestic Engineer
S.A.H.M. = **S**tay
At
Home
Mom

MECHANIC
Auto Man
Backyard Mechanic
Garage Guru
Grease Monkey
Junk Yard Warrior
Manic Mechanic
Mr. Goodwrench

PAINTER
(SEE ALSO ART)
Brushing Up
Colorful Creator
A Colorful Surprise
A Little Splat'll Do It
Master Painter
My Father The Painter
Paint By Numbers
Paint Me Colorful
Paint My Dreams
Paint My Heart
Painter Of Dreams
Painter *(Name)*
Painting Princess
Roller Man
Rollin' Along
Splattered Up
With Paintbrush In Hand...

PILOT
(SEE AIRPLANE)

PLUMBER
All Dripped Out
Drip Catcher
Pay The Piper
Pipe Dreamer

POLICE
(SEE LAW & POLICE)

POSTAL WORKER
Brown Is Better
Brownie *(UPS Person)*
Postmen Are Full Of Zip!
Those Boys In Brown *(UPS)*

PRINTER
A Colorful Type
Covered In Ink
A Man Of Much Paper
Paper Back Printer
Paper Boy

SECRETARY
All Typed Out
Doin' It By The Book
Totally Typecast

OUTDOORS TITLES

(SEE ALSO CAMPING, CLIMBING, HIKING, MOUNTAINS & NATURE)

- *Create Rocks as mats for title letters.*

Ah! Wilderness
Al Fresco
America The Beautiful
Back To Nature
Barefoot In The Park
Breathtaking...
No Bugs Allowed
A Cabin In The Woods
Call Of The Wild
Climb Every Mountain
Club Camp
Country Roads, Take Me Home
Down To Earth
Field & Stream
"Field" Trip
Fresh Air At Last
A Glorious Outdoor Day
The Good Earth
The Great Outdoors
Hard Rock Cafe/Inn
Heart Of The Wilderness
In The Still Of The Night
Natural Wonders
Nature Boy/Girl
Nature Lover
Nature's Beauty
Our Neck Of The Woods
Nighttime Visitors
One With Nature
On The Rocks
On The Trail Again
On Top Of Old Smokey
Open Your Heart To The Wild
Outdoor Adventures
Outdoor Excitement
Outdoor Fun
Outdoor Odyssey
Playing With Fire
Quiet Moments With Nature
Roughing It
Rugged Outdoorsman
A Wee Bit Of Heaven On Earth
When Smoke Gets In Your Eyes...
Wide Open Spaces
Wild In The Country
Wild, Wild Wilderness
Wilderness Earth
Wonderful Wilderness
Woodland Creatures

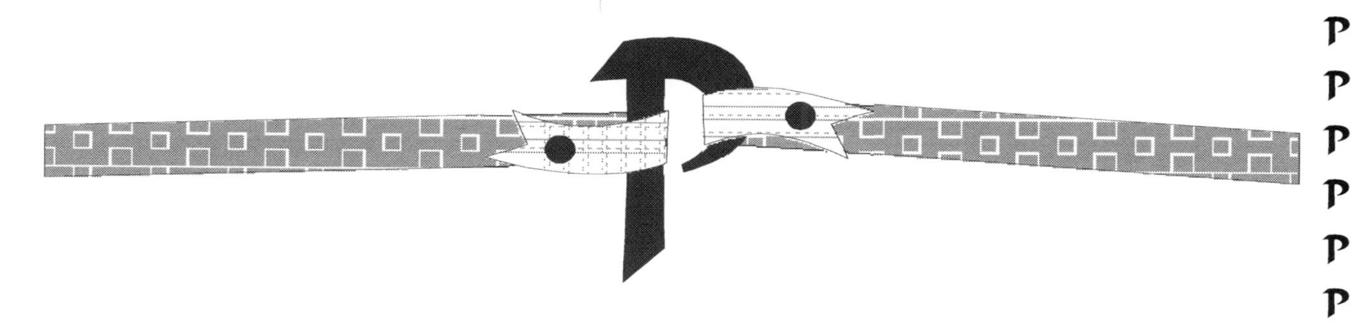

PAINTBALL TITLES

Big Shot
Bullseye
Colorful Creation
Colorful Shooter
Go Ahead, Make My Day!
Got Splatted
The Lone Paintball Wizard
A Long Shot
Marksmanship Counts
Paint Packer
Paint Packin' Paintballer
Paintball Wizard
Paintball Geek
Paintballing Takes Balls
Perfect Aim
Practice Makes Perfect
Ready, Aim, Fire!
Right On Target
Quick Draw McGraw
Sharpshooter
Shoot From The Hip
Shoot High...Aim Low!
Shoot To Thrill
Shooting Star
Snap Shooter
Splat...Out Of Luck
Splat, Splat...Ouch, Ouch...Splat!
Splat That!
Splatted Again!
Straight Shooter
Sure Shot
Survival Of The Fittest
Sweet Spotter
Target Practice
Top Gun
Trail Blazers

PARADE TITLES

- *Create letters with Batons.*
- *Make title mat look like a Street with dotted yellow line & put title on the Street.*

76 Trombones Led The Big Parade
At The Parade
Bands & Horses & Floats, Oh My!
Banner Moments
Banners & Horses & Bands, Oh My!
Bird's-eye View *(Child on shoulders)*
Champions On Parade *(Winners/Olympians)*
Christmas Parade
Circus Parade
Drum Major
Easter Parade
Everybody Loves A Parade!
Festival Parade
Fields Of Gold
A Fine Day For A Parade
Floating Along
Forward, March!
Free In The Fields
A Good Review
Green Fields
It Had Better Not Rain On Our Parade!
Keep In Step
A Kind Of Wilderness...A Kind Of Beauty
Life's A Parade!
March Of Time
Marching Bands
Marching Down The Street
Marching On
Marching Orders
Marching To The Beat Of The Drums
Masquerade Parade
May Day Parade
One-Man Parade
Parade Of Champions
Parade Of Lights
Parade Of Nations *(Olympics)*
Pomp & Circumstance
It Rained On Our Parade
Soldiers On Parade
Spring Parade
View From The Boulevard
When The Bands Go Marching Along

PARTY TITLES

(SEE ALSO BIRTHDAY & PRESENTS)

- *Use a Candle for an "I".*
- *Put title on large pieces of Confetti .*
- *Create a Party Blower for title mat.*

All Night Party
All Nighter
Another Saturday Night
Beach Party
Block Party
Born To Party
Cake Anyone?
Cake Dance
A Cause For Celebration
Celebrate!
Celebrate Freedom
Cel-e-brate Good Times
Celebrate Life
Celebrate Our Love
Celebrate The Moments Of Your Life
Celebration Cheers
Celebration Of Life
Celebration Of Love
Centennial Celebration
Cinco Di Mayo
Come As You Aren't
Crazy Little Party Girl
Dance On The Wild Side
Dancing Queens
Eat, Drink & Be Merry
Everybody Loves Saturday Night
Fiesta Frenzy
Fight For Your Right To Party
For Me?
A Gala Celebration
Garden Party
Good Time Saturday Night
Happy Hour
Having A Party
Here's To You
I Just Want To Celebrate
I Want To Party All The Time
I Want To Walk You Home
If You Want To Party...
I'm So Excited
In The Midnight Hour
It's A Celebration
It's A Date
It's My Party & I'll Cry If I Want To!
It's Never Too Late To Celebrate
It's Party Time
Let Your Hair Down
Let's Get The Party Started
Let's Party
Let's Party Hardy
The Life Of The Party
Midnight At The Oasis
The More The Merrier
The Morning After
A Night To Remember
The Night Is Still Young
Oh, What A Night!
Paint The Town Red
P-A-R-T-Y
Party All Night
Party All The Time
Party Animal
Party Boy
Party Central
Party Down
Party Girl
Party Hardy
Party Like It's 1999
Party Of The Century
The Party Place
Party 'Til The Cows Come Home
Pool Party
Put On Your Party Hat
Red Letter Day
Rock-A-Fiesta
'Round Midnight
Saturday Night Fever
Some Enchanted Evening
A Time To Celebrate
Tonight I Celebrate My Love For You
Tonight's The Night
Viva La Fiesta
Walk On The Wild Side
We're Havin' Some Fun Now
When The Sun Goes Down...
Where's The Party?

____
____
____
____
____

PASSOVER TITLES

(SEE JEWISH)

PATRIOTIC TITLES

(SEE ALSO MILITARY)

- *Use Stars for an "A".*
- *Create a Dynamite stick for an "I".*

All American Boy/Girl
All American Family
All American Kid
All Decked Out In Red, White & Blue
America, America, God Shed His Grace On Thee
America For Me
America...Home Of The Brave
America Is...
America Is Still Shining
America, Oh, America
America Sings
America The Beautiful
America The Great
America...The Land We Love
America...The Melting Pot Of Freedom
America The Unusual
America...We Salute You
American As Apple Pie
American Beauty
American Cutie Pie
American Girl
American Made
American Pride
American Spirit
Americana...
America's Dream...
America's Freedom Call
An Old Fashioned 4th
Angels Of America
B-A-N-G!!!
A Bang Up Day
A Bang Up Good Time
Beautiful America
I Believe In America
My Beloved America
The Bombs Bursting In Air!
Boom...Bang...Boom!!!
Born Free
Born In The USA
Born On The 4th Of July
Bursting In Air. - *(Great fireworks layout)*
Celebrate America
Celebrate Freedom
Celebrating Freedom
Celebrating The 4th
Celebrating The 4th With A Bang
Corn In The USA
The Cause Of Freedom, Is The Cause Of God!! - *(Rev. William Lisle Bowles)*
Diamonds In The Dark
Diamonds In The Sky
Every Heart Beats True
Every Heart Beats True, For The Red, White & Blue
Fire Cracker, Fire Cracker...Boom, Boom, Boom!
Fireworks & Firecrackers
Fireworks & Fun
Fireworks Are Scary
Fireworks Fun
Fireworks Frenzy
Fireworks On The Fourth
First Fireworks
Forever May You Wave
Fourth Of July Celebration
Freedom Is The Last Best Hope Of Earth. *(Abraham Lincoln)*
Freedom, Liberty, Pride
Freedom On The Fourth
Friends Like You Make Life "Sparkle"
From The Heart Of America...
From Sea To Shining Sea
Fryin' On The Fourth
Fun Filled Fourth Of July
Fun On The Fourth
Give Me Liberty
God Bless America
God Bless America, My Home Sweet Home
God Bless The USA
God Blessed America
God Shed His Grace On Thee
Good Morning America
Got American Spirit
In God We Trust
Goodness Gracious Great Balls Of Fire Crackers
A Grand Old Flag
Greatest American Hero
Hand On Our Hearts For America
Happy Birthday America
Happy Fourth of July
Happy Independence Day America
Hats Off To The Red, White & Blue
Havin' A Blast
Having An All American Blast
He's A Grand Old Flag
Hip, Hip, Hooray For The USA
Hip, Hip, Hooray...It's Independence Day
Home Of The Brave
Home Of The Free

Hoorah For The Red, White & Blue
Independence
Independence Day
Independence Day Was A Blast
I Love America
I Love This Land
I Love The USA
In The Winds Of Liberty
Kaboom Time
This Land Is My Land
Land Of The Free
Land Of The Free, Home Of The Brave
The Land That I Love
Let Freedom Ring
Let The Fireworks Begin
Li-BEAR-ty
Liberty & Justice For All
Liberty Belle
Liberty For All
Liberty, Justice & Sparklers For All
Light My Fire...Cracker
Lil' Fire Cracker
Little Miss Independence
Little/Littlest Patriot
Long May She Wave
Love Of Country
Made In America
Made In The USA
Memorial Monday
My All American Girl
My All American Guy
My America
My Country 'Tis Of Thee
Oh Beautiful For Spacious Skies
Oh My Stars
Oh Say Can You See
Old Glory...Forever May She Wave
One Flag, One Land
One Flag, One Land, One Heart, One Hand,
One Nation Ever More. - *(Oliver Wendell Holmes)*
One Nation Under God
Only In America
Patriotic Flames
A Patriotic Tale
Pint-Sized Patriot
I Pledge Allegiance To My Country
I Pledge Allegiance To The Flag
In Praise Of America
Proud To Be An American
Red... White... Blue
Red, White & Blue
Red, White & Blue, Through & Through
Red, White & Blue, We're True To You
Red, White & True Blue Friends
Rock In America
The Rockets Red Glare
Rockin' In The U.S.A
Salute To The Red, White & Blue
She's A Grand Old Flag
Show Your Stripes
Sing For America
Sparkler Spectacular
Sparklers, Snakes & Smoke Bombs
Sparkling July 4th
Sparkling Spectacular
The Spirit Of America
Stand Beside Her
Stars & Stripes
Stars, Stripes, Smiles
Star Spangled
Star Spangled Baby
Star Spangled Banner
Star Spangled Day
Star Spangled Fourth Of July
Star Spangled Fun
Star Spangled Kid
Star Spangled Studs
Star Spangled Sweetie
Star Struck
Stars & Stripes
Stars & Stripes & Smiles
Stars & Stripes Forever
The Sweet Echo Of Victory
Sweet Land Of Liberty
Sweet Land Of Liberty, Of Thee I Sing
Sweet Liberty
The American Spirit
The Big Bang
The Red, White & Blue
The Spirit Of America
There's No Land Like Our Land
This Is America
This Is My Country
This Land Is Your Land
Three Cheers For The Red, White & Blue
Twinkle, Twinkle Little Fire Cracker
United We Stand
United We Stand, Divided We Fall
USA Day
USA Today!
Waiting For Fireworks
We Had A Blast!

We Love America
We The People...
What A Blast
What Makes America Great...
Where The Stars & Stripes & The Eagle Flies
Yankee Doodle Baby/Daddy
You Fire Cracker Me Up!
You're A Grand Old Flag
You're A High Flying Flag

PEACH TITLES

(SEE FOOD)

PET TITLES

(SEE ANIMALS, SOME SPECIFIC ANIMALS & ZOO)

PHOTOGRAPHY TITLES

(SEE ALSO CAMERA/POSING)

- *Create a Film Canister with Film flowing out for title.*

Act Naturally
Addicted To Pics/Pictures
Big Shot
Budding Photographer
Camera Bug
Have Camera Will Shoot?
A Candid Moment
Caught On Film
Choice Cuts
A Cut Above
Film At 11
In The Spotlight
It's A Kodak Moment
Lights, Camera, Action
Memory Saver
Mom's Got The Camera Again!
Off The Cutting Room Floor
On Second Thought , Too Good To Toss
Photo Finish
Photographer Extraordinaire
Photography Lesson
Picture Perfect
Pictures Of The Past
Pictures Of Time
Pictures, Pictures, Pictures
Point & Shoot
Precious Moments
Reflections Of The Past
Reflections Of Yesteryear
Say Cheese
Show Time!!
Snapshots!

PHYSICIAN TITLES

(SEE DOCTOR)

PIANO TITLES

(SEE MUSIC)

PICNIC TITLES

(SEE ALSO COOKOUT)

- *Have Ants carrying title letters.*

The Ants Go Marching...
Backyard BBQ
Bedroom Picnic
Carpet Picnic
Fun, Food, & BBQ
Indoor Picnic
Life's A Picnic
Life's No Picnic
Lunch In The Great Outdoors
No Ants Invited
No Ifs, Ants, Or Bugs About It!
Park Picnic
Perfect Picnic
A Picnic Amongst The Flowers
A Picnic In The Meadow
Picnic In The Park
Picnic Memories
Picnic On The Beach
Star Spangled Picnic
Summer Picnic Day
Teddy Bear Picnic

PIE TITLES

(SEE ALSO FOOD)

- *Create a slice of Pie & put title on the slice.*

American Pie
Apple Pie Memories
Cutie Pie
Easy As Pie
Honey Pie
Humble Pie
Pizza Pie Fun
Puddin' Pie
Punkin Pie
Sugar Pie Honey Bunch
Sweet As Pie
Sweetest Pie
Sweetie Pie

PIG TITLES

- *Create a Pig holding the title.*

Fat As A Pig
Happy As A Pig In Mud
Hogs & Kisses
The Little Piggy Went Wee, Wee, Wee
Livin' High On The Hog
Oink! Oink! Oink!
Pig Headed
Pig Out!
Pig Pen
Pig Sty
Porky Pig
When Pigs Fly...
Year Of The Pig

PILOT TITLES

(SEE AIRPLANE)

PINK TITLES

(A great way accentuate the word Pink in the title is to create that word only in Pink. Make the word Pink larger and even in a different type style than the rest of the title)

Angel In Pink
Hot In Pink
Hot Pink
In The Pink Of Things
It's A Pink Thing
Lady In Pink
Little Pink Book
Passion Pink
Passionately Pink
Pink Cadillac
Pink Is My Color
Pretty In Pink
The Color Pink
Tickled Pink

PIRATE TITLES

- *Create an Eye Patch & place it over an "O".*
- *Use a Pirates Hook for a "U".*

Ahoy There Matey
Argh!
Argh...Matey
Avast Ya Scarvy Scum
Aye, Aye, Captain/Matey
Buried Treasure
Captain Hook
I Dig Treasure
Gar!
Going On A Treasure Hunt
Going To Treasure Island
Hidden Treasure
I Want To Be A Pirate...
I'll Get It With Me Hook!
It's A Pirate's Life For Me
Li'ly Libbered Land Lubbers
Little Treasure Hunter
My Treasure
Our Little Treasure
Pirates Cove
Pirates Of The *(Your city or state)*
A Pirate's Tale
A Pirate's Voyage

Pirate *(Name)*
Priceless Treasure
Sailing A Jolly Roger
Scoundrel On The Seas
Seeking Sunken Treasure
Shiver Me Timbers
Swab The Deck
There Be Treasure In Them Thar Hills!
Treasure Hunter
Treasure Of The Sea
Treasure Planet
Walkin' The Plank
With An "Ar, Ar, Ar," & An "Aye Matey"...
"X" Marks The Spot
Yo Ho, Ho & A Bottle Of Rum
Yo Ho, Yo Ho...It's A Pirate's Life For Me!!!

PLAY/PLAYING TITLES

(SEE ALSO GAMES)

Action Figures
Adventure Time
All Work & No Play...
Babes/Babies In Toyland
Born To Play
Caution: Child/Children At Play
Child's Play
Clap Your Hands
Come Play With Me
A Day For Play
Drama Queen/King
Fruit Loops
The Games We Play
Go Go Pogo
Got Hang Time *(Jungle Gym)*
The Great Pretender
Hard At Play
Hey, Hey...We're The Monkeys
In The Playground Zone
In The Spot Light
Inside, Outside, Upside Down
It's How You Play The Game
It's Play Time
Jumping For Joy
Just Swingin'
Kids At Play
King Of the Sandbox
Leader Of The Pack
Leap Frog Leap
Let Me/Us Entertain You
Let The Children Play
Lil Sandman
Mommy's Work Is Never Done, When
(Name) Is Busy Having Fun
Mr. Agent Man *(Child dressed as Spy)*
On A Play Date
Piggy Back Rides Are The Best
Play Children Play
Play It By Ear
Play, Play & Play
Play The Field
Play The Hand You're Dealt
Play To Win
Playin' Hard
Playin' With The Big Boys
Playing In The Park
Secret Agent Man
Simon Says...Have Fun!
Simply Slidin'
Sometimes You Feel Like A Nut
Splashing In The Sprinkler
Splendor In The Grass
Sprinkler Time
Swing Kids
Two Can Play That Game

POOH (WINNIE) TITLES

(SEE WINNIE THE POOH)

POOL TITLES

(FOR THE GAME OF POOL, SEE BILLIARDS)
(SEE ALSO SWIMMING & WATER)

- *Use a Life Ring or Water Splashes for an "O".*
- *Punch title letters out of water paper, add Rhinestones for a shimmer.*

An Angel In Floaties
Aquaholic
So Cool In The Pool
Dive In!
Don't Splash Me!
Feet First Fun
Jewel Of The Pool
Jr. Lifeguard
Just Add Water
Keepin' Cool By The Pool
Keepin' Cool In The Pool
Krazy In The Kiddie Pool
Little Mermaid
Makin' A Splash

Makin' Waves
Man Overboard
Marco! Polo!
On The Water Front
Pool Attire
Pool Fun
Pool Party
Pool Poses
Pool Potatoes
Pool Rules
Pool School
Pool Time
Poolin' Around
Poolish Pleasures
Poolside Pals
Poolside Princess
I Rule The Pool
Ruler Of The Pool
That Sinkin' Feelin'
Sinkin' Sensation
A Splash Of Fun
A Splashin' Good Time
Splashy Chics
Splish Splash
Staying Cool In The Pool
Taking The Plunge
Talent Pool
Testing The Waters *(Child barely in the pool)*
Underwater Fun
Water Wars
Water World
What Are You Wading For?
Whatta Splash!
You Rule The Pool

____
____
____
____
____

POTTY TRAINING TITLES

- *Use Toilet Paper as backing mat for title.*

Auto Sprinkler Under These Britches
Caution: Potty Training In Progress
Glad To Wear Underwear
Grin & Swish It
I'm A Big Boy/Girl/Kid Now!
It's My Potty & I'll Cry If I Want To
It's Potty Time
A King & His Throne
Once Upon A Potty
Oops, I Leaked
I Potty All The Time
Potty Pants
Potty Party
Potty Pooper
Potty Preliminaries
When Ya' Gotta Go, Ya' Gotta Go!
Who Needs Diapers? Not Me!
A Whole Lot Of Pottyin' Goin' On

____
____
____
____
____

PREGNANCY TITLES

(SEE ALSO ULTRASOUND)

- *Create a Pregnancy Test Stick, use as an "I".*
- *Use the Test Stick to underline title.*

About To Pop
Action Figure Within
Alive & Kicking
Already Adorable
Anticipation
Any Day Now!
Are You Done Yet?
As You Grew, So Did I!
At First Sight
Baby In Waiting
Baby On-Board
Baby Under Construction
The Belle Curve
Beyond Conception
Blooming Belly
Blooming In The Womb
Blooming Into Parenthood
A Bun In The Oven
Can't Wait To Hold You
Coming Soon To A Good Home
Contacting The Mother Ship
Countdown To A Miracle
Cradle Of Dreams
Developing In The Dark Womb
Diamond Under Construction
In "Due" Time
Eating For Two
Expecting...
Extra Cargo On Board
Family Under Construction
Flutters...Yeah Right!
From Here To Eternity
From The Beginning...
Great Expectations
Havin' His Baby, What A Lovely Way Of
Sayin' How Much I Love Him!
Here I Am!
I Carry Within Me A Special Treasure

I Have **PMS**...Pre-Mom Syndrome
I'm Pregnant...This Is As Perky As I Get!!
I'm Waiting For You
In Full Bloom
In The Beginning...
The Inside Story
It Started With A Kiss & Ended Like This
It's Spring & Look Who's Blooming
Kid Under Construction...
Labor Day *(Having baby)*
Labor Of Love
Lady In Waiting
Lamazing Grace
Let Me Out Of Here
Let's See What Develops
Life On The Inside
Little Boy/Girl/One Under Construction
Look Who's Blooming!
Make Room For *(Name)*
The Miracle Of Life
Mission Accomplished...
Mission Impossible
Mom In Waiting
Mommies To Be
Month By Month
Mother Lode
My Skin Just Cannot Stretch Anymore!!!
My Unborn Child
Nine-Month Miracle
Now Appearing
Oh, Baby
Oh, That Glow
Pea In A Pod
Pregnant Pause *(Pregnant pics)*
Positively Pregnant *(Test sticks)*
Ready For Baby
Ready Or Not, Here I Come
Ready To Pop
She's Havin' My Baby
Showers Of Blessings
A Shower Of Joy
Some Miracles Take Nine Months!
Someone Is Waiting
Somersault Cutie
Special Things To Come
A Splendid Surprise
Stretch Marks Are Pregnancy Service Stripes. *(Joyce Armor)*
Sweet Beginnings
Sweet Mystery Of Life
Swollen Ankles, Stretch Marks & The Miracle Of Love...
There Is A Great Joy Coming
Thinkin' Pink
True Blue
A Twinkle In Progress
Twinkle, Twinkle Little Star
Twinkle, Twinkle Little Star, How We Wonder What You Are!
Under Construction
Waiting For Baby
Watch Me Grow
We're Pregnant
What A Belly
What A Difference A Day Makes
What A Wondrous Thing God Has Made
Which Will It Be...A He Or A She?
While You Were Sleeping...
The Womb Mate
Wonderful Weight *(Pregnant pics)*
You Glow Girl
You Knit Me Together In My Mother's Womb.
- *(Psalm 139:13-14)*

PRESENTS TITLES

(SEE SPECIFIC HOLIDAYS & CELEBRATIONS)

- *Use Presents in place of some letters.*

All Wrapped Up
The Best Gift Of All Was...
Big Things Come In Small Packages
"Buried" In Love
"Buried" In Paper
Children Are God's Greatest Gifts
Gift Exchange
A Gift From Heaven
A Gift From The Heart
The Gift Of Giving
The Gift Of Life
Gift Of Love
The Gift Of You
God's Precious Gift...
Greatest Gift
I Am The Gift
It's All About The Presents
Just What I've Always Wanted...
Love Is A Gift
My Gift To You...
No Greater Gift...
Our Most Precious Gift
The Past & The Presents
The Perfect Present Is "YOU" Heaven Sent
Present Time
Presents, Presents & More Presents

"Presents"tation Is Everything
That's A Wrap
There's No Time Like The "Presents" Time

PRETTY TITLES

(SEE BEAUTY OR CUTE)

PRINCE/PRINCESS TITLES

(SEE ROYALTY)

PROM TITLES

(SEE ALSO DANCING)

All Dressed Up & Off To The Prom I Go!
Cutest Couple
Dancing Queen
Dancing The Night Away
Dream Date
A Formal Affair
Formal Elegance
A Formal Flair
Formal Fun
Lookin' Snappy
Memories In The Making
My First Formal
A Night To Remember
Oh, What A Night
Prom Queen & King
Prom Night Delight
Winter Formal

PUMPKIN TITLES

(SEE ALSO HALLOWEEN)

- *Use a Pumpkin as an "O".*
- *For a carving title, make Pumpkin Slime Splats on title.*

3 Little Pumpkins Sitting On The Fence
Carvin' Time
Cutest Little Pumpkin In The Patch
The Great Pumpkin
The Great Pumpkin Adventure/Caper
I'm A Pleasing Pumpkin
Images From The Patch
It's Pumpkin Time
I've Been Slimmed!!!
Jack-O-Lantern
Jazzy Jack-O-Lantern
Mom's Little Pumpkins
On The Cutting Edge *(Carving)*
Once Upon A Pumpkin Patch...
Our Little Pumpkin
The Perfect Pumpkin
Pick Of The Patch
Pickin' Pumpkins
Pumpkin Patch Pickin'
Pumpkin Patch Princess
Pumpkin Picasso
Pumpkin Pickin' Time
Pumpkin Pondering *(Trying to choose the perfect pumpkin)*
Pumpkins On The Vine
Rockin' Round The Pumpkin Patch
Queen Of The Pumpkins
The Seed, The Vine, The Pumpkin, The Jack-O-Lantern!!!
Slimmed By A Pumpkin
Welcome To Our Patch
(Name) O-Lantern
(Name, Name) The Pumpkin Carver

PURPLE TITLES

(A great way accentuate the word Purple in the title, is to create that word only in Purple. Make the word Purple larger and even in a different type style than the rest of the title)

The Color Purple
Deep Purple
Purple Haze
Purple Heart
Purple Nurple
Purple Passions

PUZZLE TITLES

- *Make little Puzzle Pieces & put the title letters in them.*

Bits & Pieces
Falling To Pieces
Hmm, "Puzzle"ing
It's A Puzzle To Me
The Missing Link
Pieces Of My Heart
Pieces Of My/Your Life
Pieces Of You
The Puzzle Of Love
Puzzle Pals
Puzzle Place
Puzzled Mind
Puzzled To Pieces
Puzzling Looks

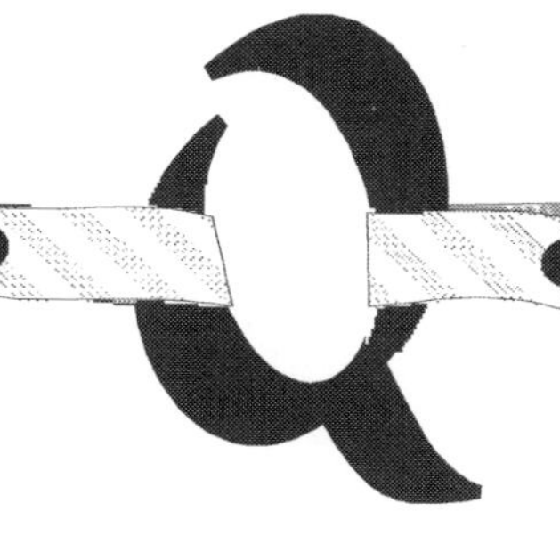

QUEEN TITLES
(SEE ROYALTY)

QUILTING TITLES
(SEE ALSO CRAFTS & SEWING)
Blessed Are The Piece Makers
Crazy Quilter
Crazy Quilting "B"
A Family Is A Patchwork Of Love!
Gramma's Quilt...
Grandma's Quilts Have Love In Every Stitch
Memories Are Stitched With Love
A Quilt Is A Blanket Of Love
A Quilt Of Colors
A Quilt Of Life
A Quilt Of Love
Quilt 'Til You Wilt!!
Quilters Don't Do Buttons...
Quilters Come With Strings Attached!
Quilters Make Better Comforters!
Quilters Never Cut Corners...
Quiltin' 'Til I Be Wiltin'
Quilting Forever...Housework Never!!
When Life Hands You Scraps...Make A Quilt
Will Work For Fabric!

RABBIT TITLES

(SEE ALSO EASTER)

Bad Hare Day
Bunny Crossing
Bunny Hip Hop
A Bunny's Tale
Cute & Fluffy As A Bunny
Ears To You!
Everybody Deserves Somebunny!
Flippy Floppy Bunny Ears
Hippity, Hoppity Fun
Hopping Down The Bunny Trail
Honey Bunny
Hunny Bunny
Jumping Jack Rabbit
Little Angel Bunny
Magic Rabbit
No Bunny Like You
Somebunny Loves You
Somebunny Special
Sweet Little Bunny
There's No Bunny Like You

RACE/RACING TITLES

(SEE ALSO CAR & DRIVING)

- *Make title mat look like a small Race Track or Road.*
- *Use black & white checkered paper for title mat.*
- *Use a Tire for an "O".*

Along For The Ride
...And He's Off
...And The Winner Is...
At The Track
Away He Goes
Back On Track
Born To Race
Box Car Racer
Breaking Away
Breakneck Speed
Built For Speed
Burning Rubber
By A Length
Can't Wait To Get On The Road Again!
Caution...Yellow Flag
Checkered Flag Dreams/Finish
The Competition
Crazy Racer
A Day At The Races
Demolition Derby
Demolition Racer
Downhill Racer
Drag King
Drag Racer
Driver Wanted
In The Driver's Seat
Driving Force
Easy Rider
Enjoying The Ride
Fast & Furious
Fast, Faster, Fastest
On The Fast Track
I Feel The Need To Speed
A Fighting Chance
Final Circuit
The Finish Line
Finish Line Frenzy
Four On The Floor
Full Throttle
Garage Guru
Gentlemen...Start Your Engines
GO! GO! GO!
Go Speed Racer
Going For The Gold
Going In Circles
Going The Distance
Good Timin'
Good To Go
The Grand Prix
The Great Race
Green Means Go!
Hairpin Turns
High Anxiety
High Hopes
Hot Rod Dreamer
Hot Wheels
I'd Rather Ride Around With You
It's The Journey, Not The Destination
Ladies & Gentlemen...START YOUR ENGINES!
The Last Lap
Life Doesn't Begin Until 150 m.p.h.!
Life In The Fast/Slow Lane
Life's Not A Race
I Live My Life A Quarter Mile At A Time
The Long & Winding Road
The Long Race
Loop The Loop
Lovin' The Victory Lap
Motocross Racer
Mr. Goodwrench
A Need For Speed
Never Drive Faster Than Your Guardian Angel Can Fly

Not So Fast
On The Right Track
On The Road Again
On The Road Again...& Again...& Again
On Track
On Your Mark...Get Set...Go ! ! !
One Lap To Go!
Ooh! That Had To Hurt!
Outpaced
Pace Car Pit Crew
Passed With Flying Colors
Pedal To The Metal
Pit Stop
Pit Stop...Portrait Of A Winner
Posi-traction
Power Race
Pro-Circuit...Here I Come
Put The Pedal To The Metal
Qualifying Quivers
Race Day
The Race For Life
The Race I Face
The Race Is On
Race To The End
Race To The Finish
Race Warrior
Racer *(Name)*
Racing Radicle
Racing To The Red Light
Rat Race
Ready For The Pro-Circuit
A Red Flag Warning
Red Light, Green Light
Road Adventures USA
Road Hog
Rough Racer
'Round & Around
Sitting In The Pitts
Slow & Steady Wins The Race
Space Race
Speed Demon
Speed Racer
Speedy Gonzalez
Spin-Out
Super Charger
Survival Of The Fastest
Tailgating
Take It To The Limit
Taking The Checkered Flag
Taste Of Victory
There's No Looking Back Now
The Thrill Of Victory
Thrill Ride
Today's Heroes
Tools Of The Trade
Top Speeder
A Track Record
Uneasy Rider
Unrivaled Competition
Vanishing Race
The Wheels On My Car Go 'Round & 'Round
When The Week Ends, The Fun Begins!
Where The Black Top Ends...
Where The Rubber Meets The Road...
White Knuckles
Winner Of The Race
Winning With Style
I WON The Race!

____
____
____
____
____

RAFTING TITLES
(SEE ALSO WATER)
- *Create a Raft as the mat for the title.*

Bumping Across The Water
A Bumpy Ride
Conquered The Rapids
A Grand Voyage
The Grandest Rapids
Man Overboard
Riding The Rapids
Roaring Rapids
White-Water Adventure
White-Water Rapids

____
____
____
____
____

RAIN TITLES
(SEE ALSO RAINBOWS & WATER)
- *Make Clouds & have the title in the Clouds with Raindrops falling from the clouds.*
- *Make the title words look like they are Raining.*
- *Use an Umbrella as a title mat.*

After The Rain, Comes A Rainbow
After The Rain Has Fallen
All We Needed Was The Reed
Always In The Rain
Amazon Rains
...And Me Without My Umbrella
...And The Heavens Opened Up
...And The Rain, Rain, Rain, Came Down, Down, Down...

Another Rainy Day
April Showers Bring May Flowers
A Beautiful Rainy Day
Blame It On El Niño
Blame It On The Rain
Blessed By The Rains
Bring On The Rain
I Can See Clearly Now The Rain Has Gone
Can You Stand The Rain?
Celebrate The Rain
City Slickers
Clean Fresh Rain
Clouds Of Silver Rain
Come Rain Or Come Shine...
Covered In Rain
Cryin' In The Rain
A Damp Dark Day
Days Of Thunder
Desert Rains
Don't Rain On My Parade
Drenched
Early Morning Rain
Every Cloud Has A Silver Lining
The Falling Of Raindrops...
Feel The Rain
Fool In The Rain
A "HAIL" Of A Storm!
Have You Ever Seen The Rain?
Here Comes The Rain
How Is The Weather?
I'm No Stranger To The Rain
Into Our Lives A Little Rain Must Fall
It Ain't Gonna Rain No More
It's A Wonderful Rainy Day
It's Raining Again
It's Raining...It's Pouring
Joy Is Like The Rain
Kiss The Rain
Laughing In The Rain
Let A Smile Be Your Umbrella
Let It Pour
Let It Rain, Rain, Rain!
Listen To The Rhythm Of The Falling Rain
A Little Black Rain Cloud
A Little Rain Must Fall
Listen To The Rhythm Of The Falling Rain
May The Rain Bring You Rainbows. - *(Scarlett)*
Mommy's Little Mud Puppy
Mud Bath
Mud Bath! .5 Cents
Mud Pies! .10 Cents
Nobody Here But Us Ducks!
Nothing Like A Wallow In The Mud!
Oops!! My Name Is Mud
Our Rainy Day Sunshine
The Perfect Storm
Puddle Jumper/Jumpin'
Rain In The Summertime
Rain Is Falling All Around
Rain On Me
Rain Or Shine...You're A Friend Of Mine
Rain, Rain Go Away
Rain...The Ornament Of Nature
It Rained On Our Parade
Raindance
Raindrops & Rainbows
Raindrops & Smiles
Raindrops & Sunshowers
Raindrops Keep Fallin' On My Head & Toes &...
Raindrops On Roses...
Raining Cats & Dogs
Raining Pitchforks
Rainy Day Fun
Rainy Day People
Rainy Days & Mondays
Rainy Days Always Get Me Down
Rhythm Of The Rain
Riding Out The Storm
Rockin' To The Rhythm Of The Rain
Running Thru The Raindrops
Saving Up For A Rainy Day
Showered With Love
Showers Of Blessings
Singin' In The Rain
So Fell Autumn Rain
Soft Is The Rain
Some People Walk In The Rain, Others Just Get Wet. - *(Roger Miller)*
Splish Splash!
Sprinkle! Sprinkle! Sprinkle!
Sprinkled With Love
Sprinkles On Top
Summertime Raindrops
The Sun'll Come Out Tomorrow!
Sweet Sounds Of The Falling Rain
Tasting The Rain
Thunder & Lightning...Very, Very Frightening
Thunder Is Just God Bowling
Tut, Tut It Looks Like Rain - *(Winnie The Pooh)*
Under The Falling Raindrops
Under The Umbrella
Waiting & Wishing For Raindrops
Walk In The Spring Rain
Warm Summer Rain

When It Rains, It Pours
Who'll Stop The Rain?
Wishes Of Raindrops
You Are A Sun Drop Among The Raindrops

RAINBOW TITLES

(SEE ALSO RAIN)

- *Create a Rainbow & have the title in it.*
- *Arch title as a Rainbow with differently colored letters or words.*

After The Rain...
After The Rain, Comes A Rainbow
All The Colors Of The Rainbow
Better Than A Pot Of Gold
Chasing Rainbows
Color My World
The Colors Of The Rainbow
Finding Rainbows Thru The Clouds
God's Resplendent Rainbows
I Got A Pocketful Of Rainbows
If I Could Catch A Rainbow...
May The Rain Bring You Rainbows. - (Scarlett)
My End Of The Rainbow
Nature's Resplendent Rainbows
Never Blame The Rainbows For The Rain
Over The Rainbow
The Rainbow Connection
Rainbow Fields
A Rainbow In The Sunshine
Rainbow, Rainbow, Across The Sky
Rainbow's End
Rainbows Apologize For Angry Skies. (Sylvia Voirol)
Rainbows Are God's Glowing Covenant. (Hosea Ballou)
Rainbows Are Proof That God Keeps His Promises
The Rainbows Of Life Follow The Storms
Raindrops & Rainbows
Rainy Day Reward
Somewhere Over The Rainbow
Summer Rainbows
The Whole Spectrum
Wishes & Rainbows

READING TITLES

(SEE BOOKS)

RECITAL TITLES

(SEE DANCE, MUSIC, PLAY & SHOW BUSINESS)

RED TITLES

(A great way accentuate the word Red in the title, is to create that word only in Red. Make the word Red larger & even in a different type style than the rest of the title)

Big Red
Caught Red-Handed
Code Red
Courtesy Of The Red, White & Blue
Fields Of Red
Flaming Red
In The Red
Lady In Red
Little Red Corvette
Little Red Riding Hood
My Heart's Like A Red Rose
Paint The Town Red
Red Alert
Red As A Beet
Red As A Lobster
The Red Badge Of Courage
The Red Carpet Treatment
The Red Dress
Red Head
Red Hi-Heels
Red Hot
Red Hot Chilly Peppers
Red Hot Lover
Red In The Face
Red Letter Day
Red Neck
Red, Red Rose
Red, Red Wine
Red Rock Canyon Rockin'
Red Roses For A Blue Lady
Red Rubber Ball
The Red Sox
Robin Red Breast
Rolled Out The Red Carpet
Roses Are Red, Violets Are Blue...
Ruby Red
Seeing Red
Sexy Red Lips
Shades Of Red

REINDEER TITLES

(SEE DEER)

RELAXING TITLES

(SEE SLEEPING)

RELIGIOUS TITLES

(SEE ALSO RELIGIOUS PASSAGES)

- *Make a Church Roof with the Cross on it & put the title under the roof.*

All That We Have...
All That's Good & Great & True...
Amazing Grace
Angels Watching Over Me
Awesome God
Be Still & Know That I Am God
Bless Me, Heavenly Father
Blessed With Blessings
A Blessing From Above
A Blessing To Behold
By The Grace Of God
I Can Do All Things Through Christ
Celebration Of Faith
A Child Of God
Church Bizarre
Church Mouse
Count Your Blessings
A Day Of Grace
A Day Of Rest
Faith Can Move Mountains
Faith Doesn't Panic
I Fear No Evil In My Father's House
Fingerprints Of God
For He Is Always There Behind You, Beside You & Before You
A Friendship Is A Blessing Of Times
Get Me To The Church On Time
Glory Be To God
God & Me...
God Answers Knee Mail
God Bless You
God Gave Me Everything
God...Give Me Strength
God Guides My World
God Is Great...God Is Good!
God Is Love
God Is Watching Us
God Made Me
God Made You For Me
God Moves In Mysterious Ways
God Must Have Spent A Little More Time On You
God Only Knows...
God Reads Our Hearts
In God We Trust
God's Blessing Of Love & Wisdom...
God's Country
God's Creation
God's Day Of Thanks
God's Door Is Always Open
God's House
God's Little Songbird
God's Rainbow
God's Time Is Best
God's Truth Will Always Stand
God's With You
Got Jesus?!
Got Me To The Church On Time
Have Faith
He Who Kneels Before God Can Stand Before Anyone!
He Will Hold You In The Palm Of His Hand
Hear Me Lord
Heaven & Earth Are Full Of His Glory
His Word Is True, His Promise Kept & His Love Is Unending
His Eye Is On The Sparrow
How Great Thou Art!
I Am A Child Of God
I Thank God For You
Jesus Is Like A Sunbeam
Jesus Loves All The Children Of The World
Life Is A Blessing
Life Is Fragile...Handle With Prayer
Little Words Of Kindness, Little Acts Of Love...
Livin' In The Light Of The Lord
Livin' On A Prayer
The Lord Is Good To All
My Lord Is My Strength & My Song
Never Alone
Oh, The Lord's Been Good To Me
On The Wings Of A Dove
Our Children & God's
Our Precious Gift From God
Our Sunday Best
The Power Of God
Praise God From Whom All Blessings Flow
Prayer Is Kind Of Like Calling Home Every Day
Precious In His Sight
Showers Of Blessings
Spirit In The Clouds
Stand Up & Bless The Lord
Sunday's Child Is Full Of Grace
Sweet Blessings
Thank The Lord For The Nighttime
Thank You Lord For The Blessings Of Today
There Are Many Mansions
There Is Joy In The Lord
To Be Alone With Silence Is To Be With God

Touched By The Hand Of God
Turn Your Eyes Upon Jesus
We Leave Thy House, But Leave Not Thee
When God Opened Heaven's Gate
When Prayers Go Up...Blessings Come Down
Wings Of God
With God's Blessings...

JOY
Jesus 1st
Others 2nd
You Last

RELIGIOUS PASSAGES TITLES
(SEE ALSO CHURCH)
As For God, His Way Is Perfect. - *(Psalm 18:30)*
As For Me & My House, We Will Serve The Lord. - *(Joshua 24:15)*
Children, Obey Your Parents. - *(Ephesians 6:1)*
Depart From Evil & Do Good. - *(Psalm 37:14)*
Even A Child Is Known By His Doings. *(Proverbs 20:11)*
Every Good & Perfect Gift Is From Above. *(James 1:17)*
The Eyes Of All Look To You, Lord. - *(Psalm 145:15)*
A Glad Heart Makes A Cheerful Countenance. *(Proverbs 15:13)*
God Blesses Those Whose Hearts Are Pure. *(Matthew 5:8)*
Have No Greater Joy Than To Hear That My Children Walk In Truth. - *(John 4)*
The Heavens Declare The Glory Of God. *(Psalm 19:1)*
I Can Do All Things Through Christ. *(Philippians 4:13)*
I Will Praise Thee For I Am Fearfully & Wonderfully Made. - *(Psalm 139:14)*
If Ye Shall Ask Anything In My Name, I Will Do It. - *(John 14:14)*
It Is God Who Arms Me With Strength & Makes My Way Perfect. - *(Psalm 18:32)*
Keep Me Safe, O God, For In You I Take Refuge. - *(Psalm 16:1)*
Let The Little Children Come To Me. - *(Luke 8:16)*
Let Us Walk In The Light Of The Lord. *(Isaiah 2:5)*
The Lord Is My Light & Salvation. - *(Psalm 27:1)*
The Lord My God Will Enlighten My Darkness. - *(Psalm 18:28)*
The Lord Watches Over All Who Love Him. *(Psalm 145:20)*
Praise Be To The Lord...Who Made Heaven & Earth. - *(2 Chronicles 2:12)*
Send Forth Your Light & Your Truth, Let Them Guide Me. - *(Psalm 43:3a)*
Sing To The Lord A New Song. - *(Psalm 96:1)*
This Is The Day The Lord Has Made, Let Us Rejoice & Be Glad In It. - *(Psalm 119:105)*
Thy Word Is A Lamp To My Feet, & A Light To My Path. - *(Psalm 119:105)*
You Knit Me Together In My Mother's Womb. *(Psalm 139:13-14)*

REMEMBER TITLES
Best Friends Always Remember
I Can Remember
Can You Remember?
Do You Remember When...
A Face To Remember
I'll Always Remember You
I'll Remember
Just Remember
Just Remember...I Love You
A Kiss To Remember
A Night To Remember
Please Remember Me
Remember Always...
Remember Me
Remember The Feeling...
Remember The Time...
Remember This...
Remember Walking In The Sand...
I Remember You
Remembrance Of Days Gone By
Remembrance Of Moments
A Rememorable Moment
Silent Remembrances
A Smile To Remember
Something To Remember
Sweet Remembrances

REMODELING TITLES

(SEE ALSO CONSTRUCTION & TOOLS)

- *Cut & chalk title mat to look like Wood & add brads for nails.*
- *Use different Tools as some letters.*

Cement Shower *(Pool being poured)*
Complete Redesign
Destruction Construction
Destruction Crew
Destruction Man
The Destruction Of *(Room, House, etc.)*
Fixer Upper
From Start To Finish
Home Improvements
My Honey Do Crew
On The Road To Reconstruction
The Process Of Destruction
Raise The Roof
Reconstruction Construction
Rome Wasn't Built In A Day Either!
Room For Improvement
Ruins Of The Old
Tear The Roof Off
Tools Of Mass Destruction
Total Destruction
Under Reconstruction
A Work In Progress

____
____
____
____
____

RENAISSANCE TITLES

A Faire Day
Faire Lady
The Fare Lady
Fare Thee Well To The Faire
Fearless Knights
A Fine Rogue Is Thee
Hear Ye, Hear Ye!
Huzzah Faire
Huzzah To The Day
Huzzah Wench
I Dub Thee...
In Majesty Glorious
Jester Fun
Joust For Fun
The King & His Castle
Magic Kingdom
Mid Evil Times
Mid Evil Woman
A Most Buxom Day
Mistress *(Surname)*
My Knight In Shining Armor
My Lady
My Lord
My Royal Jester
Needin' Mead (*A drink)*
A Most Prettyful Poppet
Renaissance Affaire/Faire
Renaissance Man
A Shire's Thee Place
Thou A Lusty Bar Maid
Thou Nonpareil
Ye Art Most Beautacious Faire
Ye Fare Maidens
Young Lords Of *(Surname)*
Your Grace

____
____
____
____
____

RENAISSANCE LINGO

- *Make tags & put Renaissance words & their definitions on them around your page for interest.*

Ale - The nectar of the Gods or dark beer
Anon - Until later
Aye/Yea - Yes or I agree
Bodice - A tight fitting vest worn over a dress by wenches of olde
Breeches - Men's short pants
Certes - Certainly
Come Hither - Come here
E'en - Evening or Night
Enow - Enough
FareThee Well - Good Bye
Gesundheit! - God save you!
Good Day/Good Morrow/Goode'en - Greeting
Good Den - Greetings reply
Grammarcy! - Thank you!
Harken - Listen
Huzzah! - Super! Great! Yippee! Yahoo!
In Sooth - I believe or I think
Jakes - Bathroom
Jerkin - A males vest usually worn over a shirt proper
M'lord/lady - Greeting
Mayhap - Maybe

Mead - An alcoholic drink made of fermented honey
Morrow - The following day
Na'er often! - Never, No, No Way, Nope
Nonpareil - A beauty
Oft - Often
Perchance - Maybe
Poppet - A small child or doll
Pray Pardon - Excuse Me
Pray tell - Please tell me
Prithee/Pray - Please
Privy - Outdoor bathroom
Rogue - The finest men at any renaissance festival!
Shire - Is usually the area where the Faire is being held, a fantasy township
Snood - Woman's hair adornment
Thou - You
Tosspot - Drunkard
Verily - Very or Truly
Very Well - OK
Wench - A serving woman
Wherefore - Why
Yonder - Over There
Zounds - Wow!

____
____
____
____
____

RETIREMENT TITLES

(SEE ALSO WORK)
Finally On The Go
A Forever Weekend
Forever Young
The Golden Years
Goodbye Tension, Hello Pension
I'm Outta Here
I'm RETIRED I'm Not Dead!
Life Begins At Retirement
Life Goes On
Look Out Fish...I'm Retired Now!
My Permanent Coffee Break
Never Too Old To Fish
Now What?
Remember...Old is Gold!!!
Retired But Not Tired
Retired...Now I Have A Life!!!
Retirement Blues
Retirement Eulogy
Retirement Rendezvous
Spring Chickens United
Time For A Little R&R
Time Marches On...
I Thought This Day Would Never Come!
Varied Visions Of Retirement
Warning!!! Retired Person, Moves Slowly, Naps Often!!!
Well-Seasoned
What Will They Do Without Me?
World Traveler

____
____
____
____
____

REUNION/REUNITED TITLES

(SEE ALSO FRIENDS & MEMORIES)
Among My Survivors...
Be True To Your School
Bits Of Yesterday
The Best Antiques To Collect Are Old Friends
The Class Of '57 *(Any year)* Had Its Dreams
Do You Remember These?
Friends Forever
Friends Never Say Goodbye
Friendship...The Older It Grows, The Stronger It Is
It Was The Best Of Times
It's Easier To Get Older Than It Is To Get Wiser
It's Been Too Long!
Life Long Friends
I Love Remembering
Love Reunited
Many Joys Come & Go, But Friendship Is Forever
Moments In Time
Nothing Is As Comfortable As An Old Friend
Old Friends Are The Best Antiques
Once Upon A Time...
Only Yesterday
Our Gang
Photographs & Memories
Remember When...
Reunited After All These
Reunited And It Feels So Good...
Seems Like Yesterday
Somewhere In Time
Special Friends Bring Special Memories
Sweet Connections
Those Were The Days
Thru The Years
A Time To Remember
Together Again

Together At Last
Travel Thru The Pages Of Time
A Walk Down Memory Lane
The Way We Were
Whatever Happened To The Class Of '65?
(Any year)
When Friends Meet, Hearts Warm!
Where Have You Been All My Life?
The Wonder Years
Yesterday Once More
Yesterme, Yesteryou, Yesterday
You Are Among My Souvenirs

RIDE/RIDING TITLES

(SEE ALSO BICYCLE, DIRT BIKE & MOTORCYCLE)

- *Use a Tire or Bike Wheel in place of an "O".*

Along For The Ride
An "E" Ticket Ride
Black Horse Rider
Born To Ride
"E" Ticket Ride
Easy Rider
Enjoying The Ride
Free Ride
Get In...Sit Down...Hold On...Shut Up!
Glory Ride
Got Air!?!
Hitchin' A Ride
It's Not The Destination, It's The Journey
I've Got A Ticket To Ride
Joy Ride
Keep The Faith...Ride Safe
Learning To Ride
Let It Ride
Let's Ride
Live To Ride...Ride To Live
Lonesome Rider
Low Rider
Midnight Ride/Rider
Night Rider
Not-So-Easy Rider
One Last Ride
Ride A Hog
The Ride Goes On Forever
Ride Like The Wind
The Ride Of Life
To Ride Or Not To Ride...Stupid Question!!!
Ride, Ride, Ride The Wild Road
Ride The Lightning
Rider In The Wind
Riding Around In My Automobile
Riding Free
Riding High
Riding In Style
Rip Roarin' Ride
Rough Rider
Rowdy Rider
Rugged Rider
She Wants To Ride
Taken For A Ride
Ticket To Ride
A White Knuckle Ride
Wild Ride

ROCK/ROCKING TITLES

- *Make Rocks by cutting or ripping & crumpling cardstock & use them as title mats.*

Between A Rock & A Hard Place
Born To Rock-N-Roll
The Boulder & The Beautiful
Caught Between A Rock & A Hard Place
Cleveland Rocks
Cradle Rock
Crocodile Rock
Dixieland Rock
Don't Rock The Boat
Don't Rock The Jukebox
Freedom Rock
Giddy-Up Mr. Rocking Horse
Gramma Rocks
Hard As Rock
Hard Rock Cafe
Hillbilly Rock
House Of Rock
I Think I'm Gettin' Horsey Sick
It's Only Rock-N-Roll To Me
Jailhouse Rock
Jingle Bell Rock
Keep On Rockin'
Let's Get Rocked
Like A Rock
Long Live Rock
Love Me Like A Rock
Love On The Rocks
I Love Rock-N-Roll
I Love To Rock
Lover's Rock
A Milestone

Off My/Your Rocker
Plymouth Rock
Pop Rocker
Pop The Rock
Punk Rocker
Red Rock Canyon Rockin'
Rock-A-Bye-Baby
Rock-A-Bye Horsey
Rock All Night
Rock Around The Clock
Rock Bottom
Rock City
Rock Freak
Rock House
Rock In The USA
Rock Is King
Rock Me Gently
Rock Me Slowly
Rock Me Tender
Rock-N-Roll
Rock-N-Roll Band
Rock-N-Roll Cowboy
Rock-N-Roll Dreams/Fantasy
Rock-N-Roll Girl
A Rock-N-Roll Heart/Love
Rock-N-Roll Kids
Rock-N-Roll Lady/Mama
Rock-N-Roll Party
Rock-N-Roll Soul
Rock-N-Roller
Rock Of Ages
Rock On!
Rock Out!
The Rock Rolls On
Rock Solid
Rock Star
Rock Steady
The Rock That Makes Me Roll
Rock This Country/Town
Rock 'Til You Drop
Rock With You
Rock You Baby
Rock You Like A Hurricane
Rock Your Body
Rockabilly
Rockin' Along
Rockin' America
Rockin' Good Time
Rockin' 'N Rollin'
Rockin' The Cradle
The Rocking Boy
To Shoot The Rock
Skippin' Rocks
Solid As A Rock
Southern Rock
Space Rock
Third Rock From The Sun
This Town Rocks
We Will Rock You
We're Rockin' Now
You Got Me Rocking
You Rock My World

ROLLING OVER TITLES

Flipped Out
Just Roll With It Baby
Gambler's Roll
High Roller
Holy Roller
Let The Good Times Roll
Let The Rhythm Roll On
Let's Roll
On A Roll
On The Roll Again
Over & Over Again
Papa Was A Rolling Stone
Ready...Set...Roll
Ready To Roll
Rock-N-Roll
Rockin' & Rollin'
Roley Poley
Roll Call
Roll 'Em Over
Roll In The Sand
Roll It
Roll It Over
Roll Of The Dice
Roll On!
Roll On Down
Roll Over
Roll With It
Roller Coaster Girl
Roller Coaster Queen
Roller Skater
Rollin' & Tumblin'
Rollin' Along
Rollin' On The Highway
Rollin', Rollin', Rollin'
Rolling Hills
Rolling Rock
Rolling Stone
Rolling Thru Life
Rolling Thunder

Shake...Rattle...& Roll
Stop, Drop & Roll
Summertime Rolls
The Thunder Rolls
As Time Rolls By
Wheels On My Heels
Wheels Rollin' On

____
____
____
____
____

ROYALTY TITLES

- *Make a Crown decorated with rhinestones & use it as the title mat.*
- *Place smaller crowns on some title letters.*

All The Queen's Men
Beauty Queen
Being A Princess Is A Full-Time Job
Burger King
California King
Candy Coated Princess
Crown Me King
Crowned Royal
Cuz I'm The Princess...That's Why!
Daddy's Little Princess
Dancing Queen
Drama Queen
Duke Of *(Your House/Town/State/Country/ Surname)*
Enchanting Princess
Fairy Princess
Fit For A King
Flower Princess
Fresh Prince/Princess Of *(Your State or Town)*
From A Jack To A King
From Prince To King
From Princess To Queen
I Found My Prince Charming
Future King/Queen
Hail To Our Princess
Handsome King
He Who Fears Nothing Is King
He Who Seems/Acts Kingly Is King!
Her Royal Highness/Majesty
Homecoming King/Queen
I Am A Princess
I Am The King/Queen
Ice Queen
If I Were King...
I'm A Princess...A Princess In Training!
In A King's/Queen's World...
In The Presence Of A Princess...
It's Good To Be King
It's Not Easy Being A Princess
I Just Can't Wait To Be King/Queen
The King & I
King For A Day
The King In His Castle
King Kong
King Me
King Of Diamonds *(Jeweler)*
King Of Hearts
King Of His Castle
A King Of Kings
King Of Love
King Of My House/Room
King Of Queens
King Of Rock
King Of Royal Badness
King Of Swing
King Of The Hill
King Of The Jungle
King Of The Mountain
King Of The Road
King Of The Throne
King Without A Crown
King *(Child's name)*
Lion King
The Little Prince/Princess
The Littlest King/Queen
March Of The King
My Princess, My Sweetheart
Our Mother Queen
Pee Wee Princess
Pouty Princess
Precious Princess
Pretty Princess
Prince Charming
Prince In Training For King
Prince Of All Charms
Prince Of My/Our Hearts
Prince Of Peace
The Princess & The Sea
Princess Bride
Princess In Training For Queen
Princess In Training For Goddess
Princess Of All Charms
Princess Of Almost Everything
Princess Of The House
Princess Today, Goddess Tomorrow!
Princess *(Child's name)*
Princessa
Queen Bee
Queen For A Day
Queen Of All Heart's
Queen Of Braids

Queen Of Diamonds
Queen Of EVERYTHING!!!
Queen Of Hearts
Queen Of My Heart
Queen Of My Room
Queen Of Royal Badness
Queen Of The Kingdom
Queen Of The Nile
Queen Of The Night
Queen Of The Universe!
Queen *(Name)*
Royal Flush
Royal Love
Royal Pain In Training
Royal Prince/Princess
Royal Rose
Sleeping Prince/Princess
Snow Queen
Speed King
Thou Art Queen
A True Princess
We Three Kings
What Part Of Princess Don't You Understand?
Worth A King's Ransom
Yes, Your Royal Highness
Your Royal Highness
You're My King/Queen
You're My Prince/Princess

____
____
____
____
____

RUN/RUNNING TITLES

(SEE ALSO TRACK & FIELD)

Always On The Run
Athlete's Feet *(Runner)*
Baby On The Run
Blade Runner
Born To Run
Come Run Away With Me
Free To Run
From Start To Finish
Go For The Gold
Going, Going, Gone!
Havin' A Field Day
Hit 'N Run
Hit The Ground Running
In The Long Run
Just Run With It!
Just Try & Catch Me!
Keep On Runnin'
Let Your Imagination Run Wild
Long May You Run
The Long Run
The Longest Mile
Love On The Run
Makin' Tracks
My Little Run-A-Away
Nowhere To Run
Off & Running
On The Fast Track
On The Run
On Your Mark, Get Set, Go
One Last Run
Racin' To The Finish Line
Ready, Set, Go!
Road Runner
The Run Away
Run Away Little Girl
Run Baby Run
Run For Cover
Run Free
Run Like The Wind
Run, Run, Run, Run, Run-Around
Run To Him
Run To Me
Run With Me
Runner Up
Running For Life
Running Free
Running In Circles
Running Late
Running Man
Running On Empty
Running Out Of Time
Running Scared
Running Thru The Night
Running Wild
It Runs In The Family
Sprint
Take It On Your Run
Take The Money & Run
'Til The River Runs Dry
Time To Run
Twinkle Toes
U-Haul *(Fast runner)*
Who Will You Run To?
Wings On My Feet

____
____
____
____
____

R
R
R
R
R
R
R
R
R
R
R
R
R
R
R
R
R
R
R
R
R
R
R
R
R
R
R
R
R
R

SAD TITLES

(SEE ALSO CRYING & MAD)

Baby's Got The Blues
Bad Weather Blues
Beach Boy Blues
Blues Boy
Blues In The Night
Blues Man
Certified Blues
Christmas Blues
Don't Worry...Be Happy!
Feelin' Blue
I Got The Blues
Honky Tonk Blues
Little Boy Blue
Little Girl Blue
Lonesome Blues
A Mess Of Blues
The Moody Blues
Morning Blues
Night Time Blues
Please Don't Cry
Rock-A-Bye Baby Blues
Sad Eyes
Singing The Blues
Sooooo Sad!
Such A Sad Little Face
Why The Long Face?

SAILING TITLES

(SEE ALSO BOAT & CRUISE)

- *Place title on a large Boat Ore.*
- *Use an Ore as an "I".*
- *Put title on a Boat Sail.*

Ahoy Matey's
As They Sail Off Into The Sunset...
Come Sail Away With Me
Crazy About Kayaking
Don't Rock The Boat
Forever I Will Sail
I'd Rather Be Sailing Than Anything Else
Let Your Dreams Set Sail
Let's Sail Away
Making Waves
A Need For Speed
On The Water Front
Only Sailors Get Blown Off Shore
Red Sails In The Sunset
Riding The Waves
Row, Row, Row, Your Boat
Row The Boat Ashore
Sail Away
Sail On
Sail On Silver Waves
Sail On To Your Dreams
Sailing Across The Seas
Sailing On A Sea Of Joy
Sailing, Sailing Away
Sailing, Sailing...Over The Ocean Blue
Sailing, Sailing...Over The Ocean's Roar
Sailing Takes Me Away
Sailing The Open Seas
Sailing Under A Sailor's Moon
Sailing Under A Silvery Moon
Sailing Wave Over Wave
Sailing With The Angels
Sailing With The Breeze
The Sailor & The Sea
Sea Fever
That Sinking Feeling
Smooth Sailing
Sunset Sailing
Testing The Waters
The Unsinkable *(Boat's name)*
We Set The Sail; God Makes The Wind
Whatever Floats Your Boat
Where The Ocean Meets The Sky, I'll Be Sailing

SANTA CLAUS TITLES

(SEE ALSO CHRISTMAS)

- *Make a Santa's Cap & put title on the brim.*
- *Make a Scroll & put title on scroll.*

Bearded Stranger
Cheeks Like Cherries
Dear Santa
Dear Santa...I've Been Good!
Delivered In A Twinkle
Do You Believe?
Hear Comes Santa Claus...
Ho! Ho! Ho!
Jolly Old Soul
Jolly Ole St. Nick
Naughty Or Nice?
Santa & Me
Santa Baby
Santa Claus Is Coming To Town
Santa's Little Helper
I Saw Mommy Kissing Santa Claus
I Still Believe

____
____
____
____
____

SCARE TITLES

Boo!
Did You Hear That?
Do I Look Afraid?
Don't Be Scared
Isn't He Scary
Monster Scary
Running Scared
Scare Tactics
Scared Of His Own Shadow
Scared Silly
Scaredy Cat
The Scarecrow & Me
A Scary Night
The Scary Spot
To Scare Or Not To Scare...
What Scares Me Most...
What Was That?
You Don't Scare Me!

____
____
____
____
____

SCHOOL TITLES

(SEE ALSO BOOKS, BUS, GRADUATION & TEACHER)

- *Use a Pencil or Crayon for an "I" or "L".*
- *Make a Ruler & put title on the Ruler.*
- *Create little Books & use as mats for title.*
- *Make title look like a Certificate or Diploma.*
- *Put title on a large Apple.*

1st Day Of School
2 Teach + 2 Touch A Life = 4 Ever
"A" No Brainer
"A" 4 Effort
A+ Student
ABC's & 123's
Adding It All Up
After School Special
All Booked Up
All Knowledge Begins With Wonder
Always Time For Learning
An Apple For The Teacher
Apple Of My Eye
Back 2 Class
Back 2 School
Back 2 The Books
Be All You Can Be
Be True To Your School
Beauty School Drop-out
Big Man On Campus
Black Board Jungle
Book Buddies
Book Worm
Brain Building
Brain Busting
Brain Overload
Brainiac With Papers To Prove It
Campus Cut-Up
Caught Thinking
Charm School Success...
Class Act
Class Clown
Classy Student
College Bound
College Life
College Or Bust
Cool School
Cyber Student
The Days Of School
Do The Math
Dorm Sweet Dorm
Education Is The Key
Explore The Genius Within
Fast Times At *(Your H.S.)*
Finally!!! *(Graduation)*
First Rate Classmate

Follow Your Dreams
Frat Brat
The Freshman!
From Diapers To Diploma!!!
Genius In Training
Gettin' Smart
Getting The Educational Edge
Go Figure
Golden Rule Days
Good Old Fashioned School Days
Goodbye Dorm
Got/Getting Edgicated
Got Smart
The Grim Reader
I Hate Mondays
Head Of The Class
High School Drama
High School Heart Attacked
Hi-ho, Hi-ho, It's Off To School I Go
Homework Makes You Ugly
Homework Time
Honor Student
I Is A College Student
I'm A Year Smarter
In A Class Of Her/His Own
In A School Daze
Intellectual Property
It's As Easy As 1,2,3/A,B,C
I've Got A Lot To Learn
I've Lost My Mind...I Think The Kids Took It
The Junior!
A Kid With Class
Kindergarten Caper
Kiss My Class Good-Bye
All Knowledge Begins With Wonder
Land Of The Learning
Learn & Get Learned
Learning Can Never Be Erased *(Eraser & chalk or pencil & eraser)*
Learning How To Learn
The Learning Zone
Lessons In Logic
Letter Perfect
Life Is An Open Book...So Study!
Live & Learn
Lots Of Learning Going On
Made The Dean's List
Magic School Bus
Makin' The Grades
The Mark Of Class
Me & My Bright Ideas
Me & *(Name)* Down On The Schoolyard
Miss Smarty Pants
Mr. Smarty Pants
My Alma Mata
My Favorite Subjects Are: Lunch & Recess
My Future's So Bright, I Gotta Wear Shades
National Achiever
No Brainer
Now I Can Get A Real Job
Now I Will Consider The CEO Position
Opportunity Knocks
This Paper Says I Have Brains In My Head!
Pep Rally
Phi Beta Capa
Playing By The Book
Pre-School Blues
Pretty & Smart
Reach For The Stars
Read To Succeed
Readin', Writin' & Rithmatic
Reading Is The Key To The World
Reading Rocks
Recess Rules
Return To Education
Roommates 'R Us
The Scholar
School Blues
School Days/Daze
School House Rock
School Is Where The Homework Is
School Life
School Rules
School Spirit
School Yard Days
School Zone
School's Out For The Summer
See You In September
Sensational Student
Sharp As A Tack
Skool Days/Daze
Smart As A Whip
Smart Guy
Smarty Pants
The Sophomore!
Sorority Sister
Spirit, Let's Hear It!
Spring Break
Spring Fling
Star Student
Still Learning
Study Buddies
I Study For Weekends
Stylish Student
Summer's Over
Super Scholar
Super Science Student
The Super Senior!

A Tassel Worth The Hassle
Teacher's Pet
These Are The Best Of Times
Thirty Days Hath September
Too Cool At School
Too Smart
A Touch Of Class
Towering Achievement
University You!
UCLA All The Way
USC Is For Me
I Wanna Learn
Well, Ain't You Somethin!
We're Not Freshman Anymore
We've Only Just Begun
When Is Lunch/Recess?
Wise As An Owl
The Written Word
You Are The "U" In University
You Can "Count" On Me
Zainy Brainy

SCRAPBOOKING TITLES

(SEE ALSO CRAFTS)

- *Scrap pieces of paper make great title mats.*
- *Use Pens or Pencils for an "I" or "L".*
- *Replace a "T" with Scissors.*

Acid Free Zone
Any Time Is Scrapping Time
At The Crop
Been There, Done That, Have The Layout!
Birds Of A Feather Scrap Together
Born To Scrap...Forced To Work
Camp Crop-A-Lot
Capturing The Memories
Caution: Scrapbooker In The House
A Celebration Of Life's Story
Come Night Or Day...I Scrap Away
Cream Of The Crop
Crop Circle
Crop Crop
The Crop Files
A Crop Load Of Good Friends
Crop Shop Girls
Crop Shop Junkie
Crop Soup
Crop The Madness
Crop 'Til Ye Drop
Cropped 'Til I Dropped
Cropped With Care
Croppers Connection
Croppin' 4 Fun
Cropping Crew
Cut The Scrap
Cuttin' Up
A Day Without Scrapping Is A Day Without Sunshine
Don't Just Stand There, Scrap Something
Down Memory Lane
Fall Scrapbooking...
Harvesting The Crop
For Generations To Come...
From One Late Night Scrapper To Another
Fun With Scissors
Gone Scrappin'
Good 'Til The Last Crop
Gotta Scrap
Had A Scrap Attack!
Happy Scrappy Day
Have Scraps Will Travel
Havin' A Scrappy Day
Hearts & Scraps
I Could Have Scrapped All Night
I Only Scrap On Days That End In "Y"
I'd Rather Be Scrapping
I'm A Page-Planning, Sticker-Art Making, Punch-Art Assembling, Scissor Cutting, Acid-Free Testing, Supply Shopping Fool
Inspiration Station
It May Not Be The Best, But It's Not Bad...
Just Call Me Scrappy
Just Scrap It
I Just Wanna Scrap
Let's Go To The Crop
Life Begins At The Crop
Life Is Simple...Eat, Sleep & Scrap
Little Scrapper
Love Is...Acid Free
Memory Saver
Memory Zone
My Adventures In Scrapbooking
My Scrappin' Lair
My Name Is *(Name)* & I'm A Scrapaholic!!!
No Time To Crop...Too Busy Deciding Where To Shop
Non-Stop Cropping
Old Scrappers Never Die...They Just Punch Out!
On The Cutting Edge
Pages Of The Ages
Pages Thru Time
Paper Trails
Picture Perfect
Pictures Of Days Gone By

PMS = Pretty Mean Scrapper
Precious Moments
Pulled An All-Nighter
Queen Of The Crop
Ready! Set! Crop/Scrap!
Reality Is Scrap
Same Old Scrap
Scrap Addict
Scrap Happy
Scrap In The Name Of Love
I Scrap, Therefore I Am...Broke!
Scrap Your Heart Out
Scrapaholic
Scrapbook Adventures
Scrapbook Corner
Scrapbook Heaven
Scrapbook Treasures
Scrapbooking Is Life...The Rest Is Details!
Scrapbooking Is The Life For Me!
Scrappily Ever After
Scrappin' 4 Memories
A Scrappin' Good Time
Scrapping Is My Life!
A Scrapping Of Remembrances
Scrapping The Past
Scrappy Birthday
The Secret To Creativity Is Knowing How To Hide Your Sources
She Who Dies With The Most Scrapbooks, Lives On!
So Many Photos, So Little Time
Sticker 'Em Up
Sticker Shock
Stop, Crop & Roll
Stop 'N Crop
Tag Your It
Thanks For The Memories
VISA...It's Everywhere My Scrapbook Wants To Be
When Life Hands You Scraps, Make Scrapbooks
When Life Happens, Scrap It
Will Scrap For Punches
(Name) Scissor Hands

SEA TITLES

(SEE BEACH)

SEWING TITLES

(SEE ALSO CROSS STITCHING & QUILTING)

- *Make title letters look like Dotted Stitching with a Needle attached at the end.*
- *Use a Needle as an "I".*
- *Place a Button in place of an "O".*
- *Closed Scissors make a cute "T".*

1 Yard Of Fabric, Like 1 Cookie, Is Never Enough!
Anytime's A Stitchin' Time
As Ye Sew, So Shall Ye Rip
Bustin' At The Seams
Button, Button...Who's Got The Button?
Cut From The Same Cloth
Cute As A Button
Don't Needle The Seamstress
I Feel Sew Sew
Hands To Work...Hearts To God
Hi Ho, Hi Ho, It's Off To Sew I Go
I Am A Material Girl
I'd Rather Be Stitchin' Than In The Kitchen!!
Itching To Be Stitching
I Love Being Materialistic
Love Is The Thread That Binds Us
I Love To Sew & Have A Material Witness
Material Girl
Memories Are Stitched With Love
Mend Your Britches
My Heart Sings Joyfully With Each Stitch I Take!!
A Perfect Fitting
Put The Treadle To The Metal
Ready...Set...Sew
I See A Pattern Here!
Sew Adorable
Sew Busy
Sew Kindness...Gather Love
Sew Much Fabric, Sew Little Time
Sew Much Fun
Sew Simple
Sew What?
Sew-ciology
Sewing For Success
Sewing Mends The Soul
Sharing The Love Of Sewing
A Stitch In Time...Saves Nine
Stitch Your Stress Away
Stitchers Bear Their Crosses Better
Stitchin' Makes Me Sew Happy
Thanks Sew Much
I Think...Sew
Will Work For Fabric

You Are Cut From A Pattern I Love
You Are Sew Special
You Keep Me In Stitches

SHAVING TITLES

- *Create a Shaving Can with the Cream coming from it & place title inside cream.*
- *Use old fashioned razor in place of "T".*

The Art Of Shaving
A Clean Shave
Comfort Glide
Creamy Fun
Day Light Shaving Time
Got The Cutting Edge
I've Been Creamed
Lather Up
"Nik" "Nik"
Old Spice...New Spice *(Dad & child)*
Romancing The Beard
Rough Cut
Sensitive Skin
Smooth As A Baby's Bottom

SHELLS TITLES

(SEE BEACH)

SHINE TITLES

- *Sprinkle Rhinestones or glitter on title or use Diamond Dust paper for a shiny look.*

All That Glitters Is Not Gold!
As The Stars Shine...
Born To Shine
Girl, You Shine
I'm Gonna Let It Shine
Let Her/Him Shine In Your Life
Let It Shine, Let It Shine
Let Your Soul Shine
Look On The Bright Side
Rain Or Shine
Rise & Shine
Shine On!
Shine On You
Shine! Shine! Shine!
Smile & Shine
Sparkle & Shine
Sparkles Of Night
Under Star Shine...
Your Eyes Shine Like Stars
Your Night To Shine

SHIP TITLES

(SEE BOAT, CRUISE & SAILING)

SHOE TITLES

- *Tie or Lace a Ribbon or String around title.*
- *Make a Shoe & put title in the shoe.*

Agony Of De High Heels
All Shoe'd Up
Amelda Jr.
Amelda Wanna Be *(Someone who has a lot of shoes or just loves shoes)*
Blue Suede Shoes
Boys In Boots
Cool Your Heels
The Cutest Shoe On Earth
Diamonds On The Souls Of Her Shoes
Fit To Be Tied
Goody Two Shoes
Gotta Hole In My Sole
Heels On Wheels
Hell On High Heels
High Heel Shoes
If The Shoe Fits...
I'm Shoe Happy
In These Shoes...

It's Shoetime
Kick Up Your Heels
My Heart & Soul
New Shoes
No Shoes...No Shirt...No Problem
A Perfect Pair
Put On Your Dancing Shoes
Put Your Best Foot Forward
Put Yourself In My Shoes
Red High Heels
Ruby Shoes
Shoe Adorable
Shoe Girl
A Shoe In
The Shoe Must Go On!
Shoeholic
Shoeless *(Name)*
Show Me The Shoes
So Shoe Me!
Sole Perfect
Sole Pretty
Steppin' Out
There's No Love Like Shoe Love
Tie One On!
Twinkle, Twinkle Little Shoes
Walkin' Shoes Blues

SHOPPING TITLES

- *Use Shopping Bag as background for title.*

Bargain Basement Queen
Bargain Shopper
Born To Shop
Charge It!!!
Coupon Queen
A Day At The Mall
Friends Of A Feather Shop Together
Garage Sale Goddess/Junkie
Goin' On A Shoppin' Spree
Got Money...Need To Shop
I Came...I Saw...I Shopped
I've Got Shopping Fever
Mall Rat
Shop Talk
Shop 'Til You Drop
Shopaholic
A Shoppin' Expedition
A Shopping I Will Go
Shopping Is Good For My Health
Shopping Makes The World Go Around
Shopping Or Bust!!!
Shopping Spree Fun
Talk Shopping
A Tired Little Shopper
When The Price Is Right...Buy It!
Window Shopping Wonders

SHOW BUSINESS TITLES

(SEE ALSO DANCE, MUSIC & PLAY)

- *Create a Reel-To-Reel Camera or Roll of Film with Film unreeling with title on Film Strip.*
- *Place Drama Masks in corners of title mat.*
- *Put title on Megaphone or coming out of it.*
- *Create a Director's Action Board for title.*
- *Make a large Film Strip to put the title on.*

Act It Out
Action!
Action Packed
All The World's My Stage
Another Opening, Another Show!
The Appearance Of A Star
Applause! Applause!
Baby I'm A Star
Beauty On The Big Screen
Behind The Scenes
Big Screen Dreamer
Bowing Out
Bravo
Break A Leg
Broadway Baby
Broadway Bound
Broadway...Here I Come
Broadway Rhythm
Cattle Call
Casting Call King/Queen
Caught In The Act
Center Stage
A Chorus Line
A Class Act
Critic's Choice
Critic's Corner
Curtain Call
Cuuut!
Drama Queen
Drama Time
Dramatic Fanatic
Dreams Of The Apollo

Dreams Of The Silver Screens
Dressing The Part
Encore
Enter Stage Left/Right
Entertainment Tonight
Everyone's A Critic
Exit Stage Right
Front Page News
Future Star
Get Reel
Give My Regards To Broadway
The Greatest Show On Earth
The Great White Way
Hi-diddle-dee-dee, An Actor's Life For Me
Hollywood...Here I Come
Hooray For Hollywood
Hot Ticket
The Hottest Show In Town
The Hottest Tickets In Town
In Cognito
In The Director's Chair
In The Limelight/Spotlight
In The News
It's Make-up Time
It's Showtime At The Apollo
It's Showtime Folks!
It's Time To Dress-up...Right!
It's Time To Light The Lights
It's Time To Put On The Make Up
The Late Show
Let It Show
Let Me/Us Entertain You!
Let The Show Begin
Life Is Her Stage
Lights...Camera...Action!!!
Little Entertainer
Little Miss Broadway/Hollywood
Look Out Broadway
Look Out Hollywood...Here I Come
Making A Scene
Master Thespians Now Appearing
Nights On Broadway
Now Appearing...
On With The Show
One Big Act
Our Rising Star
Playing The Part
Queen Of The Casting Calls
Ready...Set...Action!
Scene 3, Take 2
Shining Star
Show Girls
The Show Must Go On
Showtime
Silver Screen Dreams
Stage Fright
Stage Of Stars
Standing Room Only
A Star Is Born
The Star Of The Show
A Star Performance
Strike A Pose
Super Star
Taking Center Stage
The Talented Mr./Miss *(Surname)*
That's Entertainment
There Are No Small Parts, Only Small Actors
There's No Business Like Show Business
There's No Time Like Show Time
Twinkle, Twinkle, Our Little Star
Two Thumbs Up
Which Way To Hollywood
You Otta Be In Pictures

____
____
____
____
____

SICK TITLES
(SEE DOCTOR, ILLNESS, INJURY & NURSE)

SILLY TITLES
Don't Be Silly
Feelin' Silly
Funny Business
Funny Faces
Laughing At The Silliness
My Silly Friends
Oh, The Silliness You Possess
Pure Silliness
Silliness Brought To You By *(Name)*
Silly All Over
Silly As A Love Song
Silly Boy
Silly Faces
Silly Fool
Silly Girl
Silly Habits
Silly Is As Silly Does
Silly Love
Silly Ole Me
The Silly Things You Say & Do
So Silly Together
Sometimes I've Just Got To Be Silly
Too Silly For Words

You're So Silly
You're So Silly, Oh So Silly

____
____
____
____
____

SILVER TITLES

(A great way accentuate the word Silver in the title, is to create that word only in Silver. Make the word Silver larger and even in a different type style than the rest of the title)

Born With A Silver Spoon In Her Mouth
Clouds Of Silver Rain
Long John Silver
Look For The Silver Lining
On The Silver Screen
Sails Of Silver
Served On A Silver Platter
Silver & Gold
Silver Bells
Silver-Haired Lady
Silver Lining
Silver Medal/Medalist
Sterling Silver
You Got The Silver

____
____
____
____
____

SING/SONG TITLES

(SEE MUSIC & SHOW BUSINESS)

SISTER TITLES

(SEE ALSO FRIENDS & GIRL)

Always My Sister
Am I My Sisters Keeper?
Being Sisters Is Something Special
Being Sisters Is The Best
Best Buddies
Best Buddies Are We...My Sister & Me!
Big Sister Is Watchin' Over You
Birds Of A Feather
Celebrating Sisterhood
Celebration Of Sisters
Double Blessing
Double Trouble
First A Sister...Now A Friend
Forever My Sister, Always My Friend
Hold On To Your Sister
Just Like Big Sister
Little Sister...
I Love My Sister
The Love Of A Sister
Me & My Sis
My Sister, My Friend...
Near & Dear
Oh Brother, She's My Sister
Oh, Sister!
She Ain't Heavy, She's My Sister!
She's My Sister
Sibling Rivalry
Sister Act
Sister & Friend...Two Words That Mean The Same
Sister Golden Hair
Sister, Hold My Hand
A Sister Is A Forever Friend
A Sister Is A Special Kind Of Friend
Sister Of Mine
Sister Of My Heart
Sister, Sister
Sisterhood
Sisterhood Is Powerful
Sisterly Love
Sisterly Ties
Sisters Are A Special Hug From God
Sisters Are A Work Of Heart
Sisters Are Forever
Sisters Are Special...Especially Mine
Sisters Are The Best Kind Of Friends
Sisters Are Two Different Flowers From The Same Garden
Sisters By Chance, Friends By Choice
Sisters For Life
Sisters From The Start, Friends From The Heart
Sisters...Gotta Love 'Em!
Sisters In Arms
Sisters Make The Best Friends
Sisters...Giggles, Secrets & Sometimes Tears
Sisters Share A Love Tied With Heartstrings
Sisters Since The Beginning...Friends 'Til The End
Sisters Warm The Heart
Sometimes Enemies, Sometimes Friends, Always Sisters
The Spirit Of A Sister
Sweet Sister
Two Of A Kind
We Share A History
What A Pair!
When A Child Is Born, So Is A Sister
When I Get Big, I'll Get Even!!!
You Drive Me Nuts
(Name) Has Been Promoted To Big Sister

SIS
Simply
Incredible
Sister

SISTER
Sweet
Incredible
Sassy
Trying
Expressive
Radiant

SKATING TITLES
- *Use Skate Wheels as an "O".*
- *Border the title with Wheels.*
- *Have title riding on Skateboard.*
- *Make a halfpipe & place title in or on it.*

All Skate
Ballerina On Skates
Blade Runner
Concrete King
Dreams Of The Ice Capades
Five Wheelin'
Free Stylin'
Glidin' Along
Gliding Lightly
Go Figure Eight
Hittin' The Ice
Holiday On Ice
Ice Bound
Ice Dancer
Ice, Ice Baby
Ice Maiden
Icing On The Season
Just Skate It!!!
Let The Good Times Roll
Miracle On Ice
On Golden Pond
On One Blade
Our Little Ice Princess/Queen
Perfect Figure Eight
Princess On Ice
Queen Of The Ice
Roller Bladdin' Boogie
Rollin' Along
Rollin' At The Rink
Rollin', Rollin', Rollin', Keep Those Skates A Rollin'
Skate Mate
Skatin' Into Winter
Skatin' On Thin Ice
Smooth As Glass/Ice
Spinning Like A Top
A Winter Morning Skate

SKATEBOARD TITLES
50-50 Fanatic
Acid Drop King
Backside Flipper
Big Air!!!
Big Spin
Cement Surfers
Crooked Grindin'
Drop-In
Extreme Fun
Fakie
Flip-It!!!
Free Flyin'
Free Wheelin'
Good Golly, I Did An Ollie
Great Goofy Footer
Half-Pipe Dreams
Heel Flippin'
Kick Flippin'
Kickin' It
Kinkin' The Rail
Lord Of The Boards
Ollie Oops!
Ollie Pop!
Rail Rider
Ramp Rider
Riding The Pipes/Rail
Rock & Roll
Scootin' Around
Sidewalk Racer
Sidewalk Ridin'
Sidewalk Surfer
Skit Skatin' Away
Skate Mates
Skate Rats
Skateboard Craze/Crazy
Skateboard Lord
Skatin' The Ramp

Vicious Vert Ramp Rider
Wizard On Wheels

SKIING TITLES

(SEE ALSO SNOW)

- *Use Skis or Poles for an "I".*

Awesome
Bearing The Elements
Black Diamonds Are Dangerous
Boardin' Babe
Boots & Bindings & Skis Oh My!
Bunny Slopes Rule
Bustin' Big Air
Call The Ski Patrol
Cliff Dweller
Dashing Thru The Snow
Don't Forget The Wedge
Double Diamond Daredevil
Downhill Delight
First Run Rider
Free Heeling
Gliding On Water
Hill Rodder
Hittin' The Slopes
Hot Dogger/Doggin'
Icing On The Season
If You Can't Ski Down...Slide!!!
It's All Downhill From Here
Kickin' Up Powder
King Of The Slopes
A "Lifting" Experience
Limpin' To The Lodge
Mogul Mania
Mountain Magic/Magician
Mountains Or Moguls?
Oh! You're Supposed To Stand Up On The Skis
On the Downhill Slide
Perfect Powder
Plowin' Thru
Powder Play
Powder Puff Girls
Queen Of The Slopes
Riding Down The Bunny Hill
Riding The Wakes
Ri"Ski" Business
Ski Bums
Ski Bunnies
Slippin' & Slidin'
Smooth As Ice
Smooth As Glass
Snow Ballet
Snow Bunny
Stay Away From The Orange Fence
Tips Up
Walkin' On Water
Water Wonderland
White Out
Who Needs Poles?
Wild On The Water
Wipe Out
Xtreme

SKY DIVING TITLES

Between The Earth & The Sky
Caution...Jumps From Perfectly Good Airplanes
Cloud Climber
Cloud Diving
Coasting On Air
Don't Forget To Pull
Down, Down & Away
Dreams Of Dropping
A Fall From The Sky
Floating Thru The Friendly Skies
Flying As He/She Falls
Flying Like The Angels
Flying Without Wings
Free As A Bird
Free Faller
Free Fallin'
Gliding Thru The Air With The Greatest Of Ease
I Have Flown!
I've Got Air
Jump Master Says Jump
Natural High
Off I Soar Into The Wild Blue Yonder
Sailing The Skies
The Sky's The Limit
Soaring Like An Eagle
Soaring Thru The Skies
Take Flight
What Goes Up...Must Come Down

SLED/SLIDING TITLES

(SEE ALSO SNOW)

- *Place title on the side of a Sled.*

Down The Hills & Over The Snow
Gliding Over The Crunchy Snow
If You Can't Ski Down...Sled!!!
It's All Downhill From Here
Let It Slide
On The Downhill Slide
Sled Away
Sled Racer
Sled Rider
Sledding Buddies
Sledding Down The Bunny Hill
Sledding Thru The Snow
Sledding Thru The Winter White
Sleigh Bells Ring
Slide, Swerve & Tumble
Slidin' & Ridin'
Slidin' Thru Life
Sliding Over A Blanket Of Snow
Slip Sleddin' Away
Slip Slidin' Away
Weeeee!
Whooooosh!

____
____
____
____
____

SLEEP TITLES

(SEE ALSO DREAMS)

- *Put title on a Cloud, cut small slits in clouds & slide bottom of letters down into slits to look like they are snuggled in the clouds)*

All Is Calm
All Tucked In
All Tuckered Out
...And To All A Good Night
...And We Bid You Good Night
Angel Of Sleep
As I Lay Me Down To Sleep...
As Snug As A Bug In A Rug
As The Children Sleep...
As You Lie Embraced In A Dream...
Attacked By A Nap
Away In The Manger
Beary Sleepy
Beautiful Dreamer
Bed Head
Bedtime Angel
Bedtime Kisses
Bedtime Rituals
The Big Sleep
Boy, Am I Pooped!
Bring On The Night
I Can Sleep Thru Anything
Cat Napping
Catchin' 40 Winks
Catchin' A Few Winks
Catching A Few Zzzzzz's
Caught Napping
Caution: Snoring Zone
Close Your Sleepy Little Eyes
Conked Out
Counting Sheep
Crib Notes *(Baby banging on crib)*
Dancing In The Stars
Deep In A Dream
Down For The Count
Dream A Little Dream
I Dream Of You...
Dream On Little Dreamer
Dream Sweet Dreams
Dream Time
Dream Weaver
I Dreamed A Dream...
Dreamer Boy/Girl
Dreamin'
Dreamland Express
Dreams Are Flowers Blooming In Your Heart
My Dreams Are Getting Better All The Time
Dreams I Dream Of You
Early To Bed...Early To Rise
Endless Sleep
Enter Into The Land Of Nod
Getting Ready For Bed
The Gift Of Slumber
Golden Slumbers
Good Night Kisses
Good Night Moon!
Good Night, Sleep Tight
Good Night Sweetheart
Good Night *(Name)*
Gotta Get Some Shut-Eye
Happy Hour Is Nap Hour
Heavenly Peace
Hello Darkness My Old Friend
Here Comes The Night
Hush-A-Bye Baby
I Ain't Going Down 'Til The Sun Comes Up
I Told You I Was Tired
If I Can Dream...
If Only He/She Was Sleeping & Not Recharging
I'm Not Sleeping...I'm Meditating
I'm Still Sleepy
In My Dreams

It Was Only A Dream
Just Lion Around
Lazin' Around
Let Sleeping Children Lie
Life Is But A Dream
Lil Little Dozer
The Lion Sleeps Tonight *(Grouchy child)*
Lost In Dreams
Lullaby & Good Night
May All Your Dreams Come True
Meet Me In My Dreams
Midnight Giggles & Grins
Miles To Go Before I Sleep...
Mr. Sandman Bring Mommy/Daddy/Baby A Dream
Mr./Miss Sleepyhead
My Angel...Only When He/She's Sleeping!!!
Nap Time
Night Night Little One *(Or child's name)*
Nite! Nite!
No Day Is So Bad It Can't Be Fixed With A Nap. - *(Carrie Snow)*
Now I Lay Me Down To Sleep...
Off To Bed
Oh, How I Hate To Get Up In The Morning
On The Wings Of A Dream
Only In My Dream
Our Little Sleeping Angel
People Who Snore Always Fall Asleep First
Pillow Pals *(Sleep over or child & their comfort pal)*
Pillow Talk
Power Napping
Recharging
Redemption In Progress/Underway
Rock-A-Bye Baby
Shhhh! Angel Dreaming
Shhhh! Dad's Sawing Logs
Silence Is Golden
Silent Night
Sleep Baby Sleep
Sleep Dreamily
Sleep In Heavenly Peace
Sleep My Lil One
Sleep Now, Oh Sleep Now...
Sleep, Oh Blessed Sleep
Sleep Peacefully My Child
To Sleep Perchance To Dream/Snore
Sleep Tight My Sweet Sight
Sleep Tight Sleeping Beauty
Sleep To Dream
Sleep Walking
Sleep Well, Angel Sweetness
Sleeping Angel
Sleeping Beauty
Sleeping In
Sleeping Like A Baby
A Sleeping Rose
Sleeping Under The Stars
Sleepless In Seattle *(Substitute your town)*
Sleepy Eyes
Sleepy Head
Sleepy Time Gal/Guy
Slumber Time *(Sleep over)*
Slumber's Sweet Surrender
Snoozin'
Softly Snuggled In Your Slumber
Straight Past The Sunrise
Strange Bedfellows
Sweet Angelic Slumber
Sweet Dreams
Sweet Dreams Little One
Take Me To A Dream
There Is No Such Thing As Too Much Sleep
There Is Nothing So Precious As A Sleeping Baby
These Dreams
This Is How An Angel Sleeps!
Time For A Dream/Nap!
Time For Bed, Sleepy Head
'Til The Morning Light
Too Beat To Eat
A Well-Spent Day Brings Happy Sleep. *(Leonardo da Vinci)*
When I Dream Of You...
When In Doubt, Take A Nap
When You Sleep...
Whenever I Want You All I Have To Do Is Dream
Woke Up On The Wrong Side Of The Bed
www.sleeping.calm.com
You Are The One I Dream About
You Snooze...You Lose!
Zonked Out
Zzzzzz ZZZzzzz...Is My Favorite Letter

SLOW TITLES

Can't Slow Down
Nice 'N Slow
Slow & Easy
Slow & Steady
Slow As A Snail
Slow As Molasses
Slow Dance
Slow Goes It

Slow Motion
Slowly But Surely
A Snail's Pace

SLUMBER PARTY TITLES

(SEE ALSO SLEEP)

- *Place title on a Sleeping Bag.*
- *Make little Pillows & place title on them.*

...And To All A Good Night
Beautiful Dreamer
Down For The Count
I'll Rise But I Refuse To Shine
I'm Still Sleepy
It's My Party & I'll Sleep If I Want To...
Midnight Confessions
The Morning After
Over-Nighter
Pajama Party
Peace & Quiet
Peace At Last
Pillow Fight
Pillow Fun
Pillow Pals
Pillow Talk
Sleep Over
Sleep Over Slumber
Sleeping Beauties
Sleepless In Seattle *(Substitute your town)*
Sleepy Sillies
Slumber Party
Slumber Party Music Fest
Slumber Time
Strange Bedfellows
Wake Up Little Suzy
Wake Up Sleepyhead
In The Wee Small Hours Of The Morning
Who Needs Some Sleep?
You're Never Too Old For Slumber Parties
Zonked Out

SMILE TITLES

(SEE ALSO LAUGH)

- *Put a Happy Face in place of an "O".*

3 Mile Smile
All Smiles
Blue Ribbon Smile
Can't Smile Without You
I Can't Stop Smiling
Carry Laughter With You Wherever You Go. *(Hugh Sidney)*
A Child's Smile Soothes The Soul
Enchanting Smile
God Put A Smile On Your Face
Golden Grin
Great Grins
Grin & Bear It
Grins & Giggles
Grinning From Ear To Ear...
Happy Eyes & Smiling Lips
In Your Smile...
It's All In The Smile
It's The Smile That Keeps Me Out Of Trouble
Just Smile & Act Nice
Just To See You Smile...
Keep On Smiling
A Laugh Is A Smile That Bursts. - *(Mary H. Waldrip)*
Let A Smile Be Your Umbrella
I Love It When You Smile
I Love To See You Smile
Magical Smile
Midnight Giggles & Grins
Miles Of Smiles
More Precious Than Stardust Or Raindrops, Is Your Smile
Piles Of Smiles
The Power Of Your Smile...
Put On A Happy Face
Read My Lips
Show Me Your Dimples
Show Us Those Pearly Whites
Smile A Little Smile For Me
A Smile A Mile
Smile A Sweet Smile For Me
A Smile As Sweet As Spring
The Smile Broke The Camera
A Smile Can Brighten Your Darkest Days
A Smile Confuses An Approaching Frown
Smile For Me
A Smile In Your Heart...
A Smile Is A Curve That Sets Everything Straight. - *(Phyllis Diller)*
A Smile Is A Frown Turned Upside Down
A Smile Is A Whisper Of A Laugh
A Smile Lights Up The Day

A Smile Like Yours...
Smile Of Grace
The Smile On Your Face...
Smile! You're On Digital Camera
Smiles Bring Sunshine
Smiles, Love & Laughter
Smiling Face Of Love
Smiling Faces, Smiling Faces Sometimes...
Snap Shots & Smiles
The Sunshine Of Your Smile...
Sweet Emotion
Sweetest Smile
Tender Smiles
There Smiles A Happy Boy/Girl
This Smile...
Thoughts Of You Always Make Me Smile
We Love To See You Smile
What Curvaceous Lips You Have...
When I See You Smile...
When I Think Of You, I Smile Inside
When Irish Eyes Are Smiling...
When My Baby Smiles At Me...
When You Smile At Me...
When You Smile, The Whole World Smiles
Whenever I See Those Smiling Eyes
Whenever I See Your Smiling Face...
Who Could Resist A Smile Like This?
A Wink & A Smile
You Have A Smile That Lights Up The World
You Melt My Heart With Just A Smile
You Would Smile Too If It Happened To You
Your Smile...
Your Smile Could Melt The World
Your Smile Is Like The Sun
Your Smiles Are My Stars
You're Never Fully Dressed 'Til You Smile
You're Worth Smiling About

SNAKE TITLES

- *(Make an "S" into a Snake)*

Here's The Sssssssssstory...
Scaled Perfection
Slithering Sukatash
Snake Charmer
Snake Eyes
Snake In The Grass
Snakes Alive!!!
Snakes & Snails & Puppy Dog Tails
Sssssssnakes

SNOW TITLES

(SEE ALSO COLD, SKIING, SLEDDING, SNOWMAN & WINTER)

- *Use a Snowflake or Snowball in for an "O".*
- *Use white cardstock as 2nd background mat, leave about 1 in. at the top, rip top edge, fold down over top of title to look like snow falling onto title. (This effect can be used for photo matting as well.)*

All Bundled Up
All Covered With Snow
All Flakes Welcome
All That Glitters Is Snow
Angel In The Snow
Arctic Blast
As White As Snow
The Beauty Of The Falling Snow
Beware Of The Melting Zone
Bring On The Snow
Brrrrr...It's Cold
Brrr Shiver Brrr
...But The Snow Is So Delightful
Children Of The Ice Age
The Chill Factor
Chill Out!
Chilly Weather
Cold Hands, Warm Heart
Cool Cats
Cuddlin' With Cocoa
Dashing Thru The Snow
Digging Out
Dressed For Snow & Ready To Go
Dressed To Chill
Dressed Up Like Eskimos
Dry Socks & Mittens .5 Cents A Pair
Endless Snow
Fabulous February

Feeling Frosty
Fire & Ice Kind Of Day
The Fire Is So Delightful
First Snow
First Snowball Of The Season
First Snowfall
Flaky Fun
Flurries Of Flakes
Footprints In The Snow
Frosty & Friends
Frosty Fun & Friends
Frosty The Snowman
Frosty's Winter Wonderland
Fun In The Snow
Fury Of Flurries
The Gift Of A Snowflake
Give Me Hot Chocolate Any Day
Glisten & Glide
Got Snow?
The Great White Way
The Greatest Snow On Earth
Have Snow, Will Shovel
Heaven Sent Down Snowflakes Of White Silver Grace
Hit Me With Your Best Shot *(Snowballs)*
Ice, Ice Baby
The Ice Man Cameth
Ice Wars
The Icing On The Season
In The Frosty Air
In The Lane, The Snow Is Glistenin'...
In The Meadow, We Can Build A Snowman!
It's A Fire & Ice Kind Of Day
It's A Little Flaky Here
It's Snow Cold Outside
It's Snow White Out
It's Snow Wonder
It's Snowtime!
It's Winter
Jack Frost Visited In The Night
Jack Frost Nipping At Your Nose
Just Add Snow
Just Say Snow
Keeping Warm *(Bundled up or by the fireplace)*
Let It Snow! Let It Snow! Let It Snow!
The Magic Of Snow
Making A New Friend *(Snowman pictures)*
A May Snow Fall
May We Never Forget The Flavor Of Snowflakes
Michelangelo Of Snow
Mitten MAN
Mitten Weather
No Snow Blues
No Two Alike
Northern Exposure
Oh, Hail!
Oh, The Weather Outside Is Frightful
Once There Was A Snowman
Our Little Eskimos
Our Snow Angel
Our Snow Day
The Perfect Storm
The Polar Express
Powder Play
Pure As The Driven Snow
Ready For Winter
Romping In The Snow
Season Of Snow
Season Of White
A Silent Snowfall
Silent, Soft & Slow...Descends The Snow!
Ski Bum
Sledding Buddies
Sleigh Ride
Slip & Slide
Slip Sleddin' Away
Slip Sledding/Sliding Away
Snow Adorable
Snow Adventure
Snow Angels
Snow Baby
Snow Blossoms
Snow Buddies
Snow Bunny
Snow Business
Snow Cold/Cool
Snow Comes For All
Snow Cones For Sale...While Supplies Last
Snow Craze/Crazy
Snow Days/Daze
The Snow Dazzled The Air...
Snow Diggin'
Snow Dreams
A Snow Drop Garden
Snow Dusted
Snow Falling On Cedars
Snow Friend Like You
Snow Fun
Snow Fun Without You
Snow Happens
Snow In Love...
Snow Is Glistening
A Snow Job
Snow Kidding
Snow King
Snow Kissed

Snow May Fall, Winds May Blow, But Love Keeps Us Warm
Snow Me Your Lips
Snow Much Fun
Snow Play
Snow Parking Here
Snow Picasso
Snow Prince/Princess
Snow Queen
Snow, Snow, Snow
Snow Time
Snow Wonder
Snow Wonderful
Snowball Champ
Snowball Fight
Snowballs For Sale
Snowbody Loves You Like I Do
Snowcones For Sale
Snowed In
Snowflake Crystals
A Snowflake Is Winter's Butterfly
Snowflake Tasting Time
Snowflakes Are A Short-Lived Joy
Snowflakes Are Angel Kisses
Snowflakes Are Kisses From Heaven
Snowflakes For Sale
Snowflakes Gracefully Silently Dancing Down
Snowflakes In My Hand
Snowflakes Keep Falling On My Head
Snowflakes, Like Diamonds, Brightly Shine
Snowflakes 'R Us
Snowflakes Serenely Floating
Snowflakes Spiraling Down From The Heavens
Snowflakes Touched Only By His Hand
It's Snowtime
A Snowy Cold Day
Snowy Day
Snowy Splendor
Some Of My Best Friends Are Flakes
South For The Winter
Sub-Zero
Sumo Snowman
Take Time To Taste The Flakes
There's A Chill In The Air
There's No Business Like Snow Business
There's Snow Place Like Home
Think Snow
Waiting For The Snow
Walking In A Winter Wonderland
Warm & Cozy *(Bundled up or by the fire)*
Warm Woolen Mittens
What Fun Snow Can Be
What The Hail!?!?
Winter Blues
Winter Fun
Winter Is "Snow" Much Fun
Winter White
Winter Wonder
Winter Wonderland
The Wonder Of The Falling Snow
Winter's Dawn
Yo...Snow

SNOW
Snowflakes
Noiseless
Ornaments of
White

SNOWMAN TITLES
(SEE ALSO SNOW)
The Abominable Snowman
Chilly Willy
Even SPF 10 Didn't Work *(Melting snowman)*
Frosty & Lovin' It *(Snow couple)*
Help! My Head Is Melting
Hug Your Snowman, It's Cold Out There
I Just Love Snow Storms *(Snowman holding sign)*
I'd Melt For You!
I'm A Jolly Happy Snow Man
I'm All Rolled Up
In The Meadow We Can Build A Snowman
Let It Snow Man!
North Pole Or Bust
Once There Was A Snowman *(Melting)*
"Sand"a Claus *(Xmas at the Beach)*
Snow Grown
Snow Is My Life
The Snowman Cometh
Snowman Kisses
Snowman's Prayer: Please Freeze...Amen
Snowmen Are Cool Dudes
Snowmen Fall From Heaven...Some Assembly Required
Snowmen Fall From Heaven Unassembled
Snowmen Melt, But Memories Last
Snowmen Will Melt Your Heart
Snowzilla
Starlight, Starbright, Please Don't Let Him Melt Tonight!
Sun, Sun Go Away
There's No People Like Snow People

Will Work For Freezer Space *(Snowman holding a sign)*
Willy Melt & Betty Melt *(Snow couple)*

SOCCER TITLES

(SEE ALSO SPORTS)

- *Use a Soccer Ball for an "O".*
- *Put a Goalie's Net behind the title.*

Can I Be Goalie?
Charge The Ball
Deep Kick
Goal!
Having A Ball
I Get A Kick Out Of You
Gettin' Our Kicks
Goal Girl Goal
Goalie Dude
Goalie Guru
Halfback, Keeper, Forward...Defense, Offense...I Just Want To Kick The Ball!
He Kicks...He Scores
In The Beginning, There Was Soccer
It's A Kick In The Grass
Just For Kicks
Just Kick It
Kick Back & Have A Great Time!
A Kick In The Game
Kick It Out
Kick Your Game
In A League All Your Own
My Goal Is To Play Soccer
No! The Other Way!
Our Goal Is More Goals
Pass The Ball Please
Player Down...Everyone Kneel In Place!
Power Play
Ready...Set...Goal!
Run, Run & Run Some More
Soccer Dad/Mom
Soccer Dude
Soccer Is A Ball
Soccer Is A Kick
Soccer Is A Kick In The Grass
Soccer Is My Goal
Soccer Is My Life
Soccer Kicks
Soccer Mom & Proud Of It
Soccer Players Kick Together
Soccer Season
Soccer's A Ball!
Spread Out, Spread Out...Watch Your Offsides!
Super Soccer Dude
We Get Our Kicks In Soccer
What A Kick!
What Do We Get For Snack?
You Goal Girl

SOLAR SYSTEM TITLES

(SEE SPACE & STARS)

SON TITLES

(SEE ALSO BABY, BOY & CHILD)

Here Comes The Son
If I Have A Monument In This World, It Is My Son. - *(Maya Angelou)*
Let The "Son"Shine
The Light In Our Eyes...Is The Son In Our Lives
Like Father, Like Son
Lil' Mr. Sonshine
Mommy's "Son" Flower
A Mother Works From Son Up 'Til Son Down
My Light Comes From My Son
My Son, My Precious One
My Son, My Soul, My Sun
My Three Sons
My Two Sons
Our Little Sonshine
The Prodigal Son
Rebel Son
The Son Ain't Gonna Rise
"Son" Bathing
The Son Does Rise
Son Flowers
A Son Like The Sun
A Son Makes Every Dawn Brighter
Son, My Pride & Joy, As A Man & As A Boy
Son Of A Preacher Man
Son Of Mine
Son Spots
Son, You Outgrew My Lap But Never My Heart
A Sonny Day
Sons In The Sunset
When The Sun Is Up, The Son Is Up!

SPACE TITLES

(SEE ALSO MOON, STARS & WORLD)

- *Use a Planet or Star in place of an "O".*
- *Place title inside a Space Ship or Rocket.*

3rd Rock From The Sun
4.3.2.1...Ignition...BLAST OFF!!
All I Need Is A Space Suit & I'm Ready To Go
All Systems Go
To Boldly Go Where No Man Has Gone Before! - *(Star Trek)*
Celestial Bliss
Cyber Space
Deep Space
The Eagle Has Landed
Feelin' Alien-ated
Feelin' Spacey
Houston! We Have A Problem
To Infinity & Beyond
Is Anyone Out There?
Jumpin' Jupiter
The Kid/Man From Planet 'X'
Lost In Space
The Martian Chronicles
Meanwhile On Planet Earth...
Men Are From Mars
Mission Specialist
Mission To The Moon/Mars
My Little Astronaut
One Small Step For Man...One Giant Leap For Mankind. - *(Neil Armstrong 1969)*
Outta This World
Roger That
Rocket Man
Rocket's Red Glare
Solar Solace
Somewhere Out In Space...
Space Age
Space Buddies
Space Cadet
Space Camp
Space Captain.Commander
Space Cowboys
Space Explorers/Invaders
Space Jam
Space Man
Space, The Final Frontier - *(Star Trek)*
Spaced Out
Spaceship Earth
Splash Down & Recovery
Star Trekkin'
Starship Troopers
Teenagers Are From Mars
Up, Up & Away
Visions Of Mars
We Have Separation
What Planet Are You From?
When The Planets Are Aligned
Women Are From Venus

SPIDER TITLES

(SEE ALSO BUGS)

- *Use a Spider or simple Web for an "O".*

Along Came A Spider...
Caught In A Web
Creepy Crawler
Eight-Legged Friends
The Itsy, Bitsy Spider
Look Out, Here Comes The Spider Man/Kid
Oh, What A Tangled Web We Weave
The Spider & The Fly
Spider Boy/Girl
Weavers Of A Web

SPORTS TITLES

(SEE ALSO INDIVIDUAL SPORTS CATEGORIES)

Ain't No Chance If You Don't Take It. - *(Guy Clark)*
An Ace In The Hole
Action Man
The Agony Of De"Feet"
All Star Player
Amazing Athlete
American Gladiators
Are You Game?
Armchair Athlete
Athletic Supporter *(Fans)*
Baseball, Football, Soccer Anyone?
Be A Winner
The Best Team In The West
Between You & Sports
Bullseye
Catch Some Fun
I Caught The Most
The Champs
Defense Department
Department Of Defense *(Football)*
Doubters Don't Win...Winners Don't Doubt
The Dream Is Still Alive
Everyone's A Winner

Experience Wild Life...Be A Coach/Leader
Faster, Higher, Braver
First Round Draft Pick
For The Love Of The Game
Future Endorser Of Nike
Future Olympian
Game Day
The Game Isn't Over 'Til It's Over. - *(Yogi Berra)*
The Games People Play
Genius Is 1% Inspiration & 99% Perspiration.
(Thomas Edison)
Go! Fight! Win!
Go Team
Goin' For The Gold
Good Sport
Got My Game Face On!
Grudge Match
Havin' A Ball
Havin' A Field Day
He Who Stops Being Better, Stops Being
Good. - *(Oliver Cromwell)*
Heart Of A Champ
Hero Worship
Home Team Advantage
Hooray For Our Team
I Am Woman...See Me Score
If You Can Believe It, The Mind Can Achieve
It. - *(Ronnie Lott)*
If You Chase Two Rabbits, Both Will Escape
I'll Always Be #1 To Myself. - *(Moses Malone)*
I'm Ready For The Pro's
In A League All Your Own
Instant Replay
It Ain't Over 'Til It's Over
It's All In The Game
It's Not Bragging If You CAN Do It
Hey Now, You're An All Star!!!
Just Do It!
Just For Sport
Keep The Ball Rollin'
Legends In Your Own Time
Let The Game Begin
Little Sport
Look Out Big Leagues, Cause Here I Come
Makin' Tracks
Man Can Live On Sports Alone
Michael Jordan Jr.,
MVP
My World...My Life...My Game
No Pain, No Gain
No Whimps
Play Ball
Play For The Glory
Play It...And They'll Come!
Playing By The Book
Practice Makes Perfect
Prime Time Sports
Pom-Poms & Ponytails
Power Player
Put Me In Coach...I'm Ready To Play...Today!
Right Down The Line
The Rookie
Rookie Of The Year
Root, Root, Root, For The Home Team
Running Like The Wind
S-C-O-R-E
Set Your Goals High & Don't Stop 'Til You
Get There. - *(Bo Jackson)*
She's Got Game
Slow & Steady Wins The Race
Sore Losers
Sports Dreams
Sports Fanatic
Sports Spirit
Sports Superstar
Sportsmanlike Conduct
Summer's Games
Superstar
Super Sport
Survival Of The Fittest
Sweat + Sacrifice = Success
The Sweet Smell Of Victory
The Taste Of Victory
Taste The Victory
Team Leader
Team Spirit
Teaming Up
There Are Two Things In Life *(Sport)* & More
(Sport)
There Is No "I" In Team
There's No Substitute For Guts. - *(Paul Bear Bryant)*
This Is A Racket Of Fun
Threw In The Towel
To Be Prepared Is Half The Victory.
(Miguel Cervantes)
Today's Heroes
Tossing Terror
Total Dedication
Undefeated
The Underdogs
Unrivaled Competition
Unsportsmanlike Conduct
V-I-C-T-O-R-Y
Victory Seekers
I Wanna Be Like "Mike"
In War There Is No Substitute For Victory.
(Douglas MacArthur)
Water Boy

Way To Go!
We Are The Best
We Are The Champions!
We Came, We Saw, We Conquered!
We'll Get 'Em Next Time
We're #1
Winning Isn't Everything, It's The Only Thing!
If Winning Isn't Everything, Then Why Keep Score? - *(Vince Lombardi)*
Winning With Style
You Gotta Love The Game
You Win Some...You Lose Some
You're An All Star
(Sport) Is Life, Nothing Else Matters
(Sport) Is Life, The Rest Is Just Details

TEAM
Together
Each
Accomplishes
More

SPRING TITLES

(SEE ALSO MONTHS OF THE YEAR)

- *Use a Thermometer in place of an "I".*
- *Put a Flower in place of the "O".*

Anticipation Of Spring
April Fool
April Hath Put A Spirit Of Youth In Everything. *(William Shakespeare)*
April Showers Bring Many, Many Flowers
April Showers Bring May Flowers
As Fresh As Springtime
Bee-sy Spring
Blame It On The Spring Rain
A Bouquet Of Springtime
The Breath Of Spring Has Lifted Our Hearts
Breathtaking Spring
Celebrate Spring
Colors Of Spring
Come Gentle Spring
Daisy Days
A Day In May
The Dawn In Spring...
The Dawn Of Spring
Daylight & Darkness, Spring Balanced. *(Mike Garofalo)*
Don't Bug Me
Embracing Spring
Enchanted April
The Essence Of Spring
Everything Sprouts In Spring
It's Finally Spring
First Signs Of Spring
Flower Of Spring
Flower Power
Flowers & Butterflies Drift In Color... Illuminating Spring
Fresh As A Spring Daisy
In Full Bloom
The Grass Is Always Greener In Spring
Greenery Of The New Spring
Happy, Happy Spring
Happy Spring Days
Hay Fever
Here's The Buzz
Holy Spring
Hop Into Spring
Hopping Into Spring *(Frogs or rabbits)*
Hooray For Spring!
I Have Spring Fever
In The Green
In The Merry Month Of May
In The Spring Twilight
It's Finally Spring
It's Not That Easy Being Green
It's Spring & Look Who's Blooming
Kiss Of Spring
Let's Go Fly A Kite
Longing For Spring
May Day
Must Be Spring
New Beginnings
Nothing Is So Beautiful As Spring
One Fine Day
The Rite Of Spring
"S" Is For Spring
Signs Of Spring
A Smile As Sweet As Spring
Splash Into Spring
Spring...An Experience In Immortality. *(Henry D. Thoreau)*
Spring Awakening
Spring Break
Spring Breezes
Spring Chicks
Spring Cleaning
Spring Days
Spring Fever
Spring Fling
Spring Flings & Easter Things
Spring Flowers Bring New Life
Spring Goddess

Spring Happy
Spring Has Sprung
Spring Has Sprung Spring
Spring In Bloom
Spring Into Action
Spring Is Bustin' Out All Over
Spring Is Full Of Sweet Days & Roses. *(George Herbert)*
Spring Is God Thinking In Gold, Laughing In Blue & Speaking In Green... - *(Frank Johnson)*
Spring Is In The Air
Spring Is Just Ducky
Spring Is Nature's Way Of Saying, "Let's Party!" - *(Robin Williams)*
Spring Is When You Feel Like Whistling. *(Doug Larson)*
A Spring Love
Spring Sweet Spring
Spring To Life
Spring Would Not Be Spring Without Bird Songs. - *(Francis M. Chapman)*
Spring's Scenery
Spring's Shine
Spring's Sunset
Springtime Pleasure
A Springtime Rainbow
Springtime Splendor
Sweet April Showers, Do Spring May Flowers. - *(Thomas Tusser)*
Sweet Smells Of Spring
Swing Into Spring
Take Time To Smell The Flowers
Tip Toe Thru The Tulips *(Use any flower)*
Touched By Spring Love
A Very "Buzzy" Spring
Visions Of Spring
Wee Bee Friends
Welcome To Spring
When Bluebirds Gather & Sing...
Winter Is History/Past!
Wonder Of Spring
You're My Spring

____
____
____
____
____

ST. PATRICK'S DAY TITLES

(SEE COUNTRIES/IRELAND & IRISH)

STARS TITLES

(SEE ALSO NIGHT & SPACE)

- *Punch Stars Diamond Dust or Metallic paper & replace an "A" or "O".*
- *Hang title from a Star with Ribbon.*

1,000 Sparkling Stars
...And The Moon & The Stars & The World
Angel Upon A Star
As The Stars Shine...
The Awakening Of The Stars
Brightest Star In The Sky
To Catch A Falling Star...
Chasing Stars...Catching Dreams
Count Your Lucky Stars
Cupid Sent Us A Starry Night
Don't Let The Stars Get In Your Eyes
Even A Small Star Shines In The Darkness
Eyes That Shine Like Stars...
Five-Star Day
Flaming Star
The Flickering Stars Will Lead The Way
For I Will Rise & Touch The Stars
Galaxy Quest
God's Amazing Stars...
Guided By The Stars
Guiding Star
Happy Star
Hitch Your Wagon To A Star. *(Ralph Waldo Emerson)*
I See A Star
It Was Written In The Stars
I've Told Every Little Star...
Keeper Of The Stars
Lady Of The Stars
Like The Sparkles Of The Stars...
Little Star
Little Star Up So Far Away...
Lone Star
Lost In The Stars
Love Under A Starry Sky
Lucky Star
Moonbeams & Starshine
More Than All The Stars...
Morning Star
My Little All Star
Myriads Of Stars
New Star In The Star
Northern Star
Oh, Starry Night...
On My Horizon You'll Always Be The Star
On This Night Of A 1,000 Stars...
The Only Star In Heaven
Pocket Full Of Starlight
Precious Star

Quiet Nights Under Quiet Stars
Reach For The Stars
Reach High & Touch The Stars
Rendezvous Beneath The Stars
Ring Of Stars
Rising Star
Rock-N-Roll Star
Seeing Stars
She's A Star
A Shining Star
The Shining Star Within
Shooting Stars
Shooting Stars Are For Dreamers...Dreamers Are Hope!!!
Sleeping Under The Stars
Star Bright
Star Burst
Star Crossed
Star Drenched
Star Dust
Star Fields
Star Gazer/Gazing
A Star In My Sky
A Star Is Born
Star Light, Star Bright
Star Of My Heart
Star Of The Dawn
Star Of The Sea
The Star Of The Show
A Star Performance
Star Power
Star Quality
Star Shine
Star Struck
The Star That Guides Me...
A Star To Follow
Starry Eyed
Starry Skies
Starry, Starry Night
The Stars Are Brightly Shining
Stars In My/Your Eyes
Stars In The Midnight Sky
The Stars Over The Lonely Ocean
Super Star
Swinging On A Star
Thank Your Lucky Stars
Twinkle...Twinkle
Twinkle, Twinkle Little Star
Under A Blanket Of Stars
Underneath The Stars
Upon A Wishing Star
Walkin' On Starshine
Wandering Star
I Wanna Be A Star
We Can't All Be Stars, But We Can All Twinkle
When You Wish Upon A Star...
Wish Upon A Star
I Wished Upon A Star One Day...
Wishing On A Star...
You & I Forever Is My One Wish Upon A Star
You Deserve A Star
You're Gonna Be A Star
You're The Star Of My Life

STATES/CITIES TITLES

(SEE ALSO TRAVEL)

ALABAMA

Alabama Skies
Alabama...The Cotton State
Alabama...The Heart Of Dixie
Alabama...The Lizard State
Alabama...The Yellow Hammer State
Daybreak In Alabama
Midnight In Montgomery
The Stars Fell On Alabama
Sweet Home Alabama

ALASKA

Alaska...Forget-Me-Not
Alaska...Land Of The Midnight Sun
Alaska...The Last Frontier

ARIZONA

Arizona...Baby Of The Republic
Arizona...Italy Of America
Arizona...The Grand Canyon State
Arizona...The Land Of Copper
By The Time I Get To Phoenix...*(Or any state)*
The Moon Over Tucson
Phoenix In My Heart

ARKANSAS

Arkansas...Naturally
Arkansas...The Land Of Opportunity
Arkansas...The Razorback State
Arkansas...The State Of Hot Springs
Arkansas...The Wonder State
A Little Past Little Rock
Oh, Arkansas
The Rock Of Arkansas

CALIFORNIA

26 Miles Across The Sea...Santa Catalina Is Waiting For Me
Beverly Hill Billies
California Blue
California Dreamin'
California Here I Come
California Girls
California Gold
California Grown
California Nights
California On My Mind
California Soul
California Sun
California...The Golden State
California...The Grape State
California...The Land Of Milk & Honey
A "California"cation
Going Back To California
Golden California
Gone Hollywood
Hollywood Life
Hollywood Nights
Hollywood Waltz
Hotel California
I Left My Heart In San Francisco
I Love LA
I Love You California
LA Confidential
LA Story
LA You Are My Sunshine
Sacramento...The Heart Of California
Santa Catalina...The Island Of Romance
Seems It Never Rains In California
The Shores Of California
Surf City, USA
Sweet California
Which Way To Hollywood?

COLORADO

The Buffalo Plains Of Colorado
Centennial Colorado
Colorado...The Lead State
Colorado...The Silver State
Colorado...Where The Columbines Grow
Colorado's Majestic Mountains
Colorado's Pikes Peak...Garden Of The Gods
Colorado's Rocky Mountain High

CONNECTICUT

Connecticut...Beside The Long Tidal River
Connecticut...The Nutmeg State
Connecticut's Brownstone Quarries
Yankee Doodle Connecticut

DELAWARE

At The Delaware County Line
Delaware...A Jewel Among The State
Delaware...A Small Wonder
Delaware...The First State
Hot Time In Delaware
Our Delaware

FLORIDA

Deep Down In Florida
Floatin' Down Florida's Chattahoochee
Florida...Feast Of Flowers
Florida...Stocked Full Of Alligators
Florida...The Orange State
Florida...The Sunshine State
Florida's Rainbows
Forever In Texas
"Kiss"imee In Florida
Moon Over Miami
Riding Across The Overseas Highway In The Florida Keys
The Vast Everglades Of Florida

GEORGIA
Atlanta...A City In A Forest
Georgia Blue
Georgia On Our Minds
Georgia Peach
Georgia Rain
Georgia Rhythm
Georgia...The Empire State Of The South
Georgia's Great Goobers *(Peanuts)*
Oh, Atlanta
The Devil Went Down To Georgia
Meet Me Tonight In Atlantic City
Midnight Train To Georgia
The Night The Lights Went Out In Georgia
On A Slow Train Thru Georgia
Rainy Night In Georgia
Walkin' In The Georgia Rain
Way Down Yonder On The Chattahoochee
Welcome To Atlanta

HAWAII
Aloha From Hawaii
Aloha Honolulu
Avoid Sunburn...Try Some Hawaiian Moonlight
Blue HHawaii...Paradise Of The Pacific
Getting Lei'd In Maui
Hawaii Ponoi...Hawaii's Own
Hawaiian Moonlight
Hawaii's Pineapple Paradise
Here Today...Gone To Mauiawaii
Honolulu In A Mai Tai Mug
Honolulu Lulu
Little Rendezvous In Honolulu
Maui Dreams

IDAHO
Here We Have Idaho
Idaho...Gem Of The Mountains
Idaho...Little Ida
Idaho's Dawn

ILLINOIS
Back To Chicago
Born In Chicago
The Bright Lights Of Big City Chicago
Chicago Blues
Chicago! Chicago!
Chicago...My Kind Of Town
Chicago...The Windy City
The Cornbelt Of Illinois
Illinois...Garden Of The West
Illinois...The Land Of Lincoln
Illinois...The Prairie State
In Old Chicago
O'er The Prairies Of Illinois
On The South Side Of Chicago
Sweet Home Chicago
Take Me Back To Chicago
They're Dancin' In Chicago

INDIANA
Back Home In Indiana
Indiana...The Crossroads Of America
Indiana...The Hoosier State
Indiana...The Land Of Indians
On The Banks Of Indiana's Wabash

IOWA
The Cornbelt Of Iowa
Iowa...The Hawkeye State
Iowa...The Land Of The Rolling Prairie
Iowa...The Land Where The Tall Corn Grows
Iowa...Where Plenty Fills Her Golden Horn
Iowa's Yonder Fields Of Toasted Corn

KANSAS
Home On The Range In Kansas
Kansas City Blues
Kansas...Garden Of The West
Kansas...Mid-way USA
Kansas...The Battleground Of Freedom
Kansas...The Squatter State
We Aren't In Kansas Anymore

KENTUCKY
The Blue Moon Of Kentucky
The Blue Skies Over Kentucky
Kentucky Girl
Kentucky Rain
Kentucky Rose
Kentucky...The Bluegrass State
Kentucky...The Hemp State
Kentucky Wonders
My Old Kentucky Home
My Rose Of Old Kentucky

LOUISIANA
Back To Blue Bayou
Battle Of New Orleans
Blue Bayou Blues
Give Me Louisiana
Louisiana...Child Of The Mississippi
Louisiana Man
Louisiana Rain
Louisiana Where Your Heart Pounds & Your Senses Tingle
Louisiana's Bountiful Bayous
Louisiana's Pelican Pride
Moon Over Bourbon Street
New Orlean's Sultry Nights
Sweet Louisiana
Walkin' To New Orleans
Way Down Yonder In New Orleans

MAINE
"Maine" Event
Maine Memories
Maine Morning
Maine...Oh, Pine Tree State
Maine...The Polar Star State

MARYLAND
Maryland, My Maryland
Maryland...Queen Of Oysters State
Maryland's Monumental City Of Baltimore

MASSACHUSETTS
All Hail To Massachusetts
Massachusetts...From Sea To Shining Sea
Massachusetts...Large Hill Place
Massachusetts...The Baked Beans State
The Pilgrims Pride In Massachusetts
Please Come To Boston

MICHIGAN
Detroit Rock City Of Michigan
Michigan...In A State Of Great Lakes
Michigan, My Michigan
Michigan...The Great Lakes State
Michigan Winter Blues
Michigan's Water Winter Wonderland

MINNESOTA
Hail Minnesota
The Milky Waters Of The Minnesota River
Minnesota...Land Of 10,000 Lakes
Minnesota...New England Of The West
Minnesota...Star Of The North
Minnesota...The Bread & Butter State

MISSISSIPPI
Delta City Blues
Go Mississippi
Mississippi Blues
Mississippi Miss
Mississippi Moon
Mississippi Mud
Mississippi Mud-cats
Mississippi Queen
Mississippi's Magnificent Magnolias
Mississippi's River Of Dreams

MISSOURI

I'm Goin' To Kansas City, Kansas City Here I Come
Meet Me In St. Louis
Missouri Moon
Missouri...The Cave State
Missouri...The Gateway To The West
Missouri...The Land Of Dixie
Missouri Waltz
Missouri's Beautiful Ozark Mountains
On A Train From Kansas City
The Spirit Of New Orleans
The Spirit Of St. Louis
St. Louis Blues
The 1,000's Of Caves Of Missouri

MONTANA

Montana...Glory Of The West
Montana...Land Of Shinning Mountains
Montana, Montana...Glory Of The West
Montana Skies
Montana...The Stubtoe State
Montana's Big Sky Country
Montana's Melody
Montana's Sweetgrass Hills
Mountainous Montana
Wild Montana Skies

NEBRASKA

Beautiful Nebraska...Peaceful Prairieland
The Blackwaters Of Nebraska
Nebraska & Its Broad River
Nebraska...Land Of The Cornhuskers
Nebraska...The Beefiest State

NEVADA

Chillin' In Sin City, Las Vegas
The Glitz & Glamour Of Las Vegas
Hey Baby, Let's Go To Vegas
Home Means Nevada
Las Vegas...The City That Never Sleeps
Leaving Las Vegas
Loving Las Vegas
Nevada...The Battle Born State
Nevada...Where The Wind Blows Wild & Free
Nevada's Sierra Nevadas
Paradise City...Las Vegas
Sin City...Las Vegas
Strolling The Las Vegas Strip
Under The Bright Lights Of Las Vegas
Viva Las Vegas
What Happens In Vegas...

NEW HAMPSHIRE

The Hotel New Hampshire
New Hampshire...Switzerland Of America
New Hampshire...The White Mountain State
New Hampshire's Granite Hills
Old New Hampshire

NEW JERSEY

Going Down The New Jersey Shore
Jersey Fresh
Jersey Girl
I Like Jersey Best
New Jersey...America The Beautiful Only Smaller
New Jersey Clam Bake
New Jersey Skies
New Jersey...The Garden State
New Jersey's Moonlight At Cape May
New Jersey's Pathway Of Revolution

NEW MEXICO

Autumn In New Mexico
New Mexico...Land Of Enchantment
New Mexico...Land Of Opportunity
New Mexico...Land Of The Cactus
New Mexico...Land Of The Heart's Desire
New Mexico...Place Of Mexitli *(Aztec God)*
New Mexico...The Sunshine State
O, Fair New Mexico

NEW YORK
Autumn In New York
Back In The New York City Groove
The Big Apple
Bits & Bites Of The Big Apple
Broadway Baby
Broadway Rhythm
Coney Island Baby
Coney Island Crazy
I Love New York
I Want To Be A Part Of It, New York, NY
In A New York Minute
The Lights Are Bright On Broadway
Look Out Broadway
Lullaby Of Broadway
The Manhattan Project
New York City Boy/Girl
New York City Groove
New York City Minute
New York City Serenade
New York...Excelsior...Ever Upwards
New York...Home Of The Empire State Building
New York...New York
New York State Of Mind
New York...The Empire State
New York...The Knickerbocker State
New York Times
New York's Big Yellow Taxi's
New York's Finest
Nights On Broadway
On Broadway
On The Square Of New York
Only In New York
Princess Of Queens
The Sidewalks Of New York
Somewhere On Broadway
Takin' A Bite Out Of The Big Apple

NORTH CAROLINA
Carolina Blues
Carolina In The Morning
Carolina On My Mind
Great Smokey Mountains Of North Carolina
North Carolina...The Land Of The Sky
North Carolina...The Old North State
North Carolina...The Tarheel State
North Carolina's Blue Ridge Mountains
Nothing Could Be Fina Than To Be In Carolina

NORTH DAKOTA
North Dakota & Her Beautiful Skies
North Dakota...Green Thy Fields & Fair Thy Skies
North Dakota...Land Of The Dakotas
North Dakota...The Peace Garden State
So Long To The Red River Valley

OHIO
Beautiful Ohio, Thy Wonders Are In View
Cleveland Rocks
Ohio...Mother Of Modern Presidents
Ohio Winter Blues
Ohio...The Buckeye State
On The Banks Of Old Ohio
South Of Cincinnati

OKLAHOMA
The Last Trip To Tulsa...
Livin' On Tulsa Time
Oklahoma...Boomer's Paradise
Oklahoma...Land Of The Sweet Smelling Waving Wheat
Oklahoma...The Sooner State
Oklahoma...Where The Winds Come Sweeping Down The Plains
Those Oklahoma Hills

OREGON
On The Old Oregon Trail
Oregon, My Oregon
Oregon...The Beaver State
Oregon...The Land Of Promise
Oregon...The Web-footed State

PENNSYLVANIA

America Starts In Pennsylvania
Bethlehem, PA...Christmas City, USA
Hershey, PA...The Sweetest Place On Earth
On The Streets Of Philadelphia
Pennsylvania...A State Of Independence
Pennsylvania Avenue
Pennsylvania...Penn's Woods
Pennsylvania Polka
Pennsylvania...The Birthplace Of Independence
Pennsylvania...The Land Blessed By God's Own Hands
Pennsylvania...The Quaker State
Pennsylvania's Endless Mountains
Philadelphia Freedom...I Love You
Philadelphia Story
Philadelphia...The City Of Brotherly Love
Pittsburgh...The Big Little City

RHODE ISLAND

Rhode Island...It's For Me
Rhode Island...Little Rhodie, L'il Rhody, & Little Rhode
Rhode Island, Oh Rhode Island, Surrounded By The Sea
Rhode Island...The Ocean State
Rhode Island...The Plantation State
Rhode Island...The Southern Gateway Of New England
Rhode Island's Golden Radiance
Rhode Island's Red Clay Lined Shores

SOUTH CAROLINA

Carolina Blues
Carolina In The Morning
Carolina On My Mind
Nothing Could Be Fina Than To Be In Carolina
South Carolina...The Keystone Of The South Atlantic Seaboard
South Carolina's Marshy Swamps Of Rice

SOUTH DAKOTA

Hail South Dakota
South Dakota...The Coyote State
South Dakota...The Land Of Infinite Variety
South Dakota...The Land Of Plenty
South Dakota...The Mount Rushmore State
South Dakota...Your Beautiful Black Hills & Prairies...

TENNESSEE

The Great Smokey Mountains Of Tennessee
Knoxville Girl
Memphis City Rain
Memphis In May Festival Barbecuing
My Homeland Tennessee
My Tennessee
The River With The Big Bend Flows Thru Tennessee
Rocky Top Tennessee
The Tennessee Hills
Tennessee River Run
Tennessee Waltz
Walking In Memphis
We Went To Graceland, Graceland In Memphis Tennessee...
When It's Iris Time In Tennessee..

TEXAS

Amarillo By Morning
Beautiful, Beautiful Texas
Deep In The Heart Of Texas
The Eyes Of Texas
Going Back To Texas
God Blessed Texas With His Own Hands
I'd Like To Be In Texas
The Lone Texas Plains
Lost In Texas
San Antonio Rose
Summertime In Texas
Texan By Birth...Aggie By The Grace Of God
Texan To A "T"
Texas Hold'em Poker
Texas Is Aggie Country
Texas Longhorns
Texas, Our Texas
Texas...The Jumbo State
Texas...The Lone Star State
Texas Tornado

Waltz Across Texas
We Is Gone To Texas
Yellow Rose Of Texas

UTAH
Utah...Land Of The Saints
Utah...The Desert State
Utah...The Salt Lake State
Utah, We Love Thee

VERMONT
The Green Mountains Of Vermont
Hail Vermont
Moonlight In Vermont
Vermont's Green Hills & Silver Waters
Vermont's Lush Green Mountains

VIRGINIA
Autumn In Virginia
The Beaches Of Virginny
Carry Me Back To Old Virginny
Down In Shanandoah, Virginia
In The Heart Of Old Virginia
The Lush Virginia Hills
Old Dominion...Virginia
Old Virginia Moon
Sweet Virginia
Virginia City Waltz
Virginia...Down Where The Old South Begins
Virginia Lake At Midnight...
Virginia...The Mother Of Presidents
Virginia...Where The Blue Ridge Begins
Virginia's Trail Of The Lonesome Pine

WASHINGTON
Always Evergreen In Washington
Washington...Land Of The Evergreens
Washington...Land Of Verdant Forest Green
Washington...My Home

WEST VIRGINIA
The Beautiful Hills Of West Virginia
West Virginia Fantasies
West Virginia...The Panhandle State
West Virginia's Long & Winding Boarders
West Virginia's Rugged Terrain Of The Allegheny Mountains

WISCONSIN
Wisconsin...America's Dairyland
Wisconsin Cheese Heads
Oh, Wisconsin Land Of Beauty
Wisconsin...Land Of My Dreams
Wisconsin...The Grassy Place
Wisconsin's Deep Cool Woods

WYOMING
Big Wyoming
My Sweet Wyoming Home
Winds Of Wyoming
Wyoming...Land Where The Massive Rockies Stand
Wyoming...The Equality State
Wyoming...The Wonderland Of America
Wyoming...Where The Great Lakes Meet The Rocky Mountains
Wyoming's Natural Wonders
Wyoming's Wide-Open Grasslands

MISC.
...And On The 8th Day, God Created *(State)*
Down In The Boondocks
Gotham City
High Plains Drifter
Life's Too Short Not to Live It As A *(State)*
My Heart Belongs In *(State)*
Southern Accents
There's No Place Like *(State)*
(State) Is As Close To Heaven As I Have Been
(State) Spoken Here
(State) To The Bone

STICK/STICKER TITLES

I'll Stick Around
I'm Sticking With You
I'm Stuck
I'm Stuck On You
Let's Stick Together
Pickup Sticks
Stick Around
Stick 'Em Up
Stick It To Me Baby
Stick It Out
Stick Shift
Stick Thin
Sticker Picker
Sticker 'Em Up
Sticker Fingers
Sticker Shock
A Sticker Situation
Stickered By You
Sticking Together
Sticks & Stones...
Sticky Business
Sticky Fingers
A Sticky Situation
Sticky Sweet
Still Stuck On You
Stuck In The Middle
Stuck In The Moment
Stuck In Time
Stuck With Me
Walk Softly & Carry A Big Stick

STRAWBERRY TITLES

(SEE FOOD)

STROLLER TITLES

- *Make the "O" look like a Wheel.*

Cruisin'
Free Wheelin'
High Rollin'
Just Strollin' Along
Strollin' In The Sunshine
Strollin', Strollin', Strollin'
Strolling Side By Side
Takin' A Stroll

STRONG/STRENGTH TITLES

(SEE ALSO WEIGHT LIFTING)

Be Strong
Brute Strength
Give Me Strength
Hold On...Be Strong
Inner Strength
Mr. Muscles
Muscle Mania
Muscles Abounding
Only The Strong Survive
Stand Strong
Stay Strong
Strength...Courage...Wisdom
Strength In Numbers
Strong As An Ox
Strong As Steel
Tower Of Strength
United In Strength
We Are Strong
World's Strongest Boy

SUMMER TITLES

(SEE ALSO BEACH, HOT, POOL, SUN, SUNBATHING, SWIMMING & WATER)

- *Use a Sun in place of an "O".*
- *Put a Thermometer in place of an "I".*
- *Make Water drops dripping from letters as if they are sweating.*
- *Draw Flames coming from tops of letters.*
- *Place title inside Puffs of Smokes.*

Barefoot & Fancy Free
Beatin' The Summer Heat
Beauty Of A Summer's Day
Boys/Girls Of Summer
Celebrate Summer
Days Of Summer
Diving Into Summer
The Dog Days Of Summer
End Of Summer
Endless Summer
Endless Summer Days/Nights
Feel The Burn!
Feelin' Hot! Hot! Hot!
Floating Into Summer
Fun In The Sun
Fun Under The Sun
Heat Wave
Hellooooo Summer Sunshine
Here Comes The Summer Sun
Hip, Hip Hooray For The Hot Summer Day
Hot Fun In The Summertime
Hot! Hot! Hot!
Hot Stuff
Hot Summer Nights
Hot Time...Summer In The City
How I Spent My Summer Vacation...
I Know What You Did Last Summer!!!
In The Good Ole Summertime
In The Heat Of The Night
Indian Summer
June Is Bustin' Out All Over
Jumpin' Into June
Just Another Lazy Day Afternoon
Keep Your Cool
Lakeside Adventures
Lazy, Hazy, Crazy Days Of Summer
Lazy Summer Days/Daze
Let The Sun Shine In
Lickin' The Heat *(Popsicle)*
A Little Taste Of Summer *(Picnic)*
Long Hot Summer
Love In The Summertime
May The Summer Sun Shine Warm Upon Your Face
Much Fun In The Summer Sun
O Summer Day Beside The Joyous Sea! *(Henry Wadsworth Longfellow)*
Ode To Summer
Oh, Those Summer Nights
On A Summer's Day...
Once Upon A Summer Day/Night...
One Crazy Summer
One Fine Summer Day
One Summer's Day/Night...
A Place In The Summer Sun
Popsicle Weather
Red Hot Summer
The Red Hot Summer Sun
"S" Is For Summer!
Seasons In The Sun
School's Out For The Summer
Sizzlin' Summer Sun
A Slice Of Summer *(Eating Watermelon)*
Some Like It Hot
Some, Some, Summertime...
Summer At The Shore
Summer Breeze Makes Me Feel Fine
Summer Breezes
Summer Buzzin'
Summer Crazy
Summer Days & Summer Nights
Summer Days Are Here Again
Summer Dreams
Summer Fun
Summer In The City/Country
Summer Lovin'
Summer Lovin'...Had Me A Blast
Summer Memories
Summer Nights
Summer Of '42 *(Substitute any year)*
A Summer Place
Summer Rain
Summer Romance
A Summer Scene
Summer Sizzle
Summer Skies
In Summer, The Song Sings Itself. *(William Carlos Williams)*
A Summer's Day
Summer's End
Summer's Morning
Summer's Splendor
Summertime Adventures
Summertime Blues
Summertime In The City
Summertime Is...
Summertime Moments
Summertime Sun & Fun
Summertime Swim Fun

Sunkissed Summer
Sweet Summer Day
Sweet Summer Fun
Swimming Thru Summer
Swingin' Into Summer
Swingin' Into The Summer Sun
Too Cool To Be Hot
Too Much Fun In The Summer Sun
Under The Summer Moonlight
Watch Out Summer...Here I Come!
Water Fight
Water Fun
Wet 'N Wild
Where There Is Sunshine, There Is Also Shade
Where's The Lemonade?

____
____
____
____
____

SUN/SUNSHINE TITLES

(SEE ALSO HOT, SUMMER & SUNRISE)

- *Use a Sun in place of an "O".*
- *Replace an "I" with a Thermometer.*
- *Make Water drops dripping from the letters as if they are sweating.*
- *Draw Flames coming from tops of letters.*
- *Place title inside Puffs of Smoke.*

Ain't No Sunshine When...
As The Sun Falls Into The Sea...
Basking In The Sunshine
Beat The Heat
Behind The Clouds, The Sun Is Shining
Blinded By The Light
A Bright Sunshiny Day
Bring On The Sun
A Day In The Sun
Fun In The Sun
A Fun Sun Day
A Gleam Of Sunshine
Good Day Sunshine
Havin' Fun In The Sun
Having A Heat Wave, A Tropical Heat Wave. *(Marilyn Monroe)*
The Heat Is On
Heat Wave
Heeeellllllo Sunshine
Here Comes The Sun
Hot Fun In The Sun
Hot! Hot! Hot!
I Was Raised On Country Sunshine
If You Can't Stand The Sun...
I'm Gonna Let It Shine
I'm Walkin' On Sunshine
It's A Sunshiny Day
It's Hot, Hot, Hot
Kissed By The Sunshine
Let The Sun Shine
Let The Sunshine In!
Lickin' The Heat *(Popsicle)*
Little Miss Sunshine
Look On The Bright Side
Made In The Shade
May The Sun Shine Warm Upon Your Face
May The Sunshine Always Shine Upon You
Mr. Sun, Shine On Me
Much Fun In The Sun
My Place In The Sun
Our Lil' Mr. Sonshine
Our Little Ray Of Sonshine/Sunshine
Rays Of Sunshine
The Rising Sun
Seascape With Sun & Seagulls
Seasons In The Sun
Seasons Of The Sun
A Shady Kind Of Dude
Sizzlin' Sun Fun
A Slice Of Summer
So Much Fun
Soaking Up The Sun
Some Like It Hot
Soul Of Sunshine
Sun Baked
Sunday Morning Sunshine
Sun-Dried
Sun-Fried Kids
The Sun Is But A Morning Star.
Sun-Kissed
Sun Queen
The Sun Rose & Painted Whispers Of Joy
The Sun Shines When You Smile
The Sun...The Shine & The Light Of My Life
The Sun'll Come Out Tomorrow
Sunny Day Chasin' The Clouds Away *(Sesame Street)*
Sunny Days Are Here Again
Sunny Side Up
"Sun"sational
Sunshine Angel
Sunshine On My Shoulders
Sweet Summer Sun
Tastes Of Summer
Too Hot To Handle
Too Much Fun In The Sun
Twilight Sunlight
You Are My Sunshine
You Are The Sunshine In My Life

You Light Up My Life
Walk Barefoot Across Sunshine Days.
(James Kavanaugh)
We Had Joy, We Had Fun, We Had Seasons In The Sun...
When The Sun Burn Red...
Where The Sunshine Is...

SUNBATHING/SUNBURN TITLES

(SEE ALSO BEACH, HOT, SUMMER & SUN)

All Lathered Up
Baked To Perfection
Baking Beauties
Bathing Bootie
Bikini Babe/Baby
Bikini Brigade
Catching Some Rays
Feel The Burn
Girls Just Wanna Have Sun
Got Sun Block?
Itsy, Bitsy, Teenie, Weenie Bikini
Sizzlin' To Perfection
Soaking In The Sun
Soakin' Up Some Rays
Soakin' Up The Sunshine
Summer Sizzlin'
Sun-Baked
Sun God/Goddess
Sun-Kissed
Sun Queen
Sunbathing Beauties
Sunny Side Up
Sunscreen Queen
Sunshine On My Shoulders & My Face & My Back & My...
Too Hot To Handle
Well Done

SUNRISE/SUNSET TITLES

(SEE ALSO MOON, NIGHT & SUN)

...And God Said: Let There Be Light.
(Genesis I:3)
Angel Of The Morning
As Daytime Dwindles Into Dusk...
As Sunset Washes The Land...
As The Copper Sun Sets...
As The Morning Sun Crept Up...
As The Sunrise Bathed The Hills...
As Twilight Gave Birth To The Night...
The Awakening
The Beauty Of Sunrise
Before The Dawn...
Blaze On The Horizon
Breathtaking
The Breeze At Dawn Has Secrets To Tell You.
(Rumi)
The Cold Gray Light Of Dawn
Cold Morning Light
Come Early Morning...
The Crack Of Dawn
Dawn Begins At Midnight
Dawn Of Glory
By Dawn's Early Light
Dawn's First Light
Daylight's Last Glimmer
Each Dawn Is A New Beginning
Early Morning Starshine
Early Morning's Glow
The Early Show
Essence Of Twilight
Fire In The Twilight
From Dawn 'Til Dusk
From Dusk 'Til Dawn
From Sunset To Star Rise
The Glimmer Of Twilight
The Glory Of Daybreak
Good Morning, Merry Sunshine
Good Morning Starshine
Graced By God's Sunrise
Here Comes The Sun
How Glorious A Greeting The Sun Gives The Mountains! - *(John Muir)*
Impressions At Sunset
In The Twilight Hours
In Walks The Night
Just Beyond The Sunset
Kissed By The Breath Of Sunset
Let There Be Light
Light Of A Clear Blue Morning
The Magic Of Dawn
The Magical Morning's Glow
Midsummer Morning

The Morning After
Morning Has Broken
Morning's Glory
The Mountains Dripped With Sunset
The Mysterious Sea At Dusk
A New Day Is Dawning
A New World In The Morning
Oceanside Sunset
October Sky
Oh, What A Beautiful Morning!
The Purple Dusk Of Twilight Time
The Purple Sunset
Red Dawn
Red Sails In The Sunset
Rise & Shine
Risen' & Shinin'
Seaside Sunset
Sinking Beauty Of The Sunset
Southern Sunrise
Straight Past The Sunrise
The Sun Also Rises
The Sun Is But A Morning Star.
(Henry David Thoreau)
The Sun Sets Without Your Assistance
Sunday Morning Sunshine
Sunny Side Up
Sunrise & Blue Skies
Sunrise Explosion
The Sunrise Is God's Greeting Card...The Sunset His Signature
Sunrise On The Hills
Sunrise Serenade
Sunrise...The Last Breath Of Night
Sunset By The Bay
Sunset Heaven
A Sunset Is A Sunrise On The Other Side Of The World
Sunset Over The Horizon
The Sunset Painted The Sky
As Sunset Swept Across The Sky...
The Sunset's Golden Glow
Sunset's Paintbrush Graced The Sky With Golds & Reds & Purples
Sweet Silent Sunset
Tequila Sunrise
This Is The Day That The Lord Has Made
This Is The Land The Sunset Washes
'Til The Morning Light
Triumphant Sunrise
Twilight By The Sea
A Twilight Moon
Twilight's Golden Grace
Under The Sunset Sky
Valley Of The Morning Sun
Visions Of A Sunset
Walkin' On Sunshine
Watching The Sunrise
Where The Blue Of The Night Meets The Glory Of The Day
Where The Red Sun Sinks In The Hills Of Gold
The Wonder Of Sunrise
The World Is Waiting For The Sunrise

____
____
____
____
____

SURFING TITLES

(SEE ALSO BEACH)

- *Use a Surfboard as an "I".*
- *Have title Surfing on a Surfboard.*

Belly Boarding
Big Wednesday
Blue Crush
Body Surfing
Boogie Boardin' Boys
A Boy & A Wave
Catch A Wave
Cowabunga
Gettin' Some Skim *(Skim boarding)*
Gettin' Wave Reviews
Hangin' Ten
Just Skim It
The Last Wave Of Summer
Let's Go Surfin' Now...
Ride, Ride, Ride The Wild Surf/Wake
Shootin' The Waves
Skimmy Dipping *(Skim boarding)*
Skim-sational
Sun, Sea & Surf
Surf & Turf
Surf City
Surfer Girl/Guy
Surfer's Rule
Surfin' The Airwaves
Surfin' The Net
Surfin' USA
Surf's Up
Wait...Ride...Crash
Wave Over Wave
Wave Rider
Wild Surf

____
____
____
____
____

SWEET TITLES

Ain't She Sweet
Bitter Sweet
Gimmie Some Sugar
How Sweet It Is
I'm Sweet On You
Nothing Is Sweeter Than You
One Sweet Day
Short But Sweet
Short 'N Sweet
Sticky Sweet
Sugar Baby/Daddy
Sugar High
Sugar Love
Sugar Pie, Honey Bunch
Sugar Shock
Sugar, Sugar
Sweet & Sour
Sweet As Candy
Sweet As Honey
Sweet As Pie
Sweet Child O' Mine
A Sweet Deal
Sweet Dream Baby
Sweet Dreams
Sweet Face
Sweet Kisses
Sweet Little Sixteen
Sweet Nothings
Sweet On You
The Sweet Smell Of Roses
The Sweet Smell Of Success
Sweet Smooches
Sweet Sorrow
Sweet Talker
Sweet Thing
Sweet Tooth
Sweet Victory
Sweeter Than Candy
Sweetest Hearts
Sweetest Sweet
Sweetheart
Sweetie Pie
Sweets For My Sweet/Sweetie
Sweety Pie
You Are My Candy Girl

____
____
____
____
____

SWIMMING TITLES

(SEE ALSO POOL & WATER)

- *Make "O" into a Life Ring or Water Splash.*
- *Punch title letters out of Water Paper.*
- *Cut title mat into the shape of a Pool.*

Aqua Kid
Aquaholic
Belly Flopper
Belly Floppin' Fool
Bikini Babe/Baby
Bikini Brigade
Canon Ball Craze
Dangerous Divers
Dive In
Finned Friends
Floatin' Fool
Goggles & Giggles
Goggles, Giggles & Googly Eyes
Got That Sinking Feeling
H20 Boys
I Rule The Pool
In The Swim Of Things
Itsy, Bitsy, Teenie, Weenie Bikini
I've Got That Sinkin' Feelin'
A Jewel In The Pool
Jr. Lifeguard
Lickin' & Splashin' *(Popsicle by the pool)*
Little Mermaid
Little Swimmer
Makin' A Splash/Waves
Moonlight Swim
Oh, I Wish I Were A Fish!
On The Waterfront
On Your Mark...Get Set...Swim!!!
Pool Duel *(Kids wrestling in pool)*
Pool School
Poolside Pals
Sink Or Swim
Sinkin' Sensation
Splash Dance
Splash Session
Splashin' Around
Splish Splash
Star Swimmer
In The Swim Of Things
Swimming Beauty
Swimming In The Fastlane
Swimming Is A Stroke Of Genius
Swimming Like The Fishies
Swimming The Rapids
Swimming Thru Summer
Taking The Plunge
Talent Pool
Testing The Water

Tiny Tuber *(Baby in innertube)*
Underwater Fun
The Unsinkable *(Name)*
Water Baby
Water Bugs
Water Fun
Water Wars
Water World
Wet 'N Wild
Wet Wonders
What A Splash
Who Needs A Boat? I Can Swim & Float!

SWING TITLES

- *Have title hang from an A-Frame Swingset.*

Angel On A Swing
Away Up High
Baby Let's Swing
Boy's On A Swing
Gettin' In The Swing Of Things
Hang 'Em High
Hang In There Baby
Hang Loose
Hang Ten
Hangin' 'Round The House *(Baby in swing)*
Higher & Higher
In The Swing Of Things
It's Hang Time
Just A Hangin' Around/Out
Just A Swingin'
King Of The Swing
A Real Swinger
Swing By Sometime
Swing Into Spring/Summer
Swing King/Queen
The Swing Of Fun
Swing Time
Swingin' Around
Swingin' In The Sun
Swingin' In The Wind
Swingin' On A Star
Swingin' The Day Away
Swingin' Over The Water
Swingset Girl
Tired Of Swinging *(Swinging on a Tire swing)*
Up In The Air & Back Down
Up, Up & Away

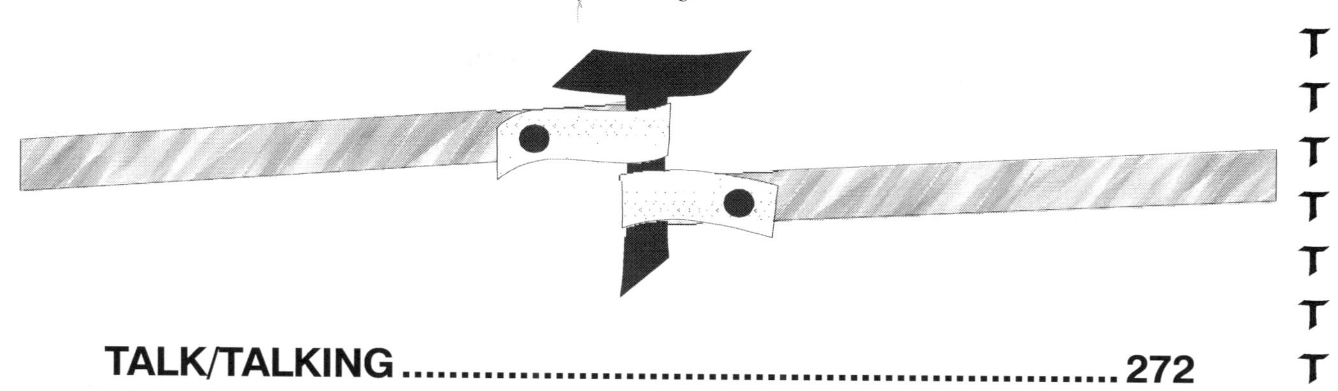

TALK/TALKING TITLES

All Talk...
Baby Talk
Bag Of Wind *(Big talker)*
Big Mouth
Chatter Box
Chatty Kathy
Chit Chat
Down In The Mouth
Endless Chatter
From The Mouths Of Babes...
Gift Of Gab
Girl Talk
Gossip! Gossip! Gossip!
Heart To Heart
I Wanna Talk About Me
If You're Going To Talk The Talk...
Jive Talkin'
Let's Talk
Look Who's Talking!
Mighty Mouth
Motor Mouth
Open Mouth, Insert Foot
Pillow Talk
Say What?
Silence Is Golden/Magical
Small Talk
Social Butterfly
Something To Talk About
Spilled The Beans
Talk About Love
Talk It Up
Talk Of The Town
Talk To Me!!!
Talk To The Animals
Talk To The Hand
Tongue In Cheek
Tongue Lashing
Tongue Tied
Whah, Whah, Whah!
Yakitty Yak

TEACHER TITLES

(SEE ALSO EDUCATION & SCHOOL)

- *Use a Pencil or Crayon for an "I" or "L".*
- *Make a Ruler & put title on the Ruler.*
- *Place title inside little Books.*
- *Make title look like a Certificate or Diploma.*
- *Use a large Apple to put title on.*

1st Class Teacher
A+ Teacher
Adding It All Up
A Classy Teacher
Education Is The Key
Experience Wildlife...Be A Teacher
A Great Teacher Loves Teaching Others To Love Learning
I Am Not A Teacher, But An Awakener. *(Robert Frost)*
Kids Are My Business
A Mark Of Class...My Class
Nutty Professor
Preschool Teachers Enjoy The Little Things In Life!!
Praise The Young & They Will Bloom
Real Learning Begins With One Good Teacher
Music Teachers Are Really Sharp
My Teacher Has Class!!
A Teacher Is A Rainbow Between Hope & Achievement
A Teacher Sees Tomorrow In A Child's Eyes
A Teacher Takes A Hand, Opens A Mind & Touches A Heart
Teachers Are In A Class Of Their Own
Teachers Bring The World Into View
Teachers Change The World...One Child At A Time
Teachers Do The "Write" Thing
Teachers Have Class
Teachers Have The "Write" Stuff
Teachers Make The Grade
Teacher's Pet
Teachers Rule
Teachers Teach Our Future
Teachers Touch Tomorrow
A Teacher's Wisdom...
Teaching Is A Work Of Heart
Teaching Is An Art Of The Heart
Teaching Is My Bag
In Teaching Others, We Teach Ourselves
Teaching Today Touches Tomorrow
Teaching With Heart & Soul
Time Spent Teaching Is Never Lost
Totally Terrific Teacher
A Touch Of Class

World Class Teacher
World's Greatest Teacher
You've Got Class

____
____
____
____
____

TEARS TITLES
(SEE CRYING)

TEEN LINGO & TITLES
(SEE ALSO CHILDREN)
Adventures In Baby-sitting
...And This Is My Room!
Attitude...??? What Attitude...???
Awesome!
B-A-D
The Best Substitute For Experience Is Being Sixteen. - *(Raymond Duncan)*
The Bomb
Bitchin'
Boogaloo
Boss
Bottomless Pit
But I Need My Own Car
But Mom, Everyone Is Wearing Them!
Caught Thinking
Chill Out!
Clueless
Cool!
Cool Chic
The Dating Game
Ditz
Don't Be Trippin'
Dream On!
Dinomite!!!
Far Out!
Fer Sure!
First Date
Flower Child
Freaky
Freedom Is A Driver's License
Funky
Gag Me
Gag Me With A Spoon
Gee Whiz
Generation Gap
Get Down
Gettin' Down With My Sounds
Gosh
Groovy
Gross
Grounded Again
Hang Loose
Hangin' Out
Hip To Be Square
Hot & Hip
How I Spent My Summer Vacation...
I'm A Teen...So That Means I'm Right!
I'm So Cool
Is This Cool, Or What?
It Won't Ever Be This Good Again...
It's A Teen Thing
It's All Good
Keen
Keep On Truckin'
Let's Not Waste Time & Just Assume I Know Everything!!!
Like...
Little Children Headache; Big Children Heartache. - *(Italian Proverb)*
Man!
MAYBE...And That Is Final!!!
My Parents, My Problem
My Telephone Is My Life
Narly Dude
Neat-O
Oh My Gawd!!!
Oh My Gosh!
Outta Sight
Peace
Pre-Teen...I Wanna Scream
Rad
Rad Man!
Radicle
Rant & Rave
Right On
Rock On
Sabrina The Teenage Witch
Say What!?
Shopping Is My Life
Slick
Snaps!
So Cool, Just Gotta Wear Shades
So Tired
Sweeeeet!
Sweet Sixteen
Swell
Talk To The Hand
Teen Angel
Teen Digest
Teen Idol
Teen Scene
Teen Seen

Teenage Mutant Ninja Turtles
Teenage Nervous Breakdown
Teens...Can't Live With 'Em, Can't Live Without 'Em
Teens Just Wanna Have Fun
Teens Rule!
That's The Pits
Tight
Torqued
Totally
Totally Cool!
Trippin'
Tubular
Tude Dude
Yo
Yo Baby Yo
You Rule
You Turkey
Wasup?
Wazzzzz Up?
What A Blast
What A Gas
What Ever
What's Happnin'
Where The Boys/Girls Are
Where The Teens Are
Wouldn't You Like To Know?
Yeah! That's The Ticket

TEENAGER

Terrific...**T**rying
Emotional...**E**xceptional
Ebullient...**E**lusive
Nice...**N**eurotic
Abrupt...**A**ngelic
Great...**G**angly
Exciting...**E**xhausting
Rebellious...**R**elentless

TEETH/TOOTH TITLES

- *Use a Tooth in place of an "O".*
- *Make little Braces Tracks to put title on.*
- *Create a large Tooth & put title in it.*
- *Use Coins in place of an "O" for Tooth Fairy pages.*

1 Tooth, 2 Tooth, Looth Tooth, Gone Tooth
All Gums
All I Want For Christmas Are My 2 Front Teeth
Black Hole *(No teeth in front)*
Brace Face
Brace Yourself *(Braces)*
Brush...Brush...Brush
Colorful Creation
Easy Money *(Toothfairy money)*
Filling The Tooth
Flossing Is Fun
Getting Mouthy
Heavy Metal Mouth
A Hole In One
If The Tooth Be Known...
I've Been Tracked
Look Mom, No Cavities
Looth Tooth & Consequences
Lost All My Wisdom *(Wisdom teeth pulled)*
Metal Mouth
My Tooth Ith Looth!
My Toothless Tale
Open Wide
Pearly Whites
Psychedelic Smile *(Colored bands)*
Show Us Those Pearly Whites
Snaggle Tooth
A Snap Of The Gap
Something Mithing
Spaced Out *(No teeth in front)*
Sparkly Whites
Sweet Tooth
Teething Bites/Sucks
Teething Is The Pits
Teething Troubles
This Is The Way We Brush Our Teeth...
Time To Brush
Tinsel Teeth
My Tooth Fairy Is Rich

A Tooth Fairy Tale
The Tooth Fairy Was Here
A Tooth In The Hand
The Tooth Ith The Matter
Tooth Or Consequences
Tooth Or Dare
Tooth Tales
The Tooth, The Whole Tooth & Nothing But The Tooth
A Toothful Tale
Toothless Beauty
Toothless Grin
Toothly Grin
Track Face
Track Teeth
Train Tracks
You're Just Too Thweet

TELEPHONE TITLES

(SEE ALSO TALKING)

1 Ringee Dingee, 2 Ringee Dingee, Hello
Bla Bla Bla!!!
Chit Chat
Cordless Mom...Recharge With Hugs
I Just Called To Say, I Love You!
Let's Talk About It
Ma Bell Didn't Have Teenagers
Phone Freak
Queen Of The Telephone
Say What?
Something To Talk About
Telephone Zone
What Did We Do Before Call Waiting?

TENNIS/TABLE TENNIS TITLES

(SEE ALSO SPORTS)

- *Put a Tennis Ball in place of an "O".*
- *Use Racket for a "P".*
- *Have a Net or Court as title's background.*

Ace Player
Banged Out A Bagel
Chopped
Drop Shot
Drop-Shot Dynamo
Flick Ball
Hit & Miss
Hittin' The Green Ball
Hittin' The Junk Rubber
I'm In Love
In The Zone
Loop De Loop
Moonball Mania
Ping Ponged
Poached
Side Spinner
Smash Man
Super Sticker
Sweet Spot King/Queen
Tanked
Tennis Anyone?
Tennis Is My Raquet
Tennis This!
This Is My Racket
Top Seeded

THANKSGIVING TITLES

- *Use a Turkey Leg for an "I".*
- *Put a Pilgrim's Hat on a few letters.*

American Pie
Be Thankful...Always
Bless This Feast...Now Let's Eat
Bless This Feast...Now Let's Eat This Beast
Blessed Are We!
Bountiful Harvest
Bunch Of Turkeys
Bushels Of Blessings
Carving The Good Times
Carving Up Thankful Memories
Cold Turkey
Cornucopia Of Bountiful Blessing
Count Your Blessings
A Day Of Thanks
Don't Worry...Be Thankful
Eat Beef *(A Turkey holding this sign)*
Family & Food...Who Could Ask For Anything More!
Family, Friends, Food & Football...Give Thanks!
Family Get Together
Family Traditions
Feast Like The Pilgrims
Feast Your Eyes On This
For Everything We Give Thanks
Gather Together With Thankful Hearts
Give Thanks
Give Thanks For The Simple Things In Life
Give Thanks With A Grateful Heart
Give Us This Day Our Daily Bread
Gobble, Gobble
Gobble 'Til You Wobble
God Is Good...God Is Great...
Happy Turkey Day
Harvest Delight
A Harvest Full Of Memories
Home-Baked For Thanksgiving
Horn Of Plenty Of Family
I'm Thankful For...
Let Us Be Thankful Unto The Lord...
Let's Eat
Let's Get Stuffed
Let's Give Thanks
Let's Talk Turkey
Little Turkeys
Live Thankfully
May The Bounty Of The Season Fill Heart & Home
O, The Lord's Been Good To Us
Our Family Is A Cornucopia Of Love
Our Table Runneth Over
The Pick Of The Patch
Pilgrims Pride
Praise God From Whom All Blessings Flow
Save A Turkey...Eat Beef
Save A Turkey...Order Pizza
Sharing The Food
Sharing The Harvest
Sharing The Love
So Much To Be Thankful For
As Stuffed As A Thanksgiving Turkey
Stuffed With Stuffing
Take Time To Be Thankful
Thank God For Elastic Waistbands
Thankful For Family...Thankful Hearts
A Thankful Heart Is A Happy Heart
Thankful Hearts & Helpful Hands
Thankful Hearts Gather Here
Thanks For The Giving
A Thanksgiving Feast
Thanksgiving Is A Circle Of Memories
Thanksgiving Is For All Creatures Great & Small
Thanksgiving Is Not A Time Of The Year, But An Attitude Of The Heart
Thanksgiving Time
Thanksgiving Traditions
A Time For Thanks
Today We Give Our Thanks
Together Is The Best Place To Be
Tons Of Turkey
Treasured Turkeys *(Kids eating)*
True Thanksgiving Comes From The Heart. *(J.A. Shedd)*
Turkey & Stuffing & Pumpkin Pie, Oh My!
Turkey Crossing
Turkey Day Gathering
Turkey In The Raw
Turkey Talk
Turkey Talk Time
Turkey Time
We Are Gathered Here...
We Are Thankful For...
We Gather Together To Ask For The Lord's Blessing
We Give Thanks For...
We Thank God For...
What A Bunch Of Turkeys!
Where's The Beef?

THOUGHT TITLES

As He Thinketh In His Heart, So Is He.
(Proverbs 23:7)
Bright Youth Passes Swiftly As A Thought.
(Theognis)
Every Pure Thought Is A Glimpse Of God.
(C. A. Bartol)
Nurture Your Mind With Great Thoughts.
(Benjamin Disraeli)
One Thought Fills Immensity. - *(William Blake)*
A Penny For Your Thoughts
Thinking: The Talking Of The Soul With Itself.
(Plato)
The Thoughtful Soul To Solitude Retires.
(Omar Khayyam)

TIME TITLES

- *Replace word Time or "I" with Hourglass.*
- *Put a little Clock in place of an "O".*

Ain't It Time...
All In Due Time
All The Time In The World...
All Time High
Anticipation
As Time Goes By...
At This Moment...
The Best Of Times
The Best Thing To Spend On Kids...Is Time
Better Late Than Never
Cryin' Time
Doing Time
Every Time...
Father Time
The Final Countdown
First Time...
First Time Ever I Saw Your Face...
For Old Time's Sake
For The First Time...
From Time To Time
The Hands Of Time
Happy Hour
Happy Times
How Did I Get So Late, So Early?
How Time Flies
I Wish I Could Stop Time
If I Could Save Time In A Bottle...
If I Could Turn Back The Hands Of Time...
If We Could Freeze Time...
In Due Time
In The Nick Of Time
In Times Like These...
It Was The Best Of Times...
It's Just A Matter Of Time...
It's My Time
It's The Most Wonderful Time Of The Year
It's Too Late To Turn Back Now
I've Got Time On My Hands
Just In Time
The Land That Time Forgot
Last Time Around
Let The Good Times Roll
Life In The Fast Lane
A Long Time Ago...
Long Time No See
Lost Time Is Never Found Again.
(John H. Aughey)
Making Every Minute Count
Minute By Minute
Moment By Moment
Moments In Time
Moments To Remember
My Favorite Waste Of Time
Next Time Around
Not Enough Time
Not In A Million Years
Not One Minute More
Nothing But Time
Nothing Is Worth More Than This Day.
(Johann Wolfgang von Goethe)
Now Is The Time
Once Upon A Time...
One Day At A Time
One Moment In Time
Only Time Will Tell
Only Yesterday
The Passage Of Time
Perfect Timing
Praying For Time
Precious Time
Remember The Time...
Right On Time
Rock Around The Clock
Same Place...Same Time
The Sands Of Time
Second Time Around
Seven Minutes In Heaven
Since The Beginning Of Time
So Much To Do...So Little Time
Somewhere In Time
Sooner Or Later
Spring Forward...Fall Back
A Stitch In Time...
Suspended In Time

Take Things One Day At A Time
Take Time To...
Take Your Time
Tea Time
Then & Now...
There Was A Time
There's No Time Like The Present
Third Time's A Charm
This Time...
This Time Around...
'Til The End Of Time...
A Time & A Place For Everything
Time & Tide Wait For No Man/One
Time & Time Again
Time After Time...
Time Brings Change
Time Does Not Change Us...It Just Unfolds Us. *(Max Frisch)*
Time Flies When You're Having Fun
Time Flies Whether You're Having Fun Or Not
Time For Love
Time Goes By So Fast
The Time Has Come...
Time Heals All Wounds
Time In A Bottle
Time Is Fleeting
Time Is Money
Time Is Not Measured By Clocks, But By Moments
Time Is On My Side
Time Is Tickin' Away
Time Keeps On Tickin' Into The Future
Time Marches On
The Time Of My Life/Our Lives
Time On My/Your Hands
Time Out Boys
Time Out For Fun
Time Out Time
Time Stood Still...
A Time To Be Born
A Time To Remember
Time Waits For No One
Time Will Tell
A Timeless Beauty
Time's A Wastin'
Time's...They Are A Changing
Time's Up
Together Time
Turning Back The Hands Of Time
Twilight Time
Wait A Minute
Well Worth The Wait
Where Did The Time Go?
Where Has All The Time Gone...
Yesterday Once More

TONGUE TITLES

Bite Your Tongue
Catching The Rain On My Tongue
Finger Lickin' Good
Hey, Good Lickin'
It Takes A Lickin' & Keeps On Drippin'
Just One Lick
Lickity Split
Speaking In Tongues
Tongue-In-Cheek
Tongue Tied
Tongue Twister
What's Wrong, Cat's Got Your Tongue?

TOOLS TITLES

(SEE ALSO CONSTRUCTION, OCCUPATIONS & REMODELING)

- *Replace an "I" with a Nail or Screw, a Bolt for an "O", or a Hammer for a "T".*

10-lb. Hammer
Big Boys Tools
A Big Enough Hammer Fixes Anything
Building A Mystery
Building Memories
Caution: Men At Work/Play
Daddy's Little Helper
Drill Instructor
Garage Guru
Grease Monkey
Hammered
Handy Dandy Man
Handy Man
Hard Hat Lover
Hard Hat *(Name)*
Hit The Nail On The Head
Home Improvement
The House That *(Name)* Built
I Came, I Tooled, I Built

If I Had A Hammer...
If You Build It, They Will Come
I'm Your Handy Man
It's Hammer Time
A "Jack" Of All Trades
Just Build It
Licensed To Drill
A Little Boys Tool Box
Man Of Many Vices
Mr. Badwrench
Mr. Goodwrench
My Very Own Tools
Nailed It
Power Tool Pride
Tool Duel
Tool Fool
Tool Time
Tool Time With Mr. Fix-it!
Tool Tyke
Tools Of The Trade
Tough As Nails
Toying With Tools
Under Construction/Destruction
When The Going Gets Tough, The Tough Use Duct Tape
When The Hammer Hits...
With Tools Like Those...

TOYS TITLES

Babes In Toyland
Big Boys & Their Big Toys
Boy Toy
A Doll Among Her Toys
Joys Of Toys
So Many Toys, So Little Time
Tinker Toy Boy
These Are A Few Of My Favorite Toys
A Toy Story
Toys 'R Us
You Can Never Have Too Many Toys

TRACK & FIELD TITLES

(SEE ALSO RUNNING & SPORTS)

- *Make a Track as background mat for title.*

1, 2, 3 Jump!
3-Legged Racer
Back On Track
Born To Run
Camptown Races
I Can Go The Distance
Chariots Of Fire
Dash Of Excitement
A Day At The Races
Field Of Dreams
Finishers Are Winners
Get Ready, Get Set, Go
Giant Leap
Go The Distance
Going The Distance
Have A Field Day
High Hopes
I'm Running For My Life
In The Running
Life In The Fast/Slow Lane
Makin' Tracks
A Need For Speed
Off & Running
On The Fast Track
On The Right Side Of The Tracks
On Track
On Your Mark, Get Set, Go
One Giant Leap For Man
One Track Mind
Outpaced
Race Against The Clock
The Race For Life
The Race Is On
Race To The Finish
Racing The Wind
Ready To Race
Running Like The Wind
Speed Demon
Speed Racer
Sprint To The Finish
Track & Field
Track Time
Trackin' To The End
The Wrong Side Of The Track

TRAIN TITLES

(SEE ALSO RIDING)

- *Create a Train & put title in a few of the cars.*
- *Make Train Tracks & put title on the Tracks.*
- *Put title in big puffs of smoke.*

All Aboard
Big Black Train
Boxcar Blues
Chattanooga Choo Choo
Choo! Choo!
Choo, Choo *(Name)*
Chug-A Chug-A Choo Choo!
Chuggin' Along
Circus Train
Come Ride Along With Me
Counting Train Cars
Crazy Train
Do The Locomotion
Down By The Station
Downtown Train
Engineer *(Name)*
Freight Train Boogie
Groovy Train
Homeward Bound Train
I Think I Can, I Think I Can...I Can!
Imagination Station
I've Been Workin' On The Railroad
A Journey By Train
Last Train Home
Leavin' On The Midnight Train To...
The Little Engine That Could
The Little Train That Could
Loco Motion
Lonesome Train Whistle
Long Black Train
Long Train Runnin'
Love Train
Makin' Tracks
Night Train
On The Right Track
One Track Mind
Peace Train
Railroad Rider
Railroad *(Name)*
Slow Train
Smooth Operator
Takin' The "A" Train
That Train Don't Stop Here
The "Tracks" Of Life
The Train Event
Train Gang
Train Hoppin'
That Train Kept A Rollin'
Train Trek
Train Whistle Blues
Train Wreck
Welcome Aboard
When Angels Ride Trains...

TRAVEL TITLES

(SEE ALSO COUNTRIES & STATES)

100 Miles From Nowhere
26 Miles Across The Sea...Santa Catalina Is Waiting For Me
500 Miles Away From Home
Across The Highways & Thru The Tunnels... To Grandmother's House We Go!
Across The Miles
Adventure Time
Adventures In Paradise
All Tripped Out
Aloha
Amazing Journey
America The Beautiful
America The Unusual
America, You're Beautiful!
Among My Souvenirs
Another Day In Paradise
Another World
Are We There Yet?
Around The World
Around The World In *(#)* Days
As We Travel The Highways...
At Journey's End...
Away We Go
Back In The Good Old USA
Back In The USA
Back On The Road Again
Bahama Mama
Been Too Long On The Road
The Beginning Of The End
Beginning Our Journey
Beyond The Sea
The Big Adventures Of *(Name)*
Big City Boy/Girl
Big City Nights
Big Yellow Taxi
Boat Journey's
Bon Voyage!
Bright Lights...Big City
Buckled Up & Ready To Roll
Building Special Memories
Burnin' Up The Interstates

California Dreamin'
The Call Of The Open Roads
Can't Wait To Get On The Road Again...
The "Car" Scene
The City By Night
City Of Angels
City Of Dreams
City Of Hope
City Of Lights
City Sights
City Streets
Come On A Safari With Me
Cruisin' Along
Destination Relaxation
Destination Unknown
Different Worlds
Dirt Road Blues
Dirt Road Riders
Disneyland Dreamin'
Distant Shores
Don't Give Up The Ship
Don't Let It End
Down By The Sea
Down By The Station
Down In The Boondocks
Eastward Ho!
Enchanted Island
Enchanted Journey
Enjoying The Ride
Escapade
European Vacation
Every Which Way But Loose
Everyday Is A Winding Road
Family Retreat
Fantastic Voyage
Far & Away
Far Away Places
Feelin' The Wind In Our Hair
Feels Like Home To Me
Final Destination
Flyin' High
Fly The Friendly Skies
Foot Loose & Fancy Free
Free & Easy
Freedom Road
From Here To Eternity
Gateway To The World
Getting There Is Half The Fun
Go Tell It On The Mountain
Go West Young Man
Goin' Places
Going Back West
Going By Planes, Trains & Automobiles
Going Bye-Bye
Going In Style
Going The Extra Mile
Going To The Theatah!!!
Going To Where The Blacktop Ends
A Going Tropical
Golden Gate Vacation
Good To Go
Got To Be There
Gotta Travel On
Great Adventure
The Great Escape
Halfway To Paradise
Happiness Is Just Around The Bend/Corner
Have Gas...Will Travel
Havin' The Time Of Our Lives
Having A Wonderful Time
Head For The Border
Headed Home
Heartbreak Hotel
Here...There...And Everywhere
Here Today...Gone Tomorrow
High Life In The City
High Plains Drifter
Highway Of Boredom/Fun
Hit The Road
Hitchin' A Ride
Home At Last!
Home Away From Home
Home On Wheels
Homeward Bound
Hot Child In The City
Hotel California
How I Spent My Vacation
How Much Longer?
I Can See For Miles & Miles...
Incredible Journey
It's The Journey Not The Destination
I've Got Two Tickets To Paradise
A Journey Around The US/World
A Journey By Boat
Journey Of A Thousand Miles
Journey To The Center Of The Earth
A Journey Thru The Moonlight
The Joy Is In The Journey, Not At The Journey's End
Just Another Day In Paradise
Just Plane Fun
King Of The Road
Ladies Of The Road
The Last Mile Home
Lazy River
Leavin' On A Jet Plane
Let The Good Times Roll
Let's Get Away From It All

T Let's Get Lost
Life In The City
T Life On The Road
Life's A Highway
T Life's A Journey, Not A Destination
Life's Highway
T Little Rendezvous In *(City/State/Town)*
The Long & Winding Road
T The Long Journey/Voyage Home
A Long, Long Road Is Winding
T The Longest Road...
Lovers In The City
T Magical Moments At The Magic Kingdom
Magical Mystery Tour
T Mama, I'm Coming Home
Memories Are Made Of This
T Merrily We Roll Along
Midnight At The Oasis
T Miles & Miles & Miles
Motel Moments
T A Mountain Paradise
No Direction In Life
T No, We Are Not There Yet
Northern Exposure
T O, Beautiful, For Spacious Skies
Off Roading We Travel
T Off We Go Into The Wild Blue Yonder
Oh, The Places We'll Go
T That Ole Lonesome Road
On A Journey Of Discovery
T On A Lonesome Highway
On A Long Lonely Road
T On The Marrakesh Express
On The Old Dirt Road
T On The Road Again
On The Road Again & Again & Again...
T On The Road Less Traveled
On The Road To Nowhere
T On Vacation
One Night In The City...
T Our Getaway
Our Journeys Thru The States
T Over The Mountain & Across The Sea
Over The River & Thru The Woods
T Pack Your Bags & Leave Tonight
Paradise
T Peaceful Easy Feeling
Permanent Vacation
T Planes...Trains...And Automobiles
Pounding The Pavement
T Professional Tourists
Ready, Set, Go/Roll
T Red Dirt Road
Red Light, Green Light...No Rest Stop In Sight

Rental Sweet Rental *(Rented RV)*
Rest & Relaxation
Ridin' The Roads
Riding On Route 66
Road Adventures USA
The Road Ahead & Behind...
Road Hog
Road Rules
Road Runners
Road Trip
Road Trips Aren't Measured By Mile Markers, But By Moments
The Roads We Travel/Tread...
Roamin' Home *(RV)*
Rollin', Rollin', Rollin' Keep Those Wheels A Rollin'
Room With A View
Rough Road Ahead/Behind
Route 66, Here We Come!
Rugged Road/Route
Run For The Boarder
RV There Yet?
Savvy Sightseers
Sentimental Journey
So Long, Farewell, Auf Wiedersehen, Good Night, I Hate To Go & Leave This Pretty Sight
Somewhere Down The Road
South Of The Border
Southern Charm/Hospitality
Southern Roads
Springtime In Paris
Start Your Engines
State Of Grace
State Of Independence
Summer In The City
Sweet Southern Comfort
Swing High...Swing Low
Take Me Home Country Roads
Take Only Memories...Leave Nothing But Footprints
Takin' A Little Trip
There Are Two Kinds Of Travel: First Class & With Children
There's A Road I'm Wandering
There's No Lookin' Back Now
They Paved Paradise To Put Up A Parking Lot
This Is Paradise
This Is Some Vacation
Those Magnificent Men In Their Flying Machines
Tired Travelers
Tour De France
Tourist Trap
Travel Time
A Traveler's Life
Travelers Of The Sea

Travelin' Man
Traveling In Style
Traveling Together
Trippin' Out
Trouble In Paradise
True Love Travelers
Two On The Road/Town
Two Tickets To Paradise
Up, Up & Away
Uptown Girl
Uptown Or Downtown, It's My Kinda Town
Traveling Down A Dirt Road...
V-A-C-A-T-I-O-N
Viva Las Vegas
Viva Lost Wages
Way To Go
We Built This City
We Sailed Thru NYC On The "Subway"
We're Off To See The Sights
We've Got A Ticket To Ride
Westward Ho
What A View
What A Wonderful World
Where In The World Is Carmen Sandiego?
Which Way Do We Go?
While The City Sleeps...
Wide Open Spaces
The Wise Man Travels To Discover Himself
Wish You Were Here
World Class Traveler
World Travelers
You "Auto" Know We Aren't There Yet
Zoom, Zoom, Zoom
The *(Name's)* Family Journeys/Travels
(Name's) Excellent Adventure
(Name's) Travels

____
____
____
____
____

TREE TITLES

- *Put title letters on the Leaves of a Tree.*
- *Use a Leaf in place of an "A" or "O".*

Barking Up The Wrong Tree
Big Oaks From Little Acorns Grow!
A Christmas Tree Hunting We Will Go!
The Greatest Oak Was Once A Little Nut
Love Under A Tree
Oh, Christmas Tree
One Tree Hill
The Old Oak Tree
Tree Of Dreams
Tree-mendous
Timber
Up A Tree
Whispering Pines

____
____
____
____
____

TRIPLETS TITLES

(SEE ALSO TWINS & CONVERT TO TRIPLETS)

- *To make a simple title fun for triplets, repeat the title words three times.*

3 For 3
3 Is Enough
3-Peat
3 Wisemen
3 X's The Fun
Act 3
...And Baby's Makes Three
...And Then There Were Three
Baby Blessings X's 3
Got Triplets!?!
Graced By Three
Just The Three Of Us
My 3 Rewards
My Three Sons
Oh, Baby! Oh, Baby!! Oh, Baby!!!
ONE, TWO, THREE!!!
Our Three Sonshines
Perfect Trio
Split Into 3's
Surprise, Surprise, Surprise!!!
Terrific Triplets
Three Angels
Three Hearts
Three Little Babies All In A Row
Three Little Maidens
Three Loves
Three Of A Kind
Three Peas In A Pod

Three Sonrises/Sunrises
Three Times The Charm
Three Times The Fun
Three Wishes Come True
Three's A Crowd/Company
Thrice Blessed
Thrilling 3's
A Trio Of Trouble
Triple Play
Triple The Pleasure
Triple Threat/Trouble
Triple Treat
We Have 3 Passions
We Three Brothers/Sisters
We Three Kings
We've Expanded Our Family By Six Feet
Womb Mates X's 3

TROUBLE TITLES

Above Suspicion
Accidents Happen
Ain't That A Shame
The Alibi
All Is Forgiven
Always Up To Something
Anger Is Only One Letter Short Of Danger
Armed & Dangerous
Armed & Innocent
Bad Attitude
Bad Company
Bad To The Bone
Bucket O' Trouble
Call Me Irresponsible
Can You Believe This?
Caught In The Act
Caught On Film
Caught With Your Hand In The Cookie Jar
Caught Red-Handed
Caution, Mom Is Stressed
Crime Doesn't Pay
Crimes & Misdemeanors
Culprit Of The Crimes
Cute, But Dangerous
Danger Chaser
Dangerous Minds
The Delinquents
Den Of Iniquity
The Devil Made Me Do It!
Devil With A Blue *(Any color)* Dress On
The Devil's Own
Did I Do That?
I Didn't Do It!!!
The Dirty Dozen
Double, Double, Toil & Trouble
Double Jeopardy
Double Trouble
I Fought The Law & The Law Won
Go Ahead, Make My Day
The Good, The Bad & The Ugly
Gotta Love 'Em Anyway
The Great Escape
Hall Of Shame
The Handwriting On The Wall...
Here Comes Trouble
I Know I'm A Handful
If You Only Knew
Imaginary Crimes
I'm Not Stubborn, I Just Like To Have My Way
I'm Not Stubborn, I'm Just Determined
I'm Only Human
In The Dog House
In Times Of Trouble
Into Everything
It's Always Something
It's Been A Rough Day
It's The Smile That Keeps Me Outta Trouble!
Just One Of Those Days
Little Devils In Action
The Little Rascals
Little Shenanigans
Little Trouble
The Long Arm Of The Law
Look What You Did...
Love Me...Love My Messes
Mad As A Hornet
Make Up? What Make Up?
Master Of Mischief
Mess? What Mess?
Mischief Makers
Mister Naughty
Mommy's Little Mess Maker
Monkey Business
My First Spanking
The Myth Of Fingerprints
Naughty Angel
Naughty 'N Nice
No Jury Would Convict Me!
No Way Out
Not Above Suspicion
Partners In "Grime"
Patience Is A Virtue
The Phantom Menace
Police Blotter

Prime Suspect
Problem Child
Raising Cain
Red-Handed
Rescue 911
Risky Business
Shenanigans
"Sin"sational
Stirring Up Trouble
Stuff Happens
Sugar & Spice..."A Whole Lotta Spice"
Suspicious Signs
Temptation Told Me To
Temptations Of Tots
There Ought To Be A Law Against That
They Call Me Trouble
Three *(Any number)* Little Monkeys Jumpin' On The Bed
To Err Is Human, To Forgive Is Divine
Too Cute To Convict
Triple Trouble
Trouble In Paradise
Trouble Is My/Your Middle Name
Trouble Maker
Trouble, Trouble, I'm In Trouble
Trouble With A Capital "T"
Uh-Oh!!!
Under Suspicion
Unsolved Mysteries
The Usual Suspects
What's All The Fuss About?
When The Moms Away...The Kids Will Play
Where The Wild Things Are
Who Dunnit?
Who Framed Roger Rabbit?
Who Me?
Who Was That Masked Boy/Girl?
Who's Sorry Now?
Wild Child
Wild & Crazy Kids
The Wild Bunch
Wild Thang/Thing
Yea! I Did It...So!
Yeah, I Know I'm Trouble, But You Love Me Anyways

____
____
____
____
____

TRUCK TITLES

- *Use Truck Wheels as an "O".*
- *Place title on a Flat Bed Truck.*

10-4 Good Buddy
4 x 4 Fun
4 x 4 On The Flour
Big Ol' Truck
Big Wheels Keep On Turnin'
A Boy/Man & His Truck
Got Dirt/Mud?!?
Heaven Is A Truck
I Love My Truck
If It Weren't For Pickup Trucks We Wouldn't Have Tailgates
I'm A Pick-up Man
Keep On Rollin'
Keep On Truckin'
Loads Of Love *(Dump truck)*
The Lone Trucker
Makin' Tracks
Mother Trucker
Mud Ridin'
Off Roading Rocks
Off Roading Rules
Only In A Jeep
Pick-Up Man
Pick-Up Truck Princess
Ridin' High
Rough Rider
Silly Boys, Trucks Are For Girls Too!
Tonka Tykes
Tricked Out Truck
Truck Drivin' Man
Truckin' Along
The Ultimate Off-Road Vehicle

____
____
____
____
____

T **TWINS TITLES**

- *Repeat title to reiterate the TWO factor.*

T 2 Cool
2-gether Forever
T 2 Gifts Of Love
2 Hot 2 Handle
T 2 Of A Kind
2 Precious
T 2 To Love
2 Unique
T 2 X's The Love
4 Hands To Hold
T 4 Hands, 4 Feet, 20 Fingers & 20 Toes, Oh My!
T Act Two
Among Two Storms
T ...And Then There Were Two
Another Day In "Pair"adise
T Army Of Two
Babies Are Terrific, But Every Once In A While, They Come "2"rrific
T Between 2 Hearts
Brother Brother Act
T Bundles Of Joy
Caution: Twins Aboard
T Copy Cats
Counting The Blessing 2 X 2
T Couple Of Cuties
Daddy's Duo
T Dangerous Duo
Delicious Duo
T Diaper Duo
Double Blessing
T Double Delicious
Double Delight
T Double Diaper Duty
Double Dribble
T Double Dose Of Infants
Double Double
T Double Duo
Double Everything
T Double Exposure
Double Feature
T Double Good
Double Header
T Double Love
Double Occupancy
T Double Play
Double Take
T Double The Fun
Double The Pleasure
T Double The Snuggles
Double Trouble
T Double Vision
Double Whammy
Doubled Up
Doubly Good
Dynamic Duo
Encore Delight
Experience
Four Hands...Four Feet
Fraternal Tornadoes
Friends Forever...Twins For Life
Good Things Come In Pairs
Got Twins ?!?!
Happy Day 2 You
Have Fear, The Twins Are Here
Have You Heard The News?...Some Blessings Come In 2's!
I May Be A Twin, But I'm One Of A Kind
If You Think I'm Cute, You Should See My Twin
I'm A Twin Engine
I'm So Beside Myself
I'm The Evil Twin
I'm The Older/Younger Twin
In A Carriage Built For Two
It Takes 2 Baby!
It's Not Double Trouble, It's Twingenuity
It's So Much Better With Two
It's Twingenuity
Just Another Day In 'Pair'adise
Just The 2 Of Us
Like 2 Peas In A Pod
Lil' Preemies
Little Brother/Sister Of Twins
Lots Of Tots
Love Times Two
Lucky To Have Twins
Me & My Womb Mate
More Than One
Mothering Multiples
Multiple Blessings
My Shadow...My Twin
Not Fair 2 Compare!
Oh Baby...Baby
Oh, Baby! Oh, Baby!!
Oops My Twins Did It
Our Family Just Grew By 4 Feet
Our Footprints
Outnumbered
A Pair Of Ones!
Paired Up
"Pair"ents Of Twins
Partners In Crime
Peek A Boo Times 2
Perfectly Paired
The Power Of Two
Seeing Double Double
Sister Brother Act

Sister Sister Act
Special Deliveries
Surprise! Surprise!
Take 2
Takes Two To Tango
A Tale Of Two
Tea For Two
Terrible Two's X 2
Terrific Twins
Terrific 2
The Babies Are Here
The BIG Pregnancy
The More, The Merrier
The Twins Go Marching 2 By 2 Hurrah! Hurrah!
There's Strength In Numbers
They Came 2 By 2
To Good To Be True
To Have 2 Is To Have Happiness
Toddlin' Twins
Too Cool To Drool
Toothless Twins
Torn Between 2 Loves
Tots X's Two
Trouble X's Two
Truckin' Twins
Tubby Time For Two
Twenty Fingers, Twenty Toes
Twice As Blessed
Twice As Fun
Twice As Much Fun
Twice As Much Love
Twice As Nice
Twice As Special
Twice Blessed
Twice Is Nice
Twice The Fun
Twice The Joy, Twice the Love, Twice The Blessing From Above
Twice The Work, Twice The Love
Twinadoes
Twinasaurus
Twincerely Yours
Twindependence Day
Twinfants
Twinly
A Twinner Wonderland
Twins, 2 for 1, I Love A Bargain
Twins Are A Kiss Blown From The Hand Of God
Twins Are A True Blessing From God
Twins Are "2" Much
Twins Are Two-Riffic!
Twins...Inter'Twin'ed
Twins Run In Our Family
Twins, Two Kids Are Better Than One
"Twin"ners
Twinship
Twinspirational Moments
Two 2 Love
Two Close For Comfort
Two Cool
Two Cute
Two Buns In The Oven
Two-By-Two
Two For The Price Of One!
Two Heads Are Better Than One
Two Is Better Than One!
Two Of A Kind
Two Peas In A Pod...Two Gifts From God!
Two Precious
Two Son In The Sunset
Two Times The Love
Two Tots
Two-gether Forever
Two-rrific
Two's Company
We Match
Welcome Little Ones
We're Awake Lets Play
We're Seeing Double
We've Expanded Our Family By 4 Feet
What A Pair
When We Are Quiet, You Better Find Us
Wild Thing #1, Wild Thing #2
Womb Mates
Yes! My Kids Are Twins
You're 2 Adorable

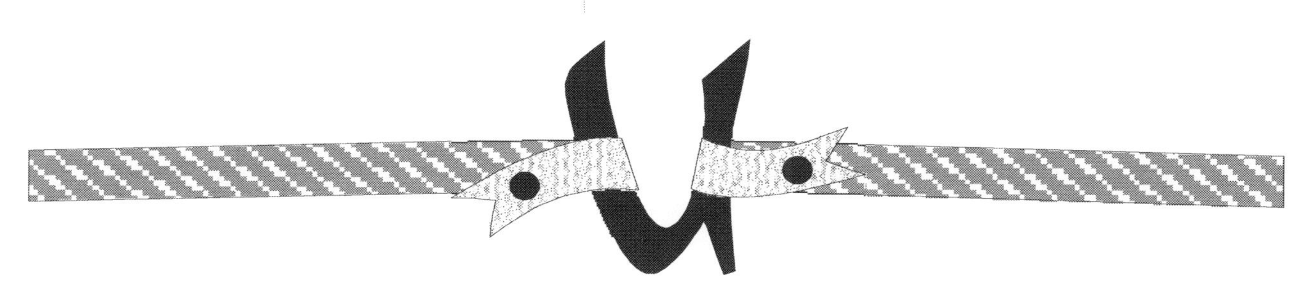

ULTRASOUND TITLES

(SEE ALSO PREGNANT)

Already Adorable
Baby's First Pics
Before I Was Born...
Camera Shy Already
Freeze Frame
Here I Am!
How Many ? ? ? ?
Look Out World Here I Come!
My First Pics
Peek-A-Boo...I See You
Peek-A-Boo...Oh! There's Two
Peek-A-Boo Perfection
Peek-A-Boo...Pink Or Blue?
Peek-A-Boo Preview
Peek-A-Boo...We Can See You!
Pictures In The Dark Of You
Silent Beginnings
Sneak-A-View
Sneak Peek
Sneak Preview
A Special Viewing
Stolen Peek
Strike A Pose
A Twinkle With Hands & Feet
Ultra Special
Womb With A View
You Peek My Interest

V V V V V V V V V V V V V V V V V V V V V V V V V V V V V V V

VACATION TITLES

(SEE COUNTRIES, STATES & TRAVEL)

VALENTINE'S DAY TITLES

(SEE ALSO HEART & LOVE)

- *Replace with a Heart an "A", "O", "V" or for the word itself.*

100% Lovable, Huggable & Snuggable
2 Hot 2 Handle
4 My Love
Addicted To Love
Basketful Of Love
Be Mine
Be My Cupid
Be My Love
Be My Sweetie
Be My Valentine
Be Still My Beating Heart
Bitten By The Love Bug
Bucket Of Kisses
Bunches Of Love
Call Me Cupid
Can You See It?...Love Is In The Air!
Candy Hearts/Kisses
Can't Fight This Feelin'
Caught By Cupid's Arrow
Celebrating Romance
Chocolate Day
Color The World With Love
Crush!
Cupid Said, "Be Mine"
Cupid Was Here!
Cupid's Arrow
Cupid's Cutie
Cupid Drew Back His Bow & Hit Right On Target
Cupid's Kisses
Cupid's Little Bundle Of Love
A Day For Love
I Don't Need Anything But You
Ever After
Everything's Coming Up Roses
First Love
Flowers & Candy & Hearts, Oh My!
For Me?
Forever Yours
I Found My Prince Charming
From My heart
Funny Face, I Love You
Gifts Of Love
Gimmie A Kiss
Give Cupid A Chance
Happy Heart's Day
Happy Love Day
Happy Valentine's Day
Heart Attack/Beat
A Heart Full Of Love
A Heart Of Gold
Heart Of My Heart
Heart To Heart
Heartland
Hearts Afire
Hearts & Kisses
Heart's Desire
Heartthrob!
Home Is Where The Heart Is
How Do I Love Thee...Let Me Count The Ways
How Sweet It Is
How Sweet It Is To Be Loved By You
How Sweet To Be Loved By You
Hugs & Kisses!
I Only Love You On Days That End In "Y".
I'm All Yours
I'm Nuts About You
I'm Sweet On You
Just 4 U
Just Say You Love Me
The Key To My Heart
A Kiss & A Hug On This Day Of Love
Kiss Me
Let Me Call You Sweetheart
Loads Of Love
Lock Me In Your Heart & Throw Away The Key
Love Bugs
Love Is A Work Of Heart
Love Is In The Air *(Have hearts floating on the page)*
Love Is The Key That Opens The Heart
Love Letters/Notes
Love Me Tender
Lovebirds
Loves Me...Loves Me Not
Mad About You
My Funny Valentine
My Girl
My Heart Explodes For You
My Heart Flutters For You
My Heart Is Lost To You
My Heart Is Yours
My Heart Leaps For You
My Heart Was Attacked By Cupid!
My Sweet Valentine
My Sweethearts
My Sweet-tart
Nothing Is Sweeter Than You
Once Upon A Valentine
Only You
The Perfect Valentine

A Piece Of My Heart
PS: I Love You
Puppy Love
Romance 101
Sealed With A Kiss
Some Bunny Loves You
State Of The Heart
Stuck By Cupid's Arrow
Sweet As Candy
Sweeter Than Candy
The Sweetest Days
Sweetest Heart
Sweethearts
Sweetie Pie
Sweets From My Sweet
There Will Never Be Another You
There's Always Time For Chocolate & Flowers
Thief Of Hearts
This Page Is Dedicated To You
Together Forever
Tokens Of Affection
Tonight I Celebrate My Love For You
U R Mine
U-R-A-Q-T
"V" Is For My Valentine
V-Day
Valentine Cuties
Valentine...I Am Hug Wild Over You!
Valentine Love
Valentine Sweet Heart
I Want You For My Valentine
Will You Be My Valentine?
With You Is Where I Like To Be
Won't You Be My Valentine?
XOXOXOXOX
You Are Always My Valentine
You Belong To Me
You Have My Heart In Your Hand
You Make My Heart Leap
You Make My Heart Sing
You Set My Heart A Flutter
You Turn Me Every Which Way But Loose
Your Heart's Desire
Your Love Sends Me Over The Rainbow
You're My Cup Of Tea
You're My Sweet Heart
You're Someone Special
You've Captured My Heart

VOLLEYBALL TITLES

(SEE ALSO SPORTS)

- *Use Volleyballs for an "O".*
- *Put title on a Volleyball Net.*

Ace!
Beautiful Rainbow
Blocked
Bump, Set, Spike!
Dig It
Diggin' The Beach Dig
Dink King/Queen
Dumped Again
Flair Play
Fooled By The Floater
Freeball!
It's A Net Thing
Joust Again
Jungle Ball Jig
King Konged!
Net Attack/Force
Pancaked Pounce
Queens Of The Court
Quickies Rule
Ready Position?
Roof Downed
Shankered
Side Out
Spike!
Spike Queen!
Tandom Triumph
Volley Girls
What A Dig!
What A Volley!
Win The Rally!

WAKING UP TITLES

Angel Of The Morning
Another Good Morning
Arise From Your Sleep
Awake From Your Slumber
I Awake Grumpy
The Awakening
I Don't Do Mornings
Each Dawn Is A New Beginning
Early Riser
The Early Show
The Glory Of Daybreak
Good Morning America
Good Morning Starshine
Good Morning, Baby Sunshine
Good Morning, Merry Sunshine
Good Morning, *(Name)* Sunshine
Here Comes The Sun
I Will Wake Up Happy
I'll Rise, But I Refuse To Shine
I'm Awake! Let's Play!
I'm Far From Tired
In The Morning When We Rise...
Let There Be Light
The Lion Rises
A New World In The Morning
Rise & Shine
Rise Like The Son
Rising With Sun
Recharged & Ready
Son Rise...Son Sit
The Sun/Son Also Rises
Sunday Morning Sunshine
Sunrise Serenade
Top Of The Mornin' To Ya
Up & At 'Em
Wake Up Little Suzy *(Name)*
Wake Up Sleepyhead
Wake Up Sunshine
Waking The Lion
Watching The Sunrise
With Every Waking Moment...

____
____
____
____
____

WALK/WALKING TITLES

(SEE ALSO FEET)

- *Place Foot Prints under title or around it.*
- *Put title inside a large Footprint.*

1,2,3,4...I Can Walk Along The Floor...
...And He's/She's Off!
I Can't Get Started
Careful Where You Step
Cruisin'
Every Step Of The Way
First Steps
Follow The Yellow Brick Road
Following Footsteps
Goin' Places
Going, Going, Gone!
He Walks On Water
High Stepper
I Walk The Line
I'm A Walkin', Yes Indeed I'm Walkin'
I'm Still Standin'
I'm Walkin' On Sunshine
In Hot Water *(Spa)*
The Journey Begins With A Single Step
The Journey Of A 1,000 Miles Begins With The First Step
Just A Step From Heaven
Look Mom! No Hands!
Look Out World, Here I Come!
Look Who's Walking
Makin' Tracks, No Turnin' Back
Next Step
The Next Step Is Love
One Day I Walked...
One Foot In Front Of The Other...
One Small Step
One Step Ahead
One Step At A Time
One Step Away/Closer
One Step Up
Pitter Patter Of Little Feet
Pounding The Pavement
Put One Foot In Front Of The Other & Soon You'll Be Walkin'...
Put Your Best Foot Forward
Ready, Set, Sit!!!
Ready, Set, Walk!!!
She Walks On Water
Solo Steps
Steady Stepper/Steps
Step Aside
Step Back In Time
Step-By-Step

Step By Tiny Step
Step Inside Love
Step Into My Life
Step Into Paradise
Step It Up
Step On It
Step Softly
A Step Too Far
Steppin' In Mommy's Shoes
Steppin' In Your Shoes
Steppin' 'N Stridin'
Steppin' Out With My Baby
Steppin' To The Rhythm
Strollin', Strollin', Strollin', Keep Those Feet A Goin'
Take A Step For Love
Take A Stroll
Teetering Toddler
These Feet Are Gonna Walk All Over You!
These Feets Were Made For Walkin'
Tip Toein'
Toddlin' Toddler
Twinkle Toes
Two Steppin'
Walk Along With Me
Walk Forever By My Side
Walk Like An Egyptian
Walk On By
Walk Softly
Walk The Walk
Walk This Way!
Walk Unafraid
Walkin' In Daddy's/Mommy's Footsteps
Walkin' In The Clouds
Walkin' In The Sand
Walkin' On Air
Walkin' On Cloud 9
Walkin' On Sunshine
Walkin' On The Wild Side
Walkin' On Thin Ice
Walkin' On Water
Walkin' The Straight Line
Walkin' The Walk
Walkin' Under A Rainbow
Walking After Midnight
Walking Hand In Hand
Walking In Memphis
Walking In My Shoes
Walking In The Sand
Walking Wizard
Walks & Talks Like An Angel
Wee Walker
Wild Walker
You Walked Funny Too When You Where My Age
You'll Never Walk Alone
You've Walked A Long Way Baby

____
____
____
____
____

WATER TITLES

(SEE ALSO POOL & SWIMMING)

- *Use a Water Splash as an "O".*
- *Place Water droplets around the letters.*
- *Have the letters sitting on a Wave of Water.*

All Wet
At The Water's Edge...
Cool, Cool Water
Deep Blue Waters
Deep Waters
Down By The Water
Got Water?
H20 Fun
In Deep Water
It's A "Water"ful Day
Just Add Water
Kersplash!
Makin' A Splash
Moonlight On The Water
Muddy Waters
On The Waterfront
Raging Waters
Sapphire Colored Waters...
Slippery When Wet
Soaking Up Summer
Spirit On The Water
Splash Dance
Splat!!!
Splish Splash
Still Waters Run Deep
Submerged
Such "Water"ful Fun!
Testing The Waters
Treading Water
Under Beautiful Waters
Underwater Fun
Water A Delight
Water Baby/Boy/Girl
Water Bug
Water Fight
Water Floats Your Boat

Water Logged
Water Me Down
Water Street Blues
Water Wars
Water Wonders
Water Works
Water World
"Water" You Looking At?
"Water" You Scared Of? *(Pics of child scared to get in the water)*
"Water" You Wading For?
Wet Behind The Ears & Legs & Arms &...
Wet N' Wild
What A "Water"ful Day
Where The Water Falls
White Water Rafting
You Part The Water
You're All Wet

WATERMELON TITLES

(SEE FOOD)

WEDDING TITLES

(SEE ALSO HEART, KISS & LOVE)

- *Use a Heart in place of an "A", "O", or "V".*
- *Hang Wedding Bells or Hearts from Title.*

2 Lives Shared, 2 Lives United As One, 2 Lives Shared As One For All Eternity
After The Boy Gets The Girl...
All Dressed In White
All My Love, All My Life
Always & Forever
...And The Story Begins
...And The Two Shall Become One
...And They're Off
...And This...Our Life...Our Beginning
The Art Of Marriage
Baby, I Do!
Baby, It's You
Behind The Scenes *(Getting Ready)*
The Big Day
The Blending Of Two Hearts/Lives
Bless You Both
Blissfully Wedded
The Bond Of Love
Bound In Love
The Boy Got The Girl
Bridal Beauty
Can You Feel The Love Tonight
I Can't Give You Anything But Love
Celebration Of Love
Chantilly Lace & A Pretty Face
Chapel Of Love
Cuttin' Up *(Cutting cake)*
Day One Of Forever
Dearly Beloved
A Dream Come True
Endless Love
An Everlasting Love
Every Bride Has Her Day
Fairy Tales Do Come True!
Father Of The Bride...So Full Of Pride
I Feel Sorry For Anyone Who Isn't Me Today!
First Love, Last Love
Flower Flingin'
Forever & Ever, Amen
Forever Yours
Forever's As Far As I'll Go
From This Day Forward...My Bride & Joy
From This Day Forward...We Are As One!
From This Moment On...
The Get Away Car
Get Me To The Church On Time
Getting Hitched
Getting Ready...
The Glory Of Love
Goin' To The Chapel & We're Gonna Get Married
I Got You Babe
The Greatest Of These Is Love
Happiest Girl In The Whole USA
Happily Ever After
Happiness Is Marrying Your Best Friend
To Have & To Hold
He Loves Me, He Loves Me, He Loves Me So We Tied The Knot!
Here Comes The Bride
The Honeymooners
Hopelessly Devoted To You
How Do I Love You...Let Me Count The Ways...
I Do, I Do, I Do!
I Give To You My Love
I Thee Wed
I'll Be Loving You, Always
I'll Build Your Dreams With These Two Hands
I'll Love You For Always...I'll Love You Forever
I'm My Beloved's & He's Mine
In The Chapel
I've Been Waiting For A Girl Like You
I Just Fall In Love Again
Just The Two Of Us
Kiss The Bride
Let It Be Me
Little Band Of Gold

Love & Marriage
Love Conquers All
Love Is The Foundation
Love One Another
Love Story
Love Tied Our Hearts Today
Love Will Find A Way
I Love You For Sentimental Reasons
I Love You Truly
Lucky To Have Each Other
This Magic Moment
Man In Black
Man Of The Hour
Match Made In Heaven
May I Have This Dance For The Rest Of My Life?
May I Have This Dance In The Moonlight
May These Two Hearts Forever Be, In Sweet & Loving Harmony
Most Of All, Let Love Guide Your Life
Much Ado About Something
My Best Friend's Wedding
My Family, Your Family...Caring, Sharing, Blending As One, A New Life's Begun
My Gift To You Is My Love
My Husband...My Love...My Friend
My Life...My Love
My Man In Black
New Beginnings
The Newly Wedded
No Greater Love
Now & Forever
Now We're Tied Together Forever In Love
Of One Heart
Officially Wed Today
On This Our Wedding Day...
One Heart, One Mind
The One I Laugh With, Live For, Dream With...And Love
Once Upon A Time...
Our Hearts & Feet Dance Today
Our Love Is Tied With Heartstrings
Our Special Day
Our Two Hearts Make One!
The Pledge
Pretty Maids All In A Row
Princess Bride
This Ring Has...No Beginning & No End... Just As Our Love
Ring Out The Old...Ring In The New
Sealed With A Kiss
Sharing The Love
Signing My Single Life Away *(Pics of signing license)*
So Happy Together
Some Dreams Come True
Something Old, Something New, Something Borrowed, Something Blue
Sounds Of Wedding Bells
Stand By Me
The Story Of Us Taking The Big Leap
This Day My Prince Came
This Diamond Ring
This Guy's In Love With You
Tied The Knot
Tiers Of Joy *(Pics of cake)*
A Time For Us
A Toast To Life, Love & Happiness
Today, I Celebrate My Love For You
Today, I Married My Best Friend
Today We Took A Leap Of Love
Together Forever
Tonight, I Celebrate My Love For You
True Companion
True Love
Two Families United Together
Two Hearts Shall Beat As One
Two Hearts, Two Lives, One Love
Two Hearts United In Love
Tying The Knot
Undying Love
United Forever In Love...
Vows Sweetly Spoken...Never To Be Broken
Walk Forever By My Side
A Walk On The Aisle Side
I Wanna Hold Your Hand
We Are Blessed
We Are Gathered Here...
We Can Last Forever
Wedded Bliss
Wedding Belles
Wedding Bells Ring
The Wedding Singer
We've Only Just Begun
What A Difference A Day Makes
When A Man Loves A Woman...
When A Woman Loves A Man...
White Wedding
Who Gives This Woman?
A Whole New World
I Will Always Love You
I Will Be Glad & Rejoice In Your Love
I Will Walk With You...
Will You Marry Me?
With Loving Hearts...
With This Ring...I Thee Wed
You & Me Against The World
You Are The Light Of My Life
You Are The Wind Beneath My Wings

W W W W W W W W W W W W W W W W W W W W W W W W W W W W W W

You Complete Me
You Mean The World To Me
You're The One

WEIGHT LIFTING TITLES

(SEE ALSO EXERCISE & STRONG)

Brute Strength
Buildin' Up The Guns
Butt Buster
Crunch-A-Bunch
Dumbbell Dynamo
Future Mr. Universe
Hard As Iron
Iron Man
Keep On Pumpin'
Man Of Iron
Mass Of Muscle
Maxin' The Reps
Mr. Muscles
Muscle Beach
Muscle Mania
Muscles Abounding
No Pain, No Gain
Popeye...But No Spinach Here
Popeye Wanna Be
Pressin' The Max
Pump, Pump, Pump It Up
Pumpin' Iron
Pushin' Weight
Six-Pack Abs
Super Sets = Super Sweats
Thigh Master
Weighting For Muscles
Workin' The Sets
Worth My Weight In Dumbbells/Gold/Steel

WHITE TITLES

(A great way accentuate the word White in the title, is to create that word only in White. Make White larger and in a different type style than the rest of the title)

Great White Hope
On The Wings Of A Snow White Dove
Snow White
White As A Ghost
White As A Sheet
White As Snow
White Hot
White Light
White Lightning
My White Knight
White Out
White Picket Fence
White Wedding

WIFE TITLES

As You Become My Wife...
Be My Wife
A Beautiful Wife
Beloved Wife Of Mine
Dear Wife...
My Beloved Wife
My Dear & Loving Wife
My Dearest Wife
My Dream Come True
My Life...My Wife
My Love...My Wife
My Loving Wife
My Success Is My Wife
My Undying Love, Given To My Wife
My Wife...Desire Of Thy Heart
My Wife My Forever
My Wife, My Heart
My Wife, My Love
My Wife, My Pride
My Wife Hands
A Wife's Love
My Life's Partner
My Love Grows For You With Every Passing Day
A Loving Heart To Rely On
The One I'll Always Love
The Perfect Wife
Sharer Of Hopes & Dreams
Soul Mate
A Strong Arm To Lean Upon
When You Become My Wife...
Wife Of Mine
Wives & Lovers

WIND TITLES

Any Old Wind That Blows
Any Way The Wind Blows
Bad Hair Day
Bite & Eat The Dust
Blow, Blow Oh Winter Wind
Blowing In The Wind
A Blustery Day - *(Winnie The Pooh)*
Brace Yourself
Breezy Days
Cold Blows The Wind
Cold Northern Breeze
Dust In The Wind
Everyone Knows It's Windy
Flapping In The Breeze
Flying High
Go Fly A Kite
Gone With The Wind
A Great Day For Kite Flying
High Winds Blow
Higher & Higher
Let The Four Winds Blow
May The Wind Be Always At Your Back
A Mighty Wind
Nature's Breath
Oh Bother! It's A Blustery Day
Ole Hickory Winds
Ride Like The Wind/Wild Wind
Sky Bound
That Wind Blown Look
Tornado Alley
Touch Of A Cold Wind
Up, Up & Away
Visited By The Santa Ana's
Wayward Winds
Whispering Winds
Wind Beneath My Wings
The Wind In My Eyes
A Wintry Breath Chills Us

WINNIE-THE-POOH TITLES

(SEE ALSO DISNEY)

Are You Ready For Some Bouncing?
Bouncing Is What Tiggers Do Best!
Bouncing Tigger
Deep In The Hundred Acre Woods
Did Somebody Say, Honey?
Don't Be Redickorus, Tigger's Don't Like Honey!
Has Anyone Seen Eeyore's Tail?
Heffalumps & Woozles Are Very Confusal...
I Promise Never To Bounce Again
I'm Not Roo, I'm Piglet
It's A "Pooh"rade
I've Got Rummbly's In My Tummbly's...Time For Something SWEET!!
No, Don't Be Redickorus!
Oh Bother!
Oh Dear, Mercy Me Too!
Oh Dear, Oh D-D-D-Dear-Dear!
A Pooh-rrific Friend
Pooh's My Tubby Little Cubby Stuffed With Fluff
Silly Old Bear!
Tat-tat, It Looks Like Rain!
That's What Tiggers Do Best!
T-I-Double-Guh-Err...That Spells Tigger!!
T-T-F-N" *(Ta Ta For Now)*
Watch Out For Heffalumps & Woozles
What's A Pooh?
The Wonderful Thing About Tiggers Is...
You Can't Fool The Bees, Pooh!

WINTER TITLES

(SEE ALSO COLD, MONTHS OF THE YEAR, SNOW & SNOWMAN)

- *Use a Thermometer as "I", show at Freezing.*

All Bundled Up
Arctic Blast
Baby It's Cold Out Here/Outside
Baby It's Warm Inside
The Beauty Of Winter
Bone Chilling Cold
Brrrrrrrrrr!!!
Brrrr It's Cold Outside
Chill Out!
Cocoa & Cuddles
Cold Day, Warm Hearts
Cold Hands, Cold Feet, Cold Everything!
Cold Kisses
Cold Lips...Warm Hearts
A Cold Winter's Day
Cool Cats
Cozy Winter Wishes
Cuddlin' With My Cocoa
Cuddling Up By The Fire
Dressed For The Chill
Dressed Up Like Eskimos
The Embrace Of Winter
Enchanted Winter

Feel The Magic
Feelin' Frosty
Frosty Days
Frosty Flakes
Frosty Kisses
The Frosty Season
The Great White Out
Hazy Shades Of Winter
Hot Chocolate Time!
The Iceman Cameth
If We Could Freeze Time...
In The Frosty Air...
In The Lane, The Snow Is Glistening
It's A Brrrrrand New Day
It's A Fire & Ice Kind Of Day
It's A Freezin' Season
It's The Chill Factor
It's The Mitten Man
Jack Frost Was Here!
Just Chillin'
Killer Frost
Kissed By Winter's Alluring Breath
Lord Of The Winter Snow
A Magical Winter's Night
A Midwinter Night's Dream
Mitten Mania
No Snow Blues
Northern Exposure
Old Man Winter Has Arrived
Once Upon A Winter's Day
The Perfect Storm
Running/Playing In A Winter Wonderland
Sweatshirt Season
A Taste Of Winter
There's A Chill In The Air
Today's A Zero
Too Cool!
Wacky Winter Weather
Walking In A Winter Wonderland
Warm & Cozy *(Bundled up by the fire)*
Warmest Wishes
The Weather Outside Is Delightful/Frightful
White Whispers Of Winter
Winter Blues
Winter Fun
Winter Marches On
Winter Memories
Winter Smiles Of Snow-Filled Days
Winter Solstice
Winter Wishes
Winter Wonderland
Winter Wonderlings
Winter's Brilliance
Winter's Delight
Winter's Flurry Fury
Winter's Frost
Winter's Kiss
Winter's Landscape
Winter's Masterpiece
A Winter's Night
Winter's Perfection
Winter's Splendor
A Winter's Tale
A Winter's Wassail
Winter's White Wonderland
Winter's Wonders
A Wintry Breath Chills Us
The Wonders Of Winter

WISDOM TITLES

The Doors Of Wisdom Are Never Shut.
(Benjamin Franklin)
The Fear Of The Lord Is The Beginning Of Wisdom. - *(Proverbs 9:10)*
A Man Of Understanding Delights In Wisdom.
(Proverbs 19:23)
Silence Is The Sleep That Nourishes Wisdom. *(Francis Bacon)*
Wisdom Begins In Wonder. - *(Socrates)*
Wisdom Is Only Found In Truth.
(Johann Wolfgang von Goethe)
Wisdom Is The Supreme Part Of Happiness.
(Sophocles)
Wisdom Outweighs Any Wealth. - *(Sophocles)*
Wonder Is The Beginning Of Wisdom.
(Greek Proverb)

WISHES TITLES

(SEE ALSO ASPIRATIONS, DREAMS & HOPES)

Best Wishes
Butterfly Wishes
Champagne Wishes
A Dream Is A Wish The Heart Makes
Few Wishes Ever Come True By Themselves
From Wishes To Kisses
I Made A Wish...
I Wish I Could...
I Wish I May...I Wish I Might...

I Wish, Oh I Wish So Hard
I Wish You Joy
I Wish You Well
If I Could Have One Wish...
If Wishes Were Kisses...
My Only Wish...
My Wishes For You
This Is My Wish...
When Things Seem Empty...I Wish You HOPE
When You Wish Upon A Star...
When You're Down...I Wish You JOY !
When You're Lonely...I Wish You LOVE !
When You're Troubled...I Wish You PEACE!
A Wishing Heart
Wishing On The Same Bright Star
Wishes & Dreams
Your Wish Is My Command

WOMAN TITLES

(SEE ALSO GIRL)

3 Little Ladies All In A Row
All The Lovely Ladies
Always A Woman
American Woman
An Angel In Women's Clothes
April Lady
Beautiful Woman
Big Girls Do Cry
Blue-Eyed Lady
Camptown
Damsel In Distress
Disco Lady
Don't Treat Me Any Differently Than You Would The Queen
Dream Lady
Enchanted Lady
Essence Of A Woman
Exclusively Feminine
Eyes Of A Woman
For The Love Of A Woman
Forever My Lady
Foxy Lady
Girl...Lady...Woman
Girl, You'll Be A Woman Soon
Girls Just Wanna Have Fun
God's Masterpiece!
Golden Lady
Good-Hearted Woman
Green-Eyed Lady
Hard Headed Woman
Heart Of A Woman
Honky Tonk Woman
I Am Woman...Hear Me Roar!
I Have Attitude & Know How To Use It ! ! !
I'm Every Woman
Independent Woman
LA Woman
Ladies First
Ladies Night
Lady Godiva
Lady In Black/Blue/Red
The Lady In My Life
Lady Love
The Lady Loves Me
Lady Luck
Lady Of The Night
Lady Sings The Blues
A Lady Takes A Chance
Lady, When You're With Me I Smile
Lady, You Bring Me Up
Lady, Your Love's The Only Love I Need
Lady, You're An Angel
The Lady's Got Potential
Little Lady
Little Old Lady From Pasadena
Lovely Lady
Luck Be A Lady
Modern Woman
More Spice Than Sugar
More Than A Woman
My Lady...My Love
My Sweet Lady
A Natural Woman
On The 6th Day, God Created Woman
One Man Woman
Power Of A Woman
The Queen Of Everything
Pretty Woman
Real Women Don't Have Hot Flashes, They Have Power Surges
Red-Headed Lady
Red Roses For A Blue Lady
Rock-N-Roll Lady
Scent Of A Woman
Sentimental Lady
She Has A Light & A Faith That Won't Die
She Moves In Mysterious Ways
She's A/My Lady
She's Got The Heart Of A Lion
She Is Woman
Sophisticated Lady
Soul Of A Woman
Sugar & Spice...A Whole Lotta Spice

Sweet Talkin' Woman
Thank God I'm A Country Girl
Three Times A Lady
What A Woman Wants
When A Woman Loves A Man
Who Was That Lady?
Witchy Woman
Woman In Black
A Woman In Love
The Woman In Me
Woman Is Thy Name
A Woman Knows
Woman Of The Year
Woman Of Women
Woman To Woman
Woman...You're Wonderful
A Woman's Love
A Woman's Touch
Women Are From Venus
Women...We're Just Better
Wonder Woman
You Go Girl!
You're A Lady Now

WONDER TITLES

A Sense Of Wonder
A Wonder Like You
All Knowledge Begins With Wonder
All The Wonders You Seek Are Within Yourself
An 8th Wonder
And I Wonder...
Believe In The Wonder Of Life
Boy Wonder
Cascades Of Wonder
Cup Of Wonder
Days Full Of Wonder
Faith's Touch...Faith's Wonder
God's Wonders
A Great Wonder
Heaven's Little Wonder
I Hope You Never Loose Your Sense Of Wonder
Little Child Of Wonder
Love Is The Wonder Of God
It Makes Me Wonder
The Most Beautiful Wonder Of All
Often I Wonder...
Sometimes I Wonder...
Thru The Eyes Of Wonder
Time To Wonder
Twinkle, Twinkle, This I Wonder...
The Wonder Of It All
The Wonder Of Life
The Wonder Of My World
The Wonder Of You
Wonder Woman
I Wonder, Wonder, Wonder, Wonder Who... Who Wrote The Book Of Love
The Wonder Years
The Wonderment Of A Child's Mind
The World's 8th Wonder

WORK/JOB TITLES

9 To 5
40-Hour Week
All In A Day's Work
All Work & Play Makes Me Tired
Another Day...Another Dollar
Be All You Can Be
Blue Collar Worker
Born To Fish/Golf/Play, Forced To Work
My Boss Made Me Come Here
Business As Usual
Busy As A Beaver
Can I Trade This Job For What's Behind Door #2?
The Car Washin' Blues
Chaos, Panic & Disorder...My Job Here Is Done
Climbing The Ladder Of Success
Creative Work
Cubicle Sweet Cubicle
Dirty Work
Doin' The Lord's Work
Dream Job
Funny Business
Got Job...Will Pay Bills
Grampa's Fixin' Shop
Hands That Work Magic
A Hard Day's Work
The Harder You Work, The Luckier You Get
How Do I Set A Laser Printer To Stun?
I Owe! I Owe! So Off To Work I Go!
In The "Company" Of Friends
Inside Job
It's All In A Day's Work
I've Been Workin' On The Railroad
Job Satisfaction
Many Hands Make Light Work

Men At Work
Men Need Signs...Women Work All The Time
Mission Impossible
My Boss Made Me Come Here
Needed Work...Got Hired
Part Of The Rat Race
A Real Workin' Man
Takin' Care Of Business
Taking Charge
T.G.I.F.
Thankless Job
The Way We Work
Time Is Money
When The Week Ends, The Fun Begins!!!
Whistle While You Work
Who's The Boss?
Will Work For Food
A Woman's Work Is Never Done
A Work In Progress
Work It Baby
Workaholic
Worker Bees
Workin' 9 To 5
Workin' At The Car Wash
Workin' It Out
Working Girl
Working Hard Or Hardly Working?
Working Stiffs
Working Together
You Gotta Work To Make It Work

____
____
____
____
____

WORLD TITLES
(SEE ALSO SPACE)

- *Create a Globe & put title in the Globe.*

3rd Rock From The Sun
All Around The World...
Amazing World
Another World
As The World Turns
The Beauties Of The Earth
Between The Earth & The Sky...
Children Of The World
Children Make The World A Magical Place
Color My World With Love
The Day The Earth Shook!
Down To Earth
Earth Angel
The Earth Laughs In Flowers
The Earth Rolls On
Earth Shattering News
The Earth...The Sun...The Rain...
Earth...Wind...Fire
Earth's Kaleidoscope
Eyes Of The World
I Feel The Earth Move Under My Feet
Four Corners Of The Earth
Gateway To The World
God's Green Earth
The Good Earth
Heaven & Earth
In A Perfect World...
In The Real World...
It's A Small World
It's A Wild World
It's A Wonderful World
Joy To The World
Living In A Material World
Looking At The World Thru Rose Colored Glasses
Meanwhile On Planet Earth...
Mother Earth
Mother Earth Is Weeping
My Place In The World
O World As God Has Made It! All Is Beauty.
(Robert Browning)
On Top Of The World
Out Of This World
Peace On Earth
Peaceful Days On Earth
The Poetry Of The Earth Is Never Dead.
(John Keats)
Salt Of The Earth
Sittin' On Top Of The World
Speak To The Earth & It Shall Teach Thee.
(Biblical Proverb)
Take The World By Storm
In Touch With The World
What A Wonderful World
What The World Needs Now...Is Love
When You Smile, The Whole World Smiles
World Class Act
The World Is A Beautiful Place
The World Is A Living Image Of God.
(Tommaso Campanella)
The World Is A Playground
I Would Go To The Ends Of The Earth For You
You Make The World A Better Place
You Mean The World To Me

____
____
____
____
____

WORM TITLES

- *Make little Worms slithering around title.*
- *Make some of the letters look like Worms.*
- *Place title atop a long, bumpy Worm.*

As The Worm Turns
Book Worm
The Early Bird Gets The Worm
Earthly Worms
Glow, Glow, Glow Worm
Here Wormy, Wormy
It's A Small Worm
Joy To The Worms
King Worm
Slip, Slimmin' Away
Squiggly, Wiggly, Squirmy Wormy
Worms Dig Dirt
A Worm's Life

WRESTLING TITLES

(SEE ALSO FIGHTING)

The All-In Wrestler
...And In This Corner *(Name)*
Banana Split
Brute Strength
Face To Face
For The Love Of Wrestling
The Great Reverser
In The Ring...
Let's Get Ready To Rumble
Miracle On The Mat
A Nice & Easy Pin
On The Mat...
On The Ropes
Pin 'Em Down
Pin To Win
Pinned
Pride In Wrestling
Ready To Rumble
Real Men Don't Play With Balls...They Wrestle
Rough & Tumble
Rumbles & Tumbles
Rumbles Of Thunder
Show No Mercy
Stick 'Em
Stuck By A Pin
Stuck 'Em
Take Down
Takin' It To The Mat
The Winner & Still Champ...
Wrestle Mania
Wrestling Warrior

WRESTLER

Weight Class
Rough
Energy Draining
Slamming
Take Down
Low Blow
Escape
Reversal

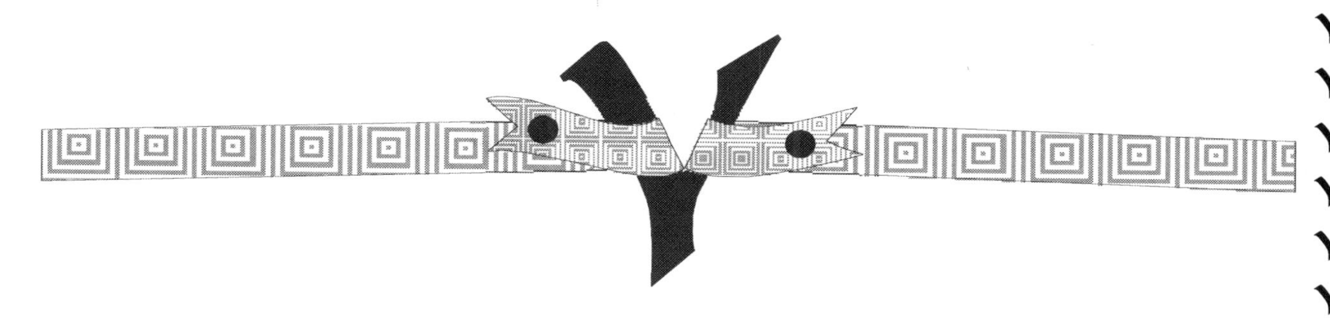

YELL/YELLING TITLES

The Call Of The Wild
Just Scream
I Just Wanna Scream
Kicking & Screaming
Scream & Shout
Scream Out Loud
I Scream, You Scream, We All Scream
 Because You Scream
Scream Your Heart Out
Screaming The New Year In
Shout & Shimmy
Shout For Joy
Shout It Out
A Silent Scream
Something To Shout About
Stand Up & Shout
Tarzan
Twist & Shout

YELLOW TITLES

(A great way accentuate the word Yellow in the title, is to create that word only in Yellow. Make Yellow larger and in a different type style than the rest of the title)

The Big Yellow Sun
Big Yellow Taxi
Good-bye Yellow Brick Road - *(Elton John)*
Mellow Yellow
The Moon Was Yellow & The Night Was
 Young
Tie A Yellow Ribbon...
Yellow Fever
The Yellow Moon
Yellow Rose Of Texas
Yellow Roses Of Friendship
My Yellow Slicker
Yellow Submarine

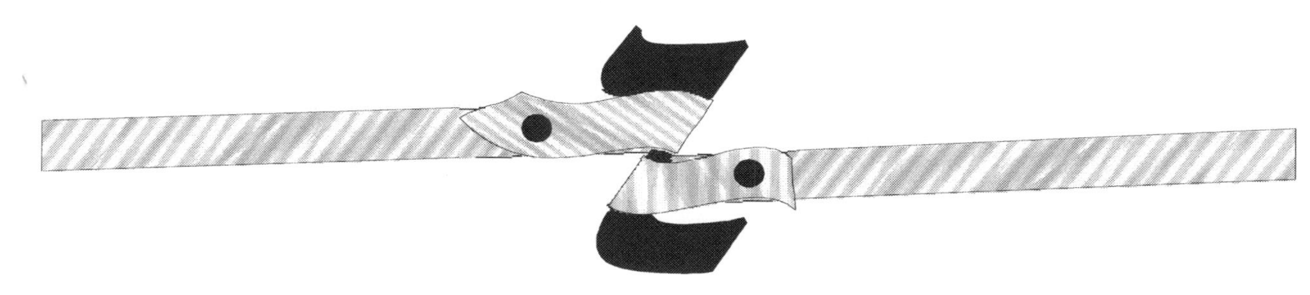

Z Z Z Z Z Z Z Z Z Z Z Z Z Z Z Z Z Z Z Z Z Z Z Z Z Z Z Z Z Z Z Z

ZOO TITLES

(SEE ALSO ANIMALS, FARM & SOME SPECIFIC ANIMALS)

- *Replace letters with different animals.*
- *Have a Giraffe come up thru word as an "I".*
- *Use a Monkey's Tail to make a letter & have him hanging below.*
- *Put a Paw print in place of an "O".*
- *Make title look like it's behind cage bars.*

All Creatures Great & Small
And God Created...
...And Let's Not Forget The... *(Elephant)*
Animal House
Born To Be Wild
Bungle In The Jungle
The Call Of The Wild
Choo, Choo At The Zoo
Come On A Safari With Me
Crawling Creatures
Creature Feature
Creatures Of Habit
Creatures Of The Night
Critter Country
Dandy Lions
A Day Among The Animals
A Day At The Zoo
Do The Zoo
Don't Feed The Animals
Don't Monkey Around!
Dr. Doolittle
Elephant Entertainment
An Elephant May Not Have Forgotten, But We Did!!!
An Elephant Never Forgets
Ever Feel Caged?
Everybody's Zooing It
The Eye Of The Tiger
The Facts Of Animal Life
Feedin' Time At The Zoo
A Few At The Zoo
The Fierce...The Wild
Funky Fur
Fuzzy Wuzzy Was The Bear
Getting In The Swing Of Things *(Monkeys)*
Giraffic Park
God's Creatures
Going Wild
Grunt & Squeak & Squawk With The Animals
Humongous! *(Elephant or Hippo)*
I Work For Peanuts *(Elephant)*
I'm A Lion...Hear Me Roar
I'm Im-paws-ible
I'm Just Wild About...
In The Jungle, The Mighty Jungle...
In The Swing Of Things *(Monkey)*
It's A Jungle Out There
It's A Zoo Around Here
It's A Zoo Life For...
It's All Happening At The Zoo
Just Hangin' Around
Just Hangin' Out
Just "Lion" Around The House
Just Monkey'n Around
Kids At Play *(Baby animals)*
Let's Not Forget... *(Elephant)*
The Lion Sleeps Tonight
Lions & Tigers & Bears...Oh My!
The Lion's Den
Look Ma! No Cavities *(Hippo)*
Look Who's At The Zoo
The Mane Attraction *(Lion)*
The Mighty Tiger
Monkey Business
Monkey See, Monkey Do
Monkeying Around
More Fun Than A Tree Full Of Monkeys!
My Furr-vorite Animal Is...
Near Wild Heaven
No Lion...Visiting The Zoo Was Grrreat!
No More Monkeying Around
Our Little Monkey
Our Private Zoo
Our Trip Was Zoopendous
Out Of Africa
Paws Here
Petting Zoo
Please Don't Feed The Animals
Rainforest Cafe
Reach For The Stars! *(Giraffe)*
A Real Swinger *(Monkey)*
The Reptile House
Roarin' Good Times *(Lion)*
Roaring For His Rights *(Lion)*
Safari Hunt
So What Are You In For *(Animal behind bars)*
Something Worth Roaring About
Splish Splash I Was Taking A Bath *(Hippo with water splashes)*
A Story Of Wild Animals
Suburban Safari
Swing My Way *(Monkey)*
Swingin' Safari
Talk To The Animals
Tall Tails *(Giraffe)*
This Place Is A Zoo
Tiger Cubs On The Prowl
Tiger Cubs Roar
Trip To The Zoo

Trunks & Tails
A Trunk Full Of Happiness
A Trunk Full Of Kisses/Love
A Trunk Full Of Peanuts
A Trunk Full Of Smiles
Two At The Zoo
The Untamed Wild
Urban Safari
A View At The Zoo
Walk With The Animals
Walking On The Wild Side
Watch Out Zoo, Here We Come!
We Belong In The Zoo
We Did The Wild Thing
We Had A Roaring Good Time
We Had Zoo Much Fun At The Zoo
Welcome To The Zoo
What A Zoo!
Where The Wild Things Are
Who's Watching Who
I'm Wild About...
I'm Wild About You
Wild & Crazy
A Wild & Crazy Place
Wild Child
Wild Life
Wild One
The Wild Ones
The Wild Side Of Life
Wild Thang!
Wild Thing
Wild Thing...I Think I Love You
Wild, Wild Life
Wild Wonders
Wild World
Winged Creatures
Wonderful Zoo
You Can Fly, You Can Fly! *(Monkeys)*
You Make Me Roar
You're Grrrrrrreat! *(Tiger)*
Zany Zoo
Zippitty Zoo Dah
Zoo Crew
Zoo Day Fun
I Zoo, Do You?
Zoo Fun
Zoo Hullabaloo
The Zoo Review
Zoo Time
Zoo-bilee
Zoobydoo
Zoo-pendous
A "Zoo"per Day/Time
Zoo-per Fun Zoo
Zooperstars
Zoorassic Park
Zoorific
A Zoo-tiful Day

____
____
____
____
____

6125697R00173

Printed in Great Britain
by Amazon.co.uk, Ltd.,
Marston Gate.